Guy of Saint-Denis
Tractatus de tonis

Medieval Institute Publications is a program of
The Medieval Institute, College of Arts and Sciences

 WESTERN MICHIGAN UNIVERSITY

Guy of Saint-Denis
Tractatus de tonis

Edited and translated by
Constant J. Mews, Carol J. Williams, John N. Crossley,
and Catherine Jeffreys

TEAMS • Varia

MEDIEVAL INSTITUTE PUBLICATIONS
Western Michigan University
Kalamazoo

Library of Congress Cataloging-in-Publication Data

Names: Guido de Sancto Dionysio author. | Mews, C. J. editor. | Williams,
   Carol J. (Carol Janice) editor. | Crossley, John N. editor. | Jeffreys,
   Catherine, 1969- editor.
Title: Tractatus de tonis = Treatise on the tones / Guy of Saint-Denis ;
   edited and translated by Constant J. Mews, Carol J. Williams, John N.
   Crossley, and Catherine Jeffreys.
Other titles: Treatise on the tones
Description: Kalamazoo : Medieval Institute Publications, [2016] | Series:
   TEAMS varia | Includes index.
Identifiers: LCCN 2016055607 (print) | LCCN 2016056599 (ebook) | ISBN
   9781580442541 (paperbound : alk. paper) | ISBN 9781580442558
Subjects: LCSH: Music theory--Early works to 1800. | Church music--Catholic
   Church--Early works to 1800. | Church music--France--Saint-Denis--Early
   works to 1800. | Tonarius. | Guido, de Sancto Dionysio. Tractatus de
   tonis. | Music theory--History--500-1400.
Classification: LCC MT5.5 .G85 2016 (print) | LCC MT5.5 (ebook) | DDC
   781.2/63--dc23
LC record available at https://lccn.loc.gov/2016055607

ISBN 9781580442992 (casebound)
ISBN 9781580442541 (paperbound)
eISBN 9781580442552

Contents

Acknowledgments   vii

Abbreviations   ix

Introduction   xi
    Outline of the *Tractatus de tonis*   xxxvii

Tractatus de tonis: Text and Translation   1

Appendices   238
    I Deleted Materials   238
    II Explanatory Material   240

Chant Sources and Concordances Table: Explanatory Notes   241

Works Cited   261
    Manuscript Sources   261
    Primary Sources   261
    Secondary Sources   265

Lexicon   271

Glossary   277

Onomastic Index   283

Acknowledgments

THIS PROJECT OF EDITING AND TRANSLATING the *Tractatus de tonis* of Guy of Saint-Denis follows up the TEAMS edition and translation prepared by the editors of the *Ars Musice* of Johannes de Grocheio from within a research group based in the Centre for Medieval and Renaissance Studies at Monash University (in Melbourne, Australia). The editors are profoundly grateful to a number of individuals who have helped us with this project, in particular Carol Appelt, who has worked as research assistant, charged with working on the sources of chant known to Guy of Saint-Denis. Others who have given assistance in various ways include Jason Stoessel, Robert Curry, Margaret Bent, and librarians at the Bibliothèque nationale de France, the British Library and the Victoria and Albert Museum. We have also benefited from support given by the ARC Centre for the History of Emotions for the opportunity to present and discuss ideas developed in our research. An interdisciplinary project such as this necessarily involves learning from a wide range of people and fields of expertise. Responsibility for any errors is of course entirely our own.

Abbreviations

AL   Aristoteles Latinus

BL   British Library

BnF   Bibliothèque nationale de France

CCCM   Corpus Christianorum Continuatio Mediaeualis

CCSL   Corpus Christianorum Series Latina

CNRS   Centre National de la Recherche Scientifique

CUP   Heinrich Denifle, ed., *Chartularium Universitatis Parisiensis*, 4 vols. (Paris, Culture and Civilisation, 1964)

CSM   Corpus scriptorum de musica

H   London, British Library, MS Harley 281

PG   Patrologia Graeca

PL   Patrologia Latina

Introduction

T HE WRITING OF GUY OF SAINT-DENIS about plainchant is not widely known. Sometime in the early fourteenth century, this monk from Saint-Denis, one of the oldest Benedictine abbeys in France, composed a treatise about the eight tones or melodic types into which all plainchant was convention-ally classified.[1] While it had often been monastic practice to list chant in this way in a *Tonale* (tonary), Guy offers an unusually sophisticated analysis in his *Tractatus de tonis*. He divides the work into two parts: the first providing a theoretical basis for understanding the tones into which all chant is divided; the second, particular examples of chants with their tones. In the first part he considers the impact of the various tones on the soul, inspired in part by teachings of Aristotle, and in the second he presents numerous specific examples drawn from his experience of the liturgy at his own abbey.

The *Tractatus* survives as the final item in an anthology of writings about music (London, British Library, Harley MS 281, hereafter referred to as Harley 281 or *H*), which he commissioned and corrected in his own hand. The first part of this anthology comprises various texts by, or attributed to, Guido of Arezzo, followed by the Cistercian *Tonale*. The second part offers three "modern" texts: the *Ars musice* of Johannes de Grocheio (John of Grouchy), from near Coutances in Normandy, written ca. 1275; the relatively brief and practical *Tractatus de tonis* of Petrus de Cruce (Pierre de la Croix), a master from Amiens in the late thir-teenth century; and then a much more developed discussion of the tones by Guy himself.[2] Guy drew on the rich liturgical traditions of his own monastery to illus-trate what he understood to be the core *raison d'être* for all plainchant, namely to enable monks to perform more fully the task of praising God daily throughout the liturgical year. Guy wanted his monks not just to know how to sing the vast body of chants they were expected to sing over the course of a liturgical year, but also to understand the rationale behind their different tones or melodic types and how they could move the human spirit.

Guy of Saint-Denis was certainly familiar with a long tradition of monks compiling tonaries that gave practical instruction about classifying chants into particular tones, including ones at his own monastery.[3] He radically transforms this tradition, however, by introducing his monks not just to the classic practical instruction of Guido of Arezzo, formulated in the early eleventh century, but to the very latest thinking about music, inspired by the thought of Aristotle, taking place in the University of Paris. He does so throughout the anthology that is now Harley 281, and his own *Tractatus de tonis* with which it concludes. Since Guy does not speak about issues of mensural notation and polyphony, as was discussed in the thirteenth century by Franco of Cologne and others, he has sometimes been described as "traditional" in his perspectives.[4] This judgment does not do justice to the originality of his achievement in transforming monastic tradition.

Guy was writing for the benefit of the monks in his abbey. Each day they were required to chant the Divine Office, which began with Vespers the previous evening, followed by Matins, Lauds, Prime, Terce, Sext, None, and Compline, reciting the entire Psalter over the course of a week. In addition, the mass had its own set of "proper" chants. These comprised introit, responsory, Alleluia or tract,[5] sequence, offertory, and post-communion. Each day had a set of chants appropriate to the liturgical season in the temporal cycle with particular antiphons introducing and closing each psalm. On the feast day of a saint, chants were needed for the antiphons and responsories relevant to readings taken from the life of that saint. In this way the Divine Office (the *opus Dei* or work of God) articulated consciousness not just of the universal Church and of a cycle of chants about the life of Christ, but also of a specific community of saints associated with Guy's own abbey of Saint-Denis. The liturgy at Saint-Denis was particularly complex, with so many feast days celebrating saints from different periods little celebrated elsewhere, such as those for King Dagobert and the little known Cucuphas.[6] There had been periodic attempts to reform chant traditions that were believed to go back to the time of Pope Gregory the Great (590–604), who is thought to have created the cycle of chants not just for the mass, but for the whole liturgical year.[7] In his *Tractatus de tonis*, Guy sought to restore what he saw as the correct understanding of the chant of the Church and to remedy the current failure to understand its true purpose and the core principles behind its composition.

Guy closed the first part of his *Tractatus*, on the principles behind the tones, with a tirade against the tendency of what he called "modern" liturgical offices to apply chants following the numerical sequence of tones from one to eight in a mechanical way, which might ensure melodic variety, but destroyed any sense of direct connection between the message of a text and the particular melody applied to it—a theme to which we shall return. After explaining the principles underpinning the tones in the first part of the *Tractatus*, he devoted the second to more practical concerns, explaining the particular musical form of the tones and their various linking passages or *differentiae* by which monks could move from the melody of any particular antiphon to the reciting tone of the psalm that it introduced.

In this way, Guy demonstrated how monks could put into practice the principles outlined in the first part. Rather than simply listing them in the manner of earlier tonaries, he wanted monks to understand the broader framework in which the tones and their *differentiae* were to be understood.

The Abbey of Saint-Denis in the Late Thirteenth and Early Fourteenth Centuries

The resting place of the kings of France from the seventh century, Saint-Denis was a very large and wealthy monastery, owning properties all over France.[8] In many ways, Matthew of Vendôme, abbot from 1258 to his death in 1286, had revitalized the abbey. He had completed the radical rebuilding of the main nave, begun by Abbot Suger in the 1130s, transforming it into one of the great Gothic churches of France.[9] From as early as 1229, the abbey of Saint-Denis had a College in Paris that served as the abbot's Parisian residence and a place of education for particularly promising monastic students. In 1263 Matthew conceived a plan to move the college from its original location near the Dominican convent at Saint-Jacques, to the Quai des Augustins, so as to be physically closer to the royal palace on the Île-de-la-cité. As senior adviser to the king, entrusted by Louis IX in 1270 with the government of France in the event of his demise, Matthew needed a Parisian base, both as his residence and as a place where gifted monks might be trained, prior to rising to positions of leadership in the abbey.[10] Matthew believed that monks should benefit from the educational opportunities offered by the University of Paris, even if they did not graduate. The new college was in operation by 1281. In 1295, Pope Boniface VIII had agreed to decisions of its abbot that monks not be accepted below the age of eighteen, or without an acceptable level of education in letters, and that the monastery be restricted in size to two hundred monks.[11] In all likelihood, this is where Guy would have been educated as a monk, probably in the late 1280s or 1290s.

Matthew also instilled in the monks of his abbey a strong sense that it was guardian of the historical memory of France, evident in the production of the *Grandes Chroniques de France* in both Latin and French during his time as abbot and that of his three successors, Renaud Giffard (1286–1304), Gilles of Pontoise (1304–26), and Guy of Châtres (1326–43). This last was the author of a *Sanctilogium*, a collection of saints' lives to which we shall return when considering whether he may be the same person as Guy of Saint-Denis.[12] Between 1285 and 1302 the accounts of the abbey reveal that the *Custos cartarum*, responsible for the archives of the abbey, was William of Nangis, who continued the *Chronicle* of Sigebert of Gembloux by drawing on the mass of historical texts in the abbey's library.[13] William's *Chronicle* was continued after his death by a series of monks of the abbey who continued its strong historical traditions, including Richard

Lescot, compiler of a chronicle covering the years between 1328 and 1344.[14] Guy inherited a fascination with dates when recording historical figures in his *Tractatus* and would make repeated reference to the *Chronicle* of Sigebert for historical information.[15]

The accounts of the abbey of Saint-Denis show how education and the copying of manuscripts at Saint-Denis were given great emphasis during these decades, with annual payments for the upkeep of students in Paris, for parchment, copying and purchase of liturgical books (including an antiphonary and psalter in 1287/88) and for school texts (including an Avicenna in 1284/85).[16] From 1284 to 1344 there were annual payments to both a *Magister iuvenum* and a *Magister puerorum* as well as to the *Custos cartarum*, the latter being a monk of the abbey. While it is not clear whether these two *magistri* were monks or outsiders paid to teach both young monks and older students, it is clear that the abbey considered education important. In 1290, there was payment for a *Magister de Grecia* and in 1323 for teachers in theology from both Dominican and Franciscan Orders.[17] From the time of Matthew of Vendôme to Guy of Châtres, the abbots of Saint-Denis believed that their best monks should benefit from being educated at the same level as other students at the University of Paris.

Saint-Denis had an unusually large collection of liturgical books going back to at least the ninth century.[18] Responsibility for this collection rested with the cantor who, among his other duties, had to arrange the readings from scripture and saints' lives in both the church and the refectory during mealtimes.[19] A distinctive feature of the Saint-Denis liturgy was that, since the ninth century, parts of the Ordinary of the mass (not just the *Kyrie,* but the Gloria, Credo, Sanctus and Agnus Dei) were sung in Greek on major feasts, while from the twelfth century an entire mass in Greek was celebrated on the Octave of St Denis.[20] This heightened consciousness of Greek in the liturgy helped promote awareness of the language at the abbey in the twelfth and thirteenth centuries. It led scholars, such as William Gap and Jean Sarrazin, to collect and translate Greek theological writings, notably of Dionysius.[21] Even if Guy did not have a profound knowledge of Greek, he inherited the awareness in Saint-Denis that the chant of the Latin Church had links to the age of the apostles, mediated through the figure they knew as Dionysius the Areopagite, imagined to be first bishop of both Athens and Paris.

The abbey did not just produce monastic chant. A French *chansonnier* attributes a collection of love songs to a monk from Saint-Denis, perhaps from around 1230, two of which also survive in polyphonic sources.[22] Guy's willingness to include the *Ars musice* of Johannes de Grocheio, who was much concerned with vernacular music, suggests he was very open to new trends in music making in Paris. Guy opens the prologue to his work with the phrase: "Knowing that the moderns rejoice in brevity;" a phrase used in mensural treatises of the late thirteenth century.[23] Fully familiar with their achievements and aware of the distinction between *antiqui* and *moderni*, Guy sought to combine the best of both ancient and more recent teaching on plainchant. One musician whom he particularly admired was Petrus de Cruce, whom he describes in the past tense as someone who had been a great cantor and observed the usage of Amiens. He included the *Tractatus de tonis* of Petrus in his anthology between the *Ars Musice* of Grocheio and his own much more sophisticated discussion of the same topic. As Petrus was still active at Amiens in 1301–2, Guy must be writing sometime after this date, perhaps in the first decade of the fourteenth century.[24]

Guy of Saint-Denis and Peter of Auvergne

Guy also draws on the last of a series of quodlibetal disputations or *Quaestiones*, which deal in part with music, delivered by Peter of Auvergne (d. 1304) ca. 1301.[25] Guy's evident dependence on this Parisian master reveals how fully connected he was to the transformation of scholastic thought taking place in Paris in the late thirteenth century. The significance of Peter of Auvergne during this period is only beginning to attract attention.[26] On 7 May 1275, Peter had been appointed by Simon de Brion, papal legate in 1275 (subsequently Pope Martin IV, 1281–85), as rector of the University of Paris, in order to resolve a serious division within the Faculty of Arts, that had led to Siger of Brabant, supported by masters from the Norman nation, being sent into exile.[27] How long Peter held this position, which required working with the provosts of the four nations (also appointed in the same document), is not clear. Nonetheless, the papal legate clearly considered that he was capable of breaking three years of internal schism in the University between followers of Siger of Brabant (supported by masters from the suffragan dioceses of Normandy) and those who followed Alberic (Aubry).[28] Peter of Auvergne's evident interest in the teachings of Thomas Aquinas is apparent from the fact that he subsequently completed the unfinished commentaries of Thomas Aquinas on Aristotle's *Politics* and *De Caelo*, probably in the second half of the 1270s.[29] These unfinished commentaries of Thomas had been requested from the Dominican Order in a letter sent from the Faculty of Arts on 2 May 1274 that also boldly asked for his physical remains.[30] Possibly Peter had a hand in that request. He differed from Thomas, however, in focusing not on theological issues, but on the scientific writings of Aristotle, namely the *Metaphysics* and writings on the movements of animals, the heavens, meteors, the soul, the senses, sleep, plants, memory, longevity, youth and age, breath, as well as the *Politics*.[31] In discussing the effects of music, inspired by Aristotle's discussion in the last book of the *Politics*, Peter followed up Thomas's interest in the emotions with much more detail about how they could be affected by different types of music. This was precisely the angle that Guy of Saint-Denis found so interesting in Peter's disputation of 1301 about whether music can arouse passions and whether it can influence moral behavior, going far beyond anything said by Thomas Aquinas on the subject.[32]

In March 1277, Stephen Tempier sought to assert his authority over the Faculty of Arts with a detailed list of 219 propositions (including some associated with Thomas Aquinas) that he deemed heretical.[33] Tempier was implicitly chiding those installed to govern the Faculty for allowing too many heterodox opinions that ran counter to his understanding of Catholic doctrine to flourish. Whether or not Peter of Auvergne still occupied a position of responsibility in 1277, his exposition of the *De caelo* without any reference to subordinating its doctrines to those of theological orthodoxy, quite different from that of Albert the Great, could be seen as being in opposition to the perspectives of Tempier.[34] Peter did not move to studying theology until the 1280s, receiving a canonry at Notre-Dame in 1296. By the early fourteenth century, when Guy of Saint-Denis followed the interpretation of Peter of Auvergne of Aristotle's discussion of music in the eighth book of the *Politics*, Aristotelian science and philosophical assumptions no longer presented any threat to a theological perspective. Peter of Auvergne played a significant part in shifting what came to be considered as the scientific mainstream in Christian thought in the last quarter of the thirteenth century. Guy of Saint-Denis sought to apply this intellectual shift to thinking about plainchant.

There is a great contrast between the ways in which Aristotle's authority is presented in the *Ars musice* of Johannes de Grocheio and in Guy's *Tractatus de tonis*. Grocheio refers to a number of works of Aristotle, but never mentions the *Politics*, even though he does comment on the social effects of different types of song. While William of Moerbeke had translated the *Politics* from Greek in the early 1260s, prompting Albert the Great, then teaching in Cologne, to produce a short commentary on the work sometime after 1267, this work was still largely unknown in Paris prior to the mid-1270s.[35] Thomas Aquinas refers very briefly to Aristotle's discussion of music in the eighth book of the *Politics* when considering the value of song in praising God in a part of his *Summa Theologia* that he wrote towards the end of his life.[36] This discussion only became widely known in Paris through Peter of Auvergne's continuation of the unfinished commentary of Aquinas.[37] Given wide Parisian interest in the *Politics* from the later 1270s, it seems unlikely that Grocheio could have written the *Ars musice* around 1300 as has been claimed.[38] Grocheio's criticism of John of Garland for ignoring the authority of Aristotle's *De Caelo* touched on issues that were still controversial in 1272–75, prior to Siger of Brabant (who was supported by a group of masters from the Norman nation), being sent into exile. By contrast, Guy of Saint-Denis incorporated the teaching of both Grocheio and Peter of Auvergne (as a commentator on Aristotle's *Politics* and through his *Quaestiones*, the quodlibetal discussion of 1301) without any sense that these were controversial authorities. Guy of Saint-Denis took for granted the authority of Peter of Auvergne's discussion, applying his theoretical understanding of the impact of melody on the soul to much more specific analyses of the different tones of plainchant.

In helping date the *Tractatus*, a further indication once considered plausible is the fact that Guy refers to the verse of a responsory (*Paratum panem*) for the Office of the Feast of Corpus Christi, which feast he calls *De eucharistia*.[39] This responsory does not occur in the published version of the Office for this feast, instituted by Pope Urban IV in 1264, and composed by Thomas Aquinas at the Pope's request (replacing the original version composed for use in Liège by Juliana of Cornillon). *Paratum panem* is found, however, in an unpublished monastic version of the Office (with twelve rather than nine readings) as composed by Aquinas, preserved in a manuscript of Saint-Vaast, Arras, from the early fourteenth century.[40] This version seems to have been adopted at Saint-Denis by this time, even though it only became widely adopted by Dominicans after 1317.[41] The earliest surviving records of the Office of Corpus Christi (some from before or around 1300) suggest that there was no consistent presentation of chant melodies. Later versions of the Office assign chants of tones one to eight in numerical sequence to each antiphon and responsory, precisely the practice to which Guy of Saint-Denis objects.[42] While a precise date for the *Tractatus* is impossible to obtain, it nevertheless seems likely that Guy completed the work during the first decade of the fourteenth century, perhaps early in the abbacy of Gilles of Pontoise (1304–26). Guy seems to have written this treatise with the express purpose of it being the consummation of the anthology of texts about chant and the principles of music that survives as Harley 281, a guide for instructing the monks of his abbey.

Guy of Saint-Denis and Monastic Tradition

At Saint-Denis, the earliest attempts to classify chants into their tones appear in a group of graduals from the early tenth century, without musical notation but containing brief references using letters to the particular tone of the chant.[43] By the early fourteenth century, the older practice of monks knowing chants by memory had given way to greater authority being given to written notation. Yet Guy of Saint-Denis was fascinated by the quest to recover the earliest authority for a so-called "Gregorian" chant by looking for a book about the tones that some said had been written by Pope Gregory the Great. He could not find it, however:

> Although I have looked for the work attributed to his name, I have been unable to find it. I have not retreated from the paths of Guido and the rules of other following musicians who imitated the paths of the venerable doctor himself. Perhaps I have even held the very book and read it attentively amongst the many and various treatises that I have seen about this matter, yet unaware or not knowing whose it was.[44]

Guy's comment hints at his impassioned desire to retrieve the oldest traces of monastic liturgical tradition in his abbey. He insisted that his exposition of chant was derived from the oldest authorities, of which the most important was Guido of Arezzo, supplemented by his knowledge of more than four hundred different chants from the liturgy of his abbey.

A good number of the chants with which Guy was familiar are likely to have been Gallican in origin, from before the reforms introduced in the eighth and ninth centuries.[45] Saint-Denis had played a key role in initiating these reforms, which were intended to make chant conform to that of the papal court, following the visit in 754 of Pope Stephen II to Saint-Denis, where he anointed Pepin. These reforms, implemented first by Abbot Fulrad (750–784) and later by Abbot Hilduin (814–841), re-defined the monastic liturgy that the abbey would follow over subsequent centuries.[46] Unlike the more florid "Roman" chant preserved in a few churches in Italy, the chant that developed in the ninth century (in part through the liturgical advisers of Charlemagne) was modally organized in that its chants could be classified into eight different melodic types, each characterized by a particular pattern of pitch hierarchies. By the early tenth century, the practice was starting to develop for composers of liturgical chant to apply each of the eight tones in numerical order within the cycle of an individual Office, as is evident, for example, in that composed for Trinity Sunday by Stephen of Liège.[47] (Whether Guy knew that the Office of the Holy Trinity, which he lists among those created by "moderns," went back to the early tenth century is uncertain.) He mentions that this practice is used "by modern musicians or cantors" for a number of feasts, not just of St. Louis, but also of the Holy Trinity, Nicholas, Mary Magdalene, Augustine, Katherine "and many others":

> The ancients and the first cantors, however, who rarely or never seem to have been concerned with such an order, (which seems to have been introduced more for a certain ornament or elegance than for the requirement of the Divine Office) seem to have been concerned more with the moderation and sobriety of chants and also with the quality of the material upon which they based their ecclesiastical chants. For just as elsewhere it is written that expressions are to be crafted according to subject matter,[48] so also it should be in this way for ecclesiastical chants. For it is fitting that ecclesiastical chants be adapted not just in any way but appropriately to the material on which they are founded.[49]

Guy's comment about expressions (*sermones*) needing to be crafted to their subject matter repeats a phrase from Aristotle's *Ethics*.[50] Guy then builds on this idea by referring to the teaching of Guido of Arezzo about chant needing to express the mood of the text. Guy's criticism of contemporary practice articulates his core theme that each of the eight tones of plainchant makes a contribution to its emotional effect and beauty. Although Guy refers to this compositional style of running through the tones in sequence within an office as "modern," it was a practice that originally started to develop in the early tenth century, as Crocker and other scholars have observed in the case of Trinity Sunday.[51] The technique became increasingly common in offices for newly composed feasts in the twelfth and thirteenth centuries. Sequential tones created melodic variety within any office, but at the risk of doing so in a predictable fashion. Guy preferred liturgical offices not to be shaped by this tradition. What matters is that he considered it a "modern" tendency that strayed from what he thought of as the true traditions of plainchant. He disliked a mechanical attitude towards the tones that did not grasp their purpose or appreciate how melody should primarily serve to communicate a text.

Guy was proud of the antiquity of the liturgical traditions of his abbey, articulated in a use (*usus*) that was, in many features—some of minor liturgical detail—quite distinct from that of any other monastery or religious community. Guy recognized that abuses had crept into liturgical chant, but he was proud of respecting the particular use or custom developed at his abbey. He revered the teaching of Guido of Arezzo, with whose writings he opened the anthology in Harley 281. Guido was very interested in using analogies from grammar to discuss how different tones could express emotion.[52] Traditionally, however, tonaries only gave information about chants, rather than discussing the nature of the rules imposed on chant. Guy followed a collection of various writings of Guido (to which he added certain prefatory passages) by a *Dialogus,* sometimes wrongly attributed to Odo of Cluny, but here attributed to Guido and providing a basic tonary.

Guy of Saint-Denis was certainly familiar with Cistercian chant practice, as attested by his decision to include in his anthology a copy of the Cistercian *Tonale*, assigned to Bernard of Clairvaux, immediately after the set of texts by, or attributed to, Guido of Arezzo. Whereas Guido of Arezzo emphasizes that chant is based on the authority of the text, the Cistercian *Tonale* adopts a more systematic framework, summarizing principles laid out more fully in the treatise of abbot Guido Augensis (Guy of Eu) on the subject in the mid-twelfth century. Cistercian practice emphasizes uniform observance rather than local practice. These principles had been formulated in a treatise dedicated to his friend, William, first abbot of Rievaulx (1131–41).[53] Rather than defining a tone as a rule judging any chant by its final, that is to say, the last note of the chant, which had been the earlier practice, Guy of Eu defined it as "a rule determining the nature and form of regular chants."[54] He defined chant as operating within certain fixed limits of pitch, according to its various *maneriae*, a term not used before the twelfth century.[55] Guy of Eu did not reflect on the specific character or the effect of individual tones, but rather focused on the core principles of chant. The *Tonale* concludes with the master responding to his student's request for clarification on the problem of *differentiae*, which seem to be of different tones, by commenting on the need for uniformity: "By the prohibition of the Cistercian General Chapter, neither in the

Gradual nor in the Antiphonary can anything be changed" and, for further guid-
ance, "consult the *Musica* of Guy of Eu, which he wrote for his most holy master,
William, first abbot of Rievaulx."[56] In providing the Cistercian *Tonale* immediately
after the *Dialogus,* Guy of Saint-Denis was enabling his readers to appreciate the
difference between its definition of the tones and that of Benedictine tradition.

Guy of Saint-Denis and Dominican Tradition

In the early fourteenth century, the privileged position of the abbey of Saint-Denis
within the kingdom of France was increasingly being challenged by the mendicant
religious orders. The Dominicans in particular were anxious to provide confessors
to Philip IV (1285–1314), in order to acquire a greater political influence than
the Franciscans, who provided confessors to the queen.[57] The canonization of St.
Louis in 1297 provides particular insight into these rivalries, since Benedictines,
Cistercians, Dominicans and Franciscans all sought to shape a liturgy appropriate
to his feast.[58] Although St. Louis had been buried at Saint-Denis in 1270, Philip
IV received papal approval from Pope Clement V (newly arrived in Avignon) to
have the major part of his grandfather's remains transferred to the Sainte-Chapelle
in 1306, where they could be venerated alongside the holiest relic in Christendom,
the Crown of Thorns.[59] While the monks of Saint-Denis followed liturgical traditions distinctive to their abbey, the Dominicans followed Cistercian practice in
mandating that all their communities should share exactly the same feasts, with
uniform chant traditions. The different offices created to honor St. Louis reflect
the competition between religious orders, each of which claimed a special connection to the king.

　　Guy's inclusion of the Office for St. Louis as one of those composed by
"moderns" in numerically sequential fashion is of particular interest because the
feast had only been established after his canonization in 1297. This office, *Ludovicus decus regnantium,* was very likely the composition commissioned from Petrus
de Cruce by Philip IV in 1298 and thus performed at Saint-Denis in that year.[60]
Elsewhere in his treatise, Guy refers to a monastic version of the office *Lauda
celestis,* the text of which, as recorded in liturgical books of Saint-Denis from the
mid-fourteenth century, seems to be a modification of a Cistercian office. Possibly
this modification reflects Guy's discomfort with its modally sequential formula.[61]
Even if he admired Petrus de Cruce as a singer and included a copy of his tonary
immediately before his own text in the Harley anthology, Guy did not refrain from
criticizing contemporary compositional practice. The fact that the form of the
Office of St. Louis finally adopted by the Dominicans (preserved for example in
the *Poissy Antiphonal*) adopts a strictly sequential approach to the choice of tones
suggests that Guy's resistance to the practice, voiced at the end of the first part of
the *Tractatus,* may have been particularly directed against what the Dominicans
were doing, and their influence on the wider liturgy of the Latin Church.[62]

This political rivalry gives a particular edge to Guy's attitude towards the *Tractatus de Musica*, compiled by the Dominican Jerome of Moray (Hieronymus de Moravia) in around 1270. Jerome's treatise is preserved in complete form in a single manuscript (Paris, BnF lat. 16663), one of 120 manuscripts bequeathed to the Sorbonne in 1306 by Peter of Limoges, a master with similar interests to Peter of Auvergne.[63] Jerome drew heavily on two major sources, the *De musica* of Boethius and an early twelfth-century treatise on chant by John Cotton (sometimes identified as John of Afflighem) that summarizes core elements of the teaching of Guido of Arezzo. Jerome's only explicit direct quotation from Guido of Arezzo is of his famous poem commenting on the distance between music theorists and cantors.[64] Jerome expanded his treatise, however, with extensive quotations from the *De mensurabili musica* of John of Garland, the *Ars cantus mensurabilis* of Franco of Cologne, and the *Ars motettorum compilata breviter* of Petrus Picardus.[65] Jerome also incorporated into his treatise a brief passage on practical instruction about the tones, beginning *Omnis igitur cantus ecclesiasticus,* covering the essential features of final notes and range.[66] This extract of Jerome's *Tractatus* relating to the tones was included at the opening of Dominican antiphonaries such as the *Poissy Antiphonal*, a copy corrected against a standard exemplar to ensure uniformity of observance throughout the Order. Guy was certainly aware of Jerome's discussion, and was likely influenced by his use of the term *licencialiter* ("by license"), which was much used by Jerome and frequently added by Guy in corrections made to his own treatise.[67] Nevertheless, Guy's *Tractatus de tonis* can be seen as a direct response to this part of Jerome's *Tractatus de musica*. Whereas Jerome identified Boethius as his authority for understanding the theory of music, Guy emphasizes the authority of Guido of Arezzo for the practice of singing.

Jerome was interested in incorporating newer treatises about music, but he does so in a traditional way without engaging in discussion of their ideas. The most recent treatise that Jerome incorporates into his compilation is a passage from the commentary of Thomas Aquinas on that part of the *De caelo* in which Aristotle criticizes the Pythagoreans for believing in any physical music of the spheres, a perspective very different from that of Boethius in the *De institutione musica* where he divides all music into cosmic (*mundana*), human (in the sense of binding body and soul) and instrumental.[68] Because this passage from Aquinas effectively interrupts a series of quotations from Richard of Saint Victor, Isidore, and Boethius about the reality of cosmic music, it may be that Jerome added this passage to an already completed work. Jerome does not offer his own opinion on the subject, nor identify Aquinas as author of the passage he quotes, as if Thomas had not yet become a celebrated authority. He simply gives it as the opinion of Aristotle contradicting the view of Boethius without coming to his own synthesis: "But which is the truer opinion of such men, we do not rashly define, but leave to be determined by our elders."[69] Because Thomas was staying at the same convent as Jerome during

Thomas's last spell in Paris (1269–72), it is quite possible that Jerome added this passage after talking to Thomas about the *De Caelo* and its criticism of the notion that cosmic music was audible to the senses.

Guy and Johannes de Grocheio

Guy's keen interest in the new directions being pursued in Paris at the turn of the fourteenth century is most evident in the way that he draws upon, and extends the ideas of, the *Ars musice* of Johannes de Grocheio, the treatise that he includes in the anthology immediately before the tonary of Petrus de Cruce.[70] Our only other witness to the *Ars musice* is a textually inferior copy belonging to the Carthusian abbey of St. Barbara, Cologne, important because it provides our only evidence for the name of its author.[71] Grocheio's treatise overturned the long-established tripartite division of Boethius of *musica* into its cosmic, human and instrumental forms. While Boethius knew about the seductive power of melody and how the Pythagoreans in the ancient world believed that certain types of melody could calm the soul, he was not interested in describing the specific types of music that he could hear in his own day. Grocheio, by contrast, was much more interested in what Aristotle had to say about music as sound, physically sensed through hearing, deriding those who followed John of Garland (d. ca. 1271) for repeating the teaching of Boethius about *musica mundana* without being aware of Aristotle's mockery in the *De Caelo* of Pythagorean teaching about the music of the spheres.[72] *Musica humana*, meaning the harmony of body and soul was, for Grocheio, a similarly absurd concept: "Nor is sound properly to be found in the human constitution. For who has heard a constitution sounding?"[73] Guy of Saint-Denis saw no problem in referring to Grocheio's critique of Pythagorean teaching within his own treatise on the tones, even if his own comments on John of Garland, with whose teaching he was fully familiar, were more deferential.[74]

Guy of Saint-Denis thought it important for his students to complement their knowledge of monastic tradition by including Grocheio's *Ars musice* within his anthology and drawing on it in his treatise (though never identifying its author by name). Grocheio still drew on many aspects of Boethian theory, in particular his analysis by numerical proportions, as defined through both consonances (two sounds united in harmony at the same moment) and concords (one note sounding after another).[75] Grocheio's concern was to describe the music "according to the use of the people of Paris," dividing this into three branches: *musica civilis* "which we call music of the people" (*musica vulgalis*); "composed or regulated or canonical music" (*musica mensurata*); and the music that was created from these two branches, but ordered for the praise of God, namely ecclesiastical music.[76] Grocheio considered that humans were unlike the angels in having bodily organs, which meant that they could not continue in praise all the time, since their organs required them to eat, drink, sleep and engage in other activities. Therefore humans needed to turn to God at appointed times.[77] Grocheio concludes his *Ars musice* by recapitulating his argument, consistent with an Aristotelian perspective, that a tone is recognized not simply by knowing how a chant begins or ends, but also by inspecting the middle: "For tone is a rule or exemplar that ought to regulate the composer just as prime truth regulates the inquirer towards the perfect search for truth."[78] This contrasts sharply with the definition of Pseudo-Odo, still much repeated in the thirteenth century, that a tone could be assessed simply by its final.[79] Guy adopts what he says is a more subtle definition, also cited by Grocheio in the *Ars musice*: a tone is a rule through which one can judge every ecclesiastical chant by assessing not just its beginning, but also its middle and end. He also claims he is following those who observe that "public and civil song (such as lyric song and *rondeaux*) and particularly measured song (such as motets, hockets and the like)" are neither subject to tones nor regulated by them—remarks drawn from Grocheio's treatise.[80] While Grocheio spoke about different kinds of music in Paris, Guy focused on applying his principles to the chants of the church. He nonetheless thought it important to include Grocheio's *Ars musice* within his anthology. Grocheio's notion that the tone was the driving principle of a chant as a whole, not necessarily fixed just by its final note, provides a framework for his appreciation of each tone as having its own expressive quality and emotional power.

Whereas Grocheio was interested in what Aristotle had to say about music as physical sound, apparent to the sense of hearing, he had no familiarity with the notion that Guy of Saint-Denis takes for granted, inspired by the eighth book of the *Politics*, that different types of melody correspond to different dispositions of the human spirit, an idea that was much developed by Peter of Auvergne. Guy of Saint-Denis was much more respectful to John of Garland, seeking to combine his teaching with the insights of Aristotle, as interpreted by Peter of Auvergne.

Guy, Peter of Auvergne, and the Emotions

Quite unlike Grocheio, Guy was particularly interested in what Peter of Auvergne had to say (drawing on ideas of Aquinas) about the soul's appetitive or desiring part as stimulated by the senses in the same way as the will (or intellectual appetite) follows the intellect.[81] The sensitive appetite varies in individual people according to their particular disposition of qualities.[82] Just as some people are hotter in disposition, others colder, thus some are bold, some jealous, and some wrathful.[83] Like the various proportions making up different kinds of music, so is there an impact on the differing constitutions of the human soul, mediated through varying moods.[84] Thus one particular type of chant has the power to make one sad, another to make one happy. Guy is aware that this is in conformity with the teaching of both Boethius and Guido, going back to the teaching of Pythagoras, but here he explains the effect of music in Aristotelian terms. Guido had commented briefly on the effect of chant, but he had not gone into this level of detail about the power of different tones of chant. Even if Guy was not a philosopher in the same way as Peter of Auvergne, he reflected much more deeply than both Guido and Grocheio on the impact of tones on the emotions.

The quodlibetal discussion of Peter, on which Guy of Saint-Denis draws heavily in his *Tractatus*, moves into areas that Thomas Aquinas never discussed in any detail. While familiar with the teaching of Boethius in his *De institutione musica*, Peter focuses his argument around Aristotle's awareness that different types of musical sound can stir the passions, understood not just through the *De Anima*, but also through the writings of two later commentators, John of Damascus and Eustratios of Nicaea, as sensitive appetites or desires. This focus on interior passion or desire is almost completely absent from Grocheio, whose interest is more in observing music as only existing insofar as it is perceptible to the senses, rather than in the particular effects of music on the soul. Implicit to Peter's discussion about the importance of the passions is acceptance of the intellectual transformation brought about by Thomas Aquinas in incorporating an extensive treatise about the passions into his *Summa theologiae*. While the passions of the soul had been the subject of academic discussion in Paris since the early thirteenth century, Thomas Aquinas identified the passions, not as disturbances of the soul, but as integral to human behavior, ethically dangerous only when taken to excess. Following Aristotle, Peter is aware of the role of "primary qualities" in the body, namely wet and dry, hot and cold, which are normally in balance, but can create differing emotional states in different situations. Peter then extends these reflections, shaped by a strong interest in physiology, to musical harmonies. He makes very few specific comments on particular expressions of music apart from claiming that the second and eighth tones stimulate feelings of compassion or mercy. For this reason, the tract and other chants of the Office of the Dead (*Cantus mortuorum*) favor these tones. While Peter confines himself to theoretical points about *harmoniae*, Guy's contribution is to reflect on the impact of specific tones.

Aristotle's discussion about music in the eighth book of the *Politics* was focused around the impact of music on the state. In these *Quaestiones* Peter moves to an area that Aristotle never touched on: the impact of music on the individual soul. Music could legitimately provoke the soul to a sense of rapture. Peter goes beyond what he had said in his commentary on the *Politics*, about the ethical impact of the traditional modes of Greek music on the young, to reflect on the impact of different types of music in a personal way. In response to a question in the course of discussion, he declares that vocal music is superior to instrumental music; he acknowledges that "a well-proportioned musical *harmonia* strengthens moral behavior (*valet ad mores*), but a poorly proportioned one has the contrary effect."[85] Following Thomas Aquinas, Peter accords particular attention to the emotion of delight or pleasure (*delectatio*) as a passion that is not sinful in itself, but rather directs the soul to the highest good. Indirectly, Guy of Saint-Denis benefited from the Thomist revolution in psychological perspective, as well as from the thought of Peter of Auvergne, about applying these notions to music. Guy went a stage further by extending these ideas to the more technical subject of the tones.

The Anthology (Harley 281) and the *Tractatus*

Guy's *Tractatus de tonis* is the final item in the anthology of texts about music, and plainchant in particular, that he commissioned in the early fourteenth century, now the manuscript volume London, British Library, Harley 281. The anthology, like the argument of his own treatise, shows how traditional and modern thinking about music could be combined. Disregarding the annotations added on fol. 1r-4v in the sixteenth century by Jean Gosselin (**H3**), the manuscript, whose core text is copied by a single hand, is organized into seven parts.[86] Although this anthology has been copied by a single scribe (**H1**), it carries corrections, extensive in the case of the *Tractatus,* in Guy's own hand (**H2**). The first three parts are devoted to an arrangement of the writings of Guido of Arezzo (supplemented by the *Dialogus de musica* of Pseudo-Odo) into three books:

1. fols. 5r–16v: Guido of Arezzo, Liber I: *Micrologus.*
2. fols. 16v–24v: Guido of Arezzo, Liber II: *Incipit liber secundus eiusdem in planam musicam quem appelat trocaicum. Prologus in quo guido muse ipsum alloquenti. Respondet ...*; *Regule rythmice, Prologus in Antiphonarium, Epistola ad Martinum* [pro *Michaelem*]
3. fols. 24v–34r: Guido of Arezzo, Liber III: *Incipit tercius liber eiusdem guidonis in musicam sub dialogo. Prologus ...* ; Pseudo- Odo, *Dialogus de musica, Discipulus. Quid est musica? Magister. Veraciter canendi scientia... tam de tonis quam de reliquis consonantiis habens artu regulam subtilitate ingenii clare discernet; Quantumcumque vero omnium...;* Guido of Arezzo, *Epistola ad Martinum* [actually *ad Michaelum,* excerpt]; *Ecce patet et non latet .... Expliciunt toni guidonis aretini.*
4. fols. 34r–38v: *Tonale Beati Bernardi: Incipit alia ars de tonis per modus dyalogi que a quibusdam intitulatur sub nomine beati bernardi.*
5. fols. 39r–52r: Johannes de Grocheio, *Ars musice.*
6. fols. 52v–58r: Petrus de Cruce, *Tractatus de tonis.*
7. fols. 58v–96v: Guy of Saint-Denis, *Tractatus de tonis.*

Only one other copy is known of this tripartite edition of Guido's writings (Oxford, St. John's College 188, copied in the twelfth century), but only Harley 281 contains additional prefaces (cited here by their incipits), which, on stylistic grounds, seem to have been added by Guy of Saint-Denis to explain why these texts are important.[87] Guy seems to have created the anthology with a deliber-ate seven-fold structure that combines both "ancients" such as Guido of Arezzo and "moderns" such as Grocheio. One way of understanding Guy's treatise is to appreciate its connection to all the texts in this anthology as well as to the broader history of the evolution of chant.

The opening three books of the anthology provide a synthesis of all the major writings of Guido of Arezzo, by whom Guy is profoundly influenced.[88] In the Harley anthology, Guy imposes order on Guidonian teaching by adding prefaces that explain how Guido of Arezzo was distancing himself from purely philosophical accounts of music to provide something of practical benefit. Thus Guido's *Micrologus* is introduced not only by his original verses, but also by additional sentences about offering "whatever [is] of musical utility" that he could provide for common benefit through rules and figured neumes."[89] In an additional preface Guido is presented as wanting to find a better way than the Greeks had of presenting the "simple reasoning of this art" for tender ears that puts aside complicated proportions of numbers:

> Turning over the ancient volumes of the Greeks, I have seriously investigated long and often if, putting aside completely proportions of numbers, the simple reasoning of this art can be fully adapted to the tender ears of singers. Having therefore considered many treatises therefore, I have found Boethius better for this, for showing what and how many are the conjunctions of pitches through modes, tropes, and species of the consonances among themselves; but the way in which he strives to explain the force and nature of pitches through the science of sound (*armonice*) is for philosophers alone and obtuse and difficult for students. For the older treatise of philosophy, mired in excessive obscurity, sets traps for inexperienced ears by the weightiness of the words of those proffering arguments.[90]

In convoluted language, the new preface presents Guido as fully familiar with learned philosophical tradition, but cautious about the potential difficulty of theoretical language. These thoughts are fully consistent with what Guy of Saint-Denis declares at the very outset of his *Tractatus*: that he is offering teaching about the tones, culled both from the *Musica* of Boethius and the writings of Guido of Arezzo, as well as from others in the discipline.[91] Guy uses these prefaces to show how Guido explained music theory on the basis of concrete examples as opposed to the theoretical style of Boethius. Guy introduces these explanatory details in the voice of Guido as a way of building up to his own synthesis, which is presented in his treatise that concludes the compilation.

The second of the three books of Guidonian teaching in Harley 281 presents the *Regule rhythmice*, introduced by an otherwise unknown, fictional dialogue between Guido and his Muse, while the third is introduced by a preface that helps explain why its author (in fact Pseudo-Odo) has chosen the genre of dialogue:

For whatever therefore that we have been able to collect for the third part, imitating moderns by the authority of philosophers about the nature of the modes we have provided for our listeners in the form of a dialogue through great forethought of facility without the addition of deceit, removing all hateful material. For what is not understood in the aforesaid volume either by the rule of neglect or because music has lain hidden for a long time is, in the final analysis, profitably perceived in an easy collection of rules for the youthful ear.[92]

This preface, like the others attached to the writings attributed here to Guido of Arezzo, explains the simplicity of its text as a conscious strategy to communicate the principles of chant to the young in a way that is easier to understand than the purely theoretical, and very mathematical, approach of Boethius.

The second half of the Harley manuscript is similarly varied in that it presents the reader with the theoretical brilliance of the *Ars musice* of Grocheio and the simpler and more practical *Tractatus de tonis* of Petrus de Cruce, whom Guy describes in his treatise as "the finest cantor and particularly observed the practice of the church of Amiens."[93] Guy may have included this tonary because he observed that some of its practices were particularly close to those of Saint-Denis. Guy's decision to conclude the anthology with his own treatise reflects his desire that monks learn to combine traditional understanding of the rules of chant with the insights not only of Grocheio, but also of Peter of Auvergne, about how different types of chant can affect the soul in different ways.

Whereas most tonaries (such as that of Petrus de Cruce) are prescriptive in character, simply giving information about the eight tones, Guy's composition is a treatise organized into two parts. The first is theoretical in character, while the second illustrates the practice of chant at Saint-Denis. In the manuscript, the opening letters of the five chapters of the first part spell out the name GVIDO, matching the acrostic that opens the *Micrologus* of Guido of Arezzo.[94] This visual highlighting of the connection of Guy's *Tractatus* to the authority of Guido of Arezzo has particular significance in relation to the structure of the anthology as a whole, which culminates in Guy's concluding treatise. Its first part introduces the reader to core principles in four chapters: (1) In how many ways tone may be understood in music and from what it takes its name; (2) How many tones there are, and by what names they are called by musicians and philosophers; (3) Concerning the nature of the tones and their differentiation; (4) On the property and effect or power of the tones. The second part is devoted to practice, with many specific musical examples, and has eight chapters: one for each of the eight tones, which also explain their appropriate *neumata* (the wordless melismatic phrases with which antiphon or intonation formulas end). Guy is explicit in acknowledging that ideas put forward in the first part are for more advanced students than the examples given in the second part: "... the more difficult and subtle is for the more studious and advanced. In the second I will deal with *praxis*, that is, the operation of these things more figuratively and by examples easier for the simpler and the young."[95] The term *praxis* that he uses is a Graecism, not much used before Thomas Aquinas, and then only rarely.[96] In this second part, Guy gives detailed instructions about how an antiphon of any given tone might connect to the reciting tone of its psalm. Guy's goal is that monks should recognize the tone of any chant, and thus connect any antiphon to its reciting tone. He argues that while most chants generally follow standard rules, these rules should not always be considered binding: exceptions can be made "by license" (*licencialiter*). Individual chants may sometimes break conventional rules in matters of detail in order to communicate their particular message, and thus move the soul. He notes that this can happen in specific responsories that he identifies as having a beautiful melody: "Such melody is unlikely to have been composed by singers inexperienced in the art of the tones and music. Whoever wishes to indulge his own taste, however, may choose what pleases them more in this matter, because in such things it is reasonable enough to have an opinion."[97] Guy allows for the subjectivity of human response in a way not found in traditional accounts. The extensive authorial corrections made to the *Tractatus de tonis*, refining arguments (including often adding the term *licencialiter*), show how Guy was concerned to steer a path between what was correct according to the theory and what was the actual practice with chants.

Guy of Saint-Denis and the *libellus antiquus*

Perhaps the most enigmatic aspect of Guy's treatise is the claim he makes about an account of the tones "which I have found in a certain truly old book, in which is also contained Guido's *Micrologus*, which I frequently quote in this treatise."[98] He reproduces a story, told by Walter of Châtillon in his *Alexandreis*, about two sisters, Scylla and Charybdis, who became rocks in the sea.[99] Guy claims that the tones were first identified in the different types of melody created by water gushing through eight holes in the rock by which Scylla seduced sailors. All melodies were reportedly variants of these different types. The Greeks, however, plugged these holes so that ships would not be lured onto the potentially destructive rocks. "Subsequently, paying attention to these eight sounds and modes of singing, which are now called tones, they brought together as many arguments as possible, formulating with great certainty the ordering of the discipline of music."[100] The eight tones comprised four authentic tones, each with its own plagal. Guy explains each authentic tone as relating to its plagal equivalent as like the nonsense word *noieane,* called from the bow of a ship, eliciting a response, *noieagis,* from the other end of the ship.

> But what those voices signify or of what language they may be, namely *noieane* or *noieagis* or the like, no one as yet knows, as is read in the same place,

unless by chance such a voice or sound, like the tongue of man, resonates through hidden pipes from the concurrence of water and the breath of the air of the wind. Some Greeks, however, to free themselves quickly from a question of this kind, interpret these words as words of joy, just as *euax* is an interjection designating joy and exultation.[101]

These "nonsense" words that simply articulate a melody were used by theorists as a way of transmitting melody. Here Guy finds a way of explaining how they might have originated. Was Guy accurately reporting what he found in this "ancient book" or was this a literary fiction to enable him to offer his own explanation of the tones, not as specific sequences of pitches, but as different forms of musical expression?

No precedent has been found in the writings of any previous monastic theorist for Guy's explanation that there were holes in these rocks through which rushing water created eight tones or types of melody, and without which no type of natural or rational song could be created. Guido of Arezzo makes no such link to classical learning. Likewise, Guy of Eu, whom we treat below, similarly avoids any association with Greek mythology in his account of the modes in his *Regulae*. Guy of Saint-Denis expresses his uncertainty about the author of the "very ancient little book," only suggesting that it must be someone who came after Guido of Arezzo because of a sentence that it reportedly contained:[102]

> Indeed I am not certain by whom those things concerning the origin of the tones—which up to now I have put forward more through citation from the aforesaid ancient little book than through assertion—were written and to what author they ought to be imputed or ascribed. It seems rather to be due to another, who came after Guido, rather than to Guido himself, especially since in the same place he expressly mentioned him and the formulas of his tones in these words: "Below we have inserted in the section about the tones the formulas of Guido the abbot, a man most distinguished in music."[103] For although Boethius and other more ancient music theorists treated the obscure and impenetrable science of music which is fully clear to God alone, more acutely and profoundly, yet he, deferring to us, composed the most lucid and useful rules for this art of singing. For an ecclesiastic has instructed us about the necessary usage of the church, giving many examples of responsories and antiphons of offices,[104] since almost all the others were completely silent.[105]

The reference to the "formulae of Guido the abbot, a most distinguished man in music" is perplexing because, throughout his *Tractatus*, Guy has referred to Guido of Arezzo simply as a "monk" (*monachus*). The "abbot Guido" to whom he is referring seems to be the author (Guy of Eu) of the Cistercian *Regule de arte musica*, now surviving in a single manuscript.[106] According to a catalogue of the

Sorbonne, these *Regulae* were also preserved in a manuscript, once belonging to Richard de Fournival, chancellor of Amiens, and given to the Sorbonne by Gerard of Abbeville (d. 1272), that also presented the *Micrologus* of Guido of Arezzo as by Guy of Eu (*Guido Augensis*). In the Sorbonne catalogue entry, however, these two authors are conflated as a single person, also thought to have composed the Pseudo-Odo dialogue in the Harley anthology.[107] It is striking, however, that Guy of Saint-Denis never makes more than a passing reference to Guy of Eu's use of the term *maneriae*, even though he included the Cistercian theory of tones in his own analogy, perhaps because they were too theoretical and foreign to the tradition of Guido of Arezzo.[108] Guy seems to have had doubts about conflating the latter with "Abbot Guido."[109]

Perhaps Guy of Saint-Denis relates the mythic origins of the Greek tones to entertain his reader, but he acknowledges that the story is far from certain. It may well be a fiction of his own invention to satisfy an audience familiar with classical allusions. He explicitly contrasts the knowledge of the ancients, in particular that of Boethius, with that of Guido (not making fully clear whether this is Guido of Arezzo, or the Guido who came after him) as compiling "most lucid and useful rules for this art of singing."[110] Guy praises him as a churchman who provided instruction in the proper usage of the church. He then elucidates the discussion, found in Guido's *Micrologus*, of the distinction between authentic and plagal tones.

Rules and Examples in the *Tractatus*

Much of the first part of Guy's *Tractatus* is taken up with general principles. Thus the first chapter is about tone, its constituent elements, namely concords and consonances and their various numerical proportions: material generally drawn from both Boethius and the *Ars musice* of Grocheio. The second chapter describes the names given to the eight tones both by musicians (specifically Guido of Arezzo) and philosophers (specifically Aristotle in the eighth book of the *Politics*), the third with their nature and differentiation, while the fourth, perhaps the most original section of the entire treatise, considers the power and effect of each of the tones. A consistent feature of the treatise, however, lies in the emphasis he places on examples. The *Ars musice* of Grocheio had laid a foundation for this technique in its emphasis on reporting the different musical observances (*usus*) being practiced in Paris, whether in relation to secular or ecclesiastical custom. Guy is similarly sensitive to different ecclesiastical observances, but draws consciously on those he knows from his own abbey.

Guy is aware that individual chants may not always conform to particular rules in relation to any tone. For this reason, the tone of a chant cannot be judged just by its final note, as argued by Pseudo-Odo.[111] The apparent irregularity of certain chants needs to be acknowledged in the same way as occasional irregularity in speech might be allowed for the sake of effect. Guy is unashamed in talking about the beauty of individual chants, which might reflect particularly intense personal emotions:

> But it should be known that it is fitting for those chants, which are commonly said to be irregular and, as said above, are considered irregular by musicians, to be restricted rather than extended, as if going beyond the regular limits of their range. This is just as we see in grammar, because some phrases and expressions or certain ways of speaking are tolerated as much in prose as in verse, clearly sometimes for the sake of meter and sometimes rationally justified by certain figures of speech, or even just by the usage of authors distinguished in grammar. In this way it does not seem at all inappropriate to our argument that some chants instituted by the ancient fathers and catholic men can, not unreasonably, be excused from irregularity sometimes because of the authority of the composers or initiators and sometimes because of the melody and consonant harmony therein. This is especially so since sometimes composers of chants of this kind rush into a kind of unrestrained ascent, either because of the sweetness of the melody they contain, or sometimes because of the matter on which chants of this kind are based. It is just as if they suffer a certain excess of mind or ecstasy in the manner of lovers or those rejoicing or sometimes of the sad and those who mourn.[112]

The emotional power of certain chants relies on the fact that they may break certain rules to create their effect. Certain chants may combine qualities of two tones: "ascending in the way of authentics and descending in the way of plagals."[113] Each tone is capable of engendering an emotional effect through its internal proportions, which act on proportions of qualities within the soul. Certain chants therefore have a particular effect on the soul, because of their internal proportions. This is coherent, he argues, with the teaching of Aristotle that "there are certain imitations and similarities of behavior in musical harmonies."[114] He also sees this as profoundly in keeping with the teaching of Boethius about the effects of particular modes on the soul. Guy quotes a passage from the Franciscan encyclopedist, Bartholomeus Anglicus, who in turn quotes Augustine to say that "musical melody conforms itself to the dispositions of the soul from a certain hidden property of the soul akin to harmony."[115] This phrase, not a verbatim quotation from any known passage in Augustine, may be a paraphrase of a comment in the *Confessions* about there being a profound, but hidden, kinship between the dispositions of the spirit, and corresponding sung modes (*modos*) in voice and spirit.[116] What matters about chants is not so much their foundation in any rule, as their internal harmonic proportions, and their capacity to affect the proportions of internal qualities in the soul. In his conclusion to the first part, Guy observes that the Church uses melodies of all eight tones, in particular those of the first and fourth tones "as clearly temperate and sober and simple and drawing back more to the mean and to virtue."[117] Those of the fourth tone differ from those of the third in being presented "not proudly nor [like a horse rider] with hair streaming in the wind like the third, but simply and modestly seated on a mule, which is more simple and more mild than a horse, holding itself more moderately compared with the third tone and in a certain way turning away from its proud impetuosity."[118] He decries the practice of modally sequential offices which, while allowing each mode to be heard in turn, did not respect this capacity of the tones, which he believed should be chosen according to the particular character of the words being set to music.

The second part of his *Tractatus* is practical in that it gives examples of chants from each of the eight tones, with all their possible variant connections or *differentiae*, to explain how antiphons can be matched to the intoning of the verses of the psalms. Nevertheless, he begins with an opening reflection on the distinction between the *neuma* (or wordless, melismatic phrase) that could follow an intonation formula, and the neumes through which chants were notated. He knew that antiphons comprised an ancient liturgical practice going back to the time of Ambrose. Unable to find any original texts of Pope Gregory the Great on the tones, Guy satisfies himself by providing samples, drawn from the repertoire of Saint-Denis itself, to demonstrate the varied character of the chants that he considers loyal to his inspiration.

What is so remarkable about the second part of the *Tractatus* is the sheer number (over 400) of examples that he presents. While Guy does not himself identify where these chants come from, perhaps relying on his own memory, they can be matched in various liturgical manuscripts from Saint-Denis. Our oldest records from the ninth century simply identify particular feasts then celebrated at the abbey. Some, as for the feast of St. Cucuphas (a Barcelona saint whose relics were honored at Saint-Denis), are non-sequential offices that may well be early in date.[119] A good proportion (although not all) of these chants are found in a twelfth-century manuscript of Saint-Denis, subsequently taken to Compiègne, which records liturgical feasts at the abbey as celebrated in the mid-twelfth century (MS Paris, BnF lat. 17296).[120] On any single page of the *Tractatus* Guy may quote from chants across the liturgical year, as if he is drawing from memory. Nevertheless, he is able to provide accurate summaries of these chants and their modes. When he gives examples in the second part the notation may well be in his own hand.

Only occasionally does he give examples from those offices, such as for Trinity Sunday that had been composed in the modally sequential manner. Similarly, there are occasional examples taken from other, more recently established, feasts that he identifies, such as those of St. Nicholas and St. Mary Magdalene. In general, however, his preference is to take examples from offices that are not modally sequential and thus represent, in his mind at least, the oldest layer of liturgical tradition at Saint-Denis. Given that it was such an ancient abbey, his examples carry the authority of tradition. Guy never described himself as doing anything more than passing on the traditions of authority. As he puts it in his final paragraph, his concern was to discuss "these things about the tones [that] have been collected from the sayings of Boethius, Guido the monk, and certain others, as far as pertains particularly to the use and custom of our monastery, to which I have endeavored to conform myself as fittingly as I could." Here Guy passes over the names of Johannes de Grocheio and Peter of Auvergne, to whom he owed so much. Yet although he insisted on his adherence to tradition, the way he explained the rules of the plainchant he loved was shaped by the philosophical discourse of his age.

More work is needed to explore what influence Guy's *Tractatus* may have exerted. One likely reader of Guy may have been the theorist Jacobus, traditionally linked to Liège (ca. 1260–after 1330), but recently identified with Jacobus de Ispania, illegitimate nephew of both Alfonso the Wise and Eleanor of Castile, through her half-brother, the Infante Enrique of Castile.[121] Jacobus spells out his own name in the opening letters of the seven books of his *Speculum musicae* in the same way as Guy spells out his name GVIDO in the opening letters of his chapters, perhaps emulating the acrostic introduced by Guido of Arezzo. As a critic of the *Ars nova*, writing in the mid- to late-1320s, Jacobus looked back to the great masters of the thirteenth century such as Franco, expressing admiration for Petrus de Cruce, but distancing himself from the achievement of "moderns" such as Johannes de Muris, who first formulated his ideas around 1321. Where Guy promoted linking Guido of Arezzo to Aristotle, Jacobus followed Jerome of Moravia in promoting the authority of Boethius, albeit combined with that of Aristotle.

Guy's dividing up his treatise into two parts, namely on theory and practice is also followed by Johannes de Muris (Jehan des Murs; ca. 1290–after 1344) in his *Notitia artis musice*, around 1321. This latter work was summarized by Petrus de Sancto Dionysio, possibly another monk of Guy's abbey (although his name could simply refer to the surrounding town of Saint-Denis).[122] While Petrus de Sancto Dionysio is concerned with mensural music rather than plainchant, he could be trying to imitate Guy in seeking to show how traditional and modern authorities could be combined together. Thus, whereas Johannes de Muris opens his treatise by quoting from Aristotle's *Metaphysics*, Petrus removes this, instead adding references to Augustine, Isidore, and Boethius in his opening discussion of the nature of sound.[123] More research is needed to establish whether Guy's *Tractatus de tonis*, and indeed the whole anthology of texts of which it forms the conclusion (Harley MS 281), may have exercised an influence on debates about music in the early twelfth century. Jacobus, for example, says that he is fully familiar with the teaching of *moderni* on plainchant (in particular with their teaching that a mode was not simply determined by a chant's final), but observes that some see constructing modally sequential Offices, a practice to which Guy of Saint-Denis objected, as beautiful.[124]

Guy of Saint-Denis and Abbot Guy of Châtres

That Guy of Saint-Denis was still a relatively young man when he wrote the *Tractatus* is suggested by his comment that he preferred to get the agreement of his elders first when proposing a change in the mode of singing a certain tone.[125] Guy of Saint-Denis emerges in his treatise as a scholarly monk who loved the liturgy of his abbey, but wanted to ensure that the choice of plainchant mode should always be dependent on the particular text being sung, going back to the liturgical practice of Saint-Denis in the ninth century. Given that he must have been writing after Peter of Auvergne's final quodlibetal disputation, delivered around Advent 1301, it seems most likely that Guy worked on his *Tractatus* and completed his anthology of texts that served to introduce his treatise during the first decade of the fourteenth century. Its composition would thus have coincided with the beginning of the abbacy of Gilles de Pontoise (1304–26), known for his commitment to ensuring the role of Saint-Denis in the writing of history.[126] Whether Guy knew Grocheio in person is difficult to say, but not impossible if Grocheio continued to teach in Paris for two decades or so after writing his *Ars musice* (ca. 1275).

Exactly the same emphasis on the primacy of text is evident in the *Sanctilogium* compiled by Guy of Châtres, who held the position of *tresorarius* in 1326, when he was elected abbot of Saint-Denis, a position he held until 1343, when he resigned on grounds of ill-health. The original copy of the *Sanctilogium* was taken to England in the fifteenth century (MS British Library, Royal 13.D.IX).[127] Guy of Châtres died in 1350, suggesting that he might have been born around 1270. If Guy of Saint-Denis had been Cantor of the abbey, he would have been responsible for organizing liturgical books and the readings undertaken in both the church and the refectory. As *tresorarius*, Guy of Châtres had overall responsibility not just for the abbey's vast treasury of precious objects, but also its books.[128] It thus seems quite possible that Guy of Saint-Denis is the same person as Guy of Châtres, who subsequently acquired responsibility for the abbey's great treasury, finally rising to become abbot. The *Sanctilogium* imitated the ninth-century *Martyrologium* of Usuard, organized according to the days of the month, from January to December, but vastly expanded by incorporating lives of the great multitude of saints whose lives were described in two great Dominican encyclopedias of the thirteenth century: the *Golden Legend* of Jacobus de Voragine and the *Speculum historiale* of Vincent of Beauvais, supplementing these texts with other material from the library of Saint-Denis. Guy of Châtres also supplied a detailed index to saints after books 1–12 of the *Sanctilogium*. In book 13 he added saints for whom no date was known, while he placed into book 14 those passages from the *Golden Legend* about the major seasons of the liturgical year, from Advent to Pentecost, followed by chapters on the feasts of Corpus Christi and the dedication of a church.[129] This was a much more efficient organizational framework than the *Golden Legend*, anticipating, in its way, that of the Bollandist *Acta sanctorum* in the seventeenth century. In including saints such as Louis IX, it was also more up to date than the compilations of either Vincent or Jacobus de Voragine. The original *Sanctilogium* manuscript, now in the British Library, was carefully prepared by a professional scribe. Small annotations and occasional corrections in the margin, as well as an opening comment on the flyleaf about the presence of an index, are written in a hand very similar to that of the corrections made to the *Tractatus de tonis* by Guy of Saint-Denis. While the *Sanctilogium* is a display manuscript, produced sometime between 1326 and 1343, and the Harley anthology a scholastic text from the first decade of the fourteenth century, both seem to have been produced in the same scriptorium, though at different times.

The problem with the *Golden Legend* for a liturgist was that it combined entries about the saints into an overview of the liturgical year, in which the date of Easter and associated feasts would vary. The *Sanctilogium* was particularly useful from a liturgical perspective because it separated out texts about any saint from feasts related to the temporal cycle of the Church. The *Sanctilogium* reinforced the foundational role of historical narratives in remembering the saints. Its composition reflects the same mentality as prompted Guy of Châtres in 1329 to engage in a major renovation of the College of Saint-Denis as a place for training young monks. In 1336, he gave particular emphasis to the role of education in a major document imposing reforms on the entire Benedictine Order at the request of Jacques Fournier, later elected as the Cistercian Pope Benedict XII (1334–42).[130] Fournier may have known Guy from the first decade of the fourteenth century when he studied and taught at the Collège Saint-Bernard in Paris to privileged Cistercian monks who would advance in the Order. The desire of Guy of Châtres to revise the compilations of Dominican scholars, with the benefit of documents preserved at the Benedictine Saint-Denis, echoes the concerns of the music theorist Guy of Saint-Denis to prioritize the role of text over melody. Unfortunately, a necrology of Saint-Denis from the mid-fourteenth century mentions a number of monks all called Guido, but does not allow any precise identification to be made.[131] Nevertheless the thematic and textual parallels between Guy's *Tractatus* and the prologue to the *Sanctilogium* argue strongly in favor of an identification.

In 1336, Guy of Châtres was asked by Fournier, then Pope Benedict XII, to reform the statutes of the Benedictine Order, creating a degree of standardization of practice among Benedictine abbeys that had never existed before.[132] As mentioned above, Fournier had once taught in Paris (where he may have known Guy), before becoming abbot of Fontfroide in 1311, and then bishop of Pamiers. In his reforms, Guy of Châtres emphasized the importance of giving the best monks a university education. In 1339, Guy instructed that the buildings of the College of Saint-Denis be restored to ensure that it continued to be in important part of the abbey.[133]

Because the Harley manuscript carries no shelf mark of the abbey, such as were given to all its manuscripts in the early fifteenth century, it is quite possible that during the fourteenth and fifteenth centuries the manuscript was preserved not there but at the College of Saint-Denis. By the mid-fifteenth century, however, Saint-Denis was no longer the abbey it had once been. The internal conflicts that tore apart so much of the kingdom resulted in many treasures of the library (such as the *Sanctilogium*) passing into English hands. In the second half of the sixteenth century, the Harley manuscript came into the hands of Jean Gosselin de Vire (ca. 1505–1604), who had been entrusted with guarding the royal library throughout the wars of religion from 1561 until his death.[134] This was a period in which many of the treasures of Saint-Denis were transferred to Paris for safekeeping, quite possibly at the College. The manuscript annotated by Gosselin subsequently entered into private hands, finding its way into the collection of Christopher Wren the younger, who presented it to Robert Harley, and was subsequently donated to the British Museum, now the British Library.

Guy's Prose Style and the Challenges of Translation

Guy's literary style presents a particular challenge to any translator. He has a love for long sentences, with many dependent clauses, carefully marked out in the punctuation of the manuscript of the *Tractatus*. Compared to the Latin of Johannes de Grocheio, Guy emerges as a scholar who likes to display his fluency with the imagery of classical rhetoric when the argument calls for it. To render his Latin into comprehensible English it has been necessary to break up his sentences and eliminate those extra terms with which he likes to embellish a phrase. Nonetheless, he is also a precise writer who has thought carefully about what he wants to say and taken care to correct both mistakes in the manuscript and occasional missteps in his own argument. Certain phrases that he uses, such as *musica falsa*, have been preserved in the English translation because there is no easy equivalent in English.

A treatise on the tones is, by its very nature, reliant on technical discussion. Yet Guy does not refrain from speaking of himself in the first person when commenting on what he himself has experienced. It is in sentences like these that we can hear him speak for himself: "For I do not see that the *neuma* of the fifth tone, as usually sung among us and many others and almost everyone, can conveniently be notated without *musica falsa*."[135] In relation to the truth of his claims to have found authority in an ancient old book, he is cautious: "What truth the aforesaid may contain, I prefer to leave to the judgment of the reader rather than say anything definite about this. Indeed I am not certain by whom those things concerning the origin of the tones—which up to now I have put forward more through citation from the aforesaid ancient little book than through assertion—were written and to what author they ought to be imputed or ascribed."[136] His willingness to adopt the first person, perhaps picked up from Johannes de Grocheio, allows him to make personal aesthetic judgments about individual chants: "For in certain ecclesiastical chants, to which our intentions are principally turned, I see clearly and frequently that some of these contain a more sufficiently beautiful melody than many others that are of the same tone."[137] Guy does not assert his personality or point of view over those of his predecessors in the manner of Grocheio, emphasizing always that he is simply transmitting the views of the ancients. Nevertheless, he cannot avoid communicating his wide knowledge of the ancient works in Saint-Denis and his personal delight in expounding the treasures of the plainchant tradition.

The Edition

This edition of Guy's *Tractatus* follows manuscript readings offered by MS London, British Library, Harley 281 closely, signaling in particular those corrections that appear to have been made by Guy himself (**H2**), correcting the work of his main scribe (**H1**). Only occasionally has an evident error in syntax been ignored by Guy in his work of correction. In such cases, readings offered by van der Klundert in her edition are signaled in the apparatus. The punctuation and sparing use of capital letters follows that of the manuscript. The *virgula suspensiva* (/) is rendered as a comma, the *punctus versus* (ƒ) as a period. With such a technical treatise, the rendering of the terminology used by Guy is inevitably difficult, in particular as his sentences are often long and obtuse. Our translation has sought to tread a fine line between respect for his technical vocabulary and the demands of clarity in the English language.

Outline of the *Tractatus de tonis*

0.0.1   Opening prayer.

1.0.0   Prologue.
1.0.1   Explanation of method and motivation.
1.0.2   Division of the treatise into two parts:
    (1) Theory of the tones;
    (2) Praxis, with illustrative examples.
1.0.3   The four chapters of the first part:
    (1) Different ways of understanding "tone";
    (2) How many tones there are and their names;
    (3) The nature of the tones and the distinction between them;
    (4) The power of the tones.

1.1.0   How "tone" is understood in music and from what it is called.
1.1.1   The two meanings of "tone."
1.1.2   The relationship between sound and motion according to Boethius.
1.1.3   The causes of high and low pitches.
1.1.4   The difference between consonance and concord.

1.1.5   The number of concords and consonances of music.

1.1.6   The tone as the distance between two pitches in a sesquioctave proportion.

1.1.7   The semitone as the concord that exists between mi and fa.

1.1.8   Two kinds of semitone, namely major and minor.

1.1.9   The property of the minor semitone, and that with the tone it constitutes all chant.

1.1.10   The ditone as a concord of two tones in proportion as 81 is to 64 in numbers.

1.1.11   The semiditone as a concord of a tone with a semitone in proportion as 32 is to 27 in numbers.

1.1.12   The *diatessaron* as a concord containing two tones with a minor semitone in sesquitertian proportion as 4 is to 3.

1.1.13   The *diapente* as a concord containing three tones with a minor semitone in sesquialter proportion as 3 is to 2.

1.1.14   The *diapason* as a concord containing five tones and two minor semitones in double proportion as 2 is to 1.

1.1.15   The analogy between the Holy Trinity and the three perfect consonances, the *diatessaron*, the *diapente* and the *diapason*.

1.1.16   That music, according to Boethius, is naturally innate in all of us.

1.1.17   The origins of music and the story of Pythagoras and the blacksmith.

1.1.18   Explanation of the Pythagorean proportions of music.

1.1.19   Discovery and description of the monochord.

1.2.0   The number of tones and their names.

1.2.1   The number of tones and basic information on pitch letter names, hexachord syllables and the hand.

1.2.2   The registers, grave, acute and superacute, and their pitches.

1.2.3   Finals and affinals.

1.2.4   Four finals but eight tones; authentic and plagal tones.

1.2.5   Scylla and Charybdis and the origin of the tones; *noannoeane* and *noeagis*.

1.2.6   The harmony of the spheres reconsidered.

1.2.7   Greek names for the tones, *protus, deuterus, tritus, tetrardus.*

1.2.8   On an ancient little book and Abbot Guido.

1.2.9   The eight authentic and plagal tones and their names.

1.2.10   Uneven numbered tones as authentic, and the even numbered tones as plagal.

1.2.11   The alternative names of tones: Dorian, Hypodorian, Phrygian, Hypophrygian, Lydian, Hypolydian, Mixolydian and Hypermixolydian.

1.2.12   The tones numbered as 1–8.

1.3.0   Concerning the nature of the tones and their differentiation.

1.3.1   Authentic and plagal tones sharing a final.

1.3.2   The difference between authentic and plagal tones.

1.3.3   The range and final of tone 1.

1.3.4   The use of license to extend the range of tone 1.

1.3.4a   Deleted passage concerning transposition of tone 1.

1.3.5   The use of the affinal for tone 1.

1.3.6   The range of tone 1 when the affinal is used.

1.3.7   The range and final of tone 2.

1.3.8   Transposition using soft b in tone 2.

1.3.9   The range and final of tone 3.

1.3.10   The use of the affinal for tone 3.

1.3.11   The range and final of tone 4.

1.3.12   Transposition using soft b when an affinal is used for tone 4.

1.3.13   The range and final of tone 5.

1.3.14   The range and final of tone 6.

1.3.15   The use of the affinal in tone 6.

1.3.16   The range and final of tone 7.

1.3.17   The use of the affinal in tone 7.

1.3.18   The range and final of tone 8.

1.3.19   The use of the affinal in tone 8.

1.3.20   Explanation of the nature of irregular chants.

1.3.21   The distinction between pure and mixed chant.

1.3.22   Mixed chants retaining the characteristics of two tones.

1.3.23   How to decide to which tone a mixed chant most properly belongs.

1.4.0   On the property and effect, or power, of the tones.

1.4.1   How harmonies, melodies, and musical consonances, regulated through the tones, can arouse different passions of the soul.

1.4.2   The relationship between the sensory appetite and passions of the soul.

1.4.3   The difference between audible and visible things in moving the passions of the soul.

1.4.4   The ability of musical harmonies to purge certain passions since what generates a particular passion weakens its opposite.

1.4.5   The capacity of musical harmonies to influence behavior.

1.4.6   Boethius and Plato on the power of music to change behavior.

1.4.7   Examples of the power of music from Boethius, Pythagoras, and Guido.

1.4.8   The capacity of music to render a happy man happier and a sad man sadder.

1.4.9   On judging which harmonies or melodies are able to arouse passions of the soul.

1.4.10   The diversity of tones as adapted to the diversity of minds.

1.4.11   A discussion of regional characteristics and customs.

1.4.12   How different planets establish diverse characteristics in us.

1.4.13   Different ways of singing and different forms of chant for different groups of people.

1.4.14   That there are as many ways of singing as there are nations of people.

1.4.15   Tone 3, the Phyrygian, by its nature leads to that passion called rapture.

1.4.16   Tone 3 as depicted like riding a horse with hair streaming in the wind.

1.4.17   Tone 7, the Mixolydian, by its nature encouraging mercy and compassion and depicted as winged and armed.

1.4.18   Melodic qualities of tones 5 and 6 as disposing more to softness or sensuousness, depicted as a man with a lance driven through his chest.

1.4.19   Melodic qualities of tones 2 and 8 as disposing more to sorrow and grief: 2 depicted as holding in its hand a peacock with its throat pierced by an arrow and 8 as holding a drawn sword in its right hand.

1.4.20   Melodic qualities of tones 1 and 4 as disposing to virtue: tone 1 depicted with a crown on its head and holding a banner in its hand.

1.4.21   Tone 4 as depicted simply and modestly seated on a mule.

1.4.22   The practice of constructing an office by proceeding according to the order of the tones.

2.0.1   **On the practice and operation of the tones.**

2.0.2   What a neume is.

2.0.3   A neume serving as a melodic passage in a chant.

2.0.4   A neume as that melodic passage made on the last syllable of the antiphon.

2.0.5   That there are eight neumes as there are eight tones.

2.0.6   The neumes as generally sung on ordinary days after only two psalms, namely the *Benedictus* and *Magnificat*.

2.0.7   How Ambrose first transferred the use of singing antiphons from the Greeks to the Latins.

2.0.8   How Charlemagne sought to use the chant of Pope Gregory throughout his lands.

2.0.9   How Pope Gregory sent the chant to the Apulians and Calabrians through Paul and taught him how to notate an antiphonary.

2.0.10   The three parts of the intonation of any psalm, namely the beginning, the middle part, and the end.

2.0.11   Verse mnemonic to remember the beginnings of intonation for each of the tones.

2.0.12   Another verse mnemonic with the same purpose.

2.0.13   The rule for establishing the median note for intonation in the tones.

2.0.14   Verse mnemonic to remember the general rule about the middle part of intonation.

2.0.15   A melodic mnemonic for remembering the beginnings of intonation for each of the tones.

2.0.16   Differences between the chant practice of Saint-Denis and those of other churches.

2.0.17   Variations of the ends of intonations or *differentiae*, commonly called seculorum amen, both within different tones and within the same tone.

2.0.18   Tones 1 and 6 as less elevated in their middle part than are the other tones.

2.0.19   How a good and expert cantor ought to look ahead toward the end of the intonation.

2.0.20   Details concerning the number of differentiae of the tones for antiphons and introits.

2.1.0   Chapter one in which are given examples of tone 1.

2.1.1   The first *differentia.*

2.1.2   The second *differentia.*

2.1.3   The third *differentia.*

2.1.4   The fourth *differentia.*

2.1.5   The fifth *differentia.*

2.1.6   The sixth *differentia.*

2.1.7   The seventh *differentia.*

2.1.8   The eighth *differentia.*

2.1.9   The ninth *differentia.*

2.1.10   The first and the seventh *differentiae* are those most commonly in use.

2.1.11   The rules of art are set down for those things that occur consistently or often rather than for those that occur rarely, so not every rule has an example. The way of intoning in the introit of the mass.

2.1.12   The first and second *differentiae* with examples.

2.2.0   Chapter two in which examples of tone 2 are given.

2.2.1   How a particular *Venite* not in the use of Saint-Denis is found in the church of Paris and in many others.

2.3.0   Chapter three in which examples of tone 3 are given.

2.3.1   The first *differentia.*

2.3.2   The second *differentia.*

2.4.0   Chapter four in which examples of tone 4 are given.

2.4.1   The first *differentia.*

2.4.2   The second *differentia.*

2.4.3   The third *differentia.*

2.4.4   The fourth *differentia.*

2.4.5   The fifth *differentia.*

2.4.6   The sixth *differentia.*

2.5.0   Chapter five in which examples of tone 5 are given.
2.5.1   The first *differentia*.

2.6.0   Chapter six in which examples of tone 6 are given.

2.7.0   Chapter seven in which examples of tone 7 are given.
2.7.1   The first *differentia*.
2.7.2   The second *differentia*.
2.7.3   The third *differentia*.
2.7.4   The fourth *differentia*.

2.8.0   Chapter eight in which examples of tone 8 are given.
2.8.1   The first *differentia*.
2.8.2   The second *differentia*.
2.8.3   The third *differentia*.
2.8.4   The fourth *differentia*.

NOTES

[1] The first critical edition of this work was produced by Sieglinde van der Klundert, *Guido von Sankt-Denis, Tractatus de tonis*, 2 vols. (Bubenreuth: Hurricane Publishers, 1998). Her critical text, reproduced at http://www.chmtl.indiana.edu/tml/14th/GUIS-TON_TEXT.html, is preceded by an important critical study. Prior to van der Klundert, Michel Huglo (n. 3 below) had commented briefly on the treatise, as had Anne Walters Robertson, *The Service-Books of the Royal Abbey of Saint-Denis. Images of Ritual and Music in the Middle Ages* (Oxford: OUP, 1991), pp. 113–28, at 335–36. The terms "tone" and "mode" are often used interchangeably; here we follow Guy's practice in referring to *toni* rather than *modi*. Broadly, *tonus* is associated with the theory of plainchant and is bound up with the practice of psalmody; *modus* draws on its roots in ancient Greek harmonic theory and is an abstraction that has little to do with practice. See Charles M. Atkinson, "On the Interpretation of *Modi, quos abusive tonos dicimus*" in *Hermeneutics and Medieval Culture*, ed. Patrick J. Gallacher and Helen Damico (Albany: State University of New York Press, 1989), pp. 147–162.

[2] For a detailed description of Harley MS 281, see Constant J. Mews, John N. Crossley, Catherine Jeffreys, Leigh McKinnon, and Carol Williams, "Guy of Saint-Denis and the Compilation of Texts about Music in London, British Library, Harl. MS. 281," *Electronic British Library Journal* (2008), art. 6, available at http://www.bl.uk/eblj/2008articles/article6.html (with references to earlier literature). See also our edition of Johannes de Grocheio, *Ars musice*, ed. and trans. by Constant J. Mews, John N. Crossley, Carol Williams, Catherine Jeffreys and Leigh McKinnon, TEAMS (Kalamazoo, MI: University of Western Michigan Press, 2011), hereafter referred to as Grocheio, *Ars musice*, and Constant J. Mews, John N. Crossley and Carol Williams, "Guy of St Denis on the Tones: Thinking about Chant for Saint-Denis c. 1300," *Journal of Plainsong and Medieval Music*, 23/2 (2014), 151–76, a study that provides more detail on issues raised in this introduction.

[3] This tradition was comprehensively studied by Michel Huglo, *Les tonaires: inventaire, analyse, comparaison* (Paris: Socété française de musicologie, 1971), with a brief discussion of Guy, but without highlighting any of his originality, pp. 336–38.

[4] Guy is described as having "completely ignored the latest developments in music" by Robertson, *The Service Books*, pp. 334–35, referring to mensural notation, which is not relevant to plainchant.

[5] Alleluias were used for most of the year but were replaced by tracts in Lent.

[6] For a listing of saints in the Saint-Denis Calendar, see Robertson, *The Service-Books*, pp. 446–61, which has an excellent commentary on the development of the Calendar, pp. 53–101.

[7] Constant J. Mews, "Gregory the Great, the Rule of Benedict and Roman liturgy: The Evolution of a Legend," *Journal of Medieval History* 37 (2011), 125–44.

[8] Guy Fourquin, "Les débuts du fermage. L'exemple de Saint-Denis," *Études rurales* 22–24 (1966), 7–81.

[9] Caroline Astrid Bruzelius, *The 13th-Century Church at St-Denis* (New Haven: Yale University Press, 1985); Anne Robertson, "The Reconstruction of the Abbey Church at Saint-Denis (1231–81): The Interplay of Music and Ceremony with Architecture and Politics," *Early Music History* 5 (1985), 187–238.

[10] Donatella Nebbiai-Dalla Guarda, "Le collège de Paris de l'abbaye de Saint-Denis-en-France (XIIIe–VIIIe siècle," in *Sous la règle de Saint Benoît: Structures monastiques et sociétés en France du Moyen Age à l'époque moderne. Abbaye bénédictine Sainte-Marie de Paris, 23–25 octobre 1980* (Genève: Droz, 1982), pp. 461–88 at p. 465.

[11] Nebbiai-Dalla Guarda, "Le collège de Paris," p. 47; Michel Félibien, *Histoire de l'abbaye royale de Saint-Denys en France* (Paris: Frédéric Lonard, 1706), p. 258, quoting a letter then in the archives of Saint-Denis.

[12] On the identification of Guy of Saint-Denis with Guy of Châtres (d. 1350), see above, pp. xxxiii–xxxvi; if they are the same person, Guy could have been born around 1270.

[13] Studied by Gabrielle M. Spiegel, *The Chronicle Tradition of Saint-Denis: A Survey*, (Brookline, Mass.: Classical Folia Editions, 1978), in particular pp. 89–112. That Guillaume de Nangis was *Custos cartarum* from 1285 to his death in 1300 was established by H.–François Delaborde, "Notes sur Guillaume de Nangis," *Bibliothèque de l'école des chartes* 44 (1883), 192–201.

[14] *Chronique latine de Guillaume de Nangis de 1113 à 1300 avec les continuations de cette chronique de 1300 à 1368*, ed. by Hércule Geraud, 2 vols. (Paris: Renouard, 1844). There were new continuators in 1314 and 1317, while the continuator from 1340 was a Carmelite friar, Jean de Venette. On the continuators, see H. Geraud, "De Guillaume de Nangis et de ses continuateurs," *Bibliothèque de l'école des chartes* 3 (1842), 17–46 and *Chronique de Richard Lescot, religieux de Saint-Denis (1328–1344) suivie de la continuation de cette chronique (1344–1364)* (Paris: Renouard, 1896), which mentions the retirement of Guy of Châtres on p. 61.

[15] Cf. *Tractatus de tonis*, 1.2.1, nn. 138 and 139 and 1.4.6, n. 206. Short references to the present edition include a location device with part number, chapter number and section, usually paragraph, as marked in the manuscript.

[16] Parts of the accounts relating to education are edited by Donatella Nebbiai-Dalla Guarda, *La Bibliothèque de l'abbaye de Saint-Denis en France du IXe au XVIIIe siècle* (Paris: CNRS, 1985), pp. 336–57, with references to the *magister iuvenum* and *magister*

puerorum from 1284/85 (p. 337) to 1342/43 (p. 355), whose payments increased from 32 to 40 *solidi* between 1303/4 and 1320/21 (when accounts resume, possibly because Guy of Châtres was now treasurer of the abbey).

[17] Ibid., pp. 340, 350.

[18] These books are listed by Nebbiai-Dalla Guarda, *La Bibliothèque*, pp. 313–17, and Robertson, *The Service-Books*, pp. 356–412.

[19] Nebbiai-Dalla Guarda, "Des rois et des moines: Livres et lecteurs à l'abbaye de Saint-Denis (XIIIe–XVe siècles)," in Françoise Autrand, Claude Gauvard, and Jean-Marie Moeglin eds., *Saint-Denis et la royauté. Etudes offerts à B. Guenée* (Paris: Publications de la Sorbonne, 1999), pp. 355–74, esp. 360–61.

[20] Michel Huglo, "Les chants de la Missa greca de Saint-Denis," in *Essays Presented to E. Wellesz,* ed. by J. Westrup (Oxford: OUP, 1966), pp. 74–83, reprinted in *Les anciens répertoires de plain-chant* (Aldershot, Hants: Ashgate, 2005) and Robertson, *The Service-Books*, pp. 285–91.

[21] Nebbiai-Dalla Guarda, *La Bibliothèque*, pp. 50–51; Roberto Weiss, "Lo studio del greco all' abbazia di San Dionigi durante il medioevo," *Rivista di storia della chiesa in Italia* 6 (1952), 426–38, reprinted in *Medieval and Humanist Greek: Collected Essays* (Padua: Antenore, 1977), pp. 44–59, and P. G. Théry, "Documents concernant Jean Sarrasin," *Archives d'histoire doctrinale et littéraire du moyen âge* 18 (1950), pp. 45–87. Whether Jean was a monk of Saint-Denis or just connected to the abbey is not clear, but he did benefit from Greek manuscripts brought to the abbey from Constantinople in 1167.

[22] Robertson, *The Service-Books*, pp. 331–4.

[23] Elias Salomo, *Scientia artis musicae*, in *Scriptores ecclesiastici de musica sacra potissimum*, 3 vols., ed. Martin Gerbert (St. Blaise: Typis San-Blasianis, 1784; reprinted Hildesheim: Olms, 1963), 3:33; Anonymous 3, *De cantu mensurabili* in *Scriptorum de musica medii aevi nova series*, 4 vols., ed. Edmond de Coussemaker (Paris: Durand, 1864–76; reprinted Hildesheim: Olms, 1963), 1:319; Anonymous, *Compendium musicae mensurabilis artis antiquae (MS Faenza, Biblioteca Communale, 117)*, ed. F. Alberto Gallo, CSM 15 ([Rome:] American Institute of Musicology, 1971), pp. 66–72.

[24] Guy, *Tractatus de tonis*, 2.4.8.

[25] The questions on music have been edited by Frank Hentschel, "Der verjagte Dämon. Mittelalterliche Gedanken zur Wirkung der Music aus der Zeit um 1300. Mit einer Edition der Questiones 16 und 17 aus Quodlibet VI des Petrus d'Auvergne," in *Geistesleben im 13. Jahrhundert*, ed. Jan A. Aertsen and Andreas Speer (Berlin, New York: 2000), pp. 395–421. The Latin text of the *questiones* is also available through the *Thesaurus Musicarum Latinarum* (*siglum* PETQUO), accessible at www.chmtl.indiana.edu/tml/start.html. See also Frank Hentschel, *Sinnlichkeit und Vernunft in der mittelalterlichen Musiktheorie: Strategien der Konsonanzwertung und der Gegenstand der* Musica sonora *um 1300*, Beiheft zum Archiv für Musikwissenschaft 47 (Stuttgart: De Gruyter, 2000), pp. 234–8; Albrecht Riethmüller, "Probleme der spekulativen Musiktheorie im Mittelalter," in *Rezeption des antiken Fachs im Mittelalter*, ed. by Michael Bernhard (Darmstadt: Wissenschaftliche Buchgesellschaft, 1990), pp. 197–201 [163–201]. Catherine Jeffreys notes this dependence on Peter of Auvergne's *Quodlibet* in "The Exchange of Ideas about Music in Paris c. 1270–1304: Guy of Saint-Denis, Johannes de Grocheio, and Peter of Auvergne," in *Communities of Learning: Networks and the Shaping of Intellectual Identity in Europe,*

1100–1500, ed. Constant J. Mews and John N. Crossley (Turnhout: Brepols, 2011), pp. 151–75. See also the reference to the *Ethics* and its interpreter in Guy, *Tractatus de tonis*, 1.4.1, which is in fact a paraphrase of Peter of Auvergne, *Quodlibet* 16, ed. by Hentschel, p. 419. Without awareness of this debt to Peter of Auvergne, Robertson follows Huglo in dating the *Tractatus* to between 1299 and 1318. Klundert, *Guido*, 1:18–19 considers the early fourteenth century, soon after the completion of the rebuilding of the abbey church, the most likely time for its composition.

[26] Christoph Flüeler, Lidia Lanza, and Marco Toste, eds., *Peter of Auvergne: University Master of the 13th century*. vol. 26 Scrinium Friburgense (Fribourg: De Gruyter, 2015), a volume that covers many of his interests, although not the field of music.

[27] Heinrich Denifle, *Chartularium Universitatis Parisiensis* (hereafter *CUP*), vol. 2, pp. 521–530 (no. 460). On the uncertainties surrounding Peter's career, see William J. Courtenay, "Peter of Auvergne, Master in Arts and Theology in Paris," in *Peter of Auvergne: University Master of the 13th century*, ed. Flüeler et al., pp. 11–28.

[28] R. A. Gauthier argued that the division was based on institutional rather than doctrinal issues, "Notes sur Siger de Brabant. II. Siger en 1272–1275. Aubry de Reims et la scission des Normands," *Revue des sciences philosophiques et théologiques* 68 (1984), 3–49. The fact that masters from suffragan dioceses of Normandy were involved may be related to their being in conflict with Eudes Rigaud, the Franciscan archbishop of Rouen 1248–75, itself an echo of the secular–mendicant dispute. Aubry (Alberic) was himself committed to philosophical inquiry in ways that Bonaventure did not like, but never became a polarizing figure like Siger of Brabant.

[29] Peter's continuations of Thomas's commentaries are edited in S. Thomae Aquinatis, *In libros politicorum Aristotelis expositio*, ed. Raymundo M. Spiazzi (Rome: Marietti, 1951) and *Thomas Aquinatis Opera omnia*, II.2 (Parma, 1866), pp. 163–202. See also Peter of Auvergne, *Quaestiones supra librum* De Caelo: *A Critical Edition with an Interpretative Essay, Ancient and Medieval Philosophy*, De Wulf-Mansion Centre, ser. 1, n. 229, (Leuven 2003). Roberto Lambertini could not date the commentary on the *Politics* precisely, but because it never draws directly on the *De regimine principum* of Giles of Rome, composed 1277–79, he suggests that it was most likely produced in the second half of the 1270s, perhaps at the same time as Giles was producing his treatise; see Roberto Lambertini, "Peter of Auvergne, Giles of Rome and Aristotle's 'Politica,'" in *Peter of Auvergne*, ed. Flüeler et al., pp. 51–69.

[30] *CUP*, vol. 2, pp. 504–5 (no. 447).

[31] On the various writings of Peter of Auvergne, most of which are unpublished, see Palémon Glorieux, *La Faculté des Arts et ses maîtres au XIIIe siècle* (Paris: Vrin, 1971), pp. 275–78, which largely reproduces that given in his *Repertoire des Maîtres en théologie de Paris au XIIIe siècle*, 2 vols. (Paris: Vrin, 1934), pp. 412–17. See also Griet Galle, "A Comprehensive Bibliography of Peter of Auvergne," *Bulletin de philosophie médiévale* 42 (2000), 53–79.

[32] See the text edited by Hentschel, in "Der verjagte Dämon;" we are indebted to Joe Dyer for sharing an advance copy of a forthcoming paper on Peter of Auvergne and his ideas about music.

[33] There is a large literature on the 1277 condemnation. See Roland Hissette, *Enquête sur les 219 articles condamnés à Paris le 7 mars 1277* (Louvain: Presses universitaires,

1977); Luca Bianchi, *Il Vescovi e i filosofi. La condanna Parigina del 1277 e l'evoluzione dell'Aristotelismo scolastico* (Bergamo: Pierluigi Lubrina Editore, 1990); J. M. M. H. Thijssen, *Censure and Heresy at the University of Paris 1200–1400* (Philadelphia: University of Pennsylvania Press, 1998), esp. pp. 40–56. The core text of the condemnation was edited by Denifle, *CUP*, vol. 1, pp. 543–558, no. 473, and reprinted with German translation and brief comments in Kurt Flasch, *Aufklärung im Mittelalter? Die Verurteilung von 1277* (Mainz: Dieterichsche Verlagsbuchhandlung, 1989). On the issues relating to Thomas, see John F. Wippel, "The Condemnations of 1270 and 1277 at Paris," *Journal of Medieval and Renaissance Studies* 7 (1977), 169–201.

[34] Luca Bianchi observes the potential challenge presented to Tempier by "eudaimonistic" opinions raised by Peter; see "Peter of Auvergne and the Condemnation of 1277," in *Peter of Auvergne*, ed. Flüeler et al., pp. 29–50. See also Henryk Anzulewicz, "Peter of Auvergne and Albert the Great as Interpreters of the *De caelo*," in *Peter of Auvergne*, ed. Flüeler, pp. 107–34.

[35] Albert the Great, "Commentarius in Aristotelis libros I-VIII Politicorum," in *Opera Omnia*, ed. E. Borgnet, vol. 8 (Paris: Vives, 1891), pp. 753–804. On the date, see Christoph Flüeler, *Rezeption und Interpretation der Aristotelischen Politica im späten Mittelalter*, 2 vols. (Amsterdam: Grüner, 1990), vol. 2, p. 2. On the diffusion of the *Politics*, see Catherine Jeffreys, "Some Early References to Aristotle's *Politics* in Parisian Writings about Music," in *Identity and Locality in Early European Music*, ed. Jason Stoessel (London: Ashgate, 2009), pp. 83–106.

[36] *Summa theologiae* IIa–IIae q. 91.2: "Manifestum est autem quod secundum diversas melodias sonorum animi hominum diversimode disponuntur, ut patet per philosophum, in viii polit., et per Boetium, in prologo musicae."

[37] Thomas Aquinas and Peter of Auvergne, *In libros politicorum Aristotelis expositio*, ed. Raymundo M. Spiazzi (Turin: Marietti, 1951). On this work, see Peter's commentary described in Lidia Lanza, "Aspetti della ricezione della 'Politica' aristotelica nel XIII secolo: Pietro d'Alvernia," *Studi Medievali* ser. 3, 35 (1994), 643–94.

[38] The *Ars musice* was dated to c. 1300 by Christopher Page, "Johannes de Grocheio on Secular Music: a Corrected Text and a New Translation," *Plainsong and Medieval Music* 2 (1993), 17–41, reprinted in *Page, Music and Instruments of the Middle Ages: Studies on Texts and Performance* (Aldershot: Ashgate, 1997). For further discussion of the date of Grocheio's treatise, see the introduction by Mews et al., to Grocheio, *Ars musice*, pp. 10–12.

[39] On the earliest version of the Office, introduced as *In Festo Eucharistie* (in The Hague, National Library MS 70.E.4, fols. 52r–63v), see Barbara R. Walters, Vincent Corrigan and Peter T. Ricketts, *The Feast of Corpus Christi* (University Park, PA: Pennsylvania State University Press, 2006), pp. 78 and 117–83, with discussion on pp. 63–65. In 2001 Michel Huglo suggested that the unusual responsory mentioned by Guy was written before widespread adoption of the version composed by Thomas Aquinas in 1315–18 "Guy de Saint-Denis," in *Grove Music Online* (Oxford University Press) [subscriber access required].

[40] *Tractatus de tonis*, 1.3.15. While *Paratum panem* is not mentioned in any of the versions edited by Walters et al., *The Feast of Corpus Christi* (although it is part of a Lauds antiphon, *Angelorum esca*, p. 188), it occurs in MS Arras, Bibliothèque municipale 893, fols. 257r and 258r, as well as in the Saint-Denis missal, MS London, Victoria and Albert

Museum, L 1346–1891, fol. 143va, though both times without music. Corrigan notes that the earliest record of the Aquinas version is that in MS Paris, BnF lat. 1143 from the second half of the thirteenth or early fourteenth century (*op. cit.* pp. 83–84). Only a single copy is known of a transitional version from Prague (MS Abbey of Strahov, D.E.I.7). The hymn *Verbum supernum prodiens* also quoted by Guy (*Tractatus de tonis*, 2.8.4) follows the melody of the Advent version of the hymn, not that of the version adapted for the feast of Corpus Christi. The Aquinas version is preserved without music in a breviary associated with Philip the Fair from the late thirteenth century (MS Paris, BnF lat. 1023), as well as in a thirteenth-century Cistercian breviary (MS Troyes, Mediathèque, 1980), and a Benedictine version, now in Graz, according to Walters, p. 59 and Corrigan, p. 85, from ca. 1280. That the Cistercian version of the Office differed from that widely attributed to Thomas Aquinas was first noted by Gervais Morin, "L'office Cistercien pour la fête-Dieu comparé avec celui de saint Thomas d'Aquin," *Revue Bénédictine* 27 (1910), 236–46; that the Liège version first spread in Cistercian circles is noted by T. J. Mathiesen, "The Office of the New Feast of Corpus Christi in the *Regimen Animarum*," *The Journal of Musicology* 2 (1983), 13–44 (at pp. 24–25).

[41] The feast is first mentioned in the Dominican General Chapter in 1304. On the affirmation of the feast by Pope Clement V in 1311 and its adoption by the Dominican Order between 1318 and 1323, see Walters et al., *The Feast of Corpus Christi*, p. 34. See n. 39 above for comments by Huglo.

[42] There is no numerical modal sequence evident in the original version as celebrated in Liège (MS The Hague, National Library 70.E.4 the only copy with the rubric *in festo eucharistie*) (*op. cit.*, pp. 93–4) or the transitional version (MS Prague, Strahov Abbey D.E.I.7) (*op. cit* pp. 95–96). There is some sequencing of modes in MS Paris, BnF 1143 (*op. cit.* pp. 97–99), MS Graz, Universitätsbibliothek 134 (*op. cit.* pp. 100–101), MS Brussels, Bibliothèque royale 139 (*op. cit.* p. 102), and much more in MS Brigham Young University, Special Collections, Harold B. Lee Library, 091 R263 1343 (*op. cit.* pp. 103–4), but none in MS Edinburgh, Edinburgh University Library, MS 211.iv (*op. cit.* p. 105).

[43] Michel Huglo analyses these manuscripts in *Les tonaires*, pp. 91–102 (with only brief comment on Guy of Saint-Denis on pp. 336–37), constructing what he calls "the tonary of Saint-Denis." Richard L. Crocker offers a valuable review of Huglo's work in the *Journal of the American Musicological Society* 26 (1973), 490–95, reprinted with other essays of his in *Studies in Medieval Music Theory and the Early Sequence* (Aldershot: Ashgate, 1993), VII.

[44] Guy, *Tractatus de tonis*, 2.0.9: "Librum autem de tonis, quem, ut dictum est, ab ipso editum quidam musici asseverant, etsi diligenter quesitum sub ipsius intitulatum nomine repperisse hucusque nequiverim, a Guidonis tamen vestigiis et aliorum sequentium musicorum regulis, qui ipsius venerandi doctoris imitati sunt vestigia, non recessi. Fortassis etiam inter multos variosque tractatus, quos de ista materia vidi, librum ipsum tenui et attente legi, ignorans tamen aut nescius cuius esset."

[45] Robertson, *The Service-Books*, pp. 261–71.

[46] On their contribution to these reforms, see Robertson, *The Service-Books*, pp. 25–42. On the difference between Gallican, Roman and other Old Italian chants, see David Hiley, *Western Plainchant: A Handbook* (Oxford: Clarendon Press, 1993) pp. 514–57.

[47] Stephen of Liège, *Officium sanctae Trinitatis*, ed. Ritva Jonsson, *Historia. Études*

sur la genèse des offices versifiés (Stockholm: Almquist & Wiksell, 1968), pp. 221–224. The attribution to Stephen (rather than to Hucbald) is affirmed by Florence Close, "L'Office de la Trinité d'Étienne de Liège (901–920). Un témoin de l'héritage liturgique et théologique de la première réforme carolingienne à l'aube du Xe siècle," *Revue belge de philologie et d'histoire* 86 (2008), 623–43. On modally sequential offices see Andrew Hughes, "Modal Order and Disorder in the Rhymed Office," *Musica Disciplina* 37 (1983), 29–51 and Richard L. Crocker, "Matins antiphons at St. Denis," *Journal of the American Musicological Society* 39 (1986), 441–90.

[48] Aristotle, *Ethics* 1.3.1094b27: "Sermones inquirendi sunt secundum materiam de qua sunt."

[49] Guy, *Tractatus de tonis*, 1.4.22: "Antiquiores tamen et primi cantores de tali ordine qui potius ad ornatum quemdam vel decorem quam ad necessitatem divini officii introductus videtur, raro vel numquam videntur curasse eo forte quod ad mediocritatem ac sobrietatem cantuum vel etiam qualitatem materie super quam cantus ecclesiasticos fundaverunt attendere potius videbantur. Sicut enim ut alibi scribitur sermones exigendi sunt secundum materiam subiectam ita etiam suo modo de ecclesiasticis cantibus debet esse."

[50] Aristotle, *Ethics* 1.3.1094b27: "Sermones inquirendi sunt secundum materiam de qua sunt."

[51] On modally sequential offices see Hughes, "Modal Order" and Crocker, "Matins antiphons" (n. 47 above).

[52] Karen Desmond, "Sicut in grammatica: Analogical Discourse in Chapter 15 of Guido's Micrologus," *The Journal of Musicology* 16/4 (1998), 467–93.

[53] The *Regulae*, attributed to "abbot Guido" in the only surviving manuscript (MS Paris, Bibl. Sainte-Geneviève 2284), were edited by Claire Maître, *La réforme cistercienne du plain-chant: étude d'un traité théorique* (Brecht: Cîteaux. Commentarii Cisterienses, 1995), pp. 108–233. The *Regulae* are followed in this manuscript by a short twelfth-century treatise on Organum, also attributed to abbot Guy: C. Sweeney, "The *Regulae organi Guidonis abbatis* and the 12th Century Organum/Discantus treatises," *Musica Disciplina* 43 (1989), 7–31.

[54] *Tonale Sancti Bernardi*, ed. Christian Meyer, "Le tonaire cistercien et sa tradition," *Revue de Musicologie* 89 (2003), 57–92, esp. p. 77: "Incipit Tonale. Discipulus. Quid est tonus? Magister. Regula, naturam et formam cantuum regularium determinans. ... Cognoscis ergo naturam cantus, si cognoveris cuius dispositionis sit, vel cuius maneriae." See also M. Cocheril, "Le 'Tonale sancti Bernardi' et la définition du ton," *Commentarii cistercienses* 13 (1962), 35–66.

[55] The term *maneria* is used in place of *modus* or *tonus* by Guido Augensis, *Regulae de arte musica*, ed. Maître, p. 110: "Hunc enim credimus esse fructum huius operis cognoscere de cantu cuius sit manerie, et cuius forme illud per dispositionem, hoc per progressionem, sive per compositionem."

[56] *Tonale Sancti Bernardi*, ed. Meyer, p. 87: "Quod quaeris, non est praesentis negotii, cum prohibente sancto Cisterciensi capitulo, nec in gradali nec in Antiphonario quidquam mutari jam liceat. Quaere tamen musicam Guidonis Augensis, quam scribit ad sanctissimum magistrum suum domnum Guillelmum primum Rievallis abbatem. Ibi de talibus sufficienter doceri poteris." Gerbert's edition, reprinted in Patralogia latinae (hereafter PL) 182, col. 1166D, erroneously reads *nec in Guidonis Antiphonario*.

[57] Constant J. Mews and Rina Lahav, "Wisdom and Justice in the Court of Jeanne of Navarre and Philip IV: Durand of Champagne, the *Speculum dominarum*, and the *De informatione principum*," *Viator* 45/3 (2014), 173–200.

[58] M. Cecilia Gaposchkin, *The Making of Saint Louis. Kingship, Sanctity, and Crusade in the Later Middle Ages* (Ithaca: Cornell University Press, 2008).

[59] Gaposchkin, *The Making of Saint Louis*, pp. 71–76.

[60] M. Cecilia Gaposchkin, "Philip the Fair, the Dominicans, and the Liturgical Office for Louis IX: New Perspectives on *Ludovicus Decus*," *Plainsong and Medieval Music* 13 (2004), 33–61; see also her monograph, *The Making of Saint Louis*, pp. 78–81.

[61] Gaposchkin, "Philip the Fair," 33–61 and "The Monastic Office for Louis IX of France," *Revue Mabillon* 20 (2009), 55–86, especially pp. 62–63 (edition on pp. 72–77); see also her Appendix 2.1 to *The Making of Saint Louis*, pp. 253–76. *Lauda celestis 3*, which is preserved in MS Oxford, Bodleian Library, Canon. Liturg. 192 (mid-fourteenth century from Saint-Denis) and MS Paris, BnF lat. 13239 (fourteenth century from Saint-Germain des Prés) seems to be modified from a version composed by Cistercians, although a secular version also survives (MS Orleans, Bibl. mun. 148).

[62] The Poissy Antiphonal (Melbourne, State Library of Victoria, MS *096.1/R66A) is available through the Medieval Music Database: http://www.lib.latrobe.edu.au/MMDB/images/Poissy/FOL_001R.htm . On its significance see John Stinson, "The Poissy Antiphonal: A Major Source of Late Medieval Chant," *La Trobe Library Journal* 51–52 (Oct 1993), 50–59, available online.

[63] Hieronymus de Moravia, *Tractatus de musica*, ed. Christian Meyer and Guy Lobrichon, CCCM 250 (Turnhout: Brepols, 2012). This edition supersedes that of Simon M. Cserba (Regensburg: Pustat, 1935). Guy Lobrichon discusses (pp. xii–xiii), without committing himself to, the possibility raised by Michel Huglo that the epithets *Moravo* and *de Moravia* given to Jerome indicate that he was from the region of Moray, Scotland, where a Dominican convent was founded at Elgin in the 1220s: "La Musica du Fr. Prêcheur Jérome de Moray," *Max Lütolf zum 60. Geburtstag*, ed. B. Hangartner and U. Fischer (Basle, 1994), 113–16. On Jerome, see also Laura Weber, *Intellectual Currents in Thirteenth-Century Paris: A Translation and Commentary on Jerome of Moravia's Tractatus de musica*, Ph.D. thesis, Yale University (2009), esp. pp. 25–42.

[64] Hieronymus de Moravia, *Tractatus*, Prologue, p. 4.

[65] Hieronymus de Moravia, *Tractatus*, 26, ed. cit., pp. 181–215 (John of Garland); pp. 214–9 (Franco of Cologne); pp. 239–44 (Petrus Picardus, sometimes identified with Petrus de Cruce); See *Ars motettorum compilata breviter*, ed. F.A. Gallo, *CSM* 15 ([Rome:] American Institute of Musicology, 1971), pp. 9–30.

[66] Hieronymus de Moravia, *Tractatus* 221, ed. Lobrichon-Meyer, pp. 147–51: "Omnis igitur cantus ecclesiasticus in mediis clauibus terminatur, hoc est in D. E. .F. .G. grauibus, et in .a. .b. .c. acutis, et hoc est quia nullus cantus ecclesiasticus supra suam finalem plus quam VIII notis potest ascendere uel sub sua finali descendere plus quam quatuor notis. ... Amen."

[67] Hieronymus de Moravia, *Tractatus*, 21, ed. Meyer and Lobrichon, p. 145; cf. Guy, *Tractatus de tonis*, 1.3.3–8, While Jerome uses *licencialiter* fourteen times in one chapter, it occurs only once in the *Introductio musice* attributed to John of Garland, in *Scriptorum de musica medii aevi nova series a Gerbertina altera*, ed. Edmond de Coussemaker, 1:168, and

once only in De musica mensurata: *The Anonymous of St. Emmeram*, ed. and trans. Jeremy Yudkin, (Bloomington: Indiana University Press, 1990), p. 158.

[68] Hieronymus de Moravia, *Tractatus* 8, pp. 23–31, quoting Thomas Aquinas, *De caelo et mundo expositio* II.9.14, *Opera omnia*, ed. Leonina, 3 (Rome, 1886), pp. 175–77. This follows Jerome's quotation of Boethius on the three forms of music: Boethius *De institutione musica* 1.2, ed. G. Friedlein (Leipzig: Teubner, 1867), pp. 187–9.

[69] Hieronymus de Moravia, *Tractatus*, p. 31: "Sed que tantorum uirorum sit uerior opinio, id non teremarie diffiniimus, sed nostris maioribus determinada relinquimus."

[70] For discussion of the date of the *Ars musice*, conventionally assigned in many dictionaries to around 1300, see the introduction to Grocheio, *Ars musice* pp. 10–12 and p. xxxiv above for further argument.

[71] On Darmstadt, Universitäts- und Landesbibliothek, MS 2663, fols. 56r–69r, see the introduction to Grocheio, *Ars musice* pp. 15–16. This fourteenth-century MS might have been acquired, along with knowledge of Grocheio's name, by Heinrich Eger von Kalkar (1328–1408), who studied in Paris, teaching there as a magister between 1355 and 1366 before becoming a Carthusian in Cologne in 1366.

[72] Grocheio, *Ars musice*, 5.6, p. 58. The date of John of Garland as music theorist has been disputed. In 2001 Rebecca Baltzer in "Johannes de Garlandia," in *Grove Music Online* (Oxford University Press) [subscriber access required] rejected the identification with the grammarian of that name (ca. 1190–ca. 1272), defended for example by William G. Waite, in "Johannes de Garlandia, Poet and Musician," *Speculum* 35 (1960), 179–95. She proposes instead a *floruit* of ca. 1270–1320, citing the arguments of Pamela Whitcomb that the music theorist could be a book seller of that name, active between 1296 and 1319, "Teachers, Booksellers and Taxes: Reinvestigating the Life and Activities of Johannes de Garlandia," *Plainsong and Medieval Music* 8 (1999), 1–13. Such dating would imply that as a music theorist, John of Garland was completely uninfluenced by awareness of Aristotle's critique of cosmic music in the *De caelo*, known within the University of Paris since the mid-thirteenth century. His authority on *musica mensurabilis* was still strong in the early fourteenth century, when further discussions were attributed to his name.

[73] See Mews, "Questioning the Music of the Spheres: Aristotle, Johannes de Grocheio, and the University of Paris 1250–1300," in *Knowledge, Discipline and Power in the Middle Ages, Essays in Honour of David Luscombe*, ed. Joseph Canning, Edmund King and Martial Staub, *Studien und Texte zur Geistesgeschichte des Mittelalters* (Leiden: Brill, 2011), pp. 95–117.

[74] Guy refers to John of Garland in *Tractatus de tonis*, 1.1.9, 1.3.8.

[75] Grocheio, *Ars musice*, 2.2, p. 46.

[76] Grocheio, *Ars musice*, 6.2, p. 60.

[77] Grocheio, *Ars musice*, 22.3, p. 90.

[78] Grocheio, *Ars musice*, 43.2, p. 114.

[79] Pseudo-Odo, *Dialogus de musica*, PL 133, col. 765A.

[80] Guy, *Tractatus de tonis*, 1.1.1: "qui cantus publicos et civiles—utpote cantilenas et rotundellos—et maxime cantus mensuratos—quales sunt moteti, hoqueti et huiusmodi dicunt tonis non subici nec per eos regulari." Cf. Grocheio, *Ars musica* 25.2, p. 94: "Non enim per tonum cognoscimus cantum vulgalem. puta cantilenam. ductiam. stantipedem. quemadmodum superius dicebatur."

[81] Guy, *Tractatus de tonis*, 1.4.1.

[82] Guy, *Tractatus de tonis*, 1.4.2.

[83] Guy, *Tractatus de tonis*, 1.4.3.

[84] Guy, *Tractatus de tonis*, 1.4.3.

[85] Petrus de Alvernia, *Quaestio* 17: "Sic igitur apparet, quod harmonia musica bene proportionata valet ad mores et per oppositum improportionata ad contrarium."

[86] The manuscript is described by Michel Huglo and Nancy Phillips in *The Theory of Music: Descriptive Catalogue of Manuscripts*, ed. Joseph Smits van Waesberghe, Peter Fischer and Christian Maas, *Répertoire internationale des sources musicales*, B/4 (Munich: K. G. Saur, 1992), pp. 74–78 and by Dolores Pesce, *Guido d'Arezzo's Regule Rithmice, Prologus in Antiphonarium and Epistola ad Michahelem. A Critical Text and Translation* (Ottawa: Institute of Mediaeval Music, 1999), pp. 112–14. The additional material added to the writings of Guido of Arezzo and Pseudo-Odo is edited in Constant J. Mews, John N. Crossley, Catherine Jeffreys, Leigh McKinnon, and Carol Williams, "Guy of Saint-Denis and the Compilation of Texts about Music in London, British Library, Harl. MS. 281," in *Electronic British Library Journal* (2008), article 6. See also the introduction to Johannes de Grocheio, *Ars musice*, pp. 12–14.

[87] Described by Pesce, *Guido of Arezzo*, pp. 162–3, 166 [O2], but in *H* the *Dialogus* follows the *Epistola*.

[88] Guido Aretinus, *Micrologus* 14, ed. van Waesberghe, p. 159: "Atque ita diversitas troporum diversitati mentium coaptatur ut unus autenti deuteri fractibus saltibus delectetur, aliud plagae triti eligat voluptatem, uni tetrardi autenti garrulitas magis placet, alter eiusdem plagae suavitatem probat; sic et de reliquis." See Klundert, 1:129.

[89] These texts in *H* are edited in Mews et al., "Guy of St Denis," pp. 155–6.

[90] *H* fol. 5v: "Sepe et multum graviter elaborare perstudui, antiqua grecorum volumina revolvens si simplex huius artis ratio numerorum proportionibus omnino posthabitis teneris auribus cantorum plenarie posset accomodari; multorum itaque consideratis tractatibus ad hoc Boetium inveni meliorem, que et quanta sit coniunctio vocum per modos per tropos per species inter se consonantium ostendentem, quo vero nititur solis intendere philosophis vim et naturam vocum armonice querentibus contrarius est et difficilis. Senior enim philosophie tractatus nimia obscuritate perplexus gravitate verborum argumenta proferentium improvectis tendit insidias auribus.," ed. Mews et al., "Guy of St Denis," p. 155.

[91] Guy, *Tractatus de tonis*, 1.0.1.

[92] *H*, fol. 24v, see Mews et al, "Guy of St Denis," p. 156: "Quicquid igitur auctoritate philosophorum imitando modernos de natura modorum tertius absque falsitatis additamento colligere potuimus, sublato omni invido, nostris auditoribus magna facilitatis providentia sub dialogo contulimus. Quod enim supradicto volumine, aut negligentie regula, vel quia longo tempore latuit musica, non intelligitur, in ultimo, puerili aure facili regularum compendio utiliter percipitur."

[93] Guy, *Tractatus de tonis*, 2.4.4: "et magistrum Petrum de Cruce, qui fuit optimus cantor et Ambianensis ecclesie consuetudinem specialiter observavit."

[94] *H*, fol. 58v: "Qui legis auctoris nomen per quinque priora / Gramata pictoris, hoc scribe celitus ora." On the *Micrologus*, see Pesce, *Guido d'Arezzo's Regule Rithmice*, p. 328.

[95] Guy, *Tractatus de tonis*, 1.0.2: "sint de bono et difficile difficilius atque subtilius pro

studiosoribus et provectis. In secunda vero quantum ad praxim idest operationem ipsorum figuraliter magis et per exempla facilius pro simplicioribus et parvulis tractaturus."

[96] Thomas Aquinas, *In Aristotelis libros Metaphysicorum* 7.6.1394.

[97] Guy, *Tractatus de tonis*, 1.3.4.

[98] Guy, *Tractatus de tonis*, 1.2.5: "sicut repperi in quodam libello de tonis ac eorum origine antiquo valde, ubi et Guidonis Micrologus continetur, quem in isto tractatu frequenter allego."

[99] Walter of Châtillon, *Alexandreis* 3.457 and 5.350; *The Alexandreis. A Twelfth-Century Epic*, trans. David Townsend (Peterborough, Ont.: Broadview Press, 2007), p. 214.

[100] *H*, fols. 65r–v: "ultra protenderet studentes postmodum et per istos octo sonos et cantandi modos qui nunc toni dicuntur argumenta quamplura certissime conicientes discipline musice seriem congesserunt."

[101] Guy, *Tractatus de tonis*, 1.2.7: "Sed quid iste voces significent vel cuius lingue sint, noieane videlicet vel noieagis aut consimiles, nemo, ut ibidem legitur, adhuc novit, nisi forte quod talis vox vel sonus quasi lingua hominis per fistulas occultas ex concursu aque et aeris spiritu ventorum resonat. Greci tamen aliqui, ut huiusmodi questione se statim liberent, istas voces interpretantur esse voces letitie sicut euax est interiectio letitiam et exultationem designans."

[102] Guy, *Tractatus de tonis*, 1.2.5.

[103] The source for this quote has not been found.

[104] "dans plurima officiorum. responsoriorum vel antiphonarum exempla." Another possible translation of this passage is "examples of introits, responsories or antiphons."

[105] Guy, *Tractatus de tonis*, 1.2.8: "Quid autem veritatis predicta contineant, lectoris arbitrio malo relinquere quam super hoc aliquid diffinire. A quo siquidem illa, que ex predicto libello antiquo hucusque de tonorum origine recitando magis posui quam asserendo, conscripta fuerint cuique auctori imputari debeant aut ascribi, certum non habeo. Videtur tamen potius quod alteri, qui post Guidonem fuerit, quam ipsi Guidoni, presertim cum ibidem de ipso eiusque tonorum formulis fiat expresse mentio sub his verbis: Formulas Guidonis abbatis viri in musica preclarissimi subter inseruimus inter tonos. Quamvis namque Boecius et ceteri antiquiores musici acutius atque profundius traverint de obscura et impenetrabili musice scientia, que soli deo ad plenum patet, iste tamen nobis condescendes lucidissimas et utilissimas ad canendum composuit regulas huius artis. Ecclesiasticus enim homo de necessario usu ecclesie nos instruxit, dans plurima officiorum responsoriorum vel antiphonarum exempla, quod omnino pene omnes alii tacuerunt."

[106] MS Paris, Bibl. Sainte-Geneviève 2284, see n. 53 above.

[107] Léopold Delisle, *Le Cabinet des manuscrits de la Bibliothèque impériale*, 4 vols. (Paris: Imprimerie impériale, 1868–1881), 2:527: "Guido Augensis liber de musica ad Willermum Rievallis abbatem. Item eiusdem micrologus ad Theobaldum, Arethiane civitatis episcopum. Item dyalogus ecclesiastice cum octo modorum formulis, demum eorum regule generales. In uno volumine cuius signum est littera E..." See Richard H. Rouse, "Manuscripts Belonging to Richard de Fournival," *Revue d'histoire des textes* 3 (1973), 253–69. Meyer, "Le tonaire," p. 66, notes that the *Micrologus* is also attributed to *Guido Augensis* in a twelfth-century manuscript, MS Rome, Bibl. Apostolica Vaticana, Reg. lat. 1616.

[108] Guy, *Tractatus de tonis,* 1.4.14: "Licet autem secundum diversitatem regionum morumque hominum tot vel plures videantur esse maneries et modi cantandi..."

[109] On Guy of Eu, see n.53 above; Guy of Eu was identified as *Guido iunior* in a Cistercian treatise, perhaps from around 1300, subsequently reported by the fifteenth-century writer, John Wylde, *Musica manualis cum tonale*, ed. Cecily Sweeney, CSM 28 ([Rome:] American Institute of Musicology, 1982), pp. 62, 70, 77, 90; see Maître, *La réforme cistercienne*, p. 68.

[110] Guy, *Tractatus de tonis,* 1.2.8.

[111] Pseudo-Odo, *Dialogus de musica*, PL 133:765A: "Tonus vel modus est regula, quae de omni cantu in fine dijudicat. Nam nisi scieris finem, non poteris cognoscere, ubi incipi, vel quantum elevari vel deponi debeat cantus." The prologue to this text is edited by Michel Huglo, "Der Prolog des Odo zugeschriebenen 'Dialogus de Musica," *Archiv für Musikwissenschaft* 28 (1971), 134–46. Cf. Guido, *Regulae rhythmice*, ed. Pesce, pp. 366 and 398.

[112] Guy, *Tractatus de tonis,* 1.3.20.

[113] Guy, *Tractatus de tonis,* 1.3.22.

[114] Guy, *Tractatus de tonis,* 1.4.5.

[115] Bartholomaeus Anglicus, *De proprietatibus rerum* 19.1393 (Lyons: Petrum Ungarum, 1482), p. 511.

[116] Augustine, *Confessiones*, ed. and trans. Albert C. Outler (Philadelphia, 1955), 10.32, p. 370: "aliquando enim plus mihi uideor honoris eis tribuere, quam decet, dum ipsis sanctis dictis religiosius et ardentius sentio moueri animos nostros in flammam pietatis, cum ita cantantur, quam si non ita cantarentur, et omnes affectus spiritus nostri pro sui diuersitate habere proprios modos in uoce atque cantu, quorum nescio qua occulta familiaritate excitentur."

[117] Guy, *Tractatus de tonis,* 1.4.21.

[118] Guy, *Tractatus de tonis,* 1.4.21.

[119] See Crocker, "Matins Antiphons at St. Denis," pp. 450 and 453.

[120] For a detailed description of this manuscript and the twenty-six *differentiae* that it offers, see JoAnn Udovich, *Modality, Office Antiphons, and Psalmody: the Musical Authority of the Twelfth-Century Antiphonal from St.-Denis*, Ph.D. thesis, University of Chapel Hill (1985), pp. 20–100. The manuscript was used by R. J. Hesbert, the first scholar to note its origin at Saint-Denis, *Corpus Antiphonalium Officii*, 6 vols. (Rome: Herder, 1963–79), 2: xi–xiv.

[121] Jacobus Leodiensis, *Speculum musicae*, ed. Roger Bragard, CSM 3, 7 vols. (Rome: American Institute of Musicology, 1955–68). Margaret Bent builds on a fifteenth-century catalogue description of the *Speculum musice* as the work of *Jacobus de Ispania* to argue that he may be an illegitimate nephew of Eleanor of Castile, wife of King Edward I, in "Jacobus de Ispania? – Ein Zwischenbericht," in *Nationes, Gentes und die Musik im Mittelalter*, ed. Frank Hentschel and Maria Winkelmuller (Berlin: De Gruyter, 2014), pp 407–22, argued more fully in *Magister Jacobus de Ispania, Author of the Speculum musicae* (Farnham: Ashgate, 2015). Bent thus rejects arguments put by Karen Desmond that he could be Jacobus de Montibus, who studied in Paris in the early fourteenth century, "New Light on Jacques, Author of the Speculum Musicae," *Plainsong and Medieval Music* 9 (2000), 19–40. On the other hand, Rob. C. Wegman has argued that "Ispania" was a district of Liège, see his "Jacobus de Ispania and Liège," *Journal of the Alamire Foundation*, 8 (2016) pp. 253–274.

[122] Petrus de Sancto Dionysio, *Tractatus de musica*, ed. Ulrich Michels, together with the *Notitia artis musicae* of Johannes de Muris, CSM 17 ([Dallas, Texas]: American

Institute of Musicology, 1972), pp. 147–66; Michels suggests (pp. 39–42) that Petrus may also be the author of the *De musica mensurabili* ascribed to Anonymous VI, which is also heavily derivative of the *Notitia artis musicae*.

[123] Petrus de sancto Dionysio, ed. by Michels, pp. 147–49.

[124] Jacobus, *Speculum musicae*, VI.87, ed. Bragard, p. 255; Jacobus speaks about his desire to examine the teaching of moderns on plainchant, going beyond Boethius and Guido, in VI.82, ed. Bragard, p. 232.

[125] Guy, *Tractatus de tonis*, 2.4.8.

[126] Nebbiai-Dalla Guarda, *La Bibliothèque*, pp. 50–51, considers that the *Vie de Saint Denis* was produced at the direction of abbot Gilles and dedicated to Philip V.

[127] H. Omont, "Le Sanctilogium de Guy de Châtres, abbé de Saint-Denis," *Bibliothèque de l'école des chartes*, 86 (1925), 407–410.

[128] See Nebbiai-Dalla Guarda, *La Bibliothèque*, pp. 336–357.

[129] For fuller detail, see Constant J. Mews, "Re-structuring the Golden Legend in the Early Fourteenth Century: *The Sanctilogium* of Guy of Châtres, Abbot of Saint-Denis," *Revue bénédictine* 120 (2010), 129–44.

[130] Nebbiai-Dalla Guarda, *La Bibliothèque*, pp. 51–52.

[131] Charles Samaran, "Etudes sandionysiennes. II. Un nécrologue inédit de l'abbaye de Saint-Denis (XIVe–XVIIe siècles)," *Bibliothèque de l'école des chartes* 104 (1943), 27–100.

[132] See Nebbiai-Dalla Guarda, *La Bibliothèque*, pp. 50–51.

[133] Nebbiai-Dalla Guarda, "Des rois et des moines: Livres et lecteurs à l'abbaye de Saint-Denis (XIIIe–XVe siècles)," in *Saint-Denis et la royauté. Études offerts à B. Guenée*, ed. by Françoise Autrand, Claude Gauvard and Jean-Marie Moeglin (Paris: Publications de la Sorbonne, 1999), p. 355.

[134] On Gosselin as guardian of the royal library and the possibility that the manuscript was preserved at the College of Saint-Denis (where the treasure of the abbey was hidden during the wars of religion), see the final appendix to Mews et al., "Guy of Saint-Denis."

[135] Guy, *Tractatus de tonis,* 1.1.9.

[136] Guy, *Tractatus de tonis,* 1.2.8.

[137] Guy, *Tractatus de tonis*, 1.4.9.

Tractatus de tonis
Text and Translation

[0.0.1]
[58v] Qui legis auctoris nomen per quinque priora. Gramata pictoris. hoc scribi
celitus ora.

[1.0.0]
Incipit prologus in tractatu de tonis.[1]

[1.0.1]
Gaudere sciens brevitate modernos et tamen ex altera parte considerans quod si forte
plus iusto timeam ne videar apparere prolixior ipse pre nimia brevitate iuxta verbum
oracii fiam obscurior. sic que scillam quodam modo evitare cupiens incidam in caribdim. aliqua que de tonis tam ex musica boecii quam venerabilis patris et monachi
guidonis aretini, ex dictis quoque aliorum quorundam in eadem peritorum scientia
studiose collegi, mediocri quadam brevitate perstringere, et sub uno tractatu ad quorundam laudabilem fratrum nostrorum instantiam compilare temptavi.

[1.0.2]
¶ Verum quia non solum simplicium fratrum immo etiam provectorum magisque
inter eos subtilium utilitati deservire cupio. libellum presentem in duas partes
principales distinxi. In prima videlicet de tonis quantum ad theoriam sive speculationem eorum artificialiter quodammodo vel scientifice et per consequens cum
omnis ars atque scientia ut alibi scribitur sint de bono et difficili difficilius atque
subtilius pro studiosioribus ac provectis. In secunda vero quantum ad praxim idest
operationem ipsorum figuraliter magis et per exempla atque facilius pro simplicioribus et parvulis tractaturus. Ut qui forte prime partis subtilitatem capere ad
plenum non potuerunt. saltem in secunde partis exemplari planitie delectentur.

[1.0.3]
¶ Prime vero parti quatuor premisi capitula que sequuntur. Capitulum primum ¶
Quot modis accipiatur tonus in musica. et quid sit, vel unde dicatur Capitulum
secundum ¶ Quot sunt toni, et quibus nominibus a musicis et philosophis appellantur Capitulum tertium ¶ De natura tonorum et distinctione eorum. Capitulum quartum ¶ De proprietate et effectu seu virtute ipsorum Explicit prologus.
Incipit pars prima tractatus de tonis.

[1.1.0]
¶ Capitulum primum. ¶ Quot modis accipiatur[2] tonus in musica. et quid sit. vel
unde dicatur.

---

[1] a fratre Guidone monacho Monas-   *right margin* **H3**.
terii Sancti Dyonisii in Francia *added in*   [2] accipipiatur **H1**.

[0.0.1]
Whoever reads the name of the author from the five first letters by the painter, pray for this to be written in heaven.

[1.0.0]
Here begins the prologue of the treatise on the tones.

[1.0.1]
Knowing that the moderns rejoice in brevity, and yet considering, on the other hand, that if I might fear, more correctly perhaps, lest I seem to appear more pro-lix, I might become (in Horace's words) more obscure through too much brevity itself,[1] and thus wanting to avoid Scylla in some way I might fall on Charybdis.[2] I have studiously collected certain things about the tones as much from the *Musica* of Boethius[3] as from the venerable father and monk Guido of Arezzo, as well as from the sayings of certain others expert in the same knowledge. At the laudable insistence of certain of our brothers I have tried to draw them together with a, degree of moderate brevity and compile them into a single treatise.

[1.0.2]
Indeed, because I wish to provide something useful not just for simple brothers but also for the more advanced and subtle among them, I have divided the present book into two principal parts. The first is about the tones in relation to theory or speculation about them through some artifice or science. In consequence, since every art and science, as is written elsewhere, is about what is good and difficult;[4] the more difficult and subtle is for the more studious and advanced. In the second, I will deal with praxis, that is, the operation of these things more figuratively and by examples easier for the simpler and the young. This is so that those who per-chance are not able to grasp the subtlety of the first part to the full are at least able to delight in the clarity of the examples in the second part.

[1.0.3]
I have set out the four chapters of the first part as follows. Chapter one: How many ways tone may be understood in music, what it is and where the name comes from. Chapter two: How many tones there are and what names they are called by music theorists and philosophers. Chapter three: On the nature of the tones and the difference between them. Chapter four: Concerning their property and effect or power. Here ends the prologue.
Here begins the first part of the tract concerning the tones.

[1.1.0]
Chapter one: In how many ways tone may be accepted in music and from what it is called.

[1.1.1]

Ut de tonis perfectior possit haberi notitia, notandum in primis, quod tonus in musica duobus modis accipitur. Uno modo videlicet pro cantandi modo quem antiquiores ac primi musici grece tropum nominant. nam tropus sive tropos grece, idem est quod conversio latine. ad modos enim cantandi seu tropos quos nunc communiter appellamus tonos quamvis abusive quodammodo secundum guidonem, in discernendis atque [59r] iudicandis cantibus convertere nos oportet. Sic autem accipiendo tonum prout communiter ab ecclesiasticis viris accipitur. Tonus secundum aliquos est regula quedam que de omni cantu in fine diiudicat. Vel sicut quibusdam aliis magis placet qui cantus publicos et civiles utpote cantilenas et rotundellos et maxime cantus mensuratos quales sunt moteti. hoqueti. et huiusmodi. dicunt tonis non subici nec per eos regulari. Tonus est regula per quam quis omnem ecclesiasticum cantum potest cognoscere et de eo veraciter iudicare, inspiciendo non solum ad cantus initium, sed etiam ad medium et ad finem. Ex quo patet quod illi profecto seipsos decipiunt, qui statim incepta antiphona vel alio quovis ecclesiastico cantu, cuius sit toni scire se infallibiliter iudicare[3] pronuntiant et affirmant. Hoc siquidem in quibusdam per usum fieri potest aliquando, sed non in omnibus. nec etiam scientifice vel artificialiter, cum sicut dictum est in iudicandis cantibus non solum principium considerare oporteat immo medium atque finem. Dicitur autem tonus sic sumptus a tonando secundum aliquos vel ab intonando eo quod psalmi secundum alium et alium tonum aliter et aliter intonantur. sicut in secunda parte huius operis apparebit. Alio modo accipitur tonus in musica, pro quodam ipsius musice principio quod a musicis concordantia appellatur. que videlicet concordantia in proportione sexquioctava consistit. Unde tonus sic acceptus est concordantia in proportione sexquioctava consistens. sicut ex dicendis plenius apparebit. Quamvis autem de tono sic accepto vel de aliis concordantiis et consonantiis musicalibus ad plenum tractare non spectet ad presens opusculum. quia tamen ista musice artis dicuntur principia. ignoratis autem omnino principiis necesse est artem penitus ignorari, inde est quod aliqua de predictis musice principiis ac eorum numero origine et natura, a boecio siquidem et aliis musicis diffusius atque subtilius pertractata breviter hic inserere superfluum non videtur. presertim cum toni de quibus supra loqui incepimus et in sequentibus principaliter loqui intendimus. non solum predicta musice principia videlicet concordantias et consonantias presupponant, immo etiam et ipsas in sui compositione et progressu ut postea magis videbitur frequenter assumant.

---

[3] iudicare *omitted Klundert.*

[1.1.1]

To acquire a more complete familiarity with the tones, it should first be noted that tone is understood in music in two ways:[5] in one way, clearly, as a way of singing, which the ancients and first music theorists called "trope" from the Greek, for *tropus* or *tropos* in Greek has the same meaning as *conversio* in Latin, indeed we ought to "convert" what we now commonly call tones (although somewhat improperly according to Guido)[6] to modes of singing or tropes in order to discern and appraise chants. In accepting "tone" thus, moreover, is as it is accepted by churchmen generally.[7] According to some, tone is that rule which assesses every chant from its final.[8] Or, as it pleases certain others more, who say that public and civil song (such as lyric song and *rondeaux*) and particularly measured song (such as motets, hockets and the like), are neither subject to the tones nor regulated by them.[9] Tone is a rule through which it is possible to recognise every ecclesiastical chant and to assess it correctly by looking not only at the beginning of the chant but also at the middle and at the end.[10] From this it is clear that those people surely deceive themselves who as soon as an antiphon or any other ecclesiastical chant has begun, pronounce and declare that they judge themselves to know infallibly of which tone it may be. Indeed, this can sometimes happen in practice in certain cases but not in all, and also not by knowledge or artifice, since, just as was said in the appraising of chant, not only the beginning, but also the middle and the end should be considered. According to some, tone is so called from *tonando*,[11] or *intonando*, since the psalms are intoned according to one tone or another, in one way or another,[12] just as will be made clear in the second part of this work. Tone is understood in another way in music, as a kind of building block of music itself, which is called "concord" by music theorists;[13] this concord clearly consists in the sesquioctave proportion.[14] Thus a tone understood in this way is a concord consisting in sesquioctave proportion,[15] as will appear more fully from what is to be said. It does not pertain to the present work to discuss tone understood in this way or other musical concords and consonances in full, since these are called foundation elements of the art of music.[16] Yet when principles are completely ignored, the art must be completely ignored.[17] Because of this, it does not seem superfluous to insert here something about the aforementioned principles of music and their number, origin, and nature, dealt with more diffusely and subtly indeed by Boethius and by other musicians,[18] especially since the tones, about which we began to speak above and intend to speak principally in what follows, presuppose not only the aforementioned principles of music, namely concords and consonances, but also frequently assume principles in their composition and progression, as will be further seen subsequently.

[1.1.2]

¶ Sciendum est ergo quod secundum boecium in primo musice. consonantia que omnem musice modulationem regit non est sine sono. sonus autem sine percussione et pulsu esse non potest. hec autem vel motus quidam locales sunt [**59v**] vel sine locali motu precedente fieri non possunt. si enim omnia quiescerent sonus omnino non esset. propter quod sonus materialiter diffinitur quod est percussio aeris continua usque ad auditum. Motuum vero localium alii sunt tardiores alii velociores. et eorum quidam sunt rariores, quidam vero spissiores. Si igitur ut dicit boecius. rarior aut tardior fuerit motus, gravem sonum efficit. nam sicut tarditas proxima est stationi ita gravitas contigua est taciturnitati. Si vero spissus aut celer vel velox fuerit motus, sonum acutum reddit. Et ideo si corda alicuius instrumenti musici intenditur, sonum acutiorem reddit. Si vero remittitur, graviorem. quando enim corda est tensior velociorem pulsum reddit celeriusque revertitur et frequentius ac spissius aerem percutit. quando vero laxior est, pulsus tardiores et raros efficit. ipsaque imbecillitate feriendi non diutius tremit. Neque enim quando corda pellitur unus tantum edi vel fieri putandus est sonus. aut unam in hijs esse percussionem, sed totiens aer feritur quotiens eum corda tremebunda percusserit. sed quoniam iuncte sunt velocitates sonorum, nulla intercapedo sentitur auribus sed unus sonus gravis vel acutus auditum pellit. quamvis uterque ex pluribus constet motibus, gravis videlicet ex tardioribus ac rarioribus. acutus vero ex celeribus atque spissis.

[1.1.3]

¶ Quoniam ergo acute voces ex spissioribus ac velocioribus causantur motibus, graves vero ex tardioribus ac raris, manifestum est ut dicit boecius, quadam additione motuum ex gravitate acuitatem intendi, detractione vero motuum ex acumine gravitatem laxari ex pluribus enim motibus tam acumen quam gravitas constat. In quibus autem pluralitas differentiam facit, ea necesse est in quadam numerositate consistere. omnis enim paucitas ad pluralitatem ita se habet ut numerus ad numerum comparatus. Eorum vero que secundum numerum comparantur quedam sunt equalia quedam autem inequalia. et ideo sonorum quidam sunt equales, quidam vero inequales et inequalitate distantes. In hijs autem sonis vel vocibus que simpliciter sunt equales non est proprie loquendo consonantia. sed magis aliquid ea perfectius. que omnium armoniarum musicalium est mensura sicut est unisonus dicendo in eodem puncto. ut. ut. vel. re. re. mi. mi. et sic de singulis vocibus. relinquitur ergo quod consonantia sit inter sonos vel voces abinvicem quadam inequalitate distantes. Unde ex predictis omnibus finaliter ibidem concludit boecius. quod consonantia est dissimilium inter se sonorum vel vocum [**60r**] redacta in unum concordia.

[1.1.2]

It should be known, therefore, that, according to Boethius in the first book of the *Musica*, consonance, which rules all melodic activity in music, is not without sound. There can be no sound without beating and pulse, which either are certain local motions or cannot happen without a preceding local motion. For if all things were quiescent, there would be no sound at all. Because of this, sound is defined materially, since it is the beating of air uninterrupted to the sense of hearing.[19] But of the local motions, some are slower, some swifter, and certain of them are sparser, while some are denser. If, therefore, as Boethius says, the motion is sparser or slower, it makes a low sound. For just as slowness is nearest to a stop, so lowness borders on silence. But if motion is dense or swift or speedy, it makes a high sound. And therefore, if the string of any musical instrument is stretched, it produces a higher sound. But if it is slackened, it produces a lower one. For when a string is more taut, it returns a more rapid pulse more swiftly and strikes the air more frequently and densely. But when it is slacker, it produces slower and thinner pulses and it does not vibrate longer on account of the weakness of the beating.[20] For when a string is struck, there is not just one sound thought to be produced or created or one pulse in them, but rather the air is struck as often as the vibrating string strikes it. But since the speeds of sounds are joined, there is no gap perceived by the ear, but one sound strikes the hearing as low or high, although it is clear that each sound comes from several motions, namely a low sound from slower or sparser ones and a high sound from fast and denser ones.[21]

[1.1.3]

Since, therefore, high pitches are caused by more frequent and swifter motions and low ones by slower and less frequent motions, it is clear, as Boethius says, that the high is intensified from the low by some addition of motions, and the low is relaxed from the high by subtraction of motions, for it is clear that the high comes from more motions than the low. However, plurality makes the difference in these matters, and it is true that it (plurality) exists in a certain great number, for every paucity is related to plurality as number is compared to number. Indeed, of those things that are compared according to number, some are equal, some are unequal. And therefore certain sounds are equal but certain ones are unequal and separated by inequality.[22] Among those sounds or pitches that are simply equal, there is, properly speaking, no consonance,[23] but rather something more perfect than it, which is the measure of all musical harmonies,[24] thus there is unison in uttering at the same point by single pitches ut-ut or re-re, mi-mi and so on. Therefore, it remains that consonance is between sounds or pitches distant from each other by a certain inequality. From the above, Boethius finally concludes in the same place that consonance is the concord of sounds or pitches dissimilar among themselves brought together into one.[25]

[1.1.4]

¶ Licet autem aliqui inter consonantiam et concordantiam, nullam aut modicam assignare videantur differentiam. secundum tamen alios loquentes subtiliter ut videtur, talis est differentia inter ista. Consonantia namque est quando duo soni vel plures simul uniti et in uno tempore a diversis prolati vel simul ab uno et eodem pulsati unam perfectam efficiunt melodiam. unde et secundum boecium in. iiij^to musice. ille voces sunt consone que simul pulse suavem et permixtum sonum faciunt. ille vero sunt dissone que non reddunt permixtum nec suavem sonum. Concordantia vero ut de ea nunc loquimur, est regularis progressus ab uno sono ad alium per arsim et thesim idest per elevationem et depressionem seu depositionem, sive per ascensum et descensum. Vel ut aliqui dicunt concordantia est intervallum sive distantia duorum sonorum vel plurium ab uno et eodem diversis temporibus prolatorum. quando videlicet unus sonus armonice continuatur alteri. sicut una pars motus vel temporis continuatur alteri, ita scilicet armonice ut unus sonus alium cui continuatur in acuitate vel gravitate secundum certam ac debitam proportionem numeralem excedat vel excedatur ab eo. Cum enim musica secundum boecium sit de numero relato ad sonum, vel de sono armonice numerato, sicut arismetica est de numero in se et[4] absolute considerato, quod est proportio in ipsis numeris hoc esse videtur concordantia in sonis musicis. Unde secundum quod inter aliquos sonos est alia et alia proportio, secundum hoc inter eos est alia et alia concordantia. Ubi vero non invenitur debita certaque proportio numeralis, nec per consequens concordantia. immo magis discordantia atque corruptio melodie. Unde et boecius in primo et quarto musice, concordantes sonos emmeles idest aptos melo sive melodie appellat. discordantes autem ekmeles nominat, idest melo sive melodie ineptos.

[1.1.5]

¶ Quamvis autem aliqui loquentes vulgariter nec opinionis sue rationem aliquam assignantes concordantias et consonantias musice esse dixerunt infinitas. Alii vero .xiii. posuerunt quas species musice appellant, videlicet. unisonum. tonum. semitonum. ditonum. semiditonum. dyatessaron. tritonum. dyapente. semitonium cum dyapente. tonum cum dyapente. semiditonum cum dyapente. ditonum cum dyapente. et dyapason. Quidam vero consonantias in principales et secundarias dividentes. principales consonantias tres esse dicunt, scilicet dyatessaron. dyapente. et dyapason. consonantias secundarias quas [**60v**] concordantias appellant sex esse ponentes. scilicet tonum. semitonum. ditonum. semiditonum. tonum cum dyapente. et semitonum cum dyapente. Secundum tamen opinionem eorum qui principia musice et eorum numerum subtilius investigare videntur. rationabiliter et satis probabiliter dici potest, quod omnes consonantie et concordantie musicales reducuntur ad .vii. que sunt, tonus. semitonus. ditonus. semiditonus.

---

[4] in se et *omitted Klundert.*

[1.1.4]

Although some people seem to assign little or no distinction between consonance and concord,[26] according to others speaking precisely it seems, the difference between these is this: consonance is when two or more sounds, either united simultaneously and pronounced at the same time by different people, or produced simultaneously by one and the same person, make one perfect melody.[27] Thus according to Boethius in the fourth book of the *Musica*, those pitches are consonant which having been produced at the same time, make an agreeable and coherent sound, but those are dissonant that do not produce a coherent and agreeable sound.[28] But concord, as we now speak about it, is regular progression from one sound to another through *arsis* and *thesis*, that is, through rising and falling or lowering, or through ascent and descent.[29] Or, as some say, concord is the interval or distance between two or more sounds produced by one and the same person at different times—namely when one sound continues to another in harmony[30] (*armonice*), just as one part of motion or time continues to another.[31] Thus it does so "in harmony," in that one sound exceeds or is exceeded by another to which it is connected in high or low pitch, according to a fixed and appropriate numerical proportion.[32] For since music is, according to Boethius, about number related to sound,[33] or about sound numbered "harmonically,"[34] just as arithmetic is about number in itself and considered absolutely,[35] because this proportion is in the numbers themselves this seems to be concord in musical sounds. Whence accordingly to the former, there is one or another proportion between certain sounds; according to the latter, there is one or another concord between them. But where an appropriate and fixed numerical proportion is not found, consequently there is no concord, but rather, on the contrary, discord, and corruption of melody.[36] Whence Boethius in the first and fourth books of the *Musica* calls concordant sounds *emmeles*, that is, "suited to a tune or melody";[37] on the other hand, he names discordant ones *ekmeles*, that is, "not suited to a tune or melody."[38]

[1.1.5]

Although some people, speaking crudely, and not assigning any reason for their opinion, have said that concords and consonances of music are innumerable,[39] others, however, have proposed thirteen, which they call "species" of music, namely unison, tone, semitone, ditone, semiditone, *diatessaron*, tritone, *diapente*, semitone with *diapente*, tone with *diapente*, semiditone with *diapente*, ditone with *diapente*, and *diapason*.[40] But certain others, dividing consonances into principal and secondary, say that there are three principal consonances, namely *diatessaron*, *diapente* and *diapason*,[41] proposing there to be six secondary consonances, which they call concords, namely tone, semitone, ditone, semiditone, tone with *diapente* and semitone with *diapente*.[42] According to the opinion of those who seem to investigate the principles of music and their number more precisely, it can be said with reason and plausibly

dyatessaron. dyapente. et dyapason, quarum ut infra videbitur .iiiior. prime concordantie dicuntur tres vero ultime non solum concordantie immo etiam consonantie nuncupantur. melius est enim principia pauca supponere. cum pluralitas principiis contradicat. Cum enim secundum Aristotelem. et Platonem, homo sit quasi quidam mundus, unde et microcosmos idest minor mundus ab eis dicitur, recte operationes et leges humane legem divinam ut est possibile debent penitus imitari. Ad diversitatem autem generationum et corruptionum totius universi septem planete cum eorum virtutibus suffecerant. sicut ergo .vii. sunt planete in celo per quos in isto sensibili mundo diversitas generationum et corruptionum efficitur. et in ebdomada .vii. dies quibus multotiens resumptis totus annus mensuratur. vii. que sunt dona spiritus sancti quibus homo quantum ad animam spiritualiter perficitur sanctificatur et regitur. Ita rationabile videtur in arte humana que musica est .vii. principia predicta ponere, que concordantie appellantur. maxime cum hec .vii. ad diversitatem musicalium sonorum causandam sufficere videantur. Etsi que sint alie preter ipsas concordantie composite et non simplices dici debent. hic autem loquimur de concordantiis ut simplices sunt et principia aliarum. Omnes namque alie, predictis .vii. cognitis satis de facili possunt cognosci. qui enim scit quid sit tonus et ditonus, per additionem toni potest efficere tritonum. qui etiam scit quid sit tonus et quid dyapente ex additione toni ad dyapente. valde faciliter tonum cum dyapente potest efficere. et sic de ceteris. Restat igitur breviter declarare quid sit unaqueque predictarum .vii. concordantiarum. quid videlicet sit tonus. quid semitonium sive semitonus. quid ditonus. semiditonus dyatessaron. dyapente. ac dyapason. et qualiter fuerint invente.

[1.1.6]

℟ Tonus igitur est concordantia distantiam illam que est inter duas voces sibi invicem immediate proximas continens que scilicet in proportione sexquioctava consistit. quando videlicet ut supra a principio tangebatur unus sonus ita continuatur alteri quod ipsum in gravitate vel acuitate secundum predictam proportionem excedit vel exceditur ab eodem. unde [61r] quod est proportio sexquioctava in numeris. hoc est tonus ut de ipso nunc loquimur in sonis musicis. Est autem sexquioctava proportio in numeris quando aliquis numerus totum alium continet et cum hoc octavam eius partem. sicut .ix. continet octo et cum hoc unitatem que est octonarii pars octava. Dicitur autem tonus sic acceptus ut volunt[5] aliqui, a ptongos grece quod est sonus latine. si enim non sonaret. non audiretur tonus. vel dicitur tonus a tonando eo videlicet quod plene vel fortiter ac perfecte sonet. Talis autem concordantia que dicitur tonus est inter .iiijor. musice voces. scilicet. inter .ut. et .re. inter .re. et .mi. inter .fa. et .sol. inter .sol. et .la. et hoc tam ascendendo quam etiam descendendo.

---

[5] voluerunt *corrected to* volunt **H2**.

enough that all musical consonances and concords are reduced to seven,[43] which are tone, semitone, ditone, semiditone, *diatessaron*, *diapente* and *diapason*.[44] Of these, as will be seen below, the first four are called concords and the last three are called not only concords but also consonances; for it is better to posit few principles, since plurality contradicts principles.[45] For since, according to Aristotle and Plato, man is like a certain world and hence is called by them a microcosm, that is, a lesser world, rightful operations and human laws ought to imitate divine law as completely as possible.[46] The seven planets with their forces suffice for the diversity of generation and decay of the whole universe.[47] Therefore, just as there are seven planets in heaven through which the diversity of generation and decay is effected within this sensible world, and there are seven days in the week by the multiple repetition of which the whole year is measured,[48] and there are seven gifts of the Holy Spirit[49] by which a person, insofar as the soul is concerned, is spiritually perfected, sanctified and governed, so it seems reasonable in the human art which is music, to propose the seven aforementioned principles, which are called concords, particularly since these seven seem to suffice for causing the diversity of musical sounds.[50] Even if there are other concords apart from those, they ought to be called composite and not simple. Here we are speaking about concords insofar as they are simple and the foundations for the others.[51] For when the seven mentioned above are sufficiently known, all the others can be easily grasped. For one who knows what a tone and a ditone is can make a tritone through the addition of a tone. Also one who knows what a tone and what a *diapente* is can make the tone–with-*diapente* very easily from the addition of a tone to the *diapente*,[52] and thus for the rest. Therefore, it remains to say briefly what each of the seven concords mentioned above is, namely what a tone is, what a *semitonium* or semitone is, what a ditone, semiditone, *diatessaron*, *diapente* and *diapason* is,[53] and how they are contrived.

[1.1.6]

So a tone is a concord containing that distance between two pitches immediately adjacent to each other, standing in sesquioctave proportion. As was touched on above at the beginning, when one sound is connected to another in this way, it exceeds it in low or high pitch according to the said proportion, or is exceeded by it,[54] so it makes a sesquioctave proportion in numbers. This is a tone, as we are now speaking about it in musical sound.[55] There is a sesquioctave proportion in numbers when some number contains the whole of the other and with this its eighth part, just as nine contains eight and with this a unity (the eighth part of eight).[56] A tone taken thus is said to be, as some wish, from *ptongos* in Greek, which is *sonus* in Latin.[57] For a tone if not sounded, will not be heard.[58] Or a tone is said to be from *tonando*, namely in that it sounds fully or strongly or perfectly.[59] A concord of this kind, called a tone, exists between four conjunctions of music, namely between ut and re, between re and mi, between fa and sol, between sol and la, and this is as much in ascending as in descending.

[1.1.7]

¶ Semitonium autem sive semitonus est concordantia illa que est inter duas reliquas musice voces. scilicet. inter .mi. et .fa. et hoc similiter tam ascendendo quam etiam descendendo. inter enim istas duas voces non est talis proportio neque tanta distantia qualis est inter ceteras .iiii^{or}. et per consequens neque tonus idest plenus ac perfectus sonus, sed solum semitonium vel semitonus, idest imperfectus et remissus sonus. Dicitur autem semitonus non quia precise medietatem toni contineat. sed quia tamquam sonus remissus a perfectione toni deficiat. sicut et semivir dicitur non quia medius vir sed quia imperfectus vir. et sicut in gramatica semivocalis dicitur non quia medietatem vocalis contineat sed quia plenam vocem per se non faciat ut vocalis.

[1.1.8]

¶ Sciendum est tamen quod duplex est semitonium. scilicet. maius et minus. tonus enim secundum boecium in duas partes equales dividi vel partiri non potest. Maius ergo semitonium quod apothome grece dicitur idest decisio. est illud quod toni medietatem excedit, et tamen ad eius integritatem non pervenit. de quo nichil spectat ad presens. Minus vero semitonium quod grece lima vel dyesis dicitur. est illud quod ad rectam medietatem toni non attingit. et tale est semitonium de quo nunc loquimur quod scilicet est inter .mi. et .fa. ascendendo vel descendendo. Et secundum doctrinam boecii iste due voces ad invicem comparate in tali proportione se habere videntur. qualis est inter ducenta quinquaginta sex et ducenta quadraginta tria. que proportio vocatur in numeris super .13. partiens ducentesimas quadragesimas tertias, sed de hoc non est vis ad presens. cum istud magis ad subtilitates arismetice pertinere noscatur.

[1.1.7]

A *semitonium* or semitone is the concord that exists between the two remaining pitches of music, namely between mi and fa, and likewise as much in rising as in falling pitch. For there is not such a proportion between these two pitches nor such a great distance as there is between the other four, and consequently there is no tone, that is a full and perfect sound, but only a *semitonium* or semitone, an imperfect and incomplete sound.[60] It is called a semitone not because it contains precisely half a tone,[61] but because just as a reduced sound lacks the perfection of a tone, [62] and just as a half-man is so called not because he is half a man but because he is an incomplete man,[63] and just as in grammar a semi-vowel is so called not because it contains half a vowel but because it does not make a full syllable on its own like a vowel.

[1.1.8]

One should know further that a semitone is of two kinds, namely major and minor.[64] For according to Boethius, a tone cannot be divided or partitioned into two equal parts.[65] Thus, the major semitone, which is called an "*apothome*" in Greek, or "remnant," is that which exceeds the midpoint of a tone and yet does not achieve its completeness,[66] and is not considered here for the moment. The minor semitone, which is called in Greek a "*lima*" or "*dyesis*," is that which does not reach the correct midpoint of a tone[67] and is the kind of semitone of which we now speak, namely between mi and fa, in rising or falling. And according to the teaching of Boethius, these two pitches, compared to each other, are seen to exist in such a proportion as is between two hundred and fifty-six and two hundred and forty-three, a proportion called in numbers *superpartiens*: one whole and 13 two hundred and forty-third parts.[68] But this is not an issue for the moment, for it is known to belong rather to the subtleties of arithmetic.

[1.1.9]

¶ Notandum est autem quod quamvis semitonii minoris hec sit proprietas. ut cum tono omnem cantum componere habeat. omnem quoque concordantiam aliam mensurare et in cantu melodiam facere. in aliis tamen omnibus signis **[61v]** gamatis ubi plures sunt voces possibilis est vocum mutatio, excepto .bfabmi. in quo situate sunt iste due voces que inter se solo maiori[6] semitonio distant. eo scilicet quod iste voces. scilicet. mi. et .fa. in eodem tono concordare non possunt. Antiqui tamen musici sicut guido et alii sequentes predicto gamatis signo .scilicet. bfabmi duas attribuerunt litteras. videlicet .b. molle sive rotundum. et etiam .♮ quadratum, per primum b semitonium. per secundum vero tonum integrum designantes. Moderni vero musici, hoc quod due predicte littere secundum rectam et communem musicam in solo. bfabmi designant. in aliis signis gamatis faciunt aliquando designare. ita videlicet quod ubi secundum rectam musicam deberet esse solum semitonus, per .♮. quadratum ad tonum ampliant. ubi vero tonus perfectus et integer esse deberet, per .b. rotundum ad semitonium minus restringunt. et hoc falsam musicam appellant. que .scilicet. falsa musica etsi causa necessitatis inventa fuerit ut melior consonantia fieri posset. et maxime in compositione. stantipedum. motetorum. et huiusmodi mensuratorum cantuum. in quibus precipue locum habet, non est tamen inconveniens ut interdum in quibusdam ecclesiasticis cantibus locum habeat, quamvis raro hoc accidat. non enim video quod neuma quinti toni prout apud nos et multos alios et quasi omnes consuevit cantari, sine falsa musica possit convenienter notari. unde et sic ipsum infra notatum repperies suo loco. sicque ipsum a magistro Iohanne de garlandia in libro quem fecit de tonis notatum inveni. Ad quid autem semitonium maius. de quo supra visum est deserviat. vel in qua proportione consistat. cur etiam tonus in duos equales semitonos non possit precise dividi aut partiri, non est[7] speculationis presentis. et qui hoc curiosius scire desiderat, necesse est ut ad musicam boecii ubi talia subtilius pertractantur studiose pariter et attente recurrat.

[1.1.10]

¶ Ditonus vero est concordantia duos tonos continens que sono precedenti sic proportionari videtur in sonis, sicut octoginta unum ad sexaginta quatuor in numeris. et talis concordantia est inter .ut. et .mi. et inter .fa. et .la. tam ascendendo quam etiam descendendo. inter istas enim secundum boecium predicta numeralis proportio repperitur.

---

[6] minori *corrected to* maiori **H2**.

[7] est *inserted from left margin* **H2**.

[1.1.9]

It should be noted that although it may be the property of the minor semitone that with the tone it may constitute all chant, it may also define every other concord and create melody in chant.[69] However, on all other signs of the gamut where there are several syllables, mutation of pitch names is possible.[70] The exception is b-fa/b-mi, where these two pitches are distant from each other by a single major semitone.[71] Of course, these syllables, that is, mi and fa, cannot make a concord on the same note.[72] For older music theorists, such as Guido and others following him, attributed two letter forms, soft or round b and also square b, to the aforesaid sign of the gamut, namely b-fa/b-mi.[73] Through the first b [soft or round b] is indicated the semitone [mi-fa] and through the second [square or hard b] is indicated the whole tone [re-mi].[74] Modern music theorists, by contrast, make the two aforesaid letter forms sometimes designate on other signs of the gamut what according to right and traditional music is only on bfabmi. In consequence what ought to be only a semitone according to *musica recta*, through square b they extend it to a tone, and where there ought to be a perfect and whole tone, through round b they draw it back to a semitone. They call this *musica falsa* which was clearly invented out of necessity so that there could be a better consonance, particularly in the composition of *stantipedes*, motets and measured songs of this kind, in which *musica falsa* has a particular place.[75] However, it is not inappropriate that it meanwhile should have a place in certain ecclesiastical chants, although this happens rarely. For I do not see that the *neuma* of the fifth tone, as usually sung among us and many others and almost everyone, can conveniently be notated without *musica falsa*. So you will find it notated in its place below, and I have found it notated thus by master John of Garland in the book that he made about the tones.[76] But what purpose the major semitone, as seen above, serves, or in what proportion it stands, or why the tone cannot be divided or partitioned precisely into two equal semitones, is not our present concern. Whoever is curious to know this needs to go back both studiously and attentively to the *Musica* of Boethius,[77] where such things are treated more minutely.

[1.1.10]

The ditone is a concord containing two tones which is seen to be proportional from the preceding sound in sounds, just as eighty-one is to sixty-four in numbers.[78] Such a concord exists between ut and mi and between fa and la, as much in rising as in falling. For according to Boethius, the aforesaid proportion of numbers is found between them.[79]

[1.1.11]

¶ Semiditonus autem est concordantia tonum cum semitonio continens. que sono precedenti sic proportionari videtur in sonis, sicut .xxxij. ad .xxvij. in numeris. et talis concordantia est inter .re. et .fa. et inter .mi. et sol. tam ascendendo quam descendendo. iste enim voces tono et semitonio minori distant ab invicem et inter eas secundum boecium talis proportio repperitur.

[1.1.12]

¶ Dyatessaron vero est **[62r]** concordantia duos tonos cum uno semitonio minori continens, que precedenti sono comparata eum in sexquitertia proportione superat et excedit, quod est enim sexquitertia proportio in numeris. hoc est dyatessaron in sonis musicis. Est autem proportio sexquitertia in numeris, quando aliquis numerus totum alterum continet et cum hoc tertiam eius partem. sicut se habent .iiij^{or}. ad .iij. et .xij. ad .ix. et talis concordantia que minima inter consonantias a boecio dicitur, est inter .ut. et .fa. inter .re. et sol. et inter .mi. et .la. tam ascendendo quam etiam descendendo. iste enim voces duobus tonis et semitonio si quis diligenter consideret distant ab invicem, ac etiam inter eas predicta proportio sexquitertia repperitur. Dicitur autem dyatessaron a dya quod est de. et tessara quod est .iiij^{or}. eo videlicet quod sit ex .iiij^{or}. vocibus.

[1.1.13]

¶ Dyapente autem est concordantia tres tonos cum semitonio minori continens, que precedenti sono comparata, eum in sexquialtera proportione supperat et excedit. quod est enim sexquialtera proportio in numeris, hoc est dyapente in sonis musicis. Est autem sexquialtera proportio in numeris. quando aliquis numerus totum alterum continet, et cum hoc alteram idest mediam eius partem. sicut se habent sex ad .iiijor. et .xij. ad octo. Et talis concordantia que media vel secunda consonantiarum dicitur, est inter .ut. et .sol. et inter .re. et .la. tam ascendendo quam etiam descendendo. iste enim voces tribus tonis ac semitonio distant ab invicem et inter eas predicta sexquialtera proportio repperitur. Dicitur autem dyapente a dya quod est de. et penta, quod est .vque. eo videlicet quod ex quinque constet vocibus.

[1.1.11]

The semiditone is a concord containing a tone with a semitone which is seen to be proportional from the preceding sound in sounds, just as thirty-two is to twenty-seven in numbers.[80] Such a concord exists between re and fa and between mi and sol, as much in rising as in falling. For these pitches are distant from each other by a tone and a minor semitone and, according to Boethius, such a proportion is found between them.[81]

[1.1.12]

The *diatessaron* is a concord containing two tones with one minor semitone that compared with a preceding sound is higher and exceeds it in sesquitertian proportion.[82] For what a sesquitertian proportion is in numbers, this is a *diatessaron* in musical sounds.[83] It is a sesquitertian proportion in numbers when some [the greater] number embraces the whole of the other number and a third of it,[84] just as four is to three and twelve to nine.[85] Such a concord, which is called the smallest among consonances by Boethius,[86] is between ut and fa, between re and sol, and between mi and la, as much in rising as in falling. For if anyone should carefully consider these pitches, they are distant from each other by two tones and a semitone; furthermore the aforesaid sesquitertian proportion occurs between them. It is called the *diatessaron* from "*dya*," which is "from," and "*tessara*," which is "four," in that it is clearly from four pitches.[87]

[1.1.13]

The *diapente* is a concord containing three tones with a minor semitone that compared with a preceding sound is higher and exceeds it in sesquialter proportion.[88] For what a sesquialter proportion is in numbers, this is a diapente in musical sounds.[89] It is a sesquialter proportion in numbers when some number [the greater] embraces the whole of the other number and a half of it,[90] just as six is to four and twelve is to eight. Such a concord, which is called a median or secondary consonance,[91] is between ut and sol and between re and la, as much in rising as in falling. For these pitches are distant from each other by three tones and a semitone, and the aforesaid sesquialter proportion is found between them. It is called the *diapente* from "*dya*," that is, "from," and "*penta*," which is "five," in that it is clearly from five pitches.[92]

[1.1.14]

¶ Dyapason vero est concordantia quinque tonos et duo minora semitonia continens, que precedenti sono comparata. eum in dupla proportione supperat et excedit. quod enim est proportio dupla in numeris. hoc est dyapason in sonis musicis. Est autem proportio dupla in numeris quando aliquis numerus bis alium continet. sicut se habent .iiijor. ad duo. et .xij. ad sex. et ista concordantia que mater consonantiarum dicitur tamquam perfectissima inter ipsas, est inter quamlibet vocem musice et suam octavam. nulla enim vox secundum guidonem alteri voci perfecte concordat preter suam octavam. Dicitur autem dypason a dya quod est de, et pason, quod est omne vel totum quasi de omnibus omnes enim concordantias precedentes non solum videlicet .tonum. semitonum. ditonum. semiditonum. immo etiam dyatessaron et dyapente que in ea iunguntur et ex quarum coniunctione resultat tamquam mater omnium in se amplectitur, continet, et includit. ex ipsa etiam **[62v]** alie due perfecte consonantie que tamen non sunt simplices sed composite oriuntur. videlicet dyapente cum dyapason et bis dyapason. quarum prima in tripla proportione consistit, secunda vero in quadrupla. Sicut ergo manifeste concluditur ex predictis .vij. sunt concordantie musicales quarum videlicet .iiijor. prime que sunt .tonus. semitonium minus. ditonus. et semiditonus. concordantie simpliciter nominantur. tres vero relique non solum concordantie immo etiam consonantie appellantur. ex quo patet etiam quod in plu[ribu]s[8] est concordantia quam consonantia. ut sic ista duo sicut superius et inferius inter se invicem debeant comparari. omnis enim consonantia est concordantia. sed non omnis concordantia est consonantia.

[1.1.15]

¶ Trinam itaque armoniam perfectam in sonis instituit a principio, sublimis omnium creator ac rector qui solus in trinitate perfecta sic permanet ut semper in unitate consistat, non solum scilicet ut in istis tribus consonantiis supradictis vel earum triplici armonia bonitatis sue participationem ostenderet, sed ut homo etiam qui ad illius summe trinitatis ymaginem et similitudinem est creatus a sui conditoris laude se ipsum excusare non posset. sed potius benedictum nomen maiestatis illius ineffabilis quoque bonitatis clementiam iugiter quantum humana permittit fragilitas collaudaret. Tres siquidem consonantie predicte. dyapason videlicet dyapente et dyatessaron non solum si simul ordinate fuerint et coniuncte unam resultantem ex tribus perfectissimam efficiunt melodiam quinimmo prima armonia que dyapason dicitur quasi mater esse videtur. dyapente vero media et quasi filia in ipsa contenta. tertia vero que dyatessaron appellatur ab eis procedens. Et[9] hoc secundum quod aliqui dicunt quidam forte senserunt pitagorici naturali inclinatione ducti. in creaturis et enim relucet quoddam vestigium trinitatis ut habet alibi declarari. hoc tamen non sunt ausi sub talibus verbis exprimere. sed de

---

[8] pl<urib>us *Klundert.*   [9] ex *struck through after* Et.

[1.1.14]

The *diapason* is a concord containing five tones and two minor semitones that compared to a preceding sound is higher and exceeds it in double proportion.[93] For what a double proportion is in numbers, this is a diapason in musical sounds.[94] It is a double proportion in numbers when some number embraces twice another,[95] just as four is to two and twelve to six. Such a concord, which is called the mother of consonances,[96] is the most perfect among these and occurs between any pitch of music and its octave. For according to Guido, no pitch agrees with another pitch more perfectly than its octave.[97] It is called a *diapason*, from "*dya*," which is "from," and "*pason*," which is "all" or "whole"[98]. Just as the mother of all encompasses, contains and includes everything in herself, so [the *diapason*] encompasses, contains and includes all the preceding concords, that is not only the tone, semitone, ditone, and semiditone, but also the *diatessaron* and *diapente* which are joined in it and from whose conjunction it results.[99] From this also arise the two other perfect consonances, which are however not simple but composite, namely the *diapente* with *diapason*,[100] and the double *diapason*, the first of which stands in triple proportion, but the second in quadruple. Hence, as is clearly concluded from the aforesaid, there are seven musical concords, of which the first four, which are tone, minor semitone, ditone and semiditone, are simply called concords, but the remaining three are not only called concords but also consonances.[101] It is clear from this that there is a concord in more places than consonance, so that the two ought to be compared together, just like the superior and the inferior,[102] for every consonance is a concord, but not every concord is a consonance.

[1.1.15]

And in this way the sublime Creator and Ruler of all things, who remains alone in perfect trinity always consisting in unity, instituted a perfect threefold harmony in sounds from the beginning.[103] That is to say not only so that he might show in these, the three aforesaid consonances, and in their threefold harmony, participation in his goodness, but also so that humans, created in the image and likeness of that most high Trinity,[104] would not be able to distance themselves from the praise of their Creator.[105] Rather they should praise the blessed name of that ineffable majesty and the mercy of his goodness as far as human frailty permits. Indeed three of the aforementioned consonances, namely the *diapason*, *diapente* and *diatessaron*, if simultaneously ordered and joined, not only make one resulting most perfect melody,[106] from the three, but also the first harmony. This is called the *diapason* which is like a mother, the *diapente* is the intermediate and contained in her like a daughter; the third which is called the *diatessaron*, proceeding from them.[107] And this, according to what some say, certain Pythagoreans perhaps sensed, led by natural inclination.[108] For a certain trace of the Trinity shines forth in creatures, as is declared elsewhere.[109] They did not dare to express this in such words, but

istis in numeris quasi sub methafora loquebantur. Quicquid autem sit de hoc per melodiam tamen ex istis tribus consonantiis resultantem refert boecius in primo musice concordantias ceteras et alia musice principia primo a pitagora philosopho reperta fuisse.

[1.1.16]

¶ Ad cuius evidentiam notandum est primo quod secundum doctrinam boecii in prologo musice, adeo musica nobis naturaliter est innata, ut nec ea carere possimus etiam si velimus. non solum enim infantes ut dicit boecius immo etiam iuvenes atque senes ita naturaliter et affectu quodam spontaneo modis musicis adiunguntur. ut nulla omnino sit etas que a cantus dulcedine sit seiuncta. unde et qui suaviter canere non possunt [63r] sibi tamen aliquid canunt, non quod eos aliqua voluptate afficiat id quod canunt sed quod quandam insitam dulcedinem ex animo proferentes, quoquomodo eam proferant delectantur. Et inde est ut dicit ibidem. quod cum aliquis cantilenam libenter auribus et animo capit, ad hoc etiam non[10] sponte convertitur. ut motum quoque aliquem audite cantilene similem corpus eius effingat, et auditum melos sibi memor animus ipse decerpat.

[1.1.17]

¶ Cum igitur musica ita nobis naturaliter sit inserta et propter hoc homines semper et quasi ab initio mundi cantaverint, usque tamen ad tempus pitagore principia musice ignorasse videntur. Licet enim quidam fabulose loquentes de musica dixerint eam a musis habitantibus iuxta aquas inventam fuisse ac etiam inde nomen traxisse. Quidam vero ab iubal fratre tubalchaim. de quo iubal dicitur in genesi quod ipse fuit pater canentium in cithara et organo. de quo etiam habetur in cronicis quod ipse delectatus[11] in sonitu malleorum fratris sui tubalchaim quem fuisse dicunt inventorem artis ferrarie et operum in metallis, proportiones perpendens in malleis ipsius primus musicam adinvenit. secundum tamen boecium et guidonem et alios loquentes de musica probabilius est dicendum, quod concordantie et alia principia musice primo a pitagora philosopho qui tempore cambisys regis persarum, filii. scilicet. regis ciri legitur floruisse, ante videlicet incarnationem domini annis quingentis et viginti vel circiter. qui que primus quamvis perfecte sapiens esset non sapientem se nominari voluit sed potius philosophum idest amatorem sapientie. ita quod deinceps ceteri sapientes philosophi sint vocati qui sapientes antea dicebantur, fuerunt inventa. Potuit tamen esse quod ipse iubal vel alii ante pitagoram aliqua instrumenta et aliqua generalia musice principia vel incerta per que magis usualiter quam artificialiter cantabant invenerint. sed certa et propria huius artis principia secundum boecium. guidonem. ceterosque modernos musicos primo a pitagora philosopho quasi quodam divino nutu modo qui sequitur certitudinaliter et magis ad plenum quam antea fuerunt inventa. Sicut enim dicit

---

[10] non *omitted Klundert.*   [11] delectatur *Klundert.*

they spoke about these things in numbers, as in metaphor.[110] Whatever the case about this, Boethius nonetheless reports in the first book of the Musica that other concords and other principles of music were first found by Pythagoras the philosopher through melody resulting from these three consonances.[111]

[1.1.16]
As evidence of this, it must first be noted that, according to the teaching of Boethius in the prologue to the *Musica*, music is naturally innate to us, so much so that we are not able to be without it, even if we wished.[112] For not only children, as Boethius says, but also the young and the old are bound together by musical modes so naturally and by a certain spontaneous effect, that no age at all is remote from the sweetness of song.[113] As a result, those who are not able to sing sweetly still sing something to themselves. They delight in it not because what they sing might affect them by a certain pleasure, but because generating a certain innate sweetness from the spirit gives delight, whatever way they produce it.[114] And so it is, as he says in the same place, that when anyone grasps lyric song freely with ears and spirit, they are not turned towards it voluntarily, so that their body also makes some motion similar to the lyric song that is heard, and the mindful spirit picks out the tune that is heard for itself.[115]

[1.1.17]
Since, therefore, music is found naturally in us and because of this people have sung always and as if from the beginning of the world, up to the time of Pythagoras they seem to have been ignorant of the principles of music.[116] For although certain people speaking in fables about music say that it was discovered by the Muses living by the waters and also took its name from there,[117] certain people indeed say that it was discovered by the brother of Tubalchaim, Jubal of whom it is said in *Genesis* that he was the father of those singing with the cithara and organ. It is reported about him in chronicles that he was delighted by the sound of the hammers of his brother Tubalchaim, who they say was the inventor of the art of iron- and metalwork. Weighing the proportions in his hammers he was the first to discover music.[118] Yet, according to Boethius and Guido and others speaking more plausibly about music, it must be said that the concords and other principles of music were first discovered by Pythagoras the philosopher,[119] who reportedly flourished at the time of Cambyses, King of the Persians, son of King Cyrus,[120] around five hundred and twenty years before the incarnation of the Lord or thereabouts. Although he was the first perfectly wise person, he did not want to be called wise, rather a philosopher, that is, a lover of wisdom, with the result that henceforth the rest of the wise people have been called philosophers who before were called the wise ones.[121] It is possible, however, that this Jubal or others before Pythagoras discovered certain instruments and certain general or vague principles of music

guido capitulo ultimo sui micrologi idest brevis sermonis in musica. Erant antiquitus instrumenta incerta et canentium multitudo. sed ceca. nullus enim hominum ut dicit ibidem vocum differentias et simphonie descriptionem poterat aliqua argumentatione colligere. neque posset umquam certum aliquid de hac arte
cognoscere, nisi divina tandem bonitas quam sequimur suo nutu disponeret. cum
pitagoras quidam magnus philosophus forte iter ageret. venitque ad fabricam in
qua super incudem quinque mallei feriebant. quorum suavem concordantiam
miratus philosophus, accessit primoque [63v] in manuum varietate seu virtute
sperans vim soni ac modulationis existere. fecit in manu ferientium mutari malleos. quo facto malleum quemque sua vis sequuta est. Subtracto itaque malleo qui
dissonus erat a ceteris, alios ponderavit. mirumque in modum divino nutu, primus
.xij. secundus .ix. tertius octo. quartus vero sex, nescio quibus certis tamen ponderibus appendebant, et sic scientiam musice in proportione et collatione numerorum versari cognovit.

[1.1.18]
¶ Sciendum est enim secundum boecium et guidonem quod pitagoras .iiijor. predictis malleis ponderatis primum malleum ad ultimum comparatum invenit in
dupla proportione se habere ad illum. sicut videlicet .xij. se habent ad sex. et sic isti
duo mallei illam consonantiam reddebant que dyapason dicitur. que ut dictum est
supra, in duppla proportione consistit. Ille vero idem primus malleus qui .xij. ponderabat, ad secundum qui ponderabat .ix. in proportione sexquitertia se habebat,
sicut se habent .xij. ad .ix. et sic consonantiam illam que dyatessaron dicitur que in
tali proportione ut supra dictum est consistit, resonabat. Ad tertium vero malleum
qui ponderabat octo, in proportione sexquialtera se habebat. sicut se habent .xij. ad
octo. et sic cum eo consonantiam que dicitur dyapente que ut supra dictum est in
tali consistit proportione reddebat. Isti etiam duo medii mallei secundus videlicet
et tertius ad quartum comparati in eisdem proportionibus se habebant. secundus
videlicet in sexquialtera. sicut sunt .ix. ad sex. et sic cum eo dyapente reddebat.
tertius vero in sexquitertia sicut sunt octo ad sex. et sic cum eo consonantiam dyatessaron resonabat. Isti autem duo medii mallei ad se invicem comparati, in proportione sexquioctava se habebant, sicut sunt .ix. ad octo. et sic unus ad alterum
comparatus cum eo concordantiam illam que dicitur tonus que ut supra dictum
est consistit in proportione sexquioctava, reddebat. Quintus vero malleus merito a
pitagora est reiectus, eo quod ceteris improportionabilis erat, et ideo nullam cum
aliquo eorum armoniam reddebat. sed eam potius corrumpebat.

through which they used to sing more by custom than by art. But according to Boethius, Guido and other modern musicians, the fixed and proper principles of this art were discovered first by Pythagoras the philosopher as if through a certain divine assent in a way that follows with certitude and more fully than had been discovered before.[122] For just as Guido said in the last chapter of his *Micrologus*, that is, the short treatise on music, there were undefined instruments and a multitude of singers in ancient times, but they were blind.[123] For, as he says in the same place, no one was able to put together by any argument the variety of pitches and the description of the harmony of sounds. Nor were they ever able to know anything certain about this art unless divine goodness, which we follow, finally grant it by its favour.[124] When Pythagoras, that great philosopher, by chance made a journey and came to a workshop in which five hammers were striking on an anvil, the philosopher, wondering at their sweet concord, approached. At first expecting that the force and modulation of the sound depended on the variety and strength of the hands, he had the hammers changed in the hands of the ironworkers. When this was done, his attention followed each hammer. And so having taken the hammer that was dissonant away from the rest, he weighed the others, and in a wonderful way by divine favour, the first weighed twelve, the second nine, the third eight, the fourth six; though I do not know their precise weights. And thus he learnt that the science of music turns on proportion and comparison of numbers.[125]

[1.1.18]
For it should be known, according to Boethius and Guido,[126] that having weighed these four hammers, Pythagoras discovered that the first hammer compared to the last was in double proportion to it, as twelve is to six, and thus those two hammers rendered the consonance called the *diapason*,[127] which, as was said above, consists in double proportion. But that same first hammer, which weighed twelve, was in sesquitertian proportion to the second, which weighed nine, as twelve is to nine and thus sounded the consonance called the *diatessaron*,[128] which, as said above, consists in such a proportion. As to the third hammer, which weighed eight, it was in sesquialter proportion, as twelve is to eight and thus renders with it the consonance called the *diapente*,[129] which, as said above, consists in that proportion. For these two middle hammers, namely the second and the third, compared to the fourth, were in the same proportions, namely the second in sesquialter, as nine is to six, and thus renders the *diapente* with it, but the third in sesquitertian, as eight is to six, and thus resounded the consonance *diatessaron* with it.[130] Compared to each other those two middle hammers were in a sesquioctave proportion, as nine is to eight, and thus one compared to the other rendered with it that concord called a tone,[131] which, as said above, consists in the sesquioctave proportion. But the fifth hammer was deservedly rejected by Pythagoras since it was not in proportion with the rest, and thus it made no harmony with any of them but rather ruined it.[132]

[1.1.19]

¶ Ex istis autem postmodum diligentius investigans pitagoras, non solum invenit quid esset tonus, quid dyesis vel semitonus, quidque ditonus. semiditonus. dyatessaron. dyapente. et dyapason. vel alia ex istis composita. immo etiam secundum guidonem ubi supra, per predicta voces ordinans primus monocordium composuit. Est autem monocordium secundum quod dicit magister Iohannes de garlandia in tractatu suo de musica instrumentum quoddam ligneum et concavum trium palmarum in longitudine, unius palme vel circa in latitudine trium vero digitorum vel circa in spissitudine, habens unicam cordam [**64r**] unde et monocordium dicitur, sub qua proportionantur omnes proportiones armonice. quod secundum guidonem sapientibus in commune placuit eo quod non ex lascivia sed ex artis musice diligenti notitia ut dictum est a pitagora fuit primo compositum et repertum. Et hoc de tono secundo modo dicto aliisque musice speciebus sive principiis quantum ad ea que infra de tonis dicentur plenius intelligenda spectare videtur, dixisse sufficiat quo ad presens.

[1.2.0]

¶ Capitulum secundum. Quot sunt toni. et quibus nominibus a musicis et philosophis appellantur.

[1.2.1]

¶ In hoc autem antiquiores primique musici de numero tonorum aliter quam posteriores quos secuntur moderni senserunt, quod priores quatuor tantummodo tonos. posteriores vero octo potius posuerunt. Ad cuius maiorem evidentiam est notandum quod secundum doctrinam in musica peritorum et maxime prefati guidonis aretini monachi viri siquidem ut habetur in cronicis in musica preclarissimi multique nominis in hoc etiam preferendi philosophis quod non solum provecti vel homines studiosi immo et pueri per ipsius artis regulas cantus difficiles et ignotos facilius quam per vocem alicuius magistri. vel etiam instrumenti musici didicerunt, et adhuc addiscunt, septem sunt littere alphabeti. a. b. c. d. e. f. g. sex vocibus quas sola musica recipit que sunt. ut. re. mi. fa. sol. la. modulatim apposite. et per .xix, manus leve iuncturas prout docet ars gamatis quam monachus memoratus, ut testantur cronice circa annum domini .mm. .xxviiim. invenisse dicitur, in locis debitis situate ac pluries repetite ex quarum elevatione et depressione sive depositione componitur omnis cantus.

[1.1.19]

From these, after more assiduous investigation Pythagoras not only discovered what is a tone, a diesis or semitone, and a ditone, semiditone, *diatessaron, diapente* and *diapason*, and others put together from these,[133] he also, according to Guido as above, was the first to put together a monochord ordering pitches according to the above.[134] According to what Master John of Garland says in his treatise *De musica*, the monochord is a certain hollow, wooden instrument three palms in length, one palm or thereabouts in breadth, but three fingers or thereabouts in thickness, having one string. Hence it is called a monochord on which all harmonic proportions are set out.[135] According to Guido, this pleased the wise in general, since it was first constructed and discovered by Pythagoras not from playfulness, but, as has been said, from careful awareness of the art of music.[136] And let this suffice for now about tone spoken about in the second way, and other principles of music, as far as seems to regard understanding those things which will be spoken of more fully below.

[1.2.0]

Chapter two: How many tones there are, and by what names they are called by musicians and philosophers.

[1.2.1]

In this the ancient and first musicians felt otherwise about the number of tones than later people, whom the moderns follow, in that the earlier ones proposed only four tones, but the later ones rather proposed eight.[137] For greater evidence of this, it should be noted what is according to the teaching of those skilled in music, and particularly of the above-mentioned monk, Guido of Arezzo, (indeed a man most distinguished and of great reputation in music, as is reported in chronicles),[138] he is even to be preferred to philosophers in this. Because not only advanced and studious people but even boys have learned and still learn difficult and unknown chants more easily through the rules of the art itself than through the voice of any master or even of a musical instrument. There are seven letters of the alphabet—a, b, c, d, e, f, g—for the six solmization syllables, namely ut, re, mi, fa, sol, la, which only music retains. These are positioned stepwise, located and repeated several times in appropriate places through the nineteen joints of the left hand, just as the art of the gamut teaches. The said monk is reputed to have discovered this around the year of our Lord 1028, as chronicles attest. From their ascent and descent or lowering all chant is composed.[139]

[1.2.2]

❡ Harum ergo vocum et litterarum quedam graves, quedam vero acute, alie autem superacute dicuntur. ille quippe graves esse dicuntur que depressum sonum efficiunt. et iste sunt octo. ille. scilicet. que sunt situate in primis octo signis totius gamatis, que videlicet signa componendo voces cum litteris vulgariter appellamus. gam aut. are. bemi¹². cfaut. dsolre. elami. ffaut. gsolreut. Acute vero dicuntur ille que sonum reddunt acutum et altum. et iste sunt septem. ille videlicet que in sequentibus septem signis gamatis situantur, que communiter appellamus. alamire. bfabmi. csolfaut. dlasolre. elami. ffaut. gsolreut. Ille autem superacute dicuntur que in .iiijᵒʳ. reliquis gamatis signis videlicet. alamire. bfabmi. csolfa. et dlasol. Situantur, eo videlicet quod superacutum idest valde acutum et altum sonum efficiant.

[1.2.3]

❡ Predictarum vero septem litterarum in signis .xix. predictis ipsius [**64v**] gamatis positarum .iiijᵒʳ. solum dicuntur esse finales. videlicet. d. e. f. g. graves. que pro tanto dicuntur finales. quia in istis .iiijᵒʳ. omnes ecclesiastici cantus regulariter et communiter finiuntur. dico autem regulariter et communiter. eo quod aliquando cantus aliqui etiam regulares sicut infra videbitur plenius qui. scilicet. propter suum ascensum vel descensum aut etiam propter sui principii modum eo modo quo consueverunt cantari non possunt sic notari quod in predictis .iiijᵒʳ. finalibus litteris terminentur, in aliis litteris que idcirco affinales dicuntur eo quod vicem finalium predictarum suppleant finiuntur. Et secundum guidonem tres sunt littere affinales. scilicet. a. b. c. acute vel quod in idem redit. a. b. c. in primis tribus acutis signis gamatis que sunt. alamire ♮ fabmi.¹³ et csolfaut. Situate, de quibus quomodo vicem finalium suppleant in sequenti capitulo tractando in speciali de quolibet tono magis et plenius apparebit.

[1.2.4]

❡ Antiquiores itaque et priores artis musice inventores .iiijor. finalium litterarum in quibus ut dictum est omnes cantus ecclesiastici regulariter finiuntur numerum attendentes secundum earum numerum .iiijor. tonos tantummodo posuerunt. Sed beatus gregorius ceterique sequentes .iiijor. tonos illos quos antiqui nominabant prothum. deuterum. tritum. et tetrardum in octo potius distinxerunt. cuius fuit ista necessitas sicut guido prefatus capitulo .xijo. sui micrologi predicti commemorat. dicit enim quod cum antiquitus antequam fieret distinctio .iiijor. tonorum in octo cantus unius toni vel modi utpote prothi idest primi per comparationem et respectum ad finem non solum graves essent et plani sed etiam acuti et alti, inde sequebatur inconveniens tale. quod. scilicet. versus et psalmi vel si quid aliud fini cantus erat aptandum, uno et eodem modo prolatum diversis aptari non poterat. quod enim subiungebatur si grave erat cum acutis non conveniebat, et si acutum

---

¹² .bmi. *Klundert.*　　　　　　　　¹³ *Should perhaps be* bfabmi?

[1.2.2]

Of these solmization syllables and letters, therefore, certain are said to be grave, certain acute, others superacute. Indeed those are said to be grave that make a deep sound, and these are eight, namely those that are situated on the first eight signs of the whole gamut. We commonly call these signs Gamma-ut, A-re, B-mi, C-faut, D-solre, E-lami, F-faut, G-solreut simply putting solmization syllables together with letters. Those called acute give an acute and high sound, and these are seven, i.e. those situated on the following seven signs of the gamut, which we commonly call a-lamire, b-fa/b-mi, c-solfaut, d-lasolre, e-lami, f-faut, g-solreut. Those are called superacute that are situated on the four remaining signs of the gamut, namely a'-lamire, b'-fa/b'-mi, c'-solfa and d'-lasol, in that they make a superacute sound, that is, very acute and high.[140]

[1.2.3]

Of the aforesaid seven letters positioned on the nineteen signs of the gamut itself, only four are said to be finals, namely D, E, F, G grave. These are called finals in as much as all ecclesiastical chants regularly and commonly end on these four. I say "regularly and commonly" in that sometimes some chants, even regular ones, as will be seen below more fully, cannot be notated in the way they are usually sung, namely ending on the four final letters, because of their ascent or descent or because of the way they begin. Rather they end on other letters, consequently called affinales in that they take the place of the aforesaid finals. And according to Guido, there are three affinal letters, namely a, b, c acute, or what turns out to be the same a, b, c situated on the first three acute signs of the gamut, which are a-lamire, b-fa/b-mi and c-solfaut.[141] It will become more fully evident how these take the place of finals in the following chapter dealing in particular with any tone.

[1.2.4]

The ancients and early discoverers of the art of music posited four final letters, on which, as has been said, all ecclesiastical chants end as a rule, and considering this number, they set at only four the number of the tones. But Blessed Gregory and others following him rather divided those four tones, which the ancients called *protus*, *deuterus*, *tritus* and *tetrardus*, into eight.[142] The aforesaid Guido records the need for this in the twelfth chapter of the aforementioned *Micrologus*.[143] For he says that, in ancient times, before the division of four tones into eight was made, the chants of one tone or mode, such as of the *protus*, that is, of the first, were not only grave and simple but also acute and lofty in comparison with and respect to the end. Then an awkwardness followed, namely if something of the verse and psalm or anything else would be adapted to the end of the chant, what was proffered could not be adapted to different chants in one and the same way. For what was added below, if it was grave, did not agree with the acute, and if it was acute,

erat a gravibus discordabat. Et ideo posteriores musici quos moderni secuntur consuluerunt, ut quilibet predictorum .iiijor. tonorum partiretur in duos in acutum videlicet et gravem ut sic acuta acutis et gravia gravibus convenirent, et sic qui prius in vocibus finales considerando litteras erant .iiijor. in cantibus deinceps essent octo.

[1.2.5]

❡ Ut autem de octo tonorum origine et eorum nominibus aliquid plenius videatur. Sciendum est quod sicut repperi in quodam libello de tonis ac eorum origine antiquo valde ubi et guidonis micrologus[14] continetur quem in isto tractactu frequenter allego. Fuit olim quedam mulier quam scillam nominatam fuisse aliqui dixerunt filiam que orci. Alii vero appellant eam circem veneficam filiam apollinis glauci uxorem. Alii autem dicunt eam filiam nisi fuisse. que secundum fabulas poetarum versa est in speciem piscis ab umbilico vel circa usque ad genua. quam etiam dicit [65r] virgilius .iij°. eneidis. succinctam fuisse caninis capitibus circa inguina ipsius latrantibus, qui canes marini nautas timidos pertranseuntes in formas diversarum bestiarum vertebant et sic eos in mare mergebant. Habuisse quoque fertur predicta scilla sororem nomine caribdim quam ipsa vertisse dicitur in caput draconis ut caridis.[15] scilicet. devoraret quoscumque illa pertimebat. Scilla autem ut fallere posset delonge nautas ignaros et eos cantilenis illiceret usque ad eorum submersionem dulces quasdam melodias iugiter in mari canebat. Capilli vero ipsius serpentini erant, et semper inter dulces sonos terribiles serpentum sonitus et canum latratus diversi audiebantur confuse. distincte vero audiebantur voces dulces. isti videlicet octo toni. videbanturque audiri quasi lingua exprimeret ita dicens. noannoeane. aliquando vero noioeane. et noeagis. Cum quibus verbis semper audiebatur vox cantilene. nunc de primo tono. nunc vero de secundo. nunc de tertio, et sic de ceteris octo tonis semperque replicabant ibidem ipse voces.

[1.2.6]

❡ Ad cuius evidentiam notandum est quod sicut ibidem legitur scilla et caribdis duo sunt in mari immania saxa inter que media virgilius ubi supra eneam oraculis deorum moderato commemorat navigasse. dicit enim eneam ipsum a diis fuisse premonitum ne in sinistrum penitus iter carperet nec in dexteram partem aliquando rates deveheret eo quod naufragia nimia ibi naute patiebantur ignari. Erant in illis duobus saxis multiplicia diversaque foramina, que permeans assidue maris unda quasi dulce canorumque melos diversis modulationibus latinorum magisque grecorum auribus ingerebat. Ex quibus melodiis vocumque diversarum sonis greci astutiores et sapientia decenter imbuti hos octo sonos vel tonos subtiliter protraxerunt conicientes nullam naturalem sive rationabilem cantilenam

---

[14] micrologius *corrected to* micrologus   [15] Cari<b>dis *Klundert*.

it was discordant with the grave. And so later musicians, whom the moderns follow, advised that each of the aforesaid four tones be divided into two, namely into acute and grave, in order that the acute matches the acute and the grave matches the grave. And thus what were previously considered in pitches to be four final letters in chant thereafter were eight.[144]

[1.2.5]

So that the origin of the eight tones and their names may be grasped more fully, it should be known that—as I found in a certain, very ancient little book on the tones and their origin, and where the *Micrologus* of Guido is also contained, which I allude to frequently in this treatise—there was once a certain woman whom some said was named Scylla and was the daughter of Phorcus.[145] Others call her Circe, the sorceress daughter of Apollo and the wife of Glaucus.[146] Yet others say she was the daughter of Nisus, who according to the fables of poets was turned into a kind of fish from the navel or thereabouts to the knees.[147] Vergil also says in the third book of the Aeneid that she was girdled with barking canine heads around her groin, and these marine dogs turned the frightened sailors, who were passing through, into the forms of different beasts, and thus they sank in the sea.[148] The aforesaid Scylla is also reported to have had a sister by the name of Charybdis, whom she is said to have turned into the head of a dragon, so that Charybdis might devour anyone she threatened.[149] So that she might deceive the unwary sailors from afar and entice them with lyric songs until they were drowned, Scylla used to sing certain sweet melodies continually in the sea. But her tresses were serpents, and among sweet sounds the various terrible hissing of the serpents and the barking of the dogs were always heard in confusion. But the sweet voices were heard clearly, namely these eight tones, and they seem to be heard as if the tongue were articulating thus, "noannoeane," but sometimes "noioeane" and "noeagis." The voicing of the lyric song was always heard with these words, now in the first tone, and now in the second, now in the third, and thus for the remainder of the eight tones, and these voices were always repeating in the same way.

[1.2.6]

As evidence of this, it must be noted that, just as is mentioned in the same place, Scylla and Charybdis are two huge rocks in the sea, between which Aeneas sailed carefully, by the oracles of the gods as Vergil recalls above.[150] For he says that Aeneas himself was warned by the gods that he should not take the path completely to the left, nor sail the boats in any way to the right, as unwary sailors had suffered too many shipwrecks there.[151] There were in those two stones many and diverse holes, through which the waves of the sea constantly poured as if they were bringing a sweet and sonorous melody with diverse modulations to the ears of the Latins and even more those of the Greeks.[152] From these melodies and sounds of diverse pitches, the

absque ipsis temperari posse. immo etiam ut ibidem legitur motus planetarum sive melos polorum celestium cum hijs octo sonis convenire apud ipsos demum probatum est. Sed istud dictum ultimo magis videtur esse pitagoricum vel platonicum quam aristotelis opinioni vel etiam veritati consentaneum. secundum enim philosophum planete non findunt orbes nec in motu suo sonum efficiunt. Greci igitur qui in ceteris artibus peritissimi erant ex melodiis octo predictis octo tonos ut dictum est invenerunt obductisque diligenter cum plumbo et marmoribus predictis foraminibus que erant in saxis illis ita videlicet ut navibus nec sonus nec vorago dampnum ultra protenderet studentes postmodum et per istos octo sonos et cantandi modos qui nunc toni dicuntur argumenta quamplura certissime conicientes discipline [**65v**] musice seriem congesserunt.

[1.2.7]

¶ Notandum est etiam quod sicut ibidem legitur octo toni lingua grecorum habent nomina que secuntur. Primus namque tonus vocatur apud eos autentus prothus idest auctoritas prima vel primus auctorizatus. quia primus nobilior est et principalior ceteris. Secundus vero plagalis vel plaga prothi idest filius vel pars primi. sic enim audiebatur a grecis sonus ille de scilla predicta ut videretur esse vox cuiusdam magni hominis quasi pater de celsa puppi navis vociferans et intonans tali voce noannoeane. et alter minor quasi filius eius econtra ex altero navis capite idest ex prora respondens cantando proferret noeagis. Tertius vero tonus apud eos vocatur autentus deuterus idest auctoritas secunda vel secundus auctorizatus qui ita dicebat noieane. Quartus vero plaga vel plagalis deuteri qui quasi filius vel pars eius respondebat dicens noieagis. Quintus autem tonus appellatur autentus tritus idest auctoritas tertia vel tertius auctorizatus qui ita clamabat noieane. Sextus vero plagalis vel plaga triti idest filius tertii auctorizati et pars eius ita respondens ex latere navis noieagis. Septimus autem tonus vocatur autentus tetrardus idest auctoritas quarta vel quartus auctorizatus ita proclamans noieane. Octavus vero plaga tetrardi idest filius quarti auctorizati. vel quarte auctoritatis et pars eius ita respondens noieagis. Sed quid iste voces significent vel cuius lingue sint noieane videlicet vel noieagis aut consimiles nemo ut ibidem legitur adhuc novit. nisi forte quod talis vox vel sonus quasi lingua hominis per fistulas occultas ex concursu aque et aeris spiritu ventorum resonat. Greci tamen aliqui ut huiusmodi questione se statim liberent istas voces interpretantur esse voces letitie sicut euax est interiectio letitiam et exultationem designans.

Greeks, more astute and fittingly imbued with wisdom, thought about these eight sounds or tones deeply, conjecturing that no natural or rational lyric song was able to be tempered without them. But also, as is mentioned there, the motion of the planets, or melody of the celestial poles, has then been proven by them to fit with these eight sounds. But this saying ultimately seems to be more Pythagorean or Platonic than in accord with the opinion of Aristotle, or indeed the truth. For according to the Philosopher, the planets do not plough through the spheres, nor do they make a sound in their motions.[153] Therefore, the Greeks, who were most skilful in the other arts, as has been said, discovered the eight tones from the aforesaid eight melodies, the aforesaid little holes that were in those rocks were carefully filled in with lead and marble, so that clearly neither the sound nor the whirlpool might further cause damage to the ships. Subsequently, paying attention to these eight sounds and modes of singing, which are now called tones, they brought together as many arguments as possible, formulating with great certainty the ordering of the discipline of music.

[1.2.7]

It should also be noted that, just as is reported there, the eight tones have names in the language of the Greeks, as follows.[154] For amongst them the first tone is called the authentic *protus*, that is, the first authorized or the first according to authority, since the first is more noble and princely than the others. The second is called plagal or in the zone of the *protus*, that is, the offspring or part of the first. For thus the former sound, from Scylla, was heard by the Greeks, seeming to be the voice of a certain great man, like a father calling from the high poop deck of a ship[155] and intoning "noannoeane" in such a voice, and the other lesser sound, like his son, who responds by singing from the other end of the ship,[156] that is, from the prow, uttering "noeagis." They call the third tone among them the authentic *deuterus*, that is, the second authorized or the second according to authority, and thus one used to say "noieane." The fourth is called the plagal or in the zone of the *deuterus*, which like a son or its part responded saying "noieagis." The fifth tone is called the authentic *tritus*, that is, the third authorized or the third according to authority, which thus proclaimed "noieane." The sixth is called plagal or in the zone of the *tritus*, that is, the son of the third according to authority and its part, thus responding "noieagis" from the side of the ship. The seventh tone is called the authentic *tetrardus*, that is, the fourth authorized or the fourth according to authority, thus proclaiming "noieani". The eighth is called the plagal of the *tetrardus*, that is, the son of the fourth according to authority, or the fourth authorized and its part, thus responding "noieagis." But what those voices signify or what language they may be, that is, of "noieane" or "noieagis" or the like, no one yet knows, as is reported in the same place,[157] unless by chance such a voice or sound, like the tongue of man, resonates through hidden pipes from the confluence of water and the breath of the air of the winds. Certain Greeks, however, in order to instantly free themselves from this kind of question, interpret those voices as voices of joy, just as "euax" is an interjection designating joy and exultation.[158]

[1.2.8]

¶ Quid autem veritatis predicta contineant lectoris arbitrio malo relinquere quam super hoc aliquid diffinire. A quo siquidem illa que ex predicto libello antiquo hucusque de tonorum origine recitando magis posui quam asserendo conscripta fuerint cuique auctori imputari debeant aut ascribi, certum non habeo. Videtur tamen potius quod alteri qui post guidonem fuerit quam ipsi guidoni presertim cum ibidem de ipso eiusque tonorum formulis fiat expresse mentio sub hijs verbis. Formulas guidonis abbatis viri in musica preclarissimi subter inseruimus inter tonos. Quamvis namque boecius et ceteri antiquiores musici acutius atque profundius **[66r]** tractaverint de obscura et impenetrabili musice scientia que soli deo ad plenum patet, iste tamen nobis condescendens, lucidissimas et utilissimas ad canendum composuit regulas huius artis. Ecclesiasticus enim homo de necessario usu ecclesie nos instruxit, dans plurima officiorum. responsoriorum vel antiphonarum exempla, quod omnino pene omnes alii tacuerunt.

[1.2.9]

¶ Quantum tamen ad ea que de numero tonorum et eorum nominibus in predicto continentur libello, satis guido et ceteri antiqui pariter ac moderni musici concordare noscuntur. Secundum enim guidonem capitulo .xiiº. predicti micrologi, ita quisque tonus vel cantandi modus in duos partitus est, ut acutus quisque diceretur autentus idest auctorizatus vel auctoralis et princeps. gravis vero plagalis vel plaga vocaretur idest lateralis et minor. qui enim ut ibidem dicit stare ad latus meum dicitur minor me est, namque si maior me esset ego aptius ad latus eius stare dicerer. unde et sequenti capitulo videlicet .xiijº. dicit quod sicut octo sunt forme beatitudinis et octo partes orationis, ita etiam octo sunt toni vel modi cantandi per quos omnis cantilena discurrens octo dissimilibus qualitatibus variatur. quos. scilicet. capitulo precedenti appellat autentum prothum et plagam prothi. autentum deuterum et plagam deuteri. autentum tritum et plagam triti. autentum tetrardum. et plagam tetrardi.

[1.2.10]

¶ Solent etiam octo toni predicti a quibusdam musicis atque philosophis aliter nominari. a musicis quippe quidam tonorum impares appellantur videlicet primus tertius. v^{us}. et .vij^{us}. quos etiam non solum principales seu autenticos sed etiam masculinos nuncupant et magistros. reliquos autem quatuor qui pares dicuntur non solum plagales seu collaterales immo etiam discipulos et femininos appellant eo videlicet quod sicut masculus femelle preficitur et magistro[16] discipulus.[17] ita et quatuor impares in elevatione cantus ut postea magis videbitur suis plagalibus preferuntur.

---

[16] magister *Klundert*; magistro **H1**.   [17] discipulo *Klundert*; discipulus **H1**.

[1.2.8]

What truth the aforesaid may contain, I prefer to leave to the judgement of the reader rather than say anything definite about this. Indeed I am not certain by whom those things concerning the origin of the tones—which up to now I have put forward more through citation from the aforesaid ancient little book than through assertion—were written and to what author they ought to be imputed or ascribed. It seems rather to be due to another, who came after Guido, rather than to Guido himself, especially since in the same place he expressly mentioned him and the formulas of his tones in these words: "Below we have inserted in the section about the tones the formulas of Guido the abbot, a man most distinguished in music."[159] For although Boethius and other more ancient music theorists treated the obscure and impenetrable science of music which is fully clear to God alone, more acutely and profoundly, yet he, deferring to us, composed the most lucid and useful rules for this art of singing. For an ecclesiastic has instructed us about the necessary usage of the church, giving many examples of responsories and antiphons of offices,[160] since almost all the others were completely silent.

[1.2.9]

Guido and equally other ancients, as well as modern music theorists, are known to agree adequately enough as far as concerns those things relating to the number of the tones and their names contained in the aforesaid little book. For according to Guido in the twelfth chapter of the aforesaid *Micrologus*, each tone or mode of singing is thus divided into two, so that any acute may be called authentic, that is, authorised or authorial and leading; but the grave is called plagal or "plaga," that is, lateral and lesser.[161] For as he says in the same place, whoever is said to stand at my side is less than me, indeed if they were greater than me, I would more fittingly be said to stand by their side.[162] Whence, in the following chapter, namely the thirteenth, he says that just as there are eight forms of beatitude and eight parts of speech, so too there are eight tones or modes of singing through which every unfolding melody may be varied through the eight dissimilar qualities.[163] These he calls in the preceding chapter authentic *protus* and the plagal of the *protus*, the authentic *deuterus* and the plagal of the *deuterus*, authentic *tritus* and the plagal of the *tritus*, and the authentic *tetrardus* and the plagal of the *tetrardus*.[164]

[1.2.10]

The eight aforesaid tones are also customarily named in another way by certain music theorists and philosophers. Certain tones are called uneven by music theorists, namely first, third, fifth and seventh, which they call not only principal or authentic but also masculine and masters. The remaining four are called even, which they not only call plagal or accompanying, but also disciples and feminine,[165] since clearly male is placed over female and master over disciple. In this way, the four uneven tones are placed before their plagals in the elevation of the chant, as will be seen more fully later.

[1.2.11]

¶ A quibusdam vero philosophis solent aliter isti toni antiquitus nominari sicut ab aristotele .viij°. politice et quibusdam aliis. Primus videlicet dorius. secundus ypodorius. tertius frigius. quartus ypofrigius. vus. lidius. .vius. ypolidius. vijus. mixolodius. octavus vero ypermixolodius.

[1.2.12]

¶ Quamvis autem secundum guidonem abusio quedam latinis tradiderit nominibus numerorum appellare vulgariter octo tonos. dicendo videlicet. primum. secundum. tertium. quartum. quintum. sextum. septimum. et octavum. quia[18] tamen nomina ista communius quam greca habentur in usu de tonorum nominibus et eorum [66v] origine aliqualiter iam disgressi ad eorum naturam et distinctionem sub latinis nominibus assignandam iterum revertamur.

[1.3.0]

¶ Capitulum tertium. De natura tonorum et distinctione eorum.

[1.3.1]

¶ Distinctionem tonorum et eorum naturam assignare seu describere ipsosque ad invicem. comparare volentes, in hoc dicunt autenticos cum suis convenire plagalibus quod utrique in eadem finali littera regulariter terminantur. primus videlicet et secundus in .d. gravi. idest in dsolre. tertius et quartus in .e. gravi idest in primo elami .vus. et .vius. in .f. gravi idest in primo. ffaut. viius. et octavus in .g. gravi idest in primo. gsolreut. Ex quo sequitur ut volunt aliqui quod omnis cantus qui finitur in. re. est primi vel secundi toni. finiens vero in mi. tertii vel quarti toni. finiens in fa. quinti vel sexti. finiens autem in sol. septimi vel octavi.

[1.3.2]

¶ In hoc autem assignatur differentia inter autenticos tonos et suos plagales, quod autentici, videlicet. primus. tertius. quintus. et septimus. ac etiam cantus qui regulantur per ipsos computando a sua finali littera sive fine regulariter[19] plus ascendunt quam suorum plagalium cantus, minusque descendunt. autentici namque supra finem suum vel finalem litteram usque ad octavam vel nonam litteram seu vocem[20] ~~regulariter~~ ascendere possunt. solum autem usque ad secundam[21] ~~vel tertiam~~ sub fine descendere. excepto tamen in hoc casu secundum aliquos primo tono de quo postea in ordine suo videbitur magis in speciali. Toni vero plagales. scilicet. iius. iiijus. vius. et viijus. cantusque regulati per eos a sua finali littera computando. econtrario plus descendunt quam cantus suorum autenticorum seu principalium et minus

---

[18] que *Klundert.*

[19] regulariter *inserted over an erasure* **H2.**

[20] regulariter *struck through after* vocem.

[21] vel tertiam *struck through after* secundam.

[1.2.11]

In ancient times, certain philosophers, such as Aristotle in the eighth book of the Politics and certain others, used to name these tones in another way:[166] that is to say the first Dorian, second Hypodorian, third Phrygian, fourth Hypophrygian, fifth Lydian, sixth Hypolydian, seventh Mixolydian, and eighth Hypermixolydian.[167]

[1.2.12]

According to Guido, a certain abuse has been transmitted by the Latins in commonly calling the eight tones by the names of numbers, namely saying first, second, third, fourth, fifth, sixth, seventh and eighth.[168] Nonetheless, because those names are more commonly used than the Greek, let us return again to their nature and differentiation assigned under the Latin names, having digressed somewhat about the names of the tones and their origin.

[1.3.0]

Chapter three: Concerning the nature of the tones and their differentiation.

[1.3.1]

Those wanting to assign a difference between the tones or describe their nature and to compare them to each other, say that authentics fit with their plagals, since both as a rule end on the same final letter, namely first and second on D-grave, that is, on D-solre; third and fourth on E-grave, that is, on the first E-lami; fifth and sixth on F-grave, that is, on the first F-faut; seventh and eighth on G-grave, that is, on the first G-solreut. From which it follows, as some wish, that every chant ending on re is of the first or second tone, ending on mi of the third or fourth tone, ending on fa of the fifth or sixth, and ending on sol the seventh or eighth.

[1.3.2]

Here the difference between authentic tones and their plagals is assigned, because the authentics—namely the first, third, fifth and seventh, and also chants that are regulated through them—regularly ascend more, and descend less, counting from their final letter or end, than chants of their plagals. For authentics ascend (by rule) above their end or final letter as far as the eighth or ninth letter or pitch, but only descend as far as the second (or third) below the end. The exception in this case according to some, however, is in the first tone, about which in particular more will be seen in its place in due course. Conversely the plagal tones—namely the second, fourth, sixth and eighth, and chants regulated through them—descend more and ascend less, counting from their final letter, than chants of their authentics or principals. For they can descend (by rule) as far as the fourth or fifth letter or pitch below their final, but ascend above their own final only up to the fifth or

ascendunt. usque enim ad quartam vel quintam litteram seu vocem sub fine suo[22] ~~regulariter~~ possunt descendere, sed supra eundem finem suum solummodo usque ad quintam vel sextam ascendere. Et ut quod nunc dictum est in generali de tonis possit plenius apparere, in speciali de unoquoque ipsorum per ordinem videamus.

[1.3.3]

¶ Primus igitur tonus est qui regulariter in .d. gravi idest in .dsolre. finitur, cuiusque acuitas vel ascensus ab eadem finali littera computando usque ad octavam litteram seu vocem. scilicet. d. acutam idest. dlasolre. regulariter se extendit[23] vel etiam usque ad nonam. scilicet. e. acutam. idest secundum elami. licentialiter.[24] eius vero gravitas et[25] descensus ab eadem finali littera computando, solummodo usque ad secundam litteram seu vocem. scilicet. c. gravem idest. cfaut[26] ~~licentialiter~~ se extendit[27] ~~et si inveniatur descendere usque ad tertiam scilicet b mi valde raro hoc accidit tamen licentialiter sit.~~ Et si ultra quam dictum est se extenderit sub vel supra, talis cantus, irregularis a musicis [67r] iudicatur, tamquam latitudinem sui toni et ipsius regulares terminos limitesque transcendens.

[1.3.4]

¶ Volunt tamen quidam antiqui musici et nonnulli moderni, quod iste tonus ratione sue prioritatis et auctoritatis pre ceteris etiam autenticis tonis in hoc privilegiatus existat. ut supra finem.[28] ultra quam dictum est per unam litteram seu vocem licentialiter se possit extendere ascendendo videlicet usque ad .f. acutam. idest secundum .ffaut. quamvis hoc raro contingat. sicut patet in responsorio. *Ecce apparebit dominus.* et in responsorio. *Qui custodiebant.* ac etiam sub fine[29] descendere[30] quandoque usque ad .a. gravem. idest are. sicut patet non solum in aliquibus gregorianis cantibus, puta in responsorio. *Universi qui te expectant.* in officio misse dominicalis. *Inclina domine* et in responsorio. *Sint lumbi.* immo et in multis aliis responsoriis pulcram habentibus melodiam. videlicet in responsoriis. *Spiritus sanctus. Candida virginitas. Cornelius centurio.* multisque aliis que non est verisimile fuisse composita a cantoribus in arte tonorum et musice inexpertis. quisque tamen qui in sensu suo habundare voluerit, eligat in hac parte quod sibi magis placuerit, quia in talibus satis est licitum opinari.

---

[22] regulariter *struck through after* suo.

[23] regulariter se extendit *inserted from the left margin* **H2**.

[24] licentialiter **H2**.

[25] et **H2**.

[26] licentialiter **H2** *struck through after* cfaut.

[27] et si inveniatur (eveniatur *Klundert*) descendere usque ad tertiam scilicet

b mi valde raro hoc accidit tamen licentialiter (omitted *Klundert*) sit **H2** *struck through after* extendit.

[28] supra finem *inserted from the right margin* **H2**.

[29] ac etiam sub fine *inserted over erasure* **H2**; sepius *struck through after* fine.

[30] descendendo *corrected to* descendere **H2**.

sixth. And so that what has now been said in general about the tones may be more fully clear, let us consider each of these in particular, in order.

[1.3.3]

Thus the first tone regularly ends on D-grave, that is, on D-solre, and its rising or ascent regularly extends, counting from the same final letter, up to the eighth letter or pitch, namely d-acute, that is, d-lasolre, or even by license up to the ninth, namely e-acute, that is, the second e-lami. But its low range and descent extends counting from the same final letter only down to the second letter or pitch, namely C-grave, that is, C-faut (by license). ~~And if it is found to descend as far as the third, that is B mi, which it may with license, it happens very rarely~~. And if it extends further than has been said, either above or below, such a chant is judged by musicians to be irregular, in that it goes beyond the range of its tone and its regular terminations and limits.

[1.3.4]

Yet certain ancient musicians, and several modern ones, want this tone to be privileged by reason of its priority and authority over other tones, even authentic ones. So it is said that it can extend by license beyond the end by one letter or pitch, namely by ascending as far as f-acute, that is, the second f-faut; however this happens rarely. Such is evident in the responsory *Ecce apparebit dominus*,[a] and in the responsory *Qui custodiebant*.[b] It can also descend below the end, and even as far as A-grave, that is, A-re, as is clear not only in certain Gregorian chants, namely in the responsory *Universi qui te expectant*,[c] in the introit of the Sunday Mass, *Inclina domine*,[d] and in the responsory *Sint lumbi*,[e] and indeed in many other responsories having a beautiful melody, namely in the responsories *Spiritus sanctus*,[f] *Candida virginitas*,[g] *Cornelius centurio*[h] and many others. Such melody is unlikely to have been composed by singers inexperienced in the art of the tones and music. Whoever wishes to indulge their own taste, however, may choose what pleases them more in this matter, because in such things it is reasonable enough to have an opinion. Yet it seems to some that it may rather be said that such chants and similar ones (of mixed chants on which see below in this chapter [i.e. deleted passage]) they savour the nature [of the tone].

[a] Third Sunday in Advent: BnF lat. 17296 f. 9r-v:

Ec - ce   ap - pa - re -   bit ... e -   o sanc - to - rum   mi - li - a

[b] Fifth Sunday of Lent: BnF lat. 17296 f. 118r:

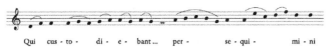

Qui cus - to -   di - e - bant ...   per -   se - qui -   mi - ni

videtur tamen aliquibus quod potius tales cantus et consimiles, mixtorum cantuum de quibus infra eodem capitulo, dicetur naturam sapiant.[31]

[1.3.5]

❡ Si vero cantus aliquos huius primi toni in aliqua affinalium litterarum utpote in .a. acuta idest in primo alamire causa necessitatis alicuius finiri contingat. tunc in fine sine .b. molli seu rotundo debent notari. ut sic videlicet non in .mi. sed [67v] in .re. finiantur. et ita .a. acuta ad .d. gravem idest ad dsolre. reducetur.

[1.3.6]

❡ Est etiam notandum quod quando cantus aliquos huius toni vel aliorum tonorum sicut infra videbitur in aliqua affinalium terminari vel finiri contingit tunc de ascensu et descensu illorum debet iudicari ab affinali littera computando. sicut iudicaretur de eis a finali littera computando si in suam finalem litteram finirentur.

---

[31] **H1** *struck through after* sapiant negligentia depravatos. de quorum sibi quia similium correctione *(omitted Klundert)*. See Appendix I for full treatment of this passage. ~~Sciendum est autem quod si contingat cantus aliquos huius toni finiri in .g. grave, idest in primo .gsolreut. causa videlicet necessitatis alicuius vel quia aliter notari non possunt prout consueverunt cantari. tunc in fine cum .b. rotundo vel molli notari debent, ut sic videlicet non in .ut. vel .sol. sed in .re. finiantur, et ita .g. gravis ad .d. gravem idest ad dsolre. reducetur. et talis reductio locum habere videtur~~ ~~in Responsorio~~ **H1** ~~Germanus plenus spiritu sancto et in antiphona illa Oramus te. et in Responsorio. Pater insignis. Deus omnipotens. et quibusdam aliis cantibus~~ **H2** ~~quorum nonnullos si vera sunt. immo quia vero sunt que de tonis senserunt musici salva nostrorum pace non solum irregulares esse constat immo nec umquam ab expertis in musica prout apud nos cantantur ad presens fuisse compositos. Sed magis scriptorum vicio vel correctionis negligentia depravatos. de quorum sibi quia similium correctione alias forsitan erit locus.~~

[1.3.5]

But if by necessity it happens that some chants of this first tone are ended on one of the affinal letters, as on a-acute, that is, on the first a-lamire, then they ought to be notated without soft or round b at the start [i.e. at the clef][169], so that clearly they end not on mi but on re, and thus a-acute is conceived as D-grave, that is, D-solre.

[1.3.6]

For it should be noted that, when it happens that some chants of this tone, or of other tones, terminate or end on another of the affinals, as will be seen below, then their ascent and descent ought to be judged counting from the affinal letter, just as they are judged counting from the final letter if they end on their final letter.

---

^c First Sunday in Advent: BnF lat. 1107 f. 1r:

U - ni - ver - - - si qui_ te ex - pec - tant

^d Fifteenth Sunday after Pentecost: BnF lat. 1107 f. 192v:

In - cli - na do - mi-ne //quo ni - am ad__re cla ma - vi to - ta_____di - e

^e All Saints: BnF lat. 17296 f. 242r:

Sint lum - bi

^f Vigil of Pentecost: BnF lat. 17296 f. 162v:

Spi - ri - tus //ig - ne - is //lu - ia_____

^g First Sunday in Advent: BnF lat. 17296 f. 1r:

Can - di - da_ vir - gi-ni-tas par - a - di - si

^h Vigil of Saint Peter: BnF lat. 17296 f. 175r:

Cor - ne - li - us cen - tu - ri - o

[1.3.7]

¶ Secundus tonus est qui regulariter in .d. gravi idest in .dsolre. finitur ut primus cuiusque acuitas et ascensus ab eadem finali littera computando, usque ad quintam litteram seu vocem. scilicet .a. acutam. idest alamire primum regulariter vel etiam usque[32] ad sextam idest primum. bfabmi licentialiter,[33] eius vero gravitas et descensus ab eadem finali littera similiter computando usque ad quartam litteram seu vocem. scilicet .a. gravem idest. are regulariter. vel etiam usque ad quintam scilicet. gamaut. licentialiter se extendit. et si[34] ~~se extendit et si supra~~[35] ultra quam dictum est se extenderit sub vel supra[36] ~~enim manifestum est non posse~~[37] irregularis reputatur a musicis cantus talis.

[1.3.8]

¶ Sciendum est autem quod si causa necessitatis alicuius cantum aliquem huius toni in aliqua litterarum affinalium puta in .a. acuta idest in primo alamire finiri contingat tunc debet cantus huiusmodi sine .b. molli seu rotundo in fine notari. ut sic videlicet non in .mi. sed in .re. potius finiatur. et ita per consequens .a. acuta ad .d. gravem idest dsolre reducetur. et hoc in .antiphona. *Assumpsit ihesus discipulos.* et in Responsorio. *Vide quia tribulor.* multisque aliis habet locum. Si vero contingat cantus aliquos huius toni in .g. gravi .ijª. idest primo[38] gsolreut terminari. quod tamen raro contingit, tunc in fine debent cum .b. molli seu rotundo notari. ut sic .scilicet. finiantur non in .ut. vel .sol. sed in .re. et ita .g. gravis ad .d. gravem idest ad dsolre que est huius toni finalis littera reducetur. sicut apparet in Responsorio illo. *Angelus domini vocavit abraham.* et in quibusdam aliis huius toni, quod tamen ut dictum est satis raro contingit. Quandoque etiam licet raro aliqui finiuntur in .d. acuta idest in .dlasolre. sicut patet in Responsorio illo de sancta agnete secundum aliquos libros.[39] *Omnipotens adorande.* et tunc .d. acuta ad .d. gravem reducitur. immo etiam secundum magistrum Iohannem de garlandia reliqua signa gamatis ad sibi similia reducuntur.

---

[32] primum regulariter vel etiam usque **H2**.

[33] licentialiter **H2**.

[34] regulariter. vel etiam usque ad quintam scilicet. gamaut. licentialiter se extendit. et si **H2**.

[35] se extendit et si supra *struck through.*

[36] sub vel supra **H2**.

[37] enim manifestum est non posse *struck through.*

[38] primo *inserted above the line* **H2**.

[39] secundum aliquos libros. *in right hand margin* **H2**.

[1.3.7]

The second tone is that which as a rule ends on D-grave, that is, on D-solre, like the first. Its acuity and ascent, by counting from the same final letter is by rule up to the fifth letter or pitch, namely a-acute, that is, the first a-lamire, or even by license up to the sixth, that is, the first b-fa/b-mi. But its low range and descent, counting similarly from the same final letter is as a rule down to the fourth letter or pitch, namely A-grave, that is, A-re, or even extends by license down to the fifth, namely Gamma-ut. And if it extends further above or below than what has been said, such chant is considered irregular by musicians.

[1.3.8]

It should be known that if, by reason of necessity, any chant of this tone happens to end on any of the affinal letters, for example on a-acute, that is, on the first a-lamire, then chant of this kind ought to be notated without soft or round b at the start,[170] so that it finishes not on mi but rather on re, and so, as a consequence a-acute is conceived as D-grave, that is, D-solre. And this takes place in the antiphon *Assumpsit ihesus discipulos*[i] and in the responsory *Vide quia tribulor*[j] and many others. But if it happens that some chants of this tone terminate on G-grave (the second G), that is, the first G-solreut—which happens rarely however—then they ought to be notated at the start with soft or round b, so that they end not on ut or sol but on re, and thus G-grave is conceived as D-grave, that is, as D-solre, which is the final letter of this tone, as appears in that responsory *Angelus domini vocavit Abraham*[k] and in certain others of this tone. As has been said, however, this happens quite rarely. Also, sometimes, albeit rarely, others end on d-acute, that is, on d-lasolre, just as happens according to some books in that responsory about Saint Agnes, *Omnipotens adorande,*[l][171] and then d-acute is conceived as D-grave, or rather, according to Master John of Garland, the remaining signs of the gamut are transposed to signs similar to them.[172]

[i] Eve of second Sunday of Lent: BnF lat. 17296 f. 101v: 1) original, ending on a-lamire; 2) transposed, ending on D-solre:

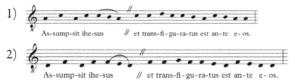

[j] Fifth Sunday of Lent: BnF lat. 17296 f. 117v: 1) original, ending on a-lamire; 2) transposed, ending on D-solre:

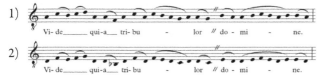

[1.3.9]

¶ Tertius tonus est qui in .e. gravi idest in primo .elami. regulariter terminatur cuiusque acuitas et ascensus ab eadem finali littera computando usque ad octavam litteram seu vocem. scilicet .e. acutam idest secundum. elami regulariter. vel etiam usque ad nonam. videlicet .f. acutam idest. secundum .ffaut. licentialiter, quamvis hoc non habeat usus. eius vero gravitas et descensus[40] **[68r]** eadem finali littera computando solummodo usque ad secundam litteram sive vocem videlicet .d. gravem idest .dsolre. licentialiter[41] ~~iijam scilicet .cfaut. licentialiter~~[42] se extendit. et si ultra quam dictum est se extenderit sub vel supra irregularis eadem ratione que supra dicta est in primo tono iudicatur a musicis.

[1.3.10]

¶ Sciendum tamen quod si cantum aliquem huius toni in aliqua affinali littera puta in .a. acuta idest in primo alamire causa necessitatis alicuius terminari contingat, quod valde raro contingit. tunc talis cantus cum .b. molli seu rotundo debet in fine notari. ut sic videlicet non in .re. sed in .mi. potius finiatur et ita per consequens .a. acuta ad .e. gravem idest primum elami. reducatur. sicut apparet in .communione. gradalis. *beatus servus.* et in *alleluya letatus sum.*

---

[40] secundum. elami regulariter. vel etiam usque ad nonam. videlicet .f. acutam idest. secundum .ffaut. licentialiter, quamvis hoc non habeat usus. eius vero gravitas et descensus *added in the lower margin* **H2**.

[41] solummodo *inserted above the line* **H2**; usque ad secundam litteram sive vocem videlicet .d. gravem idest .dsolre. licentialiter **H2**.

[42] .iij^am. scilicet .cfaut. licentialiter **H2** *struck through.*

[1.3.9]

As a rule, the third tone closes on E-grave, that is, on the first E-lami, and its rising and ascent extends, counting from the same final letter up to the eighth letter or pitch, namely e-acute, that is, the second e-lami, as a rule or even, by license, up to the ninth, namely f-acute, that is, the second f-faut. Although this might not be used, its depth and descent extends, by license, counting from the same final letter only as far as the second letter or pitch, namely D-grave, that is, D-solre. And if it extends further than has been said, either above or below, it is considered irregular by musicians for the same reasons as was said above about the first tone.

[1.3.10]

It should be known, however, that if it happens by reason of necessity that any chant of this tone terminates on some affinal letter, for example on a-acute, that is, on the first a-lamire, which happens quite rarely, then such chant should be notated at the start with a soft or round b, with the result that it ends not on re but rather on mi. And thus, as a consequence, a-acute is conceived as E-grave, that is, the first E-lami, as happens in the communion of the gradual, *Beatus servus*,[m] and in *Alleluya letatus sum*.[n 173]

---

[k] Quinquagesima Sunday: BnF lat. 17296 f. 94v: 1) original, ending on G-solreut with flat 'signature'; 2) transposed, ending on D-solre

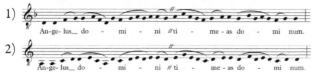

[l] St. Agnes: 1) BnF lat. 17296 f. 58v demonstrating a transposed version ending on a-lamire; and, 2) BnF lat. 15181 f. 425r illustrates the discussion by ending on d-lasolre:

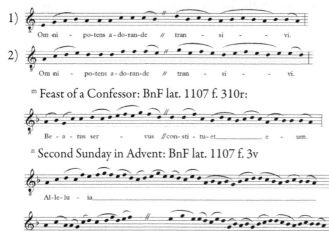

[m] Feast of a Confessor: BnF lat. 1107 f. 310r:

[n] Second Sunday in Advent: BnF lat. 1107 f. 3v

[1.3.11]

❡ Quartus tonus est qui regulariter in .e. gravi idest in primo. elami. finitur ut tertius, cuiusque acuitas et ascensus ab eadem finali littera computando usque ad[43] quintam litteram seu vocem. scilicet. b. acutam regulariter se extendit.[44] vel etiam usque ad sextam videlicet .c. acutam idest .csolfaut. licentialiter.[45] eius vero gravitas et descensus ab eadem finali littera computando usque ad tertiam litteram seu vocem. scilicet. c. gravem idest .cfaut. vel etiam usque ad. quartam. scilicet. bmi, quamvis raro hoc accidat regulariter se extendit. si vero repperiatur usque ad quintam. scilicet. are. descendere. adhuc licentialiter fit. sed si ultra sub vel supra se extenderit irregularis est.[46]

[1.3.12]

❡ Sciendum est autem, quod quando contingit causa necessitatis alicuius, cantus aliquos huius toni in aliqua affinalium utpote in .a. acuta idest in primo. alamire. finiri, tunc notari debent in fine cum .b. rotundo vel molli ut sic videlicet non in .re. sed in .mi. potius finiantur. et ita per consequens .a. acuta ad .e. gravem idest ad primum .elami. que est huius toni finalis littera reducetur. Et hoc in .antiphona. *Ex egypto. Syon renovaberis. Ante thorum. Gaude maria.* multisque aliis habet locum.

[1.3.13]

❡ Quintus tonus est qui regulariter et semper ut mihi videtur in .f. gravi idest in primo .ffaut. terminatur, cuiusque acuitas et ascensus ab eadem finali littera computando usque ad octavam litteram seu vocem. scilicet. f. acutam idest secundum .ffaut. regulariter. et etiam usque[47] ad nonam. scilicet. g. acutam idest secundum gsolreut. licentialiter. eius[48] vero gravitas et descensus ab eadem finali littera computando tantummodo usque ad secundam litteram seu vocem. scilicet. e. gravem idest primum elami. que a finali[49] littera solo minori semitonio distat ~~regulariter aut saltem~~[50] licentialiter[51] se extendit, et si ultra se extenderit sub vel supra, irregularis iudicari debet.

---

[43] computando usque ad **H2**.

[44] regulariter se extendit **H2**.

[45] licentialiter **H2**.

[46] gravem idest cfaut...se extenderit irregularis est. **H2**.

[47] .ffaut. regulariter. et etiam usque **H2**.

[48] gsolreut. licentialiter. eius **H2**.

[49] que a finali **H2**.

[50] regulariter aut saltem **H2** *struck through*.

[51] licentialiter **H2**.

[1.3.11]

As a rule, the fourth tone ends on E-grave, that is, on the first E-lami, like the third, and its rising and ascent extends counting from the same final letter up to the fifth letter or pitch, namely b-acute, as a rule or even, by license, up to the sixth, namely c-acute, that is, c-solfaut. But as a rule, its depth and descent extends counting from the same final letter down to the third letter or pitch, namely C-grave, that is, C-faut, or even down to the fourth, namely B-mi, although this happens rarely. And if it is found to descend even as far as the fifth, namely A-re, it still does so by license, but if it extends further, either below or above, it is irregular.

[1.3.12]

It should be known that when, by reason of some necessity, it happens that some chants of this tone end on any of the affinals, as on a-acute, that is, on the first a-lamire, then they ought to be notated at the start with the round or soft b, so that they clearly end not on re but rather on mi. And so, as a consequence, a-acute is conceived as E-grave, that is, the first E-lami, which is the final letter of this tone. And this occurs in the antiphons *Ex egypto*,[o] *Syon renovaberis*,[p] *Ante thorum*,[q] *Gaude maria*[r] and in many others.

[1.3.13]

As a rule, the fifth tone always, as it seems to me, ends on F-grave, that is, on the first F-faut, and its rising and ascent extends counting from the same final letter up to the eighth letter or pitch, namely f-acute, that is, the second f-faut, as a rule, and even by license up to the ninth, namely g-acute, that is, the second g-solreut. But its depth and descent extends counting from the same final letter by license only to the second letter or pitch, namely E-grave, which is, the first E-lami, which is distant from the final pitch by only a minor semitone. And if it extends further, either below or above, it ought to be considered irregular.

[o] Friday, first week in Advent: BnF lat. 15181 f. 114v [transposition found but without flat signature]:

Ex e- gyp - to vo-ca-vi fi-li - um me- um ve-ni et ut sal- vet po - pu- lum su- um.

[p] Wednesday, second week in Advent: BnF lat. 15181 f. 120r:

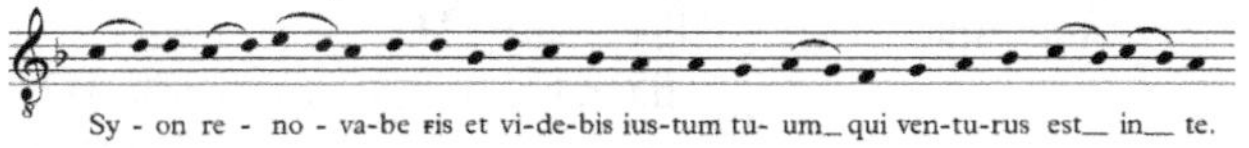
Sy - on re - no - va-be ris et vi-de-bis ius-tum tu- um_ qui ven-tu-rus est_ in_ te.

[q] Purification: BnF lat. 17296 f. 66r:

An te tho-rum hu ius vir - gi - nis fre quen ta - te no bis dul ci-a can - ti- ca drag mis.

[r] Purification: BnF lat. 15181 f. 448v: here transposed but without the flat signature.

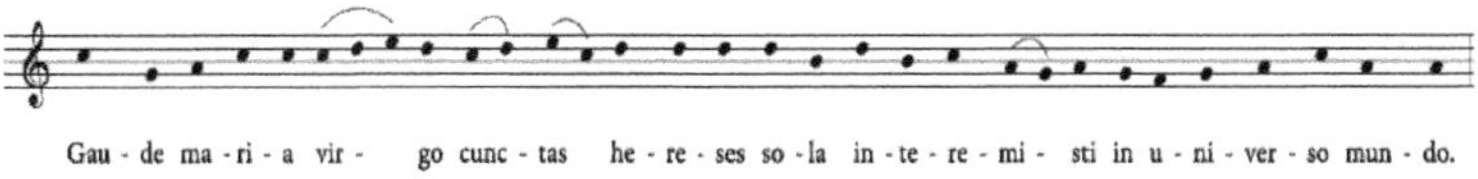
Gau - de ma - ri - a vir - go cunc - tas he - re - ses so - la in - te - re - mi - sti in u - ni - ver - so mun - do.

[1.3.14]

❡ Sextus tonus est qui regulariter in .f. gravi **[68v]** idest in primo ffaut. termi-
nator, cuiusque acuitas et ascensus ab eadem finali littera computando usque ad
quintam litteram seu vocem. scilicet. c. acutam idest. csolfaut regulariter vel etiam
usque ad sextam.[52] scilicet. d. acutam idest .dlasolre. licentialiter,[53] eius vero gravitas et descensus ab eadem finali littera computando usque ad quartam litteram seu
vocem. scilicet. c. gravem idest .cfaut. ~~similiter inclusive~~[54] regulariter se extendit. et
si ultra se extenderit sub vel supra, irregularis iudicatur a musicis.

[1.3.15]

❡ Sed notandum quod quando contingit causa necessitatis alicuius cantus aliquos
huius toni in aliqua affinali littera terminari. scilicet. in. c. acuta idest in. csolfaut.
tunc affinalis littera ad .f. gravem idest ad primum .ffaut. que est huius toni finalis littera reducetur. et hoc locum habet in .antiphona. *Ave regina celorum*. et in
Responsorio. *Cum esset in accubitu*. multisque aliis cantibus huius toni. et tunc
etiam absque irregularitate potest talis cantus licentialiter[55] usque ad quintam
descendere videlicet usque ad primum .ffaut. ut in Responsorio. *Quatuor animalia*. et in versu Responsorii. illius de eucharistia. *Paratum panem* repperitur. Hoc
tamen accidit valde raro.

[1.3.16]

❡ Septimus tonus est qui in .g. gravi secunda idest in primo .gsolreut. regulariter
terminatur. cuiusque acuitas et ascensus a predicta finali littera computando usque
ad octavam litteram sive vocem. scilicet. g. acutam idest secundum .gsolreut. regulariter[56] vel etiam usque ad nonam videlicet .a. acutam idest secundum .alamire.
licentialiter.[57] eius vero gravitas et descensus ab eadem finali littera computando
solummodo usque ad secundam litteram seu vocem. scilicet. f. gravem idest primum .ffaut. licentialiter se extendit.[58] ~~et si interdum usque ad tertium. scilicet. e.
gravem idest primum elami se extendat raro hoc et licentialiter fit~~[59] Et si ultra se
extenderit sub vel supra, irregularis[60] iudicari debet.

---

[52] csolfaut regulariter vel etiam usque ad sextam **H2**.

[53] licentialiter **H2**.

[54] similiter inclusive **H2** *struck through*.

[55] licentialiter . **H2** *inserted from left margin*.

[56] regulariter **H2** *added from right margin* .

[57] licentialiter **H2**.

[58] .ffaut. licentialiter se extendit. **H2**.

[59] et si interdum usque ad tertium. scilicet. e. gravem idest primum elami se extendat raro hoc et licentialiter fit. **H2** *struck through*.

[60] Et si ultra se extenderit sub vel supra, irregularis **H2**.

[1.3.14]

The sixth tone is that which, as a rule, ends on F-grave, that is, on the first F-faut, and whose rising and ascent, counting from the same final letter is up to the fifth letter or pitch, namely c-acute, that is, c-solfaut, as a rule, or even up to the sixth, namely d-acute, that is, d-lasolre, by license. But its depth and descent, counting from the same final letter, extends down to the fourth letter or pitch, namely C-grave, which is, C-faut, as a rule. And if it extends further, either below or above, it is considered irregular by musicians.

[1.3.15]

But it should be noted that, when by reason of some necessity it happens that some chants of this tone close on some affinal letter, namely on c-acute, that is, c-solfaut, then the affinal letter is conceived as F-grave, that is, the first F-faut, which is the final letter of this tone. And this occurs in the antiphon *Ave regina celorum*[s] and in the responsory *Cum esset in accubitu*[t] and in many other chants of this tone. And then such chant can by license descend without irregularity down to the fifth, namely to the first F-faut, as is found in the responsory *Quatuor animalia*[u] and in the verse of that responsory about the Eucharist, *Paratum panem*.[174] However, this happens very rarely.

[1.3.16]

The seventh tone is that which, as a rule, ends on G-grave (the second G), that is, on the first G-solreut, and whose rising and ascent, counting from the aforesaid final letter is up to the eighth letter or pitch, namely g-acute, that is, the second g-solreut, as a rule, or even up to the ninth, namely a-acute, that is, the second a'-lamire, by license. But its depth and descent, counting from the same final letter, extends only down to the second letter or pitch, namely F-grave, that is, the first F-faut, by license. And if it extends further, either below or above, it ought to be judged irregular.

---

[s] Marian antiphon sung between Purification and Wednesday of Holy Week: BnF lat. 12044 f. 177v:

A - ve___ re-gi__na ce - lo -   rum   sem- per_ chris-tum ex__ o -   ra.

[t] St. Louis: Melbourne, State Library of Victoria, MS 096.1 [Poissy Antiphonal] f. 313r:

Cum es -   set   in ac -   cu -   bi - tu... re -   gi - mi - nis.

[u] Common of the Evangelists: BnF lat. 17296 f. 270v:

Qua-   tu - or   a - ni - ma - li - a i -   - bant

[1.3.17]

¶ Sciendum est autem quod si cantum aliquem huius toni causa necessitatis alicuius in aliqua affinalium puta in .c. acuta idest in. csolfaut finiri contingat. cum tunc finiatur in .ut. ad .g. gravem secundam idest primum .gsolreut. que est huius toni finalis littera reducetur, et hoc licet raro valde contingat, in Responsorio tamen illo. *Una hora* locum habere videtur.

[1.3.18]

¶ Octavus tonus est qui regulariter in .g. gravi secunda idest in primo. gsolreut. finitur ut septimus. cuiusque acuitas et ascensus ab eadem finali littera computando usque ad quintam litteram seu vocem videlicet .d. acutam regulariter. vel etiam ~~interdum~~[61] usque ad sextam. scilicet. e. acutam idest secundum .elami. licentialiter.[62] eius vero gravitas et descensus ab eadem finali littera computando usque ad quartam videlicet .d. gravem idest .dsolre. regulariter[63] **[69r]** vel etiam usque ad quintam. scilicet. c. gravem idest. cfaut. ~~similiter inclusive~~[64] licentialiter[65] se extendit. et si ultra se extenderit sub vel supra irregularis ut de precedentibus tonis dictum est iudicatur.

[1.3.19]

¶ Et notandum quod si cantum aliquem huius toni in aliqua affinalium utpote in. c. acuta idest in. csolfaut causa necessitatis alicuius finiri contingat. quod tamen contingit rarissime, cum tunc finiatur in. ut. ad. g. gravem secundam idest primum .gsolreut. que est huius toni finalis littera ut immediate dictum est de tono septimo reducetur. Et hoc locum habere videtur in Responsorio. *Oravit iacob.* ~~et in illo. Conclusit vias meas~~[66] quod tamen irregulare videtur esse secundum ea que superius dicta sunt de tonis, cum videlicet computando a littera seu voce in qua finitur usque ad octavam ascendat, et sic per consequens sui toni latitudinem regularem transcendat.

[1.3.20]

¶ Sed sciendum quod et si cantus illos qui communiter irregulares esse dicuntur. et ut supra dictum est pro irregularibus a musicis iudicantur, restringi potius quam ampliari conveniat tamquam ut dictum est supra latitudinis sue regulares terminos transcendentes sicut tamen in gramatica videmus quod orationes alique

---

[61] regulariter. vel etiam **H2**; interdum **H2** *struck through*.

[62] licentialiter **H2**.

[63] regulariter **H2** *in right margin*.

[64] similiter inclusive *struck through*.

[65] licentialiter **H2**.

[66] "et in illo. Conclusit vias meas. *struck through*.

[1.3.17]

It should be known that if any chant of this tone happens, by reason of some necessity, to end on any of the affinals, for example on c-acute, that is, on c-solfaut, then when it ends on ut, it is conceived as G-grave (the second G), that is, the first G-solreut, which is the final letter of this tone. And granted that this happens very rarely, it seems to take place in the responsory *Una hora*.[v]

[1.3.18]

The eighth tone is that which, ends on G-grave (the second G), that is, on the first G-solreut, like the seventh, and whose rising and ascent, counting from the same final letter is up to the fifth letter or pitch, namely d-acute, as a rule, or even up to the sixth, namely e-acute, that is, the second e-lami, by license. But its depth and descent, counting from the same final letter is down to the fourth, namely D-grave, that is, D-solre, as a rule, or even extends down to the fifth, namely C-grave, that is, C-faut by license. And if it extends further, either above or below, it is considered irregular, as has been said about the preceding tones.

[1.3.19]

And it should be noted that if, by reason of some necessity, any chant of this tone happens to end on any of the affinals, as on c-acute, that is, on c-solfaut (which, however, happens very rarely), then when it ends on ut, it is conceived as G-grave (the second G), that is, the first G-solreut, which is the final letter of this tone, as has been said immediately above concerning the seventh tone. And this seems to take place in the responsory *Oravit iacob*,[w] which seems to be irregular according to what has been said above about the tones, when it ascends counting from the letter or pitch on which it ends up to the eighth, and consequently it goes above the regular range of its tone.

[1.3.20]

But it should be known that it is fitting for those chants, which are commonly said to be irregular and, as said above, are considered irregular by musicians, to be restricted rather than extended, as if going beyond the regular limits of their range. This is just as we see in grammar, because some phrases and expressions or certain

[v] Maundy Thursday: BnF lat. 15181 f. 282v:

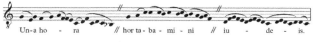

Un-a ho - ra // hor ta- ba- mi - ni // iu - de - is.

[w] Second Sunday of Lent: BnF lat. 17296 f. 103v:

O-ra - vit //do mi - ne //na - ti - vi-ta - tis // ti- me - o.

et locutiones vel modi quidam loquendi tam prosaice quam metrice sustinentur, aliquando videlicet causa metri. quandoque vero figuris quibusdam gramaticalibus rationabiliter excusati. aut etiam solo usu auctorum qui in gramatica fuerunt insignes. Ita etiam nec omnino inconveniens esse videtur in proposito nostro, cantus aliquos ab antiquis patribus virisque catholicis institutos, tum propter auctoritatem componentium seu instituentium, tum etiam propter melodiam et consonam armoniam quam continent, ab irregularitate non irrationabiliter excusari posse presertim cum interdum compositores huiusmodi cantuum vel propter melodie suavitatem quam continent, vel interdum occasione materie supra quam fundantur huiusmodi cantus, tamquam quendam mentis excessum vel extasim quodammodo passi amatorum seu letantium vel quandoque tristium atque lugentium more, in ascensum proruperint aliqualiter excessivum. Sic enim videtur esse non solum in Responsorio illo *Conclusit vias*. quod. scilicet. in illo puncto et iudica excedit limites toni octavi. et in illo Responsorio toni eiusdem. *Tenebre facte sunt* in illo puncto. deus deus ubi christi clamor validus designatur, immo etiam et in illo Responsorio. *Sicut cedrus*. quod etiam in illo puncto in monte syon excedit limites quarti toni. similiter etiam et in illo Responsorio. *Qui custodiebant*. in illo puncto. quia non est. et etiam in quibusdam aliis gregorianis cantibus. Cuius rei satis probabile argumentum ex eo conicitur, [**69v**] quod non solum in huiusmodi cantibus immo etiam et in illis in quibus nequaquam tonorum limites exierunt nec terminos regulares eorum, ubi precipue modulationis ipsius dulcedine delectati vel potius materie supra quam cantus huiuscemodi fundaverunt pia quadam devotione succensi, eis ab illo de cuius munere venit ut digne sibi ac laudabiliter serviatur misericorditer est donatum ut gustarent quam suavis est dominus, nunc ad pauca altiora quasi raptim visi sunt conscendere, sicut patet in multis punctis illius antiphone. *Alma redemptoris*. et in illa. *Salve regina,* ibi illos tuos. et deinceps. et in primo Responsorio de natali, in illo puncto gaudet exercitus, nunc vero morosius in eisdem punctis insistere sicut patet in illo Responsorio. *Insurrexerunt in me*, maxime in illo puncto, et concussa sunt omnia ossa mea et deinceps. et in primo Responsorio de pascha aliisque multis de quibus hic exempla ponere longum esset.

ways of speaking are tolerated as much in prose as in verse, clearly sometimes for the sake of meter and sometimes rationally justified by certain figures of speech, or even just by the usage of authors distinguished in grammar. In this way it does not seem at all inappropriate to our argument that some chants instituted by the ancient fathers and catholic men can, not unreasonably, be excused from irregularity sometimes because of the authority of the composers or initiators and sometimes because of the melody and consonant harmony therein. This is especially so since sometimes composers of chants of this kind rush into a kind of unrestrained ascent, either because of the sweetness of the melody they contain, or sometimes because of the matter on which chants of this kind are based. It is just as if they suffer a certain excess of mind or ecstasy in the manner of lovers or those rejoicing or sometimes of the sad and those who mourn. For this seems to be the case not only in that responsory *Conclusit vias*, which exceeds the limits of the eighth tone at that point "*et iudica*,"[x] but also in that responsory of the same tone, *Tenebre facte sunt*, at the point "*deus deus*,"[y] where the powerful cry of Christ is evoked. This is also the case in that responsory *Sicut cedrus*, which at the point "*in monte syon*" also exceeds the limits of the fourth tone,[z] and similarly in that responsory *Qui custodiebant* at the point "*quia non est*," which exceeds its limits.[aa] and also in certain other Gregorian chants. A sufficiently plausible argument can be put together from this because not only in chants like this but even in those chants that in no way exceed the limits of the tones, nor their regular finals. This happens when people, delighting in particular in the sweetness of their modulations or, rather, on the matter on which they based chants of this kind, are inflamed by a certain pious devotion. To them it has been mercifully given by Him from whose gift it comes, to taste how sweet is the Lord,[175] that He may be worthily and laudably served. At one moment they seem to ascend a little higher as if in rapture, just as is evident at many points of that antiphon *Alma redemptoris*,[bb] and in that *Salve regina* at "*illos tuos*,"[cc] and then also in the first responsory of Christmas at that point "*gaudet exercitus*."[dd] At another time they linger more at those points as in that responsory *Insurrexerunt in me*, in particular at that point "*et concussa sunt omnia ossa mea*,"[ee] and in the first responsory of Easter[ff] and many others, about which it would be tedious to provide examples here.

[x] Palm Sunday: BnF lat. 17296 f. 121v:

Con - clu -   sit vi - as ...   et   iu - di -   ca cau -   sam

[y] Good Friday: BnF lat. 17296 f. 132v:

Te - ne - bre fac - te sunt   de - us   de - us   ut   quid me

[z] Assumption: BnF lat. 15182 f. 306v:

Si - cut_ ce - drus_____   in mon - te sy - on

[1.3.21]

¶ Quia igitur ecclesiastici cantus non omnes equaliter ut iam ex predictis apparet toni sui terminos regulares observant, ad eorum distinctionis pleniorem notitiam est notandum. quod ecclesiasticorum cantuum de quibus precipue ad nostrum propositum spectat, quidam sunt puri, quidam vero mixti. Puri sunt cantus illi qui in semetipsis unius tantummodo toni naturam retinent et observant. et isti quidem secundum ea que superius de tonis sunt tradita regulares vel irregulares esse iudicari debent.

[1.3.22]

¶ Mixti vero dicuntur illi cantus, qui duorum tonorum naturam in se continere videntur. ascendendo videlicet ad modum autenticorum, et ad modum plagalium descendendo, sicut sunt multa Responsoria. precipue gradualis videlicet. *Propicius esto. Protector noster.* et multa alia que ex tono .v°. et .vi°. esse mixta videntur. talisque mixtio maxime in quibusdam sequentiis sicut in sequentia. *Laudes crucis. Letabundus.* multisque aliis cantibus satis notabiliter repperitur. De quibus regulariter est tenendum, quod si ad acuitatem vel ascensum tendant frequentius, debent pro autenticis iudicari. si vero frequentius ad gravitatem et deorsum tendant, pro plagalibus sunt habendi. si autem equaliter se habeant ad utrumque, adhuc debent pro autenticis reputari.

[1.3.21]

Since ecclesiastical chants do not all equally observe the regular endings of their tone, as appears from what has been said, it should be noted for greater awareness of how they differ from one another, that from the ecclesiastical chants particularly relevant to our argument, some are pure while others are mixed. Pure chants retain and observe in themselves the nature of one tone only. These ought to be judged regular or irregular according to those matters that have been treated above concerning the tones.

[1.3.22]

Those chants are called mixed that seem to contain in themselves the nature of two tones, namely ascending in the way of authentics and descending in the way of plagals. This is the case for many responsories, especially of the gradual, namely *Propicius esto*,[gg] *Protector noster*,[hh] and many others, which seem to be a mixture of the fifth and sixth tone. Such mixing is found in particular in certain sequences, as in the sequence *Laudes crucis*,[ii] *Letabundus*,[jj] and in many other quite well-known chants. As a rule if such chants tend more frequently to rising or ascent, they should be judged as authentic, but if they tend more frequently to depth and falling, they are understood to be plagal. If they do both equally, they still ought to be thought of as authentic.

[aa] Fifth Sunday of Lent: BnF lat. 17296 f. 118r:

Qui cus - to - di - e - bant... qui - a non est

[bb] Marian Antiphon sung between Advent and February 1: BnF lat. 17296 f. 341r:

Al -   ma   re - demp - to - ris...   que ge - nu - i - sti

[cc] Marian Antiphon sung between Trinity Sunday and Advent: BnF lat. 15182 f. 313r:

Sal - ve re - gi - na   il-los tu - os

[dd] Christmas: BnF lat. 17296 f. 20v:

Ho - di - e no - bis   ce - lo - rum rex...   gau - det ex - er - ci - tus

[ee] Palm Sunday: BnF lat. 17296 f. 123r:

In - sur - rex - e - runt in me...   et con - cus - sa sunt om - ni - a os - sa   me -   a

[ff] Easter Day 'first responsory of Easter': BnF lat. 17296 f. 137r:

An - ge - lus__ do- mi -   ni__ de - scen - dit de ce - lo -   rum

[1.3.23]

¶ Si autem queratur de illis cantibus qui tantum ascensum vel descensum non habent qui de tonis notatus est supra, sed mediocriter se tenent, de quo tono debeant iudicari dicendum est quod etsi quandoque tales cantus sint dubii vel incerti si tamen a sua finali littera computando usque ad quartam litteram seu vocem tantummodo ascendant, et ad quintam non attingant [**70r**] de plagali tono debent infallibiliter iudicari. Unde secundum istam regulam manifeste apparet, quod salva pace nostrorum illa. antiphona. *In omnem terram.* non de primo tono sed potius de secundo iudicari deberet. Si vero cantus tales qui dubii sunt aliqualiter et incerti ascendant usque ad quintam litteram seu vocem et in eadem quinta vel quarta frequenter ~~fecerint~~ steterint[67] raroque ad litteram finalem descenderint, tales absque dubio pro autenticis sunt habendi. sicut patet in. antiphona. *Ave maria. De syon veniet Levate capita* multisque aliis. Sed si cantus huiuscemodi frequenter ad finalem descenderent quamvis interdum usque ad quintam ascendant tunc magis deberent pro plagalibus iudicari. sicut patet in. antiphona. de bono andrea. *Domine ihesu christe.* et in illa de purificatione. *Senex puerum portabat,* que etiam usque ad sextam ascendit. etiam et in. antiphona. *O sapientia.* et consimilibus que ad finalem litteram descendentes in eadem vel prope frequenter persistunt. Quod autem de cantibus puris vel mixtis sive dubiis et incertis nunc dictum est non solum veritatem habet in cantibus primi toni vel secundi de quibus exempla posuisse specialius visi sumus, immo etiam quantum ad cantus aliorum tonorum, ascensum tamen et descensum eorum a suis finalibus litteris computando.

---

[67] fecerint *struck through*; steterint *added from right margin* **H2**.

[1.3.23]

If one asks about the tone to which those chants noted above that do not have so much ascent or descent but hold themselves in a middle way, ought to be assigned, it must be said that although such chants might be doubtful or uncertain, without question they ought to be considered plagal, if counting from their final letter they ascend only to the fourth letter or pitch and do not reach the fifth. Hence according to that rule, it clearly appears, keeping peace with our brothers, that the antiphon *In omnem terram*[kk] ought to be considered not of the first tone but rather of the second. But if such chants, which are somewhat doubtful and uncertain, ascend to the fifth letter or pitch and stay frequently on the same fifth or fourth and rarely descend to the final letter, without doubt they ought to be considered authentic, as happens in the antiphon *Ave maria,*[ll] *De syon veniet,*[mm] *Levate capita*[nn] and many others. But if chants of this kind frequently descend to the final, although they ascend to the fifth in the interim, then they ought to be considered rather as plagal, as is evident in the antiphon concerning Andrew the Good, *Domine ihesu christe,*[oo] and in that of the Purification, *Senex puerum portabat,*[pp] which even ascends to the sixth, and also in the antiphon *O sapientia*[qq] and similar ones, which descending to the final pitch, frequently remain on or nearby that same pitch. What has now been said concerning pure or mixed or doubtful or uncertain chants is true of chants not only of the first or second tone—about which we have put forward more specific examples—but just as much of chants of other tones, counting their ascent and descent from their final pitches.

[gg] First week of Lent, Saturday: BnF lat. 1107 f. 58r:

Pro-pi - ti-us e - sto_____ do - mi-ne

[hh] Monday, first week of Lent: BnF lat. 1107 f. 50v:

Pro - te - ctor no - ster a - spi - ce

[ii] Exaltation of the Holy Cross: Rhymed sequence for the finding of the True Cross. BnF lat. 1107 f. 377v:

Lau - des cru - cis at - tol - la - mus nos qui cru - cis ex - ul - ta - mus spe - ci - a - li glo - ri - a.

[jj] Christmas Day: Sequence for Christmas. BnF lat. 830 f. 302r:

Le - ta - bun - dus ex - ul - tet fi - de - lis

[kk] Common of the Apostles: BnF lat. 17296 f. 265r:

In om - nem ter - ram ex - i - vit so - nus e - o - rum et in fi - nes or - bis ter - re ver - ba e - o - rum.

[1.4.0]

¶ Capitulum quartum. De proprietate et effectu seu virtute tonorum.

[1.4.1]

Ostensa iam aliqualiter distinctione et natura tonorum, nunc videndum est de proprietate et effectu seu virtute ipsorum. quomodo .scilicet. armonie seu melodie vel etiam consonantie musicales, que sicut ex predictis apparet regulantur per tonos, aliter et aliter prout videlicet alterius vel alterius toni existunt, audientium mentes et animos habent disponere et in eis diversas anime passiones causare vel etiam excitare, et ita per consequens ut infra videbitur ad mores interdum conferre. Ad quorum evidentiam maiorem sciendum est quod passiones anime ut de ipsis nunc loquimur nichil aliud esse videntur quam quidam motus appetitive partis sensitive sub fantasia boni vel mali, ut dicit eustracius super secundum ethicorum. vel sub ymaginatione boni vel mali ut dicit damascenus, et in idem redit. Sciendum est enim quod sicut voluntas que est appetitus intellectualis ordine nature sequitur intellectum, ita in parte sensitiva appetitus sequitur sensum. sicut ergo voluntas non fertur in bonum nisi prius ordine nature ab intellectu apprehensum vel cognitum, invisa enim ut dicit Augustinus diligere possumus. incognita vero nequaquam, ita nec appetitus sensitivus fertur in aliquid nisi ymaginatum vel apprehensum videlicet sub ratione boni convenientis vel mali disconvenientis[68] ita quod si sequitur apprehensionem sub ratione boni convenientis cum delectatione movetur si autem sub ratione disconvenientis[69] cum tristitia movetur. recte ergo [70v] in diffinitione passionis vel passionum anime positum est sub[70] fantasia vel ymaginatione boni vel mali. Dicuntur autem passiones anime motus quidam ~~motus~~[71] esse. non quidem accipiendo motum stricte sed magis pro mutatione indivisibili que finis est motus. aliter enim in parte sensitiva non est motus ut magis probatum est a philosopho .vij. phisicorum. mutatio autem que finis est motus ordine nature sequitur motum cuius est finis. unde et passiones anime que sunt mutationes et fines motuum ordine nature secuntur alterationem factam in qualitatibus primis ~~et~~[72] activis videlicet et passivis. que sunt calidum, frigidum, siccum, et humidum. secundum quas animalium corpora primo alterantur, ut vult philosophus ubi supra.

---

[68] ita quod si sequitur apprehensionem sub ratione boni convenientis cum delectatione movetur si autem sub ratione disconvenientis **H2** *inserted from right margin.*

[69] . mali *added after* ratione *Klundert.*
[70] sub **H2** *inserted from the top margin.*
[71] motus *struck through.*
[72] et *struck through.*

[1.4.0]
Chapter four: On the property and effect or power of the tones.

[1.4.1]
Having shown something of the distinction between and nature of the tones, now we should look at their property and effect or power. Namely we should look at how harmonies, melodies and musical consonances regulated through the tones in one way or another (just as tones of one kind or another exist, as is evident from what has been said) are able to direct the minds and spirits of listeners and provoke or even arouse different passions of the soul. Thus consequently, as will be seen below, they shape behavior.[176] For greater clarity on this, it should be known that, the passions of the soul as we are now speaking about them, seem to be nothing other than certain motions of the sensitive appetitive part behind the façade of good or bad, as Eustratius says [in his commentary] on the second book of the *Ethics*, or beyond the imagining of good or bad, as the Damascene says,[177] and this amounts to the same thing. For it should be known that just as the will, which is the intellectual appetite, follows the intellect through natural order, thus appetite follows sense in the sensory part. Therefore, just as the will is not led to good unless first grasped or known by the intellect through natural order—for as Augustine says, we are able to love things unseen but things unknown not at all—thus the sensory appetite is not led to anything except that which is imagined or grasped,

---

ll Fourth Sunday in Advent: BnF lat. 17296 f. 13v:

A - ve ma - ri - a gra - ti - a ple - na do - mi - nus te - cum be - ne - di - cta tu in mu - li - e - ri - bus.

mm Fourth Sunday in Advent: Thursday: BnF lat. 17296 f. 17r:

De sy - on ven - i - et do - mi - nus om - ni - po - tens ut sal - vum fa - ci - at po - pu - lum su - um.

nn Christmas Eve: BnF lat. 17296 f. 19r:

Le - va - te ca - pi - ta ve - stra ec - ce ap - pro - pin - qua - bit re - demp - ti - o ve - stra.

oo St. Andrew: BnF lat. 17296 f. 261r:

Do - mi-ne Ihe - su Chris-te ma - gis-ter

pp Purification: BnF lat. 17296 f. 69v:

Se - nex pu - e-rum por - ta - bat_ pu-er au - tem

qq Fourth Week in Advent: BnF lat. 17296 f. 13v:

O_____ sa - pi- en - ti - a que e-ro - re

[1.4.2]

¶ Cum enim appetitiva sensibilis sit quedam virtus organica, in corpore videlicet existens et organo indigens corporali non solum in esse sed etiam in operatione sua sequitur dispositionem materie et corporis. et ideo passiones ipsius dispositionem aliquam primarum qualitatum sequuntur. unde et anime passiones per huiusmodi qualitates materialiter diffiniuntur, dicimus enim quod ira est accensio sanguinis vel spiritus circa cor. timor vero remissio quedam vel infrigidatio eorundem, delectationem autem dicimus esse diffusionem spiritus et caloris. tristitiam vero contractionem eorum. et sic de ceteris anime passionibus. Qualitates autem predicte non sunt simplices neque pure in humano corpore, sicut nec in animalibus ceteris. sed potius composite et extremis secundum aliquam proportionem numeralem permixte. nam calidum animalis non est simpliciter calidum sed remissum per frigidum nec humidum est simpliciter humidum, sed cum sicco secundum aliquam proportionem permixtum, et sic de ceteris. et ideo quamvis in omnibus hominibus sit dispositio huiusmodi qualitatum, ex istis enim sicut ex materia sunt homines omnes compositi quantum ad corpus, huiusmodi dispositio tamen non est in omnibus equaliter, secundum quod quidam homines magis sunt calidi quidam vero minus calidi, et quidam magis frigidi alii vero minus et sic de aliis. Ex quo contingit quod etsi in omnibus hominibus huiusmodi passiones existant quadam aptitudine vel virtute, in quibusdam tamen magis secundum actum et intense, in aliis vero magis secundum potentiam et remisse ita videlicet ut aliqui secundum quandam excellentiam sint audaces, alii vero mediocriter. alii etiam excellenter sint invidi alii iracundi, quidam vero mediocriter. et sic de passionibus ceteris, secundum quod huiusmodi qualitates magis vel minus a dominio aliterque[73] et aliter sunt in ipsis.

---

[73] aliter *Klundert.*

namely through reasoning about appropriate good or inappropriate bad. The result is that if it [the appetitive part] follows apprehension through reasoning about appropriate good, it is moved with delight, or if it follows through reasoning about the inappropriate, it is moved with sadness.[178] Rightly, therefore, in the definition of passion or passions of the soul, it is located under the appearance or imagining of good or bad.[179] Passions of the soul are said to be certain motions, not indeed taken as motion strictly, but rather as indivisible change, which is the end of motion. For motion is not in any other way in the sensory part, as has been further demonstrated by the Philosopher in the seventh book of the *Physics*.[180] Change, which is the end of motion, in the natural order follows the motion of which it is the end. Hence the passions of the soul, which are changes and ends of motions, in the natural order follow the alteration made in the prime qualities namely active and passive, which are hot, cold, dry and moist. The bodies of living things are first changed according to these, as the Philosopher determines as above.[181]

[1.4.2]

For since the sensory appetitive part is a certain organic power, that is to say existing in the body and lacking a bodily organ, it follows the disposition of matter and body not only in essence but also in its operation, and therefore its passions follow any disposition of prime qualities.[182] Hence, the passions of the soul are defined materially by qualities of this kind, for we say that anger is the inflaming of the blood or spirit around the heart, but fear is a certain shrinking or freezing of them. We also say that delight is the diffusion of spirit and heat, but sadness is their contraction,[183] and similarly with other passions of the soul. The aforesaid qualities are neither simple nor pure in the human body, just as in other living things, but rather are composite and mixed, within limits, according to some numeric proportion. For the warmth of a living thing is not simply warmth but something less cold; nor is moistness simply moist but mixed with dryness according to some proportion,[184] and so for the rest. And therefore, although there is such an arrangement of qualities in everyone, just as all people are composed from matter as far as the body is concerned, however such an arrangement is not identical in everyone. Following this, certain people are more warm, others are less warm, and some are more cold, others are less, and so on.[185] Thus it happens that, although passions of this kind exist in all people through a certain aptitude or power, among some, they tend more to action and intensely so, but in others they tend more to potential and mildly so. So it clearly results that some people are bold in an outstanding way, but others moderately so; and others are outstandingly jealous, others irascible, but certain people are just moderately so, and thus for the other passions. According to this, qualities of this kind vary more or less in their dominance and are differ among themselves.[186]

[1.4.3]

⁋ Hoc viso ad propositum sic potest argui. Armonie seu melodie et consonantie musicales sicut ex primo capitulo precedenti satis apparere potest. in quadam sonorum media ratione et proportione consistunt, ratione etiam soni armonici [71r] non solum movendo immo etiam alterando agunt in spiritus qui sunt primum organum auditus et universaliter omnium virtutum sensitivarum et etiam motivarum. In hoc enim est differentia inter audibilia et visibilia, quod visibilia movent visum sola quadam immutatione tenui et quasi insensibili. audibilia vero movent et secundum alterationem quandam et secundum motum localem medii et organi. omne autem agens per aliquam formam in agendo assimilat sibi passum. secundum enim commenta[to]rem in secundo de anima. passum in principio contrarium est agenti. in medio vero ex simili et contrario compositum est. sed in fine assimilatur agenti. relinquitur ergo quod armonie musice movendo et alterando spiritus secundum predictas qualitates primas eos assimilant sibi et eos alterant armonia et proportione sibi simili. Cum ergo ut probatum est supra, passiones anime sequantur dispositiones aliquas primarum qualitatum secundum aliquam proportionem numeralem commixtas, si aliqua armonia musica sit in eadem proportione vel propinqua sive consimili et agat in spiritus secundum quod huiusmodi eos sibi assimilabit, et per consequens passionem existentem in simili proportione causabit.

[1.4.4]

⁋ Et hoc idem aliter sic probatur omnis enim operatio partis anime appetitive que fit secundum inclinationem naturalem delectabilis est secundum intentionem philosophi secundo et .vij°. ethicorum. ubi dicit quod delectatio est operatio connaturalis habitus non impedita, sed operatio ipsius anime que fit ab armonia simili proportioni illi in qua consistit passio aliqua puta ira vel timor vel aliqua huiusmodi, fit secundum inclinationem naturalem eius ut in tali passione consistit vel bene dispositus est ad eam. ergo est ei delectabilis. delectatio autem secundum aliquam operationem adauget operationem illam et corrumpit contrariam, ut habetur .x. ethicorum. ergo armonia talis non solum delectationem inducit, immo etiam auget passionem que in simili proportione consistit, et corrumpit contrariam ab ipsa purgando. unde et philosophus dicit .viij°. politice. quasdam armonias musicas esse purgativas aliquarum passionum que est enim generativa alicuius passionis corruptiva est sue contrarie. sicut enim simile disponit ad simile sibi vel ipsum auget et confortat ita contraria invicem se corrumpunt.

[1.4.3]

Understanding this, we can argue the matter thus. Harmonies or melodies and musical consonances, just as may be sufficiently evident from the preceding first chapter, consist in a certain mediating ratio and proportion of sounds.[187] Also by the ratio, harmonic sounds not only by moving but also by changing, act upon the spirits, the first vehicle of hearing, and universally of all sensitive and also moving powers.[188] For in this is the difference between audible and visible things, because visible things move what is seen only by a certain slender and almost imperceptible exchange, but audible things move according to a particular change and according to a local motion of the medium and vehicle [of hearing].[189] In acting, however, every agent, assimilates to itself what is experienced through a certain form.[190] For according to the Commentator on the second [book of the] *De anima*, the thing experienced at the outset is different from the agent, in the middle it is composed of the similar and the different, but in the end it is assimilated to the agent.[191] Therefore, it remains that musical harmonies by moving and altering the spirits, assimilate them to themselves according to the aforesaid first qualities and change them by a harmony and proportion similar to themselves.[192] Since therefore, as has been proved above, the passions of the soul follow certain distributions of first qualities mixed according to some numeric proportion, if any musical harmony is in the same or approximate or similar proportion and in this way acts on spirits it will assimilate them to itself and it will consequently cause an existing passion in a similar proportion.[193]

[1.4.4]

And the same thing is proved differently thus: every operation of the appetitive part of the soul, which happens by natural inclination, is delightful according to the intention of the Philosopher in the second and seventh [books] of the *Ethics*, where he says that delight is the unimpeded operation of natural disposition.[194] But the operation of the soul itself—which comes from a harmony in that same proportion in which consists a certain passion, namely anger or fear or something of this kind—occurs according to its natural inclination, as it consists in such a passion or is well disposed to it. Therefore, it is delightful to it [the soul]. Delight increases that operation according to some process and weakens [its] opposite, as is in the tenth [book] of the *Ethics*. Therefore, such a harmony not only induces delight, but it also increases the passion, which consists in a similar proportion and, weakens [its] opposite by purging it from itself. And hence the Philosopher says in the eighth [book] of the *Politics* that certain musical harmonies purge certain passions. For what generates a certain passion weakens its opposite.[195] For just as like disposes itself to like or increases and supports itself,[196] so opposites weaken each other.

[1.4.5]

¶ Ex his itaque colligitur duplici ratione quare vel qualiter saltem in generali, armonie musice regulate per tonos, diversas anime passiones in audientibus excitare habeant vel causare. et sic per consequens apparere potest quod habeant ad mores conferre. Cum enim passiones redacte ad medium disponant ad virtutes, quia sunt materia virtutum. virtutes enim sunt moderative[74] earum manifestum est, quod, si armonie musice disponere habeant ad [71v] passiones moderatas, quod etiam per consequens ad virtutes et bonos mores. Quod autem ad passiones moderatas armonie quedam musicales disponant, ex predictis potest faciliter sic concludi. quando enim aliquid disponit ad aliud, ipsum magis factum magis habet disponere ad magis tale. quoniam si simpliciter ad simpliciter, et magis ad magis, et maxime ad maxime, sicut autem ex predictis apparet armonie quedam musice sive soni consonantes secundum earum aliquas agunt ad passiones, et eas quandoque causant vel excitant, ergo magis consonantes et redacte ad medium agunt et disponunt ad passiones moderatas et ad medium reductas, et per consequens ut dictum est sequitur quod etiam conferant et disponant ad mores. unde et philosophus dicit .viij°. politice. quod in armoniis musicalibus sunt quedam imitationes et similitudines morum.

[1.4.6]

¶ Predicta vero de armoniis musicalibus et earum virtute seu effectu quo ad passiones anime in audientibus excitandas. ipsos videlicet audientes ad anime passiones aliquas incitando et contrarias remittendo, et sic per consequens ad mores quandoque disponendo, non solum rationes premisse probabiliter videntur concludere. immo et boetius magnus ille philosophus qui anno domini .d°. xx°. vel circiter legitur floruisse. quod ita sit ut dictum est, pulcre satis ac diffuse in prologo sue musice multis auctoritatibus et exemplis nititur declarare. dicit enim ibidem quod cum sint .iiij°r. mathematice discipline. videlicet. geometria. astronomia. arismetica. musica. quarum tres prime precipue investigatione veritatis laborant. musica tamen ut dicit non solum speculationi, verum etiam moralitati adeo est coniuncta, ut nichil tam proprium sit humanitati, quam modis remitti dulcibus et astringi contrariis. unde plato ut quibusdam interpositis refert boetius, maxime cavendum existimat ne de bene morata musica aliquid permutetur. negat enim tantam morum in re publica labem esse, quam aliquid de pudenti ac modesta musica paulatim evertere. statim namque accidit audientium animos idem pati ac paulatim discedere nullumque honesti ac recti vestigium retinere, si videlicet vel per lasciviores modos cantandi aliquid inverecundum, vel [per] asperiores immane vel ferox mentibus illabatur, nulla enim ut dicit magis ad animum disciplinis via quam auribus patet. et ideo cum per eas cantus et modi cantandi ad animum usque descenderint, dubitari non potest. quin equo modo mentem et animum ad que ipsi

---

[74] moderative -tive *added over erasure* **H2**.

[1.4.5]

Therefore, why or how, at least in general, musical harmonies regulated through the tones come to excite or cause diverse passions of the soul in hearers is brought together from these things by a twofold reasoning;[197] and thus consequently it can appear that they have the capacity to influence behavior. For since passions reduced to a mean dispose to virtues, because they are the material of virtues, for clearly the virtues moderate them, if musical harmonies are able to dispose to moderated passions, they also consequently [dispose] to virtues and good behavior.[198] That certain musical harmonies dispose to moderated passions can thus easily be concluded from the aforesaid.[199] For when something influences something else, what is done more is more effectively able to influence such a thing.[200] Since if simple [disposes] to simple, and more to more, and very much to very much, just as appears from the aforesaid, certain musical harmonies or consonant sounds act according to their particular passions, and sometimes they cause or arouse them.[201] Therefore, the harmonies that are more consonant and rendered to a mean, lead and incline to passions that are moderated and rendered to a mean,[202] and consequently, as has been said, it follows that they also generate and influence behavior.[203] And hence the Philosopher says in the eighth [book] of the *Politics* that there are certain imitations and similarities of behavior in musical harmonies.[204]

[1.4.6]

But what has been said concerning musical harmonies and their power or effect, by which they arouse passions of the soul in listeners - namely [they arouse] those listeners by inciting certain passions of the soul and reducing the opposites,[205] and consequently sometimes influence behavior seems to be demonstrably established and not just by the reasoning advanced here. Indeed Boethius, that great philosopher who is reported to have flourished in the year of Our Lord 520 or thereabouts,[206] strives to declare this rather beautifully and extensively in the prologue of his *Musica* by many authorities and examples. For he says there that, since there are four mathematical disciplines—namely geometry, astronomy, arithmetic, music—of which the first three work mainly by the investigation of truth, music, however, as he says, is not only joined to speculation but also indeed to morality, so that nothing is so particular to humanity as being soothed in sweet ways and restrained by the opposites.[207] Hence, as Boethius reports further on, Plato considers the greatest precaution should be taken with music lest anyone be diverted from good behavior.[208] For he says that there is never so great a collapse of behavior in the state as gradually turning something away from fitting and modest music; for then it immediately happens that the spirits of listeners experience the same thing and gradually wander, and keep to no path of honesty and rectitude if, namely, it weakens minds either through more lascivious modes of singing something shameless, or through more harsh ones, cruelly or fiercely.[209]

sunt afficiant et conforment. Fuit autem [72r] ut postea dicit idem boetius pudens et modesta musica, dum simplicioribus organis ageretur. ubi vero tractata est varie ac permixte. sic amisit virtutis gravitatisque modum ut pene in turpitudinem prolapsa, minimum antiquam speciem servet. unde et plato precepit non oportere pueros ad omnes erudiri modos, sed potius ad valentes ac simplices. Magnam quippe rei publice custodiam arbitratus est ipse plato, musicam optime moratam pudenterque coniunctam esse. videlicet ut sit modesta et simplex, mascula non effeminata, nec fera nec varia. quod et lacedemonii cum maxima ope vel diligentia servaverunt.[75] Tanta quippe ut ibidem dicit boetius apud quosdam antiquos fuit diligentia musice. ut eam quoque arbitrarentur humanos animos obtinere. et hoc maxime sensisse videntur pitagorici. refert enim ibidem quod in tantum antique philosophie studiis vis musice artis innotuit, ut pitagorici cum diurnas in sompno curas resolverent, quibusdam cantilenis uterentur, ut eis videlicet quietus ac lenis sopor irreperet. et postea experrecti aliis quibusdam modis cantandi stuporem confusionemque sompni purgabant. credebant enim pitagorici quod humana anima tota sit musica coaptatione coniuncta.

[1.4.7]

¶ Quam sepe iracundias vel alias anime passiones noxias vel nocivas cantilene represserint. et quam multa in corporibus vel in animorum affectionibus miranda perfecerint, declarat ibi boetius per exempla, narrat enim de quodam ebrio iuvene. qui ad sonum modi frigii idest tertii toni ita ad iram vel libidinem incitatus fuerat ut domum impudice cuiusdam mulieris vellet effringere sive comburere, nec precibus amicorum desistere. quod ipsum pitagoras per mutationem modi vel soni frigii in spondeum idest in quemdam alium cantandi modum qui gravior erat et tardior, ad statum mentis pacatissime revocavit. Quod etiam ut dicit boetius marcus tullius in libro de consiliis factum esse commemorat. quamvis sub aliis verbis. dicit enim tullius quod cum quidam vinolenti adolescentes cantu tibiarum accensi, mulieris pudice fores frangerent, admonuisse tibicinam ut spondeum caneret pitagoras dicitur. quod cum illa fecisset tarditate morum[76] et gravitate canentis, illorum petulentiam[77] consedisse. Cum enim manifestum sit ut postea quibusdam interpositis dicit boetius, animos in bello pugnantium [72v] carmine tubarum accendi. et quemquam ab animi statu pacato ad furorem vel iracundiam posse proferri, non est dubium quod conturbate mentis iracundiam vel nimiam cupiditatem sive cupidinem modestior modus possit astringere. Sic etenim secundum quod guido refert .xiij°. ubi supra, quidam freneticus canente asclepiade medico ab insania legitur revocatus. sic etiam secundum eundem guidonem davitica cithara saulis demonium mitigabat. feritatemque demoniacam huius artis potenti

---

[75] servaverunt -verunt *inserted over erasure* **H2**.

[76] mo<do>rum *Klundert*.
[77] petul<a>ntiam *Klundert*.

For there is no path in teaching, as he says, more direct to the spirit than through the ears, and therefore, since through them chants and ways of singing sink into the spirit, it cannot be doubted that they affect and mould the mind and spirit in an equal way to what they themselves are.[210] As the same Boethius says later, there was chaste and modest music, yet it was made for simpler organs: but where it was treated variously and blended, thus it lost the manner of strength and seriousness, so that, having just about slipped into disgrace, it hardly kept at all to its former state.[211] And hence Plato taught that boys ought not to be educated in all the modes, but rather in the strong and simple ones.[212] Plato himself thought that the great guardian of the republic is music, well-mannered and chastely put together, so that it is modest and simple, masculine and not effeminate, neither rough nor disorganised. This is what the Lacedaemonians preserved with the greatest effort and care.[213] Indeed, as Boethius says in the same place, there was so much care for music amongst certain ancients, that they also thought that it took hold of human spirits. The Pythagoreans seemed to have felt this to the greatest degree.[214] For he relates in the same place that the power of the art of music became so well known in the study of ancient philosophy that when the Pythagoreans resolved their daily cares in sleep, they used certain lyric songs so that quiet and gentle sleep resulted. And afterwards, having woken up, they purged the stupor and confusion of sleep with certain other modes of singing. For the Pythagoreans believed that the whole human soul was integrated through appropriate music.[215]

[1.4.7]
Boethius declares there through examples how often lyric songs may restrain rages and other noxious or harmful passions of the soul and how many wonders it has worked on bodies or on the dispositions of the spirits.[216] For he tells of a certain drunken youth, who at the sound of the Phrygian mode, that is, of the third tone, was so incited to anger and lust that he wanted to break into or burn down the house of a certain immodest woman and would not desist upon the pleas of his friends. Pythagoras restored him to a very calm state of mind through the change of the Phrygian mode, or sound, into a spondee,[217] that is into another way of singing that was graver and slower. Yet again as Boethius says, Marcus Tullius, in his book *De consiliis*, relates that this happened, although in different terms.[218] For Tullius says that when certain drunken youths, incited by the sound of flutes, were about to break down the doors of a chaste woman, it is said that Pythagoras admonished the flute player to perform a spondee. When this was done their petulance subsided with the restraint of the modes and the gravity of the performer. [219] For since it is clear, as Boethius says later on, that the passions of those fighting are aroused by the call of trumpets, and that anyone can be brought from a peaceful state of mind to fury and wrath, there is no doubt that a more temperate mode can calm the wrath or excessive desire or lust of a troubled mind.[220] For

virtute frangebat. Quin immo et secundum boetium ubi supra, ismenias thebanus boetiorum quampluribus quos doloris sciatici idest umbratici tormenta vexabant modis musicis cunctas fertur abstersisse[78] molestias. Nonnullique alii musici quos ibidem boetius nominatim commemorat, gentes multas a morbis gravissimis cantus eripuere presidio.

[1.4.8]

¶ Predictas vero et quasdam alias armoniarum musice proprietates auctor de proprietatibus rerum circa finem sui libri enumerat sub hijs verbis. Armonia inquit musica contraria et disparata conciliat, gravia acutis et acuta gravibus modificat et adaptat, affectiones contrarias et adversas reconciliat, malitiosos animorum motus reprimit et refrenat, sensus debilitatos reparat et confortat, unitatem exemplaris divini in operibus contrariis ac diversis manifestissime preconizat terrenis celestia celestibusque terrena posse uniri in concordia manifestat. letos animos magis letificat. et tristes magis tristificat. quia ut dicit beatus augustinus. ex quadam occulta anime et armonie consimili proprietate, melodia musica affectionibus anime se conformat. et inde est quod auctores dicunt quod instrume[n]ta musica letum hominem reddunt letiorem et tristem efficiunt tristiorem. hec auctor prefatus.

[1.4.9]

¶ Si quis autem ulterius inquirere velit que vel quales et quorum tonorum armonie seu melodie specialiter et determinate has vel illas anime passiones in audientibus excitare habeant vel causare iudicare pro certo de talibus non est facile immo valde difficile. tum propter armoniarum ipsarum varietatem multiplicem profundam nimium et obscuram. tum etiam propter ipsorum audientium dispositionem variam et diversam. Quod enim hoc sit difficile ex parte armoniarum musicalium ex hoc patet, quamvis enim armonie seu melodie musice movendo spiritus[79] et eos secundum qualitates primas. activas. scilicet. et passivas alterando sibique eos assimilando armonia videlicet et [73r] proportione sibi simili illam anime passionem que in tali proportione consistit vel que dispositionem huiusmodi qualitatum secundum talem numeralem proportionem permixtarum ordine nature sequitur excitare habeant vel causare ut dictum est supra, huiusmodi tamen proportionum similitudines in armoniis et qualitatibus primis determinare et in speciali perpendere sive cognoscere facile non videtur. immo certe valde difficile saltem mihi. in quibusdam etiam ecclesiasticis cantibus de quibus principaliter nostra versatur intentio, manifeste video et frequenter, quod eorum aliqui pulcriorem satis melodiam continent quam alii multi qui eiusdem sunt toni. sicut apparet de responsoriis istis et eorum versiculis scilicet. *Ierusalem cito veniet.* et *O iuda.* vel secundum alios. *Iudea et ierusalem.* respectu multorum aliorum immo quasi omnium

---

[78] astersisse *corrected to* abstersisse **H2**.   [79] spiritibus *Klundert.*

thus, according to what Guido reports in the thirteenth [chapter] above, it is read that a certain madman was brought back from insanity by the doctor Asclepiades singing.[221] Thus also according to the same Guido, the Davidic harp used to soften the demon of Saul and broke the strength of the demonic ferocity by the power of this art.[222] Indeed by contrast, according to Boethius above, Ismenias the Theban is said to have taken away by musical modes all the annoyances of many Boeotians, whom the torments of the pain of sciatica, that is, idleness, troubled.[223] And Boethius remembers several other musicians by name in the same place—many peoples were taken away from serious illnesses by the help of song.[224]

[1.4.8]

The author of *De proprietatibus rerum* enumerates the aforesaid and various other properties of the harmonies of music, towards the end of his book in these words: "Musical harmony," he said, "reconciles contrary and disparate things, modifies and adapts graves to acutes and acutes to graves, reconciles contrary and adverse dispositions, suppresses and adapts the malicious motions of spirits, restores and comforts weakened senses [and] preaches most clearly the unity of the divine exemplar in contrary and diverse works. It makes clear that heavenly things are able to be united to earthly things and earthly things to heavenly things in harmony, [and] it makes joyful spirits more joyful and sad ones more sad, because, as blessed Augustine says, musical melody conforms itself to the dispositions of the soul from a certain hidden property of the soul akin to harmony. And thus it is that authors say that musical instruments render a happy person happier and make a sad person sadder."[225] Thus says the author.

[1.4.9]

If anyone wishes to enquire further as to which harmonies or melodies—or of which kind or of which tones—are especially and particularly able to arouse or cause some or other passions of the soul in hearers, it is not easy to judge for certain about such things. Indeed it is truly difficult, as much because of the manifold, excessively deep and unintelligible variety of the harmonies themselves as of the varied and diverse disposition of the hearers themselves. That this is difficult as regards musical harmonies is clear from this. For harmonies and melodies of music can excite or provoke, by moving spirits according to first qualities, namely active and passive, by altering and assimilating that passion of the soul to itself by harmony and proportion like to themselves;[226] it consists in such a proportion or it follows the disposition of qualities of this kind according to such a numeric proportion of qualities mixed together by the order of nature that they are able to excite or cause, as was said above. Yet it does not seem easy to determine the likenesses of such proportions in harmonies and first qualities and in particular to assess or know them. Rather it is certainly truly difficult at least for me. For

eiusdem toni videlicet quarti. quod etiam si quis velit diligenter inspicere, in cantibus aliorum tonorum frequenter inveniet.

[1.4.10]

¶ Ex parte vero dispositionis diverse que in hominibus[80] esse dinoscitur etiam hoc
esse difficile dubium nequaquam existit. Cum enim secundum philosophum actus
activorum sint in patiente et disposito. constat quod homines secundum diversam
eorum dispositionem diversimode se habent ad percipiendam armoniarum musicalium et tonorum efficaciam et virtutem. Unde secundum quod homines aliter et
aliter sunt corpore et mente dispositi secundum hoc armonias musicas audiendo.
per ipsas dissimiliter ad varias anime passiones contingit eos affici vel moveri. et in
ipsis motus varios. incitari. Lascivus quippe animus sicut dicit boecius ubi supra.
modis lascivioribus delectatur. vel sepius eosdem audiens emollitur aut frangitur. Rursus asperior mens vel incitatioribus gaudet. vel incitatioribus asperatur.
Ita namque secundum guidonem capitulo .xiiijo. ubi supra. troporum diversitas
diversitati mentium coaptatur, ut unus autenti deuteri idest tertii toni vel tropi
fractis saltibus delectetur. Alius vero plage triti idest sexti toni eligat voluptatem.
Et uni quidem autenti tetrardi. idest septimi toni garrulitas magis placet. Alter
vero eiusdem plage idest octavi toni suavitatem probat. et sic de reliquis. Et hec
sane humanorum mentium circa cantus et modos cantandi diversitas non tam in
hominibus eiusdem regionis apparet quam in aliis qui de diversis mundi climati-
bus trahunt originem. vel diversas inhabitant regiones.

---

[80] ominibus *corrected to* hominibus **H2.**

in certain ecclesiastical chants, to which our intentions are principally turned, I
see clearly and frequently that some of these contain a more sufficiently beautiful
melody than many others that are of the same tone, just as appears from the following responsories and their versicles, namely *Ierusalem cito veniet*,[rr] and *O Iuda*[ss]
or as others call it, *Iudea et ierusalem*,[227] compared to many others indeed, almost
all, of the same tone namely the fourth. For if anyone wishes to consider this carefully they will frequently find this in chants of other tones.

[1.4.10]

With respect to the varieties of disposition evident in mankind, there is no doubt
at all that this is also difficult. For since according to the Philosopher, the activities of active things are present in the thing that is acted upon and affected,[228] it is
clear that people conduct themselves according to their particular disposition in
perceiving in different ways the efficacy and strength of musical harmonies and
tones. Hence just as people are disposed in one way or another in body and mind
by listening to musical harmonies in this way thus it happens that through these
harmonies they are diversely affected or moved to various passions of the soul,
and various emotions are aroused in them. Indeed, a lascivious disposition, just as
Boethius says as above, takes pleasure in more lascivious modes, or is often made
soft and corrupted upon hearing them. On the other hand, a rougher spirit either
finds pleasure in more exciting modes or becomes aroused by them.[229] For thus
according to Guido in the fourteenth chapter as above, the diversity of tropes is
adapted to the diversity of minds, with the result that one person may be delighted
by the broken leaps of the authentic deuterus, that is, the third tone or trope. But
another chooses the indulgence of the plagal *tritus*, that is, the sixth tone. And
indeed to one person the babbling of, the authentic *tetrardus*, that is, the seventh
tone, is more pleasing. But another commends the smoothness of the plagal of the
same, that is, the eighth tone, and so on for the rest. And clearly this diversity of
human minds concerning song and ways of singing appears not as much in people
of the same region as in others who take their origin from different climates of the
world or inhabit different regions.

[rr] Second Sunday in Advent: BnF lat. 17296 f. 6r:

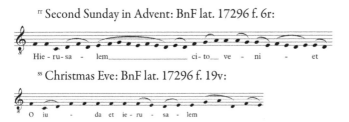

Hie - ru - sa - lem_____ ci - to__ ve - ni - et

[ss] Christmas Eve: BnF lat. 17296 f. 19v:

O iu - da et ie - ru - sa - lem

[1.4.11]

¶ Ad cuius evidentiam notandum est. quod secundum ieronimum super epistulam ad galathas. Unaqueque provincia suas habet proprietates et mores. [73v] Cretenses namque mendaces. malas bestias. ventres pigros vere. ab epimenide poeta dictos apostolus comprobat. Vanosque punicos et feroces dalmatas latinus pulsat hystoricus. Timidos quoque frigas omnes poete lacerant. Et athenis expeditiora nasci ingenia philosophi gloriantur. Grecos vero leves apud cesarem suggillat tullius. populumque israel gravi corde et dura cervice omnes scripture arguunt. Et per hunc modum arbitror ipsum apostolum galathas, ad quos scribit regionis sue proprietate pulsare cum dicit. O insensati galathe et cetera. Dicit etiam idem ieronimus super ysaiam. quod omnes hystorie referunt, romanorum et iudeorum gente nichil fuisse avarius. Videmus etiam ut auctores aliqui volunt, romanos graves. gayos[81] leves. affros vel affricos versipelles. gallos vero feroces natura et ingenio acriores.

[1.4.12]

¶ Iste autem proprietates et mores vel consimiles que hominibus diversas habitantibus regiones vel climata, noscuntur inesse. etsi ex dispositione corporali vel complexione naturali tamquam ex causa speciali et propinqua proveniant. ex diversitate tamen facierum et aspectuum celi. motu quoque et influentia celestium corporum tamquam ex causa universali magis et remota frequenter eveniunt. quamvis enim motus celi vel corpora celestia super electiones nostras non habeant vim coactivam aut necessitantem. Non enim in intellectum nostrum aut voluntatem directe influunt aut aliquam impressionem efficiunt. quia tamen in corporibus nostris dispositiones aliquas imprimunt corporales. ad quas in nobis quandoque motus passionum insurgunt. inde est quod ad nostrum liberum arbitrium per modum inclinantis ad aliquid agendum se habent, in quantum videlicet ex impressione eorum relinquitur in corpore nostro dispositio aliqua secundum quam anima ad hanc actionem vel illam prona efficitur. sicut etiam ex naturali complexione quidam homines magis sunt proni ad aliquod vitium vel virtutem quam alii. De germania siquidem loquens ysidorus dicit, quod ibi sunt homines natura feroces immanesque hominum nationes. et immania habentes corpora. que sevissime et frigoribus indurate, mores ex ipso celi rigore traxerunt. Secundum etiam damascenum alii et alii planete complexiones diversas habitusque et dispositiones in nobis constituunt.

---

[81] G<r>ayos *Klundert.*

[1.4.11]

As evidence for this, it should be noted that, according to Jerome in his *Commentary on the Epistle to the Galatians*, each province has its own characteristics and customs. The Apostle confirms that the Cretans were rightly called liars, evil beasts, lazy gluttons by the poet Epimenides. And the Latin historian hammers the vain Carthaginians and the ferocious Dalmatians. All poets also lacerate the timid Phrygians. And philosophers pride themselves on being born in the more unfettered spirit of Athens. But Cicero insults the lightweight Greeks in the company of Caesar, and all the scriptures argue that the people of Israel are with a hard heart and a stiff neck. And I judge in this way that the same Apostle hammers the Galatians, to whom he writes in the character of their region when he says, "O foolish Galatians" etc.[230] Also, the same Jerome says in his commentary on *Isaiah* that all the histories report that none were more avaricious than the people of the Romans and of the Jews.[231] Also, we see, as other authors suggest, that the Romans were serious, the Greeks light hearted, the Africans crafty, but the Gauls fierce by nature and more shrewd in character.[232]

[1.4.12]

These characteristics and customs and the like, which are known to be in people inhabiting diverse regions or climates although originating from bodily disposition or from natural constitution as much as from a particular and related cause frequently arise as much from a specific and nearby cause, namely from the diversity of appearances and aspects of the heavens as from the motion and influence of heavenly bodies as from a more universal and remote cause. This is although the movements of heaven or the heavenly bodies do not have an active or compelling force on our choices. For they do not directly influence or make any impression on our intellect or will, since they impress certain bodily dispositions upon our bodies. To these the motions of the passions sometimes swell in us. Thus they [the heavenly bodies] are able to do something to our free will through a kind of inclination, clearly in as much as, a certain disposition is left by their impression upon our body by which the soul is made prone to this or that action: just as from natural constitution, certain people are more prone to some vice or virtue than others. Indeed, speaking about Germany, Isidore says that people there, are by nature fierce, and there are frightful nations of people having frightful bodies, which, have been made savage and hard by cold, have drawn their behavior from the same harshness of the heavens.[233] For according to the Damascene, the different planets establish diverse complexions and humours and characteristics in us.[234]

[1.4.13]

¶ Sicut autem diversitas proprietatum et morum, hominibus regionum vel climatum diversorum secundum diversitatem facierum celi et influentiarum eius inesse
probatur, ita etiam de diversitate [**74r**] vel dissimilitudine quam habent homines
in diversis regionibus ad cantus et modos cantandi satis rationabiliter dici potest.
Secundum namque boetium ubi supra. Gaudet unaqueque gens suorum similitudine morum. amica est enim ut dicit similitudo. odiosa vero dissimilitudo atque
contraria. neque enim fieri potest ut mollia duris vel dura mollibus annectantur
aut gaudeant. sed amorem et dilectionem ipsa similitudo conciliat. Unde que
asperiores sunt gentium, modis cantandi durioribus, que vero mediocres sunt
mediocribus delectantur. Hinc est etiam ut ibidem paulo ante dicit boetius quod
musici modi saltem aliqui ut lidius et frigius vocabulo gentium designati fuerunt.
ita videlicet ut quo modo unaqueque gens gaudere probatur etiam ipse modus eius
vocabulo nuncupetur. Pro diversitate siquidem gentium sicut dicit guido .xvij°.
capitulo. ubi supra. quod uni displicet ab alio amplectitur. Et hunc oblectant consona. ille vero magis probat diversa. Et iste quidem continuationem vel mollitiem
secundum mentis sue lasciviam querit. ille vero utpote gravis et sobrius temperatis
ac sobriis cantibus demulcetur. Alius vero ut amens et incompositus anfractis vexationibus pascitur.

[1.4.14]

¶ Licet autem secundum diversitatem regionum morumque hominum, tot vel
plures videantur esse maneries et modi cantandi. et precipue cantilenas et alios
cantus publicos et civiles. quot per orbis circulum ydiomatum vel linguarum
sunt genera, seu gentium nationes. Alius siquidem est modus cantandi apud ger-
manos seu teutonicos et alios barbaros. Alius apud italos. alius apud hispanos.
atque alius apud gallos senones. sive parisios qui franci dicuntur. et sic de reliquis.
Unusquisque tamen patrioticum modum cantandi tamquam sibi connaturalem
quodammodo intantum amplectitur. et in eo quem profecto pulcriorem reputat
delectari conspicitur. quod etiam in hac parte ut patroni nostri precellentissimique
doctoris beati scilicet dyonisii. verbis in epistula ad policarpum utar, regale num-
misma se habere pre ceteris gloriatur. Universaliter namque secundum guidonem.
capitulo .xvij°. ubi supra. unusquisque cantum illum sonorius multo pronuntiat,
quem secundum sue mentis insitam qualitatem probat. Unde et in vita beati pape
gregorii de germanis gallis qui vocantur teutonici de quibus dictum est supra.
quod mores ex ipso celi rigore traxerunt, expresse legitur. quod etsi inter alias
europe gentes, modulationis dulcedinem ab ipso papa gregorio [**74v**] institutam
discere crebroque rediscere insigniter potuerint incorruptam tamen tam animi
levitate qua nonnulla de proprio gregorianis cantibus miscuerunt. quam etiam
feritate naturali servare minime valuerunt. Alpina siquidem idest ingentia et alta
corpora vocum suarum tonitruis altissone perstrepentia ut ibidem dicitur suscepte

[1.4.13]

For just as the diversity of attributes and behaviors of people of different regions and climates is proven to be in them according to the diversity of the aspects of the heavens and its influences, thus also it can be said reasonably enough about the diversity or dissimilarity as regards chant and the ways of singing that people have in different regions. For according to Boethius as above, each people rejoices in the likeness of their own customs, for, as he says, similarity is a friend, but dissimilarity is disagreeable and contrary.[235] For it cannot happen that soft things are bound together with or delight in hard things, or the hard in with the soft, but likeness itself brings about love and delight.[236] Hence, rougher peoples delight in harsher ways of singing, while the moderate rejoice in the moderate.[237] For as Boethius says a little earlier in the same work, at least some musical modes were designated by the name of peoples, such as Lydian and Phrygian, so that each people is shown to rejoice in that mode, called by its name.[238] For just as Guido says in the seventeenth chapter what displeases one is embraced by another because of the diversity of peoples. Consonance delights this person, but that person is more in favour of diversity. This one seeks continuity or softness according to the playfulness of his mind. But clearly one who is grave and serious is soothed by temperate and sober chants. Another, as one mindless and scattered, is nurtured by tortured troubles.[239]

[1.4.14]

For there seem to be as many or more manners and modes of singing especially lyric songs and other public and civic chants as there are kinds of idioms or languages or nations of people around the circle of the globe because of the diversity of regions and customs of men.[240] Indeed there is one kind of singing among the Germans or Teutons and other barbarians, another among the Italians, another among the Spanish, and another among the Senonian Gauls or the Parisians who are called the French. Everyone, however, embraces a patriotic way of singing as if it were in a certain way natural to them. And they are considered to delight in that which they think is clearly more beautiful, since regarding this I may use the words of our patron and most distinguished doctor, Blessed Denis, in the letter to Polycarp, where he boasts that he has a royal coin without peer.[241] For according to Guido in chapter seventeen as above, universally, each person enunciates all the more sonorously that chant that they approve according to the innate quality of their mind.[242] And hence, in the *Life of the Blessed Pope Gregory*, it is expressly read concerning the German Gauls, called Teutons, mentioned above, that they draw their behavior from the very harshness of the heavens. Although among other peoples of Europe, they [Teutons] have been able to learn or frequently relearn the uncorrupted sweetness of modulation instituted by Pope Gregory himself, yet through a laxity of spirit they mix several things of their own with Gregorian chants. Indeed by their natural wildness they have not been able to retain this sweetness at all. Indeed the Alps, that

modulationis dulcedinem proprie non resultant bibuli enim gutturis barbara feritas dum inflexionibus et repercussionibus mitem nititur edere cantilenam, naturali quodam fragore quasi plaustra per gradus confuse sonantia rigidas voces iactat. sicque audientium animos quos mulcere debuerat, exasperando magis ac obstrependo conturbat.

[1.4.15]

¶ Quamvis igitur propter predicta et alia nonnulla non sit facile immo multum difficile iudicare vel scire que vel quales armonie seu consonantie musicales quas vel quales anime passiones in audientibus excitare habeant vel causare. Probabiliter tamen circa istam materiam que satis occulta videtur et dubia opinando, secundum intentionem[82] philosophi eiusque expositoris. viij°. politice dici potest. quod sicut ibidem annuere videtur philosophus. et plenius declarat expositor. melodia tertii toni quam ibidem philosophus frigistam appellat. de natura sua ad passionem illam que dicitur raptus videtur disponere. causa enim raptus videtur esse intentio anime vehemens circa aliquid interius apprehensum. que provenit vel ex vehementi desiderio attingendi ad illud vel fugiendi ab illo. ex hoc enim quod aliquis vehementer attendit circa aliquid apprehensum interius, contingit quod anima spiritum qui ut supra dictum est est primum instrumentum sensus et motus ab exterioribus ad interiora retrahat et revocet. et maxime ad primum sensitivum et cogitativum. Hec est enim nature proprietas atque sagacitas, mittere spiritum ad locum illum ubi plus indiget et per consequens membra exteriora sensusque exteriores immobilitantur. efficiturque homo quasi immobilis. Cum igitur melodia predicta seu armonia propter fortem percussionem in vocibus, fortiter revocet spiritus ab exterioribus ad interiora, idcirco videtur secundum mentem et opinionem philosophi. quam etiam per aliqua dicta vel exempla quorundam aliorum declarat, quod ipsa ad passionem predictam que raptus dicitur disponere habeat vel eam causare.

[1.4.16]

Sed non solum ad passionem istam secundum intentionem philosophi armonia ista habet disponere, immo etiam et ad alias quasdam anime passiones. secundum enim philosophum melodia huius toni eandem [75r] videtur habere virtutem inter ceteras armonias, quam habet fistula inter musica instrumenta. ambo siquidem non solum ad iram vel audaciam immo et ad ceteras anime passiones ad que[83] disponit calidum incitant vel disponunt. et hoc forte propter fortitudinem percussionis et motus, ratione quorum habent caliditatem in spiritibus excitare. Unde etiam in libello de quo supra .ij°. capitulo. feci mentionem ubi tonorum iuxta proprietates et effectus eorum depinguntur ymagines. iste tonus. scilicet .iijus. propter huiusmodi percussionem fortem in vocibus et motum in spiritibus vehementem,

---

[82] intententionem **H1**.   [83] qu<as> *Klundert*.

is, the great and high bodies loftily resounding with the thunderings of their voices, as is said in the same place, do not reverberate with the sweetness of the modulation being properly taken up, for the barbarous wildness of the bibulous throat, when it attempts to emit a sweet lyric song with inflexions and repercussions, throws forth rigid voices with a certain natural break, like a wagon clattering higgledy-piggeldy over steps. And so it disturbs the spirits of those who hear, whom it ought to soothe, rather by vexing and disrupting.[243]

[1.4.15]

Although, therefore, because of this and several other things, it may not be easy but very difficult to judge or know which or what sort of musical harmonies or consonances are able to excite or cause which or what sort of passions of the soul in hearers. Yet about this matter, which seems quite hidden and dubious to think about, it can reasonably be said, according to the intention of the Philosopher and his expositor in the eighth book of the *Politics*, that, just as there the Philosopher seems to agree, and the expositor declares more fully,[244] the melody of the third tone, which the Philosopher there calls Phrygian, by its nature seems to lead to that passion that is called rapture.[245] For the cause of rapture seems to be the eager intent of the soul on something apprehended internally, which comes forth either from eager desire to grasp it or to flee from it.[246] From the fact that anyone eagerly attends to something apprehended internally, it happens that the soul draws back and recalls the spirit (as said above, the first instrument of sense and motion) from externals to internals, and most of all towards the first thing sensed and thought.[247] For this is the property and wisdom of nature, to send the spirit to that place where there is greater need, and consequently exterior limbs and exterior senses are immobilised, and a person is made as if immobile.[248] Therefore, when the aforesaid melody or harmony, because of strong reverberation in the voices, strongly recalls spirits from externals to internals, for that reason it seems according to the mind and opinion of the Philosopher, which he also declares through other sayings, or the examples of certain others, that it [the melody] can lead [the soul] to the aforesaid passion, namely rapture, or cause it.[249]

[1.4.16]

But not only can that melodic quality lead to that passion according to the intention of the Philosopher, but also even to certain other passions of the soul. For, according to the Philosopher, melody of this tone seems to have the same power among other melodic types that the pipe has among musical instruments, since both, indeed, not only dispose to anger or boldness, but incite or lead warmth to other passions of the soul. This is perhaps because of the strength of the beating and motions, by reason of which they can arouse warmth in the spirits.[250] Whence also in the little book, noted above in the second chapter, I mentioned

quia etiam tam in versibus quam in modulis nunc humilius nunc vero altius sonat, quasi superbe et ad modum equitantis saliens, hyrsutis vel vento erectis[84] crinibus, equum cum impetu quodam depingitur equitare.

[1.4.17]

¶ Armonia vero septimi toni quam philosophus ubi supra mixolodistam appellat. licet propter magnum acumen quod habet in vocibus quia ad .a. superacutam idest ad secundum alamire interdum attingit ad quam nullus aliorum tonorum ascendit, ab exterioribus ad interiora aliqualiter spiritum revocet vel retrahat. non tamen sic fortiter ut melodia toni tertii vel frigista. et ideo non ad raptum aut audaciam seu iram. sed potius ad misericordiam et compassionem disponit. Nam secundum philosophum ubi supra. propter huiusmodi retractionem spiritus ab exterioribus ad interiora. planctivi per eam efficiuntur homines et quasi contracti. Unde et iste tonus ubi supra alatus depingitur et armatus. alatus siquidem, eo quod in sua origine et in versibus responsoriorum quasi volare statim incipit vel quasi volando incedere. sicut patet in .antiphona. *Veterem hominem* et aliis cantibus sibi similibus. Armatus vero, eo quod quasi preliator aliquando durius et gravius. aliquando vero [53] velocius atque securius, nunc vero altius et quasi planctuosus ut dicitur ibidem sonat in modulis.

[1.4.18]

¶ Armonie autem quinti toni et sexti ad mollitiem magis sive lasciviam videntur disponere. et hoc forte sicut predictus expositor et quidam alii dicunt propter semitonia que in eorum compositione frequenter occurrunt. nam .b. molli vel rotundo sepe cantus istorum tonorum utuntur. Unde et sextus tonus qui inter ipsos tamquam magis delectabilis et voluptuosus habetur. et ad quandam mentis lasciviam ut dictum est videtur disponere. et per consequens ad amorem lanceatus ideo fortassis depingitur transfixa videlicet per pectus lancea fracta tamen, eo quod vulnus illud non mortem inferat [75v] sed delectationem potius et amorem. iuxta illud cantici canticorum. Vulnerasti cor meum soror mea sponsa et cetera. Precipue vero versus Responsoriorum istius toni pre ceteris delectabiliores existunt. quia ut plurimum totam latitudinem sui toni sub et supra comprehendunt pulcherrime et includunt. ut apparet in versiculis illis. *Potestas eius potestas eterna. Deponet omnes iniquitates nostras* et eorum similibus. Quintus etiam tonus qui et nudus depingitur. eo videlicet quod sonis modicis ac raris frequenter versum faciat currere quasi nudum, tenet in manu cignum qui olor dicitur. qui in fine suo aliquid dulce canit. per quod istius toni melodia satis congrue designatur.

---

[84] ereptis *corrected to* erectis **H2**.

this where next to the properties and the effects of tones images of them are portrayed. That tone, namely the third, because of this kind of strong beating in the voices and eager motion in the spirits, as much in verses as in measures, now sounds lower now higher, is depicted riding a horse with a certain fury, with hair bristling and streaming in the wind, as if proudly and leaping in the way of a rider.

[1.4.17]
But the melodic quality of the seventh tone—which the Philosopher, as above, calls the Mixolydian on account of the great height that it has in pitch, because it sometimes reaches as far as a'-superacute, that is, the second a'-lamire, to which none of the other tones ascends—recalls or draws back the spirit from exterior things to interior ones in some way. This is not, however, so strongly as the melody of the third or Phrygian tone, and thus it does not dispose towards rapture or audacity or anger, but rather to mercy and compassion.[251] For according to the Philosopher as above, people are made mournful through it and as if withdrawn, on account of the retreat of the spirit in this way from exterior things to interior ones.[252] And hence, that tone is depicted as above as winged and armed. Winged indeed in that, in its origin and in the verses of the responsories, it immediately begins as if flying or to advance as if flying, as is clear in the antiphon *Veterem hominem* and other chants similar to it.[tt] Armed indeed, since sometimes in measures it sounds harder and graver, just like a warrior, some times indeed speedier and more carefree, other times indeed higher and as if mournful, as is mentioned in the same place.

[1.4.18]
Melodic qualities of the fifth and sixth tone, however, seem to dispose more to softness or sensuousness. This is perhaps just as the commentator mentioned above and certain others say, because of the semitones that frequently occur in their structure,[253] for chants of these tones often use soft or round b. Hence the sixth tone, which of the two is held to be more delectable and voluptuous, seems to dispose towards a certain sensuousness of mind, as has been said, and consequently towards love. Perhaps therefore it is depicted as a man pierced in this way, that is to say, by a lance driven through his chest but broken, since that wound does not bring death but rather delight and love, as in that [verse] of the *Song of Songs*: "You have wounded my heart, my sister, wife" etc.[254] Indeed, the verses of the responsories of this tone (sixth) especially, are more delightful than the others, because, as much as possible, they very beautifully comprehend and embrace the whole range of their tone below and above,

[tt] Sunday within the Octave of Epiphany: BnF lat. 17296 f. 50r:

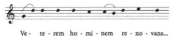

Ve - te - rem ho - mi - nem re - no - vans...

[1.4.19]

¶ Armoni[e][85] vero secundi et octavi toni ad tristitiam magis vel merorem et luc-
tum incitare videntur. et hoc forte propter quandam tarditatem quam in sua pro-
gressione vel motu necnon propter duritiem quandam et asperitatem quam in sua
compositione videntur habere. Unde et secundus tonus pavonem sagitta iugula-
tum tenere in manu depingitur. que avis vocem habet terribilem. et octavus tenet
in manu dextera nudum ensem. que profecto signa sunt non letitie sed magis tristitie et meroris. Et inde est quod cantus illi ecclesiastici qui dicuntur tractus qui sunt
cantus lugubres. utpote qui in missa pro mortuis et in illis temporibus in quibus
sancta mater ecclesia cantus deponendo letitie cantus tristitie vel meroris assumit
consueverunt cantari, puta a .lxx[a]. usque ad pascha, communiter et quasi omnes
sunt istius vel illius toni secundi videlicet vel octavi. secundi. ut *Qui habitat. Deus
deus meus respice. Ave maria. Ecce vir prudens* et huiusmodi. octavi vero ut *De
profundis. Sicut cervus. Qui seminant. Sepe expugnaverunt.* et consimiles.

---

[85] Armonia **H1**.

as appears in those versicles *Potestas eius potestas eterna*,[uu] *Deponet omnes iniquitates nostras*[vv] and the likes of them. Also, the fifth tone, which is depicted unencumbered, in that it often makes a verse run, as if naked, with measured and spare sounds, holds a swan [*cignus*] in its hand, called the swan [*olor*] that sings something sweetly at its end, by which melody of this tone is fittingly enough denoted.

[1.4.19]

Now the melodic qualities of the second and eighth tones seem to incite towards sadness more, or to sorrow and grief;[255] this may be because of a certain slowness that there is in their progression or motion, also because of a certain hardness and severity that they seem to have in their construction. And hence the second tone is depicted as holding in its hand a peacock with its throat pierced by an arrow—this bird has a frightful voice—and the eighth holds a drawn sword in its right hand. These certainly are not signs of joy but rather of sadness and sorrow. And so it is because those ecclesiastical chants that are called Tracts, which are mournful chants such as those in the Mass for the Dead,[256] are customarily sung in those seasons namely from Septuagesima up to Easter when Holy Mother Church, putting aside chants of happiness, takes up chants of sadness or sorrow. In general these are all either of the former or latter tone, namely of the second or the eighth: of the second, as with *Qui habitat*,[ww] *Deus deus meus respice*,[xx] *Ave maria*,[yy] *Ecce vir prudens*[zz] and the like, and of the eighth, as with *De profundis*,[aaa] *Sicut cervus*,[bbb] *Qui seminant*,[ccc] *Sepe expugnaverunt*[ddd] and the like.

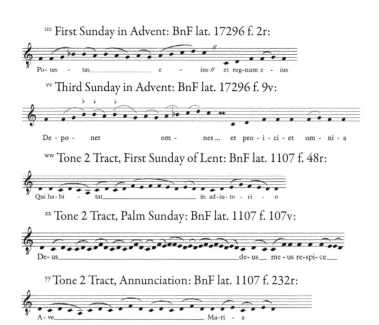

[uu] First Sunday in Advent: BnF lat. 17296 f. 2r:

Po- tes - tas ___ e - ius // et reg-num e - ius

[vv] Third Sunday in Advent: BnF lat. 17296 f. 9v:

De - po - net om - nes ... et pro - i - ci - et om - ni - a

[ww] Tone 2 Tract, First Sunday of Lent: BnF lat. 1107 f. 48r:

Qui ha - bi - tat ___ in ad-iu- to - ri - o

[xx] Tone 2 Tract, Palm Sunday: BnF lat. 1107 f. 107v:

De- us ___ de- us ___ me - us re-spi- ce ___

[yy] Tone 2 Tract, Annunciation: BnF lat. 1107 f. 232r:

A - ve ___ Ma-ri - a

[1.4.20]

¶ Armonie vero primi et quarti toni tamquam mediocriter se habentes, ad virtutem que consistit in medio magis videntur disponere quam alie precedentes. et
maxime melodia primi toni quam philosophus doristam appellat. de qua, ut dicit,
confitentur omnes, quod maxime sit moralis. morem enim magis habet virilem,
stabilissimaque existit. et per consequens convenit cum virtute, ad quam videlicet in hijs que sunt secundum rationem requiritur mentis constantia. Quod enim
armonia toni istius in medio se teneat, ex hoc apparet, quod non est ita excellenter
acuta sicut armonie quinti et septimi. nec ita fortiter percutere videtur spiritus et
movere sicut armonia tertii [**76r**] sed nec ita depressa est vel gravis sicut armonie
secundi. quarti. sexti. vel octavi. Unde etiam tonus iste non solum propter sui
primitatem vel auctoritatem immo forte propter approximationem seu propinqui-
tatem maiorem quam habet ut dictum est ad virtutem et mores. tamquam ceteris
virtuosior. atque ornatior, coronam habere in capite et vexillum in manu tenere
depingitur ubi supra.

[1.4.21]

¶ Alma etiam mater ecclesia que celesti et superne ierusalem que secundum apostolum mater est omnium nostrorum ecclesie scilicet triumphanti ut humana sinit
mortalitas se conformans modis omnibus quibus potest suum nititur laudare
iugiter creatorem, quamvis omnium melodiis tonorum alternatim utatur, precipue

[1.4.20]

Indeed, the melodic qualities of the first and fourth tone, as if keeping to a middle path, seem to dispose more than the others preceding towards virtue, which consists in the mean. This applies most of all, to the melody of the first tone. This the Philosopher calls *Dorian*, concerning which, as he says, all confess that it is highly moral.[257] For it is more virile and is most stable, and consequently it fits with virtue, for which, clearly, constancy of mind is required in those things that are rational.[258] For since the melodic quality of this tone maintains moderation, from this it is clear that it is not in this way especially high like the melodic qualities of the fifth and the seventh,[259] nor does it seem to hammer and move spirits strongly,[260] as with the melodic quality of the third,[261] but neither is it depressed or low as in the melodic quality of the second, fourth, sixth or eighth.[262] Thus also this tone is depicted with a crown on its head and holding a banner in its hand not only on account of its primacy or authority, but also perhaps because of its greater approximation or closeness, to virtue and behavior, as if it were more virtuous than the others and more ornate, as was said above.

[1.4.21]

Nurturing Mother Church, which is in the celestial and supernal Jerusalem, and which according to the Apostle is the mother of us all,[263] namely the Church Triumphant, adapting to all the ways it can as far as human mortality allows, strives continually to praise the Creator. Yet it uses melodies of all the tones by turn, especially,

[zz] Tone 2 Tract, St. Hilary: BnF lat. 17329 f. 86r

Ec-ce vir___ pru - dens

[aaa] Tone 8 Tract, Septuagesima Sunday: BnF lat. 1107 f. 36r:

De pro- fun - dis___ cla - - vi ad___ te

[bbb] Tone 8 Tract, Holy Saturday: BnF lat. 1107 f. 138v:

Si-cut cer - vus___ de - si - de-rat

[ccc] Tone 8 Tract, St. Agatha: BnF lat. 1107 f. 225v:

Qui se - mi - - - nant

[ddd] Tone 8 Tract, Passion Sunday (Fifth Sunday of Lent): BnF lat. 1107 f. 97r:

Se- pe___ ex - pug- na - ve- runt___ me

tamen cantibus primi toni. et post eos cantibus quarti toni. tamquam videlicet temperatis et sobriis atque simplicibus magisque ad medium et virtutem reductis. Nam et simbolum patrum quod cantatur in missa, et himnus *Te deum laudamus* quem sicut testatur honorius in speculo ecclesie augustinus et ambrosius in baptizatione ipsius augustini alternatim composuisse dicuntur. et *gloria in excelsis* quod cantatur in festis precipuis, multique cantus alii sobrii, huiusmodi quarti toni esse noscuntur. Unde et iste quartus tonus non superbe nec erectis[86] a vento capillis ut tertius sed simpliciter ac modeste mulo qui simplicior et mitior est equo sedere depingitur ubi supra, tamquam. scilicet. respectu tertii toni mediocriter se habens. et ab eius superba quodammodo impetuositate declinans.

[1.4.22]

¶ Sciendum est autem quod licet posteriores modernique musici vel cantores qui ecclesiasticos cantus ultimo composuisse videntur plerumque secundum ordinem octo tonorum processerint. et eum maxime in antiphonis responsoriisque nocturnis servaverint, ut apparet in hystoria sancte trinitatis. Marie magdalene. beati nicholai. Iudovici. Augustini. Katerine. multisque aliis. presertim quando eodem cantantur ordine quo fuerunt composite. et sicut illi qui novem lectionibus sunt contenti eas decantare noscuntur. Antiquiores tamen et primi cantores de tali ordine qui potius ad ornatum quemdam vel decorem quam ad necessitatem divini officii introductus videtur. raro vel numquam videntur curasse eo forte quod ad mediocritatem ac sobrietatem cantuum vel etiam qualitatem materie super quam cantus ecclesiasticos fundaverunt attendere potius videbantur. Sicut enim ut alibi scribitur sermones exigendi sunt secundum materiam subiectam [**76v**] ita etiam suo modo de ecclesiasticis cantibus debet esse. Decet enim ecclesiasticos cantus materie super quam fundantur non qualitercumque sed convenienter aptari. ita videlicet ut secundum guidonem. capitulo .xv°. ubi supra. sic rerum eventus cantionis imitetur effectus quod in rebus tristibus graviores sint neume idest vocum

---

[86] ereptis *corrected to* erectis **H2**.

however, chants of the first tone and after those, chants of the fourth tone, as clearly temperate and sober and simple and drawing back more to the mean and to virtue. And for both the Creed of the Fathers,^{eee} which is sung in the Mass, and the Hymn *Te deum laudamus*,^{fff} which Augustine and Ambrose are said to have taken turn in composing for the baptism of Augustine himself,[264] (as Honorius confirms in the *Speculum Ecclesie*,)[265] and the *Gloria in excelsis*,^{ggg} sung on special feasts, and many other sober chants of this kind are known to be of the fourth tone. And hence this fourth tone is depicted, as above, not proudly nor with hair streaming in the wind like the third, but simply and modestly seated on a mule, which is more simple and more mild than a horse, holding itself more moderately compared with the third tone and in a certain way turning away from its proud impetuosity.

[1.4.22]

It should be known, however, that although later and modern musicians or cantors, who seem to have composed ecclesiastical chants recently, have generally proceeded according to the order of the eight tones, and they have kept this mainly in the antiphons and night responsories, as appears in the Offices of the Holy Trinity, Mary Magdalene, Blessed Nicholas, Louis, Augustine, Katherine, and many others, especially when they are sung in the same order in which they were composed, and in the way those who are satisfied with nine readings are known to sing them. The ancients and the first cantors, however, who rarely or never seem to have been concerned with such an order, (which seems to have been introduced more for a certain ornament or elegance than for the requirement of the Divine Office) seem to have been concerned more with the moderation and sobriety of chants and also with the quality of the material upon which they based their ecclesiastical chants. For just as elsewhere it is written that expressions are to be crafted according to subject matter,[266] so also it should be in this way for ecclesiastical chants. For it is fitting that ecclesiastical chants be adapted not just in any way but appropriately to the material on which they are founded. Thus clearly, according to Guido in chapter fifteen, as above, the effect of singing imitates the flow of things, namely that in

^{eee} I.e. the Nicene Creed, a Mass chant, which in tone 4 is:

Cre-do in u-num de-um

^{fff} Matins hymn: Melbourne, State Library of Victoria, MS 096.1 [Poissy Antiphonal] f. 396r:

Te de - um lau-da - mus_ te do - mi-nus con-fi - te - mur

^{ggg} Christmas: BnF lat. 17296 f. 24v:

Glo - ri-a in ex-cel - sis de - o

modulationes seu emissiones earum in transquillis autem iocunde. et in rebus prosperis exultantes. Et hoc de proprietate et effectu vel virtute tonorum et armoniarum musice cuius virtus secundum auctores adeo est impenetrabilis et obscura ut secundum guidonem soli divine sapientie ad plenum pateat, ex diversis auctoribus quantum ad theoriam spectat, sufficiat collegisse. Explicit prima pars tractatus de tonis.

[2.0.1]
Incipit secunda pars.
Expedita per dei gratiam prima parte presentis operis in qua videlicet tractatum est utcumque de tonis quantum ad theoricam[87] seu speculationem ipsorum. nunc restat in hac parte secunda tractare de ipsis quantum ad practicam et operationem eorum, declarando. scilicet. per exempla in octo capitulis que secuntur secundum numerum ordinemque tonorum qualiter ipsi toni non solum ad intonationes psalmorum secundum antiphonas et missarum introitus applicari seu adaptari debeant. immo etiam ad quosdam alios cantus ecclesiasticos tam antiphonarii quam gradalis.

[2.0.2]
¶ Verum quia ab intonatione psalmorum inchoando in principio toni cuiuslibet premittenda est quedam .antiphona. ad tonum pertinens cum suo neumate sive neuma. Videndum est primo quid sit neuma. Sciendum est ergo quod neuma quandoque accipitur pro spiritu, et tunc est neutri generis et declinatur hoc neuma .tis. et hoc sive accipiatur[88] pro spiritu qui est tertia in trinitate persona. ut apparet in sequentia illa .*A<u>rea virga*. ubi dicitur .sanctum neuma descendet in te casta. sive etiam in plurali sumptum angelicis attribuatur spiritibus. sicut patet in sequentia illa. *Ad celebres*. ubi dicitur sic .Novies distincta neumatum sunt agmina per te facta.

---

[87] theoriam *Klundert*.   [88] accipitur *corrected to* accipiatur **H2**.

sad matters the neumes—the modulations of pitch or their projection—are lower, in peaceful things they are happy, and in fortunate things they are exultant.[267] And let what has been collected from different authors suffice as far as theory is concerned, about the property and effect or power of the tones and the melodic qualities of music, the power of which is so impenetrable and obscure according to the authors, that according to Guido, it is fully clear to Divine Wisdom alone.[268] Here ends the first part of the tract concerning the tones.

[2.0.1]

The second part begins.

Having completed through the grace of God the first part of the present work, in which the tones have been considered in relation to theory or speculation about them, it now remains in this second part to deal with them in regards to their practice and operation. That is by declaring through example in the eight chapters that follow—according to the number and order of the tones—how those tones ought to be applied or adapted not only to the intonations of the psalms according to the antiphons and introits of masses, but also to certain other ecclesiastical chants as much of the antiphonary as of the gradual.

[2.0.2]

Indeed, because from the start of the intonation of the psalms a certain "antiphon" belonging to that tone is to be placed at the beginning of any tone with its neumes or neume, it should first be seen what a neume is. Therefore, it should be known that neume is sometimes used for "spirit," and then it is of the neuter gender and is declined thus: *neuma, neumatis*.[269] And if it is used for "spirit"—which is the third person in the Trinity, as is clear in that sequence *A[u]rea virga*,[hhh] where it says "the Holy *Neuma* [Spirit] descends upon you, chaste woman"—or whether taken in the plural, it is attributed to angelic spirits, as is clear in that sequence *Ad celebres*,[iii] where it is said thus: "the distinct lines of *neumata* [spirits] have been made through you."

[hhh] Sequence for the Assumption: BnF lat. 1107 f. 364v.

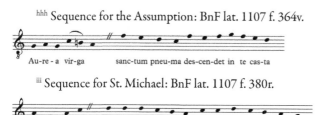

Au - re - a vir-ga   sanc-tum pneu-ma des-cen-det in te cas-ta

[iii] Sequence for St. Michael: BnF lat. 1107 f. 380r.

Ad ce - le-bres   No - vi - es dis-tinc-ta neu-ma-tum sunt ag - mi - na

[2.0.3]

¶ Aliquando vero neuma ad cantum pertinet, et sic quandoque accipitur generaliter et large, videlicet pro debita vocum modulatione sive vocum modulata emissione in quocumque cantu talis fiat modulatio, videlicet sive in antiphonis sive .Responsoriis. sive sequentiis. sive aliis cantibus quibuscumque. et sic accipitur in illa sequentia de natali *Nato canunt omnia.* ubi dicitur in secundo versu. Sillabatim neumata perstringendo organica. et in sequentia. [77r] *Epiphaniam domino.* in illo versu. Omnis nunc caterva tinnulum iungat organi laudibus neuma.

[2.0.4]

¶ Aliquando vero accipitur neuma non ita generaliter et large. sed magis specialiter et stricte, pro illa vocum modulatione et emissione que sequitur cantum antiphone sicut eius cauda vel exitus. quemadmodum in viella videmus quod post stantipedem seu cantum coronatum vel alium quemlibet viellatum, a viellatoribus fit quidam exitus, quem viellatores ipsi modum appellant. Quamvis autem secundum guidonem, neuma ut ad cantum pertinet semper sit generis feminini communius tamen a modernis dicitur quod sit generis neutri, tam in singulari quam in plurali. sicut et neuma acceptum pro spiritu de quo supra dictum est. a quo etiam neuma pro modulatione cantus acceptum et maxime pro modulatione illa que fit supra ultimam sillabam antiphone decantate de qua nunc loquimur propter similitudinem quandam quam ut aliqui dicunt habet ad spiritum nomen traxisse videtur. Sicut enim spiritus ut ipsi dicunt est aliquid simplex et purum. unde et salvator dicit in iohanne spiritus carnem et ossa non habet. ita neuma quodammodo puritatem quandam et simplicitatem habere videtur. nam absque dictionibus et sillabis supra ultimam sillabam antiphone simpliciter et pure prolatum leniter et cum quadam modulatione suavi antiphonam ipsam secundum[89] preteriti cantus tenorem et modum ad finem perducit.

---

[89] seu *corrected to* secundum **H2**.

[2.0.3]

Sometimes a neume belongs to a chant, and thus it is sometimes understood generally and broadly, namely as the required alteration of pitches or the sung projection of pitches, in whatever chant where there is such a melodic passage. For example in either antiphons or responsories or sequences or any other chants, and it is understood thus in that sequence for Christmas, *Nato canunt omnia,*[jjj] where it is said in the second verse, "By stringing together neumes syllable by syllable from the organ," and in the sequence *Epiphaniam domino*[kkk] in that verse "Now the whole band joins the ringing *neuma* of the organ in praises."

[2.0.4]

But sometimes a neume is understood not generally and broadly in this way, but more specifically and strictly as in the changing pitches and melodic passage that follows the chant of an antiphon as its tail or close. We see this in the vielle in that, after an *estampie* or *grand chant* or any other vielle piece, there is a certain closing by vielle players that the vielle players themselves call "mode."[270] According to Guido, "neume," as it pertains to chant, is always of the feminine gender,[271] yet it is more commonly said by moderns that it is of the neuter gender, as much in the singular as in the plural.[272] And just as *neuma* is also understood as spirit, which we spoke about above, so *neuma* is also understood as inflection of chant, and particularly as that melisma that is made upon the last syllable of the antiphon being sung, about which we now speak. It seems to have taken the name because of a certain similarity, which, as some say, it has to spirit.[273] For just as "spirit," as they say, is something simple and pure—and hence the Savior says in John, "the spirit does not have flesh and bone"[274]—thus *neuma* seems to have a certain purity and simplicity in this way, for it leads the antiphon itself to the end according to the tenor and mode of the previous chant without words and syllables above the last syllable of the antiphon, produced simply and slowly and with a certain suave melody.

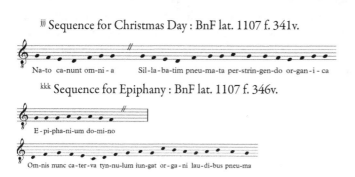

[jjj] Sequence for Christmas Day : BnF lat. 1107 f. 341v.

Na-to ca-nunt om-ni - a   Sil-la-ba-tim pneu-ma-ta per-strin-gen-do or-gan-i - ca

[kkk] Sequence for Epiphany : BnF lat. 1107 f. 346v.

E - pi-pha-ni-um do-mi-no

Om-nis nunc ca-ter-va tyn-nu-lum iun-gat or-ga-ni lau-di-bus pneu-ma

[2.0.5]

¶ Sciendum est igitur quod loquendo de neumate sive neumatibus isto modo. octo sunt neumata secundum numerum octo tonorum. quorum modulationes in tono quolibet exemplariter postmodum describentur. que. scilicet. secundum guidonem reperta fuerunt ad modos in cantibus discernendos. Sicut enim ex aptitudine corporum humanorum sepe que cuius sit tunica vel vestis alia repperimus. ita etiam ut dicit. capitulo. xiijº. ubi supra. ex ipsarum aptitudine neumarum modum cantionis agnoscimus. Mox enim ut dicit postea. ut cum fine alicuius antiphone neumam huius. antiphone. *Primum querite regnum dei* que est primi toni. bene videris convenire. quod sit autenti prothi idest primi toni non est opus aliqualiter dubitare. et sic de ceteris.

[2.0.6]

¶ Licet autem hec neumata que secuntur antiphonas, diebus profestis simplicioribusque festis post duos tantummodo psalmos. scilicet. *benedictus* et *magnificat*. propter eorum auctoritatem quia psalmi euvangelici sunt communiter consueverint decantari, quandoque tamen in festis sollempnibus ad laudem divinam precipue attollendam quodque incomprehensibilis[90] et ineffabilis[91] sit exprimendum. post psalmos [77v] ceteros decantantur. Nam secundum magistrum guillermum altissiodorensem in summa de officio ecclesie. Neuma est quidam iubilus sive iubilatio idest quedam mentis exultatio habita de eternis que ad plenum non potest exprimi nec omnino taceri.

[2.0.7]

¶ A quo autem predicta neumata que secuntur antiphonas ut dictum est reperta fuerint vel a quibus usus eorum in ecclesia primo fuerit introductus, certum usquequaque non habeo. De antiphonis quidem bene legi in cronicis. quod beatus ambrosius qui circa annum domini trecentesimum nonagesimum legitur floruisse ritum canendi antiphonas in ecclesia primus a grecis transtulit ad latinos. qui. scilicet. ritus iamdudum maxime apud grecos inoleverat ex instituto beati ignacii antiocheni episcopi et apostolorum discipuli. de quo et beatus dyonisius in epistula ad policarpum commemorat. sicut inquit divinus ait ignacius. amor meus crucifixus est. hic siquidem divinus ignatius per visionem in celum raptus audivit et vidit quomodo angeli per reciprocationem huiusmodi cantuum videlicet antiphonarum hympnos summe trinitati canebant. Unde etiam et ipse beatus ambrosius post beatum hylarium qui ante ipsum sanctum ambrosium floruisse legitur videlicet circa annos domini. cccᵒˢ. xl. hympnos in ecclesia canendos primus constituit.

---

[90] incomprehensibile *Klundert.*   [91] ineffabile *Klundert.*

[2.0.5]

Therefore, it should be known that, in speaking about a neume or neumes in this way, there are eight neumes according to the number of the eight tones, the melodies of which are subsequently described through example in whatever tone.[275] According to Guido, these were devised for identifying the modes in chants.[276] For just as we have found to whom a tunic or other clothing belongs from its bodily fit, so too, as he says in the thirteenth chapter above, we know the mode of song from the fit of the neumes themselves.[277] For soon, as he says later, as you well see at the end of any antiphon that the neume of this antiphon, *Primum querite regnum dei*,[III] which is of the first tone, fits. There is no need to doubt in any way that it is of the authentic *protus*, that is, of the first tone, and so on for the rest.[278]

[2.0.6]

Although these neumes, which follow antiphons, are in general customarily sung on ordinary days and simpler feasts after only two psalms, namely the *Benedictus* and *Magnificat*, on account of their authority because they are Gospel psalms, they are also sung after other psalms whenever the transcendent and ineffable is to be expressed on solemn feasts, especially for the purpose of giving divine praise.[279] For according to Master William of Auxerre in the *Summa de officio ecclesie*, a neume is a certain joyful melody or jubilation, that is, a certain exultation of the mind habitual from eternity, which cannot be expressed to the full nor completely passed over in silence.[280]

[2.0.7]

I am not certain in every case who devised the aforesaid neumes that follow antiphons, or by whom their use was first introduced into the church. I have certainly read about antiphons in a chronicle that blessed Ambrose, who was reported to have flourished around the year 390 AD, first transferred the use of singing antiphons in the church from the Greeks to the Latins. This use had already long developed, particularly among the Greeks, from its institution by blessed Ignatius, Bishop of Antioch and disciple of the apostles,[281] whom blessed Denis also recalls in the *Letter to Policarp*, as he said the divine Ignatius says, "My love has been crucified."[282] Indeed, the divine Ignatius taken up to heaven through a vision heard this and saw how the angels were singing through the alternation of chants of this kind, as in antiphonal hymns to the Supreme Trinity.[283] Hence, blessed Ambrose himself also first established hymn singing in church after blessed Hilary,[284] who is said to have flourished before Saint Ambrose, namely around 340 AD.

[III] Model antiphon of the first tone with its neuma :

Pri - mum que-ri-te__ re- gnum de - i

[2.0.8]

¶ Legitur etiam in vita beati pape gregorii. qui circa annum domini sexcentesimum legitur floruisse. quod ipse vir domini propter musice compunctionis dulcedinem tamquam cantorum studiosissimus in domo domini more sapientissimi salomonis non solummodo antiphonarium nimis utiliter compilavit. sed etiam scolam cantorum instituit, eis quoque nonnullis datis, prediis duo habitacula preparavit et usque hodie rome lectus[92] eius quo recumbens modulabatur. flagellumque ipsius. quo pueris minabatur veneratione congrua cum antiphonario eius autentico reservatur. unde et postea karolus magnus francorum rex ac patricius romanorum cum antiphonaria gallie vitiata fuisse et a predicto antiphonario rome sibi ostenso discordare videret malens ut ibidem et etiam in quibusdam cronicis legitur. de puro fonte antiphonarii memorati bibere quam de rivo aliorum turbato, duos de suis clericis qui autenticum cantum a romanis discerent et gallos docerent, pape adriano reliquit. per quos postmodum satis eleganter instructos, primo metensis ecclesia que inter ceteras ab illo cantu minus recesserat, et postea tota gallicana ecclesia ad eiusdem cantus [**78r**] dulcedinem fuisse legitur revocata. Quod autem ipse sanctus papa gregorius qui pro certo multa instituit ad decorem divini officii et ornatum spectantia, ista neumata seu neumas primo composuerit aut primus instituerit, adhuc certitudinaliter et ad plenum nescio. Sane scio quod guido monachus de quo supra frequenter memini in .ijo. libro de plana musica quem appellat trocaicum loquens de neumis sive neumatibus ita dicit. Ita sane procuratum sit antiphonarium per apulienses cunctos et vicinos calabros. Quibus tales misit neumas per paulum gregorius. Sed hec verba guidonis utrum de predictis neumatibus sive neumis intelligi debeant, aut potius de notis vel notulis quas guido predictus sepe neumas appellat et per quas in antiphonariis et aliis libris notatis voces musice designantur, certum non habeo. Posset tamen videri aliquibus ea ratione de[93] utrisque supradicta verba probabiliter posse intelligi, quod specialem expressam de utrisque paulo ante fecerat mentionem.

---

[92] letus *corrected to* lectus **H2**.   [93] Letter u *at end of line, deleted.*

[2.0.8]

For one also reads in the *Life of Blessed Pope Gregory*, who is said to have flour-ished around 600 AD,[285] that very man of the Lord, most studious in the house of the Lord in the manner of the most wise Solomon, because of the sweet-ness of the force of music as much as of chant, not only composed a very useful antiphonary, but also established a school of singers. When some things had been donated to them, he prepared two dwellings on the estates. To this day his bed at Rome (where he used to sing lying down) and his whip (with which he used to threaten the boys) is preserved with fitting veneration together with his authentic antiphonary.[286] Hence afterwards, Charlemagne, King of the Franks and Patrician of the Romans, when he saw that the antiphonary of Gaul had been corrupted and was in discord with the aforesaid antiphonary shown to him in Rome,[287] prefer-ring, to drink from the pure fountain of the aforementioned antiphonary rather than from the turgid river of the others,[288] as is read in the same place and also in certain chronicles,[289] left two of his clerics with Pope Adrian to learn the authentic chant from the Romans in order to teach the Gauls. Afterwards, through those who had been sufficiently well instructed, first the church of Metz, which of the rest had departed less from that chant, and later the whole Gallic church is reported to have been called back to the sweetness of that chant.[290] I still do not know with certainty or fully that holy Pope Gregory himself, who certainly established many things concerning the beauty and adornment of the Divine Office, composed or first established these *neumata* or neumes. Indeed, I know that the monk Guido, whom I have frequently recalled above, said as follows speaking of neumes or *neu-mata* in the second book on plain chant, which he calls the *Trocaicus*: "So let an antiphonary be appropriately administered among all the Apulians and neigh-boring Calabrians, to whom Gregory sent such neumes through Paul."[291] But I am not certain whether these words of Guido ought to be understood as being about the aforesaid *neumata* or neumes, or rather about notes or *notulae*, which the aforesaid Guido often calls neumes,[292] and through which musical pitches are depicted in antiphonaries and other notated books. It can seem to some people however, that for this reason the above words can plausibly be understood about both, because he made express, special mention of both a little earlier.[293]

[2.0.9]

Ita videlicet ut ea sic intelligendo beatus gregorius apuliensibus et calabris per paulum quem guido commemorat et neumata sepedicta transmiserit, et quomodo[94] quibusque notis vel notulis antiphonarium neumare idest notare deberent per eundem docuerit. Cui sententie illud etiam attestari videtur, quod aliqui tractantes de tonis, hunc venerabilem et sacrum doctorem quemdam librum de arte tonorum edidisse et a boetio eliciusse dicunt in quo predicta neumata continentur. Sed et communis usus loquentium, octo tonos sepedicto doctori attribuit communiter et ascribit. Ita ut probabiliter possit dici predicta neumata ab ipso potius instituta fuisse quam ab aliquo subsequentium musicorum presertim cum guido prefatus qui post ipsum de plana musica tractavit diffusius, ea dicat ante tempus suum fuisse reperta. Librum autem de tonis quem ut dictum est ab ipso editum quidam musici asseverant. etsi diligenter quesitum sub ipsius intitulatum nomine repperisse hucusque nequiverim. a guidonis tamen vestigiis et aliorum sequentium. musicorum regulis qui ipsius venerandi doctoris imitati sunt vestigia non recessi. fortassis etiam inter multos variosque tractatus quos de ista materia vidi, librum ipsum tenui et attente legi. ignorans tamen aut nescius cuius esset. Verum quia de istis neumatibus aliqualiter iam disgressi sumus, ad operationem tonorum deinceps accedentes, primo de [**78v**] intonatione psalmorum aliqua breviter videamus.

[2.0.10]

¶ Notandum est igitur quod circa intonationem cuiuslibet psalmi tria sunt precipue consideranda. scilicet. principium. mediatio sive medium. atque finis. Quantum ad principium intonandi sciendum est quod primus tonus et sextus inter se conveniunt et ab aliis differunt. Similiter. ij^{us}. iii^{us}. et. viij^{us}. inter se quoad principium intonandi conveniunt et ab aliis differunt. quilibet vero ceterorum trium tonorum habet specialem sibique proprium et a predictis quinque distinctum modum intonandi quoad principium. Et hec patent in versibus sequentibus, qui de principiis intonandi dant regulam generalem.

[2.0.11]

¶ Primo cum sexto .fa. sol. la. semper habeto. Tertius octavus .ut. re. fa. sicque secundus. La. sol. la. Quartus .ut. mi. sol. sit tibi quintus. Septimus est .mi. fa. sol. sic omnes esse recordor. Vel sic aliter et in idem redit.

---

[94] *Repeated* et quomodo *struck through.*

[2.0.9]

Thus, for understanding these things in this way, blessed Gregory both sent the oft-mentioned *neumata* to the Apulians and Calabrians through Paul (whom Guido recalls),[294] and also taught through him how and with what notes or *notulae* they ought to "neume," that is notate, an antiphonary. That also seems to confirm this opinion because, some people dealing with the tones say that this venerable and holy doctor published a book about the art of the tones in which the aforementioned neumes are contained.[295] But the common usage of speakers generally attributes and ascribes the eight tones to the oft-mentioned doctor. As a result, the aforesaid neumes can reasonably be said to have been established by him [Gregory] rather than by any of the later musicians, especially since the said Guido, who dealt more widely with plainchant after him, said that these things had been discovered before his own time.[296] Certain musicians had asserted that the book about the tones was produced by him [Gregory], as was said above. Although I have looked for the work attributed to his name, I have been unable to find it. I have not retreated from the paths of Guido and the rules of other following musicians who imitated the paths of the venerable doctor himself. Perhaps I have even held the very book and read it attentively amongst the many and various treatises that I have seen about this matter, yet unaware or not knowing whose it was. Indeed, because we have digressed somewhat concerning these neumes, let us, turning next to the operation of the tones first look briefly at certain things about the intonation of the psalms.

[2.0.10]

It should be noted, therefore, that three things in particular are to be considered concerning the intonation of any psalm, namely the beginning, the mediant or middle part, and the end.[297] As regards the beginning of the intonation, it should be known that the first tone and the sixth agree with each other and differ from the others. Likewise the second, third, and eighth agree amongst themselves as regards the beginning of the intonation and differ from others. Indeed, as regards the beginning, any of the other three tones has a special way of intoning proper to itself and distinct from the aforesaid five. And these things are clear in the following verses, which give a general rule for the beginnings of intoning:

[2.0.11]

"In the first with the sixth you shall always have fa sol la. The third and the eighth, and also the second, ut re fa. La sol la, fourth, fifth shall be ut mi sol for you. The seventh is mi fa sol, thus I remember them all to be."[298] It comes to the same thing otherwise, thus:

[2.0.12]

¶ Primo cum sexto cantu .fa. sol. la. teneto. Tertius octavus .ut. re. fa. sicque secundus. Septimus incipiet . mi. fa. sol. Quartusque .la. sol. la. Hunc quintum dicas quem. fa. la. re. fa. bene cantas.

[2.0.13]

¶ Quantum autem ad mediationem sive medium intonandi. Primus tonus sextus et septimus inter se conveniunt et ab aliis differunt. Similiter .ii^us. quintus et octavus inter se conveniunt quoad medium intonandi et ab aliis differunt. quisque vero aliorum duorum habet medium intonandi speciale sibique proprium et a sex tonis predictis differens ac distinctum. ut apparet in tribus versibus sequentibus qui circa medium intonandi dant regulam generalem.

[2.0.14]

¶ Septimus et sextus dant. fa. mi. re. mi. quoque primus. Quintus et octavus. fa. fa. sol. fa. sicque secundus. Sol. fa. mi. fa. tertius. re. ut. re. mi. re. quartus. Et iste quidem regule de modo intonandi. psalmos. quantum ad principium et medium sive mediationem eorum vere sunt, quando. psalmi. simpliciter intonantur, et per consequens in omnibus psalmis exceptis duobus. scilicet benedictus ad laudes. et magnificat ad vesperas. qui ut supra dictum est propter eorum reverentiam quia psalmi euvangelici sunt sollempniter intonantur. Qualiter autem isti duo debeant sollempniter intonari postea in exemplis toni cuiuslibet apparebit. Principia tamen intonationis ipsorum describuntur ab aliquibus in istis octo dictionibus que secuntur et deserviunt per ordinem octo tonis. ita videlicet ut prima dictio deserviat primo tono. et secunda secundo. et sic de ceteris.

[2.0.15]

¶ Pater. In filio. [**79r**] Filius. in patre. Spiritus. Sanctus. Ab utroque. Procedens.

Pa - ter.   In fi - li - o.   Fi - li - us.   In pa - tre.

Spi - ri - tus.   Sanc - tus.   Ab ut - ro - que.   Pro - ce - dens.

[2.0.12]
You shall have fa sol la in the first with the sixth chant. The third and the eighth and also the second: ut re fa. Let the seventh begin mi fa sol, and the fourth la sol la. You may say for the fifth what you sing well as: fa la re fa.[299]

[2.0.13]
As regards the mediant or middle part of intoning, the first, sixth and seventh tones agree amongst themselves and differ from the others. Likewise, the second, fifth and eighth agree amongst themselves as regards the middle part of intoning and differ from the others.[300] Indeed each of the other two has the middle part of intoning particular to itself and different and distinct from the aforesaid six tones, as will be clear in the three following verses, which give the general rule about the middle part of intoning:

[2.0.14]
The seventh and the sixth give fa mi re mi, likewise the first. The fifth and the eighth, fa fa sol fa and similarly the second. Sol fa mi fa the third, re ut re mi re the fourth.[301] And indeed, these rules concerning the way of intoning the psalms are true as regards their beginning and the middle part or median or when the psalms are intoned simply. Consequently this happens in all psalms except two, namely the Benedictus at Lauds and the Magnificat at Vespers, which, as said above, are intoned solemnly on account of reverence for them since they are Gospel psalms. How these two ought to be solemnly intoned will appear later in examples of whatever tone. The beginnings of the intonations themselves, however, are described by some in those eight phrases that follow and apply to the eight tones in order. Thus it is clear that the first phrase applies to the first tone, and the second to the second, and thus for the rest:[302]

[2.0.15]
The Father is in the Son, the Son in the Father, the Holy Spirit proceeding from both.

[See Appendix II for clarification of this mnemonic.]

[2.0.16]

❡ Quamvis autem usus noster quantum ad ea que dicta sunt de intonatione psalmorum tam simplici quam sollempni cum usu aliarum ecclesiarum sepe conveniat, inchoando scilicet et etiam mediando. in modo tamen intonandi sollempniter secundum differentias aliquorum tonorum non omnino concordat. nam secundum usum nostrum idem est modus intonandi tam simpliciter quam sollempniter secundum aliquas differentias toni quarti et octavi. ut postea videbitur plenius suo loco. Cum tamen apud alios modus intonandi sollempniter in omnibus differentiis istorum duorum tonorum a simplici sit diversus. sicut patet intuenti tractatus aliorum de tonis.

[2.0.17]

❡ Quantum autem ad finem intonandi sciendum est quod fines intonationum seu differentie quas communiter appellamus seculorum amen. non solum in diversis tonis immo etiam frequenter in eodem tono sunt varie ac diverse. nec certum aut determinatum earum numerum aliqua musice artis regula declaravit. immo secundum quod in diversis ecclesiis sunt usus diversi varieque consuetudines, secundum hoc etiam alias et alias differentias constat esse. pluresque interdum in una ecclesia. in alia vero pauciores, secundum diversitatem consuetudinis et usus ipsarum. Sicut autem alii in hac parte ecclesie sue consuetudinem et usum secuntur communiter. ita etiam quantum ad modum intonandi consuetudinem in monasterio nostro hactenus approbatam in hiis precipue que regulis musice artis aut eis que supra de tonis sunt tradita non repugnant, sequi principaliter hic intendo. De utroque nimirum curam gerere vir ecclesiasticus debet. ut. scilicet. et artis regulas consuetudini cuilibet vel usui non postponat. et tamen a consuetudine in ecclesia sua rationabiliter[95] observata nimis de facili non recedat. Sicut enim ab artis regulis declinare non debet ita cum occasione modica et que arti omnino non obviat, ab antiqua consuetudine statim resilire non decet. Sed eidem se ipsum potius conformare. et in ea frequenti exercitio et usu laudabiliter exercere. Nam secundum guidonem predictum. capitulo .xvij. ubi supra. Omnis cantus more puri argenti quo magis utitur coloratur, in tantum. scilicet. ut quod modo alicui fortassis displicet. ab eodem postmodum quasi lima politum per usum et consuetudinem collaudetur.

---

[95] rotionabiliter **H1**.

[2.0.16]

Although our use may often agree with the use of other churches regarding those things which have been said concerning the intonation of the psalms, both simple and solemn, namely in the beginning and also the middle part, yet it does not agree at all in the way of intoning solemnly according to the *differentiae* of some tones. For according to our use, the way of intoning, both simply and solemnly, is the same according to certain *differentiae* of the fourth and eighth tone, as will be seen more fully later in its place. Amongst others, however, the way of intoning solemnly in all the *differentiae* of those two tones, may be different from simple intoning, as is clear to one looking at the treatises of others on the tones.

[2.0.17]

With regard to the end of intonings it should be known that the ends of intonations, or *differentiae*, which we commonly call *seculorum amen,* are not only varied in the different tones but even frequently within the same tone.[303] Neither has any rule of the art of music decreed a specific or fixed number of them. Rather, just as there are diverse uses and various customs in the different churches, so also it happens that *differentiae* vary one from another. Sometimes there are more in one church but fewer in another, according to their diversity of custom and use. For just as others commonly follow the custom and use of their church in this respect, so also, as regards the way of intoning, I intend here to principally follow the custom approved in our monastery up to now. This is in regard to these things that do not especially oppose the rules of the art of music or those things about the tones that have been mentioned above. A churchman should certainly be concerned for both, so that he neither subordinates the rules of the art to any custom or use, nor, yet recedes from a custom reasonably observed in his church. For just as he ought not depart from the rules of the art so, when on a specific occasion and one that does not follow the art at all, it is not appropriate to depart immediately from ancient practice. But let him rather conform himself to the art and train himself in it worthily by frequent exercise and practice. For according to Guido in chapter seventeen as noted above, all chant is burnished like pure silver, the more it is used. In other words it may perhaps somehow displease someone but later be praised by the same as if it had been polished with a file through use and custom.[304]

[2.0.18]

¶ Notandum est tamen quod, si quis regulas de intonatione psalmorum quantum ad principium et mediationem superius datas velit [**79v**] advertere diligenter, ex ipsis perpendere manifeste poterit quod primus tonus et sextus in mediatione sua computando a suo discursu communi minus elevantur quam ceteri toni. Elevatio namque et ascensus duorum predictorum tonorum ultra .bfabmi. cum .b. rotundo vel molli notatum nequaquam extenditur. communis autem eorum discursus est in primo .alamire. inter que duo. scilicet. alamire. et .bfabmi. cum .b. molli. notato minus semitonium tantummodo repperitur ut in prima parte huius operis plenius est ostensum. Alii vero toni supra suum communem discursum ad minus per unum tonum integrum elevantur. sicut patet discursum et mediationem cuilibet secundum predictas regulas intuenti. Et inde fortassis accidit quod sicut illi psalmi qui equaliter magis et quasi sub uni sono in directum canuntur sicut fit ad horas tempore paschali non ita cito deprimuntur aut cadunt ut ceteri. ita etiam et psalmi qui secundum duos tonos predictos cantantur non ita de facili deprimuntur aut gravantur ut illi qui secundum tonos ceteros intonantur tamquam .scilicet. ab equalitate[96] unisoni minus distantes suamque mediationem ut dictum est a suo communi discursu per solum semitonium elevantes.

[2.0.19]

Ex quo patet ulterius. quod sicut bonus cantor et expertus si antiphonam aut alium cantum moderate et artificialiter velit incipere. ascensum illius et descensum debet sollicite previdere. sic et illi qui psalmos intonant, cuius toni sit .antiphona. secundum quam intonandus est psalmus previdere debent mediocriter .scilicet. secundum duos tonos predictos, Altius vero secundum ceteros intonando. et maxime apud illos hoc observari debet, apud quos psalmodia deponitur citius et gravatur. Quamvis enim descensus huiusmodi ex vitio cantus vel defectu tonorum nequaquam eveniat, immo solum ex cantorum vitio vel defectu. ita tamen apud quosdam partim quidem ex ignorantia, partim[97] ex consuetudine que dicenda est potius corruptela, partim vero ex quadam mollitie et quasi sompnolenta pigritia paulatim cadentes et deorsum tendentes huiusmodi psalmodie descensus adeo notabilis repperitur, ut eam interdum ante finem etiam modici psalmi per integrum diapason et ultra frequenter in profundo dimersam valeas experiri. et maxime quando secundum tonos alios a duobus supradictis discurrit. Quod profecto non est dubium tam deo quam hominibus non mediocriter displicere. et quicumque in hoc casu culpabiles se esse conspiciunt, errorem huiusmodi deberent corrigere. et se ipsos in hac parte dirigere dictumque abusum in bonum [**80r**] quantotius immutare.

[96] a qualitate *corrected to* ab equalitate   [97] partim *omitted Klundert.*
H2.

[2.0.18]

It is to be noted, however, that if anyone wishes carefully to heed the rules given above concerning the intonation of psalms in the beginning and middle part, he will clearly be able to assess from these that, counting from the usual reciting tone, the first tone and the sixth are less elevated in their middle part than other tones. For the elevation and ascent of these two tones does not extend beyond b-fa/b-mi—notated with round or soft b—their usual reciting tone is on the first a-lamire, between which two (namely a-lamire and b-fa/b-mi with soft b notated), however, is found the minor semitone, as has been shown more fully in the first part of this work. But the other tones are elevated above their usual reciting tone by at least one whole tone, just as is evident to anyone considering the reciting tone and mediant note according to the aforesaid rules.[305] And hence perhaps it happens that just as those psalms that are sung more evenly and as if directed at a single sound, as, in the hours of the Easter season, they are not lowered or fall as quickly as the others. Thus also the psalms that are sung according to the two aforesaid tones are not as easily lowered or pulled down in this way as those that are intoned according to other tones: they are less removed from the evenness of one sound, raising their mediant note by only a semitone from their usual reciting tone, as was said.

[2.0.19]

From which it is further clear that, a good and expert cantor—if he wishes to begin an antiphon or other chant moderately or skillfully—ought to be concerned to look ahead to its ascent and descent. Thus those who intone the psalms ought ordinarily to envision of which tone the antiphon may be, according to which the psalm is to be intoned, namely according to these two tones [first and sixth]. But for the others in intoning higher and, especially for them, the following ought to be observed: for them, psalmody is lowered more quickly and falls. For a descent of this kind never happens from a fault of the chant or weakness of the tones, but rather only from a fault or weakness of the singers. Thus, among certain people, partly from ignorance, partly from custom, which should rather be called corruption, partly indeed from a certain weakness and a kind of sleepy sloth, a descent of this kind of psalmody falling little by little and tending downwards, is found to be truly conspicuous. So you may find it plunged into the depths through the whole octave, and frequently further, before the ending of even a modest psalm, and especially when it wanders off according to tones other than the two abovementioned. When this happens there really is no doubt that it displeases God as much as humans in no small way, and whoever sees themselves to be culpable in this matter ought to correct an error of this kind and steer themselves in this respect and turn the aforesaid abuse into good as much as possible.

[2.0.20]

¶ Sciendum est igitur quod quantum colligere potui ex nostro antiphonario et gradali, primi toni secundum usum nostrum quantum ad antiphonas novem sunt differentie. et quantum ad officia sive introitus due. Secundi vero toni quantum ad .antiphonas. una tantum. et similiter quantum ad introitus unica. Tertii autem toni quantum ad .antiphonas. due sunt differentie. et quantum ad introitus una tantum. Quarti vero toni quantum ad .antiphonas. sex sunt differentie. quantum autem ad introitus una tantum. Quinti autem toni quantum ad .antiphonas. una tantum est differentia. et similiter quantum ad introitus tantum una. Sexti vero toni etiam quantum ad .antiphonas. unica est differentia. et similiter quantum ad introitus tantum una. Septimi autem quantum ad .antiphonas. quatuor sunt differentie. et quantum ad introitus tantum una. Octavi vero toni similiter quantum ad .antiphonas. quatuor sunt differentie et quantum ad introitus una tantum. De quibus omnibus et qualiter octo toni non solum ad intonationem psalmorum immo etiam ad antiphonas. nocturnalia Responsoria. Invitatoria. venite. hympnos. missarum introitus. Responsoria. alleluia.[98] tractus. sequentias. offerendas. et postcommuniones. adaptari convenienter et applicari debeant. sequendo precipue ut dictum est supra ecclesie nostre consuetudinem et usum per exempla subsequentia plenius apparebit.

[2.1.0]

Capitulum primum in quo ponuntur exempla de primo tono. Antiphona. primi toni cum suo neumate.

Pri - mum que - ri - te   re- gnum dei

Modus intonandi super psalmos.

Pri - mus to - nus sim - pli - ci - ter sic in - ci - pit et sic me - di - a - tur.

So - lemp - ni - ter sic in - ci - pit et sic me - di - a - tur.

---

[98] alleluia *inserted from right margin* **H2**.

[2.0.20]

It should be known, therefore, that as far as I have been able to put together from our antiphonary and gradual, according to our use as far as concerns antiphons, there are nine *differentiae* of the first tone, and as regards *officia* or introits there are two. Of the second tone, as regards antiphons there is only one, and similarly one as regards introits. Of the third tone, there are two *differentiae* as regards antiphons, and only one as regards introits. Of the fourth tone, there are six *differentiae* as regards antiphons, but only one as regards introits. Of the fifth tone, there is only one *differentia* as regards antiphons, and similarly only one as regards introits. Of the sixth tone, there is also a single *differentia* as regards antiphons, and similarly only one as regards introits. Of the seventh, there are four *differentiae* as regards antiphons, and only one as regards introits. Of the eighth tone, there are similarly four *differentiae* as regards antiphons, and only one as regards introits. Concerning all these things and how the eight tones ought to be suitably adapted and applied—not only to the intonation of the psalms but also to antiphons, night responsories, invitatories, *Venites*, hymns, introits of masses, responsories, the Alleluias, Tracts, sequences, offertories and post-communions, especially, as was said above, in following the custom and use of our church—will appear more fully through the following examples.

[2.1.0]

Chapter one, in which are given examples of the first tone. The antiphon of the first tone with its *neumata*:

[Matthew 6:33 provides the text for the model antiphon for tone one.]

The way of intoning upon psalms:

[Simple psalm intonation for the first tone]

[Solemn psalm intonation for the first tone][306]

[2.1.1]
Prima differentia.

Et sic fi - ni - tur. E u o u a   e

[80v] Et ista differentia secundum usum nostrum loquendo debetur antiphonis illis que incipientes a. cfaut ascendunt per .dsolre. superius isto modo.

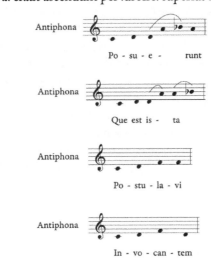

Antiphona

Po - su - e -   runt

vel sic.

Antiphona

Que est is -   ta

vel sic.

Antiphona

Po - stu - la - vi

vel sic.

Antiphona

In - vo - can - tem

vel sic.

Antiphona

Do - mus me - a

vel sic.

Antiphona

Val - de ho - no - ran - dus est

Item illis que incipientes a. dsolre primo descendunt in .cfaut. et postea reascend-unt superius isto modo.

Antiphona

Ec - ce   no - men do - mi - ni

vel sic.

Antiphona

Lo - que - re do - mi - ne

[2.1.1]
The first *differentia*:

[Termination formula with *seculorum amen*]

And this *differentia,* in our way of speaking ought to be assigned to those anti-phons that beginning from C-faut rise through D-solre above, or this way:

[Good Friday : BnF lat. 17296 fol. 133v.]

Or thus:

[Second week of Advent, Saturday : BnF lat. 17296 fol. 9r.]

Or thus:

[Easter Sunday : BnF lat. 17296 fol. 136r.]

Or thus:

[Common of a Confessor : BnF lat. 17296 fol. 280r.]

Or thus:

[First Sunday of Lent : BnF lat. 17296 fol. 100v.]

Or thus:

[St. John the Evangelist : BnF lat. 17296 fol. 32r.]

Likewise for those that, beginning from D-solre, at first descend to C-faut and then re-ascend above in this way:

[First Sunday in Advent : BnF lat. 15181 fol. 106r.]

Or thus:

[First Sunday after Trinity : BnF lat. 17296 fol. 289v.]

vel sic.

Pro - phe - te pre - di - ca - ve - runt

Illis etiam que incipientes a .dsolre. primo ascendunt in. ffaut et postea descendendo iterum reascendunt hoc modo.

Cum ap-pro-pin - qua - ret

vel sic.

Pu - e - ri he - bre - o - rum

Illis quoque que incipientes a .dsolre. statim in alamire saliunt isto modo.

De sy - on

vel etiam ultra sic.

Pre - di - cans

vel sic.

Tan - tam_ gra-ti-am

Antiphona [99]
vel que quasi gradatim ascendu<n>t[100] sic.

Ger - mi - na - vit ra - dix

vel sic.

Lau - da_____ ce - les - - tis

Item debetur eis que incipientes ab. ffaut primo descendunt in. cfaut et sic postea reascendunt.

Antiphona

A - ve ma - ri - a

---

[99] Tamtam *Klundert, here corrected to* Tantam.

[100] ascendut *corrected to* ascendunt *Klundert*

Or thus:

[Fourth week in Advent, Wednesday : BnF lat. 17296 fol. 17r.]

Likewise, those also beginning from D-solre first ascend to F-faut and, after descending, re-ascend again in this way:

[Palm Sunday : BnF lat. 17296 fol. 324r.]

Or thus:

[Palm Sunday : BnF lat. 17296 fol. 125v.]

Also, for those which beginning from D-solre immediately leap to a-lamire in this way:

[Fourth week in Advent, Thursday : BnF lat. 17296 fol. 17r.]

Or even beyond, thus:

[Common of Martyrs : BnF lat. 17296 fol. 276r.]

Or thus:

[St. Benedict: BnF lat. 17296 fol. 79v.]

Or those that likewise gradually ascend thus:

[Octave of Christmas : BnF lat. 17296 fol. 44r.]

Or thus:

[St. Louis : BnF lat. 13239 fols. 383va-397vb.][307]

Likewise, there ought to be assigned to these, those that, beginning from F-faut, at first descend to C-faut and then re-ascend thus:

[Fourth Sunday in Advent : BnF lat. 17296 fol. 13v.]

vel sic.

San - cti - fi - ca - vit

[2.1.2]
[81r] Secunda differentia.

Et sic fi - ni - tur.   E u o u a e

Et ista proprie solum debetur illis antiphonis que incipientes ab ffaut gradatim in dsolre descendunt isto modo. antiphona.

Vo - lo pa - ter

Re - ges thar - sis

[2.1.3]
Tertia differentia.

Et sic fi - ni - tur. E u o u a e

Et ista debetur proprie illis .antiphonis. que incipiunt ab alamire verbi gratia.

Ve - ni - et do - mi - nus

Cla - ma - vi

Fa - cti su - mus

et consimiles.
Item illis que incipientes ab. ffaut statim in alamire saliunt isto modo.

Antiphona

A - per - tis

Or thus:

[Dedication of one virgin: BnF lat. 17296 fol. 287v.]

[2.1.2]
The second *differentia*:

[Termination formula with *seculorum amen*]

And this is properly assigned only to those antiphons that, beginning from F-faut, gradually descend to D-solre in this way:

[Common of a Martyr: BnF lat. 17296 fol. 279r.]

[Epiphany: BnF lat. 17296 fol. 44v.]

[2.1.3]
The third *differentia*:

[Termination formula with *seculorum amen*]

And this ought properly to be assigned to those antiphons that begin from a-lamire, for example:

[Third Sunday in Advent: BnF lat. 17296 fol. 10v.]

[Mondays or Tuesdays throughout the year: BnF lat. 12044 fol. 33v.]

[Tuesdays throughout the year: BnF lat. 12044 fol. 34r.]
and the like.

Likewise to those that, beginning from F-faut, at once jump to a-lamire in this way:

[Epiphany: BnF lat. 17296 fol. 48r.]

[2.1.4]
Quarta differentia.

Et sic fi - ni - tur.   E u o u a e

Et ista debetur proprie illis antiphonis que incipientes ab. ffaut gradatim in alamire ascendunt et gradatim iterum in ffaut descendunt hoc modo.

Antiphona

Ad - iu - to - ri - um nos - trum

Antiphona

Fun - da - men - ta ei - us

[2.1.5]
Quinta differentia.

Et sic fi - ni - tur.   E u o u a e

Et ista debetur proprie illis antiphonis. que incipientes ab. ffaut gradatim cum quadam reflexione ascendunt hoc modo.

Antiphona

Do - mi - nus

Antiphona

La - za - rus

Licet enim statim quandoque non sit in principio antiphone talis reflexio debet tamen sequi postea satis cito isto modo.

Antiphona

Do- mi - ne pu- er__ me-us

Antiphona

Do- mi - ne non sum_ dig - nus

Quandoque etiam debetur hec differentia licet raro antiphone. que sic incipit.

Antiphona

Ex quo fa - cta

[2.1.4]
The fourth *differentia*:

[Termination formula with *seculorum amen*]

And this ought properly to be assigned to those antiphons that, beginning from F-faut, gradually ascend to a-lamire and again gradually descend to F-faut in this way:

[Tuesdays throughout the year: BnF lat. 15181 fol. 191v.]

[Fridays throughout the year: BnF lat. 15181 fol. 195r.]

[2.1.5]
The fifth *differentia*:

[Termination formula with *seculorum amen*]

And this ought properly to be assigned to those antiphons that, beginning from F-faut, gradually ascend with a certain turn in this way:

[Fourth week of Lent, Friday: BnF lat. 15181 fol. 193r.]

[Fourth week of Lent, Friday: BnF lat. 17296 fol. 115v.]

For although whenever there is not such a turn immediately at the beginning of an antiphon, it ought however to follow quite quickly afterwards in this way:

[Thursday in Quinquagesima: BnF lat. 17296 fol. 96v.]

[Thursday in Quinquagesima: BnF lat. 17296 fol. 96v.]

Sometimes this *differentia* ought to also be assigned, albeit rarely, to an antiphon that begins in this way:

[Thursday, fourth week in Advent: BnF lat. 12044 fol. 3v.]

[2.1.6]

[81v] Sexta differentia.

Et sic fi - ni - tur.   E   u   o   u   a   e

Et ista attribuitur tantummodo isti .antiphone.

Antiphona

Lau - da - te do - mi - num de   ce - lis

[2.1.7]

Septima differentia.

Et sic fi - ni - tur.   E   u   o   u   a   e

Et ista differentia debetur .antiphonis. illis que incipientes a .cfaut. sic ascendunt.

Antiphona

Qui ce - lo - rum

vel sic.

Antiphona

Non au - fe - re - tur

vel sic.

Antiphona

O_____ be - a - ta

Item incipientibus in dsolre que primo ascendunt et postea descendentes reascendunt hoc modo.

Antiphona

O____ pa - stor e - ter - ne

vel sic.

Antiphona

Pec - ca - ta   me - a

vel sic.

Antiphona

Di - xit ihe - sus   ad le - gis

[2.1.6]
The sixth *differentia*:

[Termination formula with *seculorum amen*]

And this is to be assigned in such a way to the antiphon:

[Sexagesima Sunday: BnF lat. 17296 fol. 92r.]

[2.1.7]
The seventh *differentia*:

[Termination formula with *seculorum amen*]

And this *differentia* ought to be assigned to those antiphons that, beginning from C-faut, ascend thus:

[Prophets: BnF lat. 17296 fol. 309r.]

Or thus:

[Second week in Advent, Saturday: BnF lat. 17296 fol. 9r.]

Or thus:

[Holy Trinity, Saturday: BnF lat. 17296 fol. 168r.]

Likewise, to those beginning on D-solre that first ascent and, after descending, ascend again in this way:

[St. Nicholas: BnF lat. 17296 fol. 261r.][308]

Or thus:

[Sunday after Epiphany: BnF lat. 17296 fol. 312v.]

Or thus:

[Seventeenth Sunday after Pentecost: BnF lat. 17296 fol. 325v.]

Item illis que incipientes similiter in dsolre econtrario primo descendunt et postea ascendunt isto modo.

Sal - va - tor

vel sic.

Be - a - tus   ste - pha - nus

vel sic.

Quod au - tem

Illis quoque que similiter a .dsolre. incipiunt magis tamen uniformiter quam precedentes ascendunt. ut sic.

O   be - a - te dy - o - ni - si

vel sic.

Vos qui re - li - qui - stis

Item incipientibus ab ffaut. que descendunt et ascendunt hoc modo.

Pa - ter   man - i - fes - ta - vi

vel sic.

Vir - go   glo - ri - o - sa

vel sic.

U - nus   est   e - nim

[2.1.8]
Octava differentia.

Et sic fi - ni - tur.   E   u   o   u   a   e

Likewise to those that, beginning similarly on D-solre, by contrast first descend and then ascend in the same way:

[All Saints: BnF lat. 17296 fol. 243vr.]

or thus:

[St. Stephen: BnF lat. 17296 fol. 27r.]

or thus:

[Sexagesima Sunday: BnF lat. 17296 fol. 92v.]

Also, to those that similarly begin on D-solre ascend more uniformly, however, than the preceding ones, just as this:

[St. Denis: BnF lat. 17296 fol. 152r.]

or thus:

[St. Paul: BnF lat. 17296 fol. 193v.]

Likewise to those beginning from F-faut that descend and ascend in this way:

[Vigil of the Ascension: BnF lat. 17296 fol. 156r.]

or thus:

[St. Cecilia: BnF lat. 17296 fol. 253r.]

or thus:

[Second week of Lent, Tuesday: BnF lat. 17296 fol. 105r.]

[2.1.8]
The eighth *differentia*:

[Termination formula with *seculorum amen*]

[82r] Et ista debetur illis tamen .antiphonis. que incipientes a .cfaut. tres notas super primam sillabam habent isto modo.

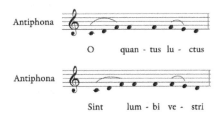

Antiphona

O quan - tus lu - ctus

Antiphona

Sint lum - bi ve - stri

[2.1.9]
Nona differentia.

Et sic fi - ni - tur. E u o u a e

Et ista debetur illis .antiphonis. que incipientes ab ffaut ascendunt et descendunt isto modo.

Antiphona

Cri - sti vir - go

Antiphona

Ip - si so - li

vel hoc modo cum quadam reflexione.

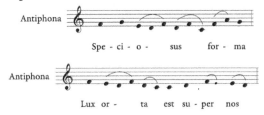

Antiphona

Spe - ci - o - sus for - ma

Antiphona

Lux or - ta est su - per nos

[2.1.10]
Sciendum est tamen quod inter omnes predictas differentias primi toni principaliores et que communius habentur in usu sunt prima et septima. et ideo forte contingit aliquando quamvis raro hoc accidat quod alique antiphone. quibus[101] prima differentia attribuitur simili modo videantur incipere sicut alique alie quibus differentia septima applicatur. Sicut videtur esse de .antiphona.

Antiphona

Ful - ge - bunt iu - sti

[101] cui **H1** *corrected to* quibus *Klundert*

And it ought to be assigned, however, to those antiphons that, beginning from C-faut, have three notes above the first syllable in this way:

[St. Martin: BnF lat. 17296 fol. 251r.]

[All Saints: BnF lat. 17296 fol. 240v.]

[2.1.9]
The ninth *differentia*:

[Termination formula with *seculorum amen*]

And this ought to be assigned to those antiphons that, beginning from F-faut, ascend and descend in this way:

[St. Agnes: BnF lat. 17296 fol. 56r.]

[St. Agnes: BnF lat. 17296 fol. 57r.]

or this way with a certain turn:

[January 1: BnF lat. 17296 fol. 43r.]

[Christmas Day: BnF lat. 17296 fol. 25r.]

[2.1.10]
It must be known, however, that among all the aforesaid *differentiae* of the first tone, the more important and those that are held more commonly in use are the first and the seventh [*differentiae*]. And similarly perhaps it happens sometimes, although rarely, that some antiphons, to which is assigned the first *differentia*, seem to begin in a similar way, as some others to which the seventh *differentia* is applied, just as is seen for the antiphon:

[Holy Innocents: BnF lat. 17296 fol. 38v.]

Cui applicatur prima differentia respectu istius cui applicatur differentia septima.

Ambe enim ut hic patet simili modo incipiunt. Si quis tamen diligenter velit utri-usque progressum inspicere. ita in progressu post sua principia variantur. quod utraque differentie sue convenienter et satis proprie adaptatur. Et quod dico de istis duabus .antiphonis. per respectum ad suas differentias etiam suo modo intel-ligendum arbitror de .antiphonis. et differentiis aliorum tonorum si talem in eis fortasse similitudinem reperiri contingat.

[2.1.11]

Sciendum insuper quod si forte. antiphonas. aliquas huius toni vel ceterorum tonorum inveniri contingat que aliter quam supra dictum est vel infra dicetur incipiant. de hiis tamen exempla ponere non semper curavi. eo quod raro hoc acci-dat. ad illa siquidem que convenienter vel frequenter eveniunt potius quam ad ea que raro contingunt artis regule describuntur.

[82v] Exempla de responsoriis.

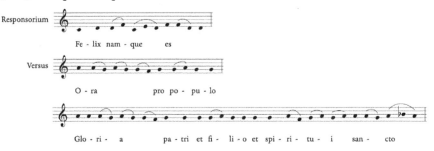

Et nota quod iste modus cantandi in .Responsoriis. non solum predictam gloriam huius toni immo etiam ceterorum tonorum sicut infra in suo ordine notantur communiter a monachis observatur. licet ab aliis ecclesiasticis viris aliter habean-tur in usu. ambianensis tamen ecclesia secundum tonos magistri petri de cruce et exempla que ponit ibidem nostro potius et ceterorum monachorum usui quo ad hoc conformari videtur et nos ipsi.

Exemplum de invitatoriis.

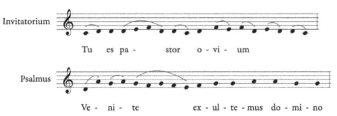

To this is applied the first *differentia*. With respect to the following the seventh *differentia* is applied.

[Sexagesima Sunday: BnF lat. 17296 fol. 92v.]

For both [antiphons], as is clear here, begin in the same way. If anyone, however, wishes to carefully inspect the progression of each, they are varied in progression after their beginnings, because each is adapted appropriately and properly enough to its *differentia*. And what I say about these antiphons with respect to their *differentiae* I also judge to be understood even in its own way concerning the antiphons and *differentiae* of other tones, if perhaps it happens that such a likeness can be found in them.

[2.1.11]

Additionally it should be known that, if perhaps it happens that other antiphons of this tone or of the other tones can be found that begin differently from what was said above or what will be said below, I have not always taken the trouble, however, to present examples of these, because this happens rarely. Indeed, the rules of art are set down for those things that occur consistently or often, rather than for those that occur rarely.

Examples of responsories:

[Immaculate Conception of Mary: BnF lat. 15181 fols. 381r-v.]

And note that this way of singing the aforesaid *Gloria* in responsories, not only of this tone but also of other tones as are noted below in order, is commonly observed by monks, although there is a different use among other churchmen. The church of Amiens, however, according to the tonary of Master Petrus de Cruce and the examples that he puts there, and ourselves, seems to conform to our use and that of other monks.

Example of the invitatory:

[Invitatory *Tu es pastor ovium* St. Peter: BnF lat. 17296 fol. 180v; Psalm *Venite exultemus domino* Purification: BnF lat. 17296 fol. 116r.][309]

Exempla de hympnis.

Modus intonandi in officiis misse.

[2.1.12]
Prima differentia.

Et ista debetur illis officiis que incipiunt. a. cfaut ut.

Item illis que incipiunt a. dsolre. ut.

Item que incipiunt a ffaut.[102] descendendo ut.
[83r]

---

[102] cfaut **H1** *corrected to* ffaut *Klundert.*

Examples of hymns:

[Annunciation: BnF lat. 15181 fol. 467r.]

[All Saints: Melbourne, State Library of Victoria, MS 096.1 [Poissy Antiphonal] fol. 416v (with some slight variations).]

The way of intoning in the introit of the mass:

[Intonation formula for the first tone.]

[2.1.12]
The first *differentia*:

[Termination formula with *seculorum amen*]

And this is assigned to those introits that begin from C-faut, as:

[First week in Advent, Wednesday: BnF lat. 1107 fol. 6v.]

[St. Agatha: BnF lat. 1107 fol. 225r]

Likewise to those that begin from D-solre, as:

[Sexagesima Sunday: BnF lat. 1107 fol. 37r.]

[John the Baptist: BnF lat. 1107 fol. 243r.]

Likewise to those that begin from F-faut descending thus:

[Apostles Philip and James: BnF lat. 1107 fol. 235r.]

[St. Stephen: BnF lat. 1107 fol. 21r.]

Secunda differentia.

Et sic   fi - ni -   tur. E u   o u a   e

Et ista debetur illis officiis que incipiunt ab ffaut. ascendendo ut sic.

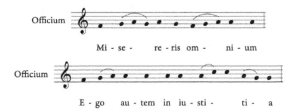

Officium

Mi - se -   re - ris om -   ni - um

Officium

E - go   au - tem in iu - sti -   ti - a

Item illis que incipiunt in alamire. ut sic.

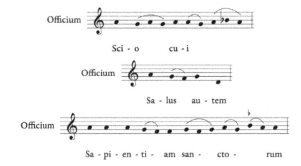

Officium

Sci - o   cu - i

Officium

Sa - lus   au - tem

Officium

Sa - pi - en - ti - am san -   cto -   rum

et consimilibus.

Exempla de responsoriis.

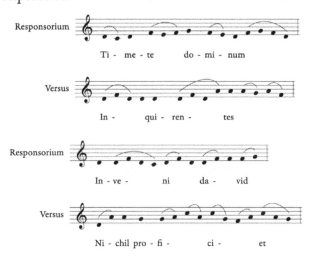

Responsorium

Ti - me - te   do - mi - num

Versus

In -   qui - ren -   tes

Responsorium

In - ve -   ni   da -   vid

Versus

Ni - chil pro - fi -   ci -   et

The second *differentia*:

[Termination formula with *seculorum amen*]

And this is assigned to those introits that begin from F-faut ascending thus:

[Quinquagesima: BnF lat. 1107 fol. 42r.]

[Second week of Lent, Friday: BnF lat. 1107 fol. 68r.]

Likewise to those that begin on a-lamire thus:

[St. Paul: BnF lat. 1107 fol. 220r.]

[Several Martyrs: BnF lat. 1107 fol. 297r.]

[Several Martyrs: BnF lat. 1107 fol. 297r.]

and similar ones.
Examples of responsories:

[Several Martyrs: Responsory (*Timete dominum*) Verse (*Inquirentes*): BnF lat. 1107 fols. 299r-v.]

[Common of one Confessor: Responsory (*Inveni David*); Verse (*Nichil proficiet*): BnF lat. 1107 fol. 308v; fol. 309r.]

Exempla de alleluya.

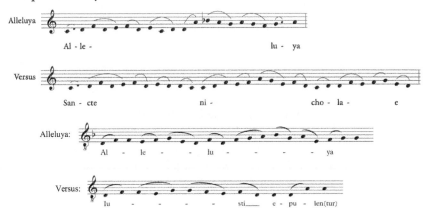

Exempla de sequentiis.

alia.

Exempla de offerendis.

aliud.
[83v]

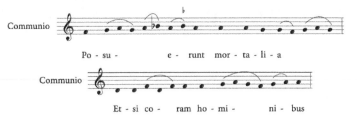

Exempla de communionibus.

Examples of the Alleluia:

[St. Nicholas: BnF lat. 1107 fol. 282r.]

[Ascension Day: BnF lat. 1107 fol. 163ar.]

Examples of sequences:

[St. Nicholas: BnF lat. 1107 fol. 389v.]

another:

[St. Denis: BnF lat. 1107 fol. 381r.]

Examples of offertories:

[Second Sunday after Epiphany: BnF lat. 1107 fol. 32r]

another:

[St. Michael: BnF lat. 1107 fol. 269r.]

Examples of communions:

[Several Martyrs: BnF lat. 1107 fol. 302v.]

[Several Martyrs: BnF lat. 1107 fol. 303r.]

[2.2.0]

Capitulum secundum in quo ponuntur exempla de secundo tono. antiphona. huius toni cum neumate.

Se - cun - dum au - tem　si - mi - le est hu - ic

Modus intonandi super psalmos.

Sec - un - dus ton - us sim - pli - ci - ter sic in - ci - pit et sic me - di - a - tur

Sol - lemp - ni - ter sic in - ci - pit et sic　me - di - a - tur.

Et sic sem - per a - pud nos fi - ni - tur.　E u o u a e

Antiphona　　O　　sa - pi - en - ti - a

Antiphona　　Te -　　u - num

Antiphona　　Be - a - ta ma - ter

Exempla de responsoriis:

Responsorium　Do - ce - bit nos

Versus　Ve - ni - te a - scen - da - mus

Responsorium　E - ru - e___ fra - me - a

Versus　De o - - re le - o - nis

[2.2.0]
Chapter two, in which examples of the second tone are given. The antiphon of the second tone with its *neumata*:

[Matthew 22:39 provides the text for the model antiphon for tone two.]³¹⁰

The way of intoning upon psalms:

[Simple psalm intonation for the second tone.]

[Solemn psalm intonation for the second tone.]

[Termination formula with *seculorum amen.*]

[Fourth week in Advent: BnF lat. 17296 fol. 13v.]

[Holy Trinity: BnF lat. 15182 fol. 90v.]

[Vigil of the Assumption: BnF lat. 17296 fol. 206r.]

Examples of responsories:

[Second Sunday in Advent: BnF lat. 17296 fol. 6r.]

Glo - ri-a pa - tri et fi - li-o et spi-ri - tu - i__ san - cto.

[84r] Exempla de invitatoriis.

Invitatorium

Re - gem ce - lo - rum do - mi - num a - do - re - mus

aliud.

[Invitatorium]

Re - gem sem - pi - ter - num pro - nis men - ti - bus

Psalmus

Ve - ni - te ex - ul - te - mus do - mi - no

[2.2.1]

Nota tamen quod istud venite non habemus in usu. nec aliquod huius toni. gratia vero exempli quod hic mihi deficiebat malui ponere exemplum de illo quam deficere in exemplo. istud enim venite habet in usu non solum parisiensis. ecclesia. immo etiam plures alie et quasi omnes.

Exempla de hympnis.

Hympnus

Ti - bi Chri - ste splen - dor pa - tris

alius.

[Hympnus]

Ut que - ant la - xis re - so - na - re fi - bris

Modus intonandi in officiis.

Se - cun - dus to - nus in of - fi - ci - is sic in - ci - pit et sic me - di - a - tur

Et sic sem - per fi - ni - tur. E u o u a e

Officium

Sal - ve san - cta pa - rens

[Fifth Sunday of Lent: BnF lat. 17296 fol. 119r-v.]

Examples of invitatories:

[Dedication of the Church of St. Michael: BnF lat. 17296 fol. 222v.]

Another:

[Invitatory *Regem sempiternum* for St. Lawrence: BnF lat. 17296 fol. 188v.][311]

[2.2.1]
Note, however, that we do not have this *Venite* in our use, nor any in this tone. So, for the sake of an example, because I am short of one here, I preferred to give an example of that rather than to be short of an example, for that *Venite* is in use not only in the church of Paris but also in many others and almost all.
Examples of hymns:

[St. Michael: BnF lat. 15182 fol. 375r.]

Another:

[St. John the Baptist: BnF n. a. lat. 1235 fol. 166r.]

The way of intoning in introits:

[Intonation for the second tone]

[Termination formula with *seculorum amen*]

[Blessed Virgin Mary: BnF lat. 1107 fol. 322v.]

Officium — Vul - tum   tu -   um

Exempla de responsoriis.

Responsorium — Re -   qui - em

Versus — Qui la - za - rum

[84v]

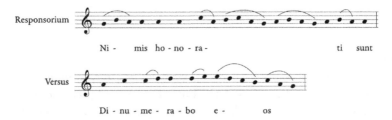

Responsorium — Ni -   mis ho - no - ra-   ti   sunt

Versus — Di - nu - me - ra - bo   e -   os

Exempla de alleluys.

Alleluya — Al - le - lu - ya

Versus — Di -   es   san - cti - fi - ca - tus

[Alleluya] — Al - le -   lu - ya

Versus — Sur - re - xit   chri - stus

Exempla de tractibus.

Tractus — Qui ha - bi -   tat

[Several Confessors: BnF lat. 1107 fol. 316r.]

Examples of responsories:

[Requiem Mass: BnF lat. 1107 fols. 329r-v.]

[Common of Apostles: BnF lat. 1107 fol. 286r.]

Examples of Alleluias:

[Christmas Day: BnF lat. 1107 fol. 20r.]

[Second Sunday after the Octave of Easter: BnF lat. 1107 fol. 157r.]

Examples of Tracts:

[First Sunday of Lent: BnF lat. 1107 fol. 48r.]

Tractus — A - ve ... ma - ri - a

Exempla[103] de sequentiis.

Sequentia — Lau - dum car - mi - na

Exempla de offerendis.

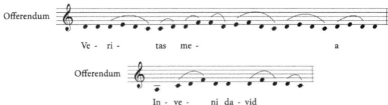

Offerendum — Pre - ter re - rum se - ri - em

Offerendum — Ve - ri - tas me - ... a

Offerendum — In - ve - ni da - vid

Exempla de communionibus.

Communio — Ihe - ru - sa - lem sur - ge

Communio — Na - ti - vi - tas glo - ri - o - se

[2.3.0]

Capitulum tertium in quo ponuntur exempla de tertio tono antiphona huius toni cum suo neumate.

Ter - ti - a di - es est quo hec fa - cta sunt ————

Modus intonandi super psalmos.
[85r]

Ter - ti - us to - nus sim - pli - ci - ter sic in - ci - pit et sic me - di - a - tur.

———
[103] "Exemplum" **K**

[Annunciation: BnF lat. 1107 fol. 232r.]

Examples of sequences:

[St. Benedict: BnF lat. 1107 fol. 362r.]

Examples of offertories:

[Blessed Virgin Mary: BnF lat. 1107 fol. 398v.]

[Common of one Confessor: BnF lat. 1107 fol. 309v.

[Common of one Confessor: BnF lat. 1107 fol. 310r [transposed].]

Examples of communions:

[Second Sunday in Advent: BnF lat. 1107 fol. 4r.]

[Blessed Virgin Mary: BnF lat. 1107 fol. 264r.]

[2.3.0]
Chapter three, in which examples of the third tone are given. The antiphon of the third tone with its *neumata*:

[Luke 24:21 provides the text for the model antiphon for tone three.]

The way of intoning upon psalms:

[Simple psalm intonation for the third tone.]

Sol - lemp - ni - ter sic in - ci - pit   et sic   e - ti - am me - di - a - tur

[2.3.1]
Prima differentia.

Et sic fi - ni - tur.   E u o u a e

Et ista debetur proprie illis .antiphonis. que incipientes a gsolreut. per alamire sine repercussione aliqua vel repetitione notule illius que est in alamire ascendunt in csolfaut isto modo.

Antiphona

Tu beth - le - em

Antiphona

Do - mi - nus le - gi - fer no - ster

Item illis que a. gsolreut incipientes per. bfabmi ascendunt in csolfaut isto modo.

Antiphona

O - ri - e - tur

Item illis que incipientes ab alamire ascendunt hoc modo.

[Antiphona]

Ser - vi - te do - mi - no

Item illis que a. csolfaut. incipiunt isto modo.

Antiphona

U - num o - pus fe - ci

Antiphona

Do - mi - ne mi   rex

[Solemn psalm intonation for the third tone.]

[2.3.1]
The first *differentia*:

[Termination formula with *seculorum amen*]

And this is properly assigned to those antiphons, that, beginning from G-solreut, ascend through a-lamire without any repercussion or repetition of that little note [b-mi], which is on [above] a-lamire, to c-solfaut in this way:

[Fourth week in Advent, Tuesday: BnF lat. 17296 fol. 16v.]

[Fourth week in Advent, Thursday: BnF lat. 17296 fol. 17v.]

Likewise to those that, beginning from G-solreut, ascend through b-fa-b-mi to c-solfaut in this way:

[Christmas Day: BnF lat. 17296 fol. 20r.]

Likewise to those that, beginning from a-lamire, ascend in this way:

[First week after Epiphany, Monday: BnF lat. 12044 fol. 32v.]

Likewise to those that begin from c-solfaut in this way:

[Fourth week of Lent, Tuesday: BnF lat. 17296 fol. 115r.]

[John the Baptist: BnF lat. 17296 fol. 209v.]

[2.3.2]
Secunda differentia.

Et sic fi - ni - tur. E u o u a e

Et ista debetur proprie illis antiphonis. que ab elami incipiunt descendendo vel etiam ascendendo. descendendo sic.

Antiphona

Qui de ter - ra est

Antiphona

Quan - do na - tus est

Ascendentibus hoc modo.

Antiphona

Hec est que ne - sci - vit

Antiphona

Ho - stem pe - stis

Item illis que incipiunt a. gsolreut.[104] tam descendendo quam etiam ascendendo modo qui sequitur. descendendo videlicet isto modo.

Antiphona

Que - ren - tes e - um

vel sic.
[85v]

Antiphona

Ser - ve ne - quam

Antiphona

Au - ge in no - bis

---

[104] gsolreut . solreut *unecessary repetition.*

[2.3.2]
The second *differentia*:

[Termination formula with *seculorum amen*]

And this is properly assigned to those antiphons that begin on E-lami, descending or even ascending, descending thus:

[Circumcision: BnF lat. 17296 fol. 43r.]

[Circumcision: BnF lat. 17296 fol. 43v.]

With ascents in this way:

[Purification: BnF lat. 17296 fol. 66r.]

[St. Louis: the melody for *Hostem pestis* is not found][312]

Likewise to those that begin from G-solreut, descending as much as ascending in the way that follows—clearly, descending in this way:

[Second week of Lent, Friday: BnF lat. 17296 fol. 105v.]

Or thus:

[Twenty-second Sunday after Pentecost: BnF lat. 17296 fol. 327r.]

[Vigil of Pentecost: BnF lat. 17296 fol. 164r.]

ascendendo vero primo sic.

vel sic.

Ita scilicet ut nota que est in alamire repercutiatur aut bis accipiatur ad differentiam prime differentie de qua dictum est supra.

Exempla de responsoriis.

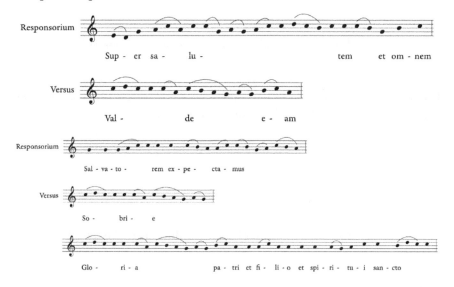

Exempla[105] de invitatoriis.

[105] Exemplum *Klundert*

but ascending at first thus:

[St. Mary Magdalene: BnF lat. 17296 fol. 350v.]

[St. Nicholas: BnF lat. 17296 fol. 261v.]

or thus:

[Thursday of Holy Week: BnF lat. 15181 fol. 90v.]

[Thursday of Holy Week: BnF lat. 15181 fol. 91r.]

Thus the note on a-lamire is repeated or sounded a second time, for this *differentia* as for the first *differentia*, spoken about above.
Examples of responsories:

[Assumption: BnF lat. 15182 fol. 309v.]

[First Sunday in Advent: BnF lat. 17296 fol. 3r.]

Examples of invitatories:

[John the Baptist: Invitatory *Regem precursoris* BnF lat.15182 fol. 207r; Psalm *Venite exultemus* BnF lat. 15181 fol. 547r.]

Psalmus

Ve - ni - te   ex - ul - te - mus do - mi - no

Exempla de hympnis.

Hympnus

Pan - ge lin - gua glo - ri - o - si

Hympnus

E - ter - na   cri - sti   mu - ne - ra

Modus intonandi in officiis misse.[106]

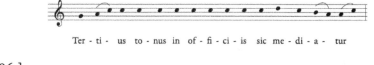

Ter - ti - us to - nus in of - fi - ci - is   sic me - di - a - tur

[86r]

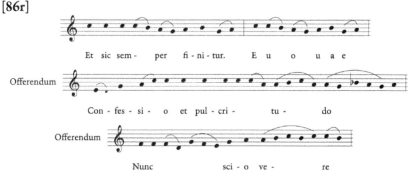

Et sic sem -   per   fi - ni - tur.   E   u   o   u a e

Offerendum

Con - fes - si - o   et pul - cri -   tu -   do

Offerendum

Nunc   sci - o ve -   re

Exempla de responsoriis.

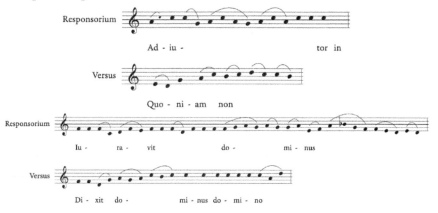

Responsorium

Ad - iu -   tor in

Versus

Quo - ni - am   non

Responsorium

Iu -   ra - vit   do -   mi - nus

Versus

Di - xit do -   mi - nus do - mi - no

---

[106] *Repeated word* misse *struck through*

Examples of hymns:

[Passion Sunday: BnF lat. 15181 fol. 261v.]

[Several Martyrs: BnF lat. 15181 fol. 518v.]

The ways of intoning in the introits of the mass:

[Intonation for the third tone]

[Termination formula with *seculorum amen*]

[First week of Lent, Thursday: BnF lat. 1107 fol. 55r.]

[Apostles, Peter and Paul: BnF lat. 1107 fol. 245v.]

Examples of responsories:

[Septuagesima Sunday: BnF lat. 1107 fol. 35v.]

[Confessor: BnF lat. 1107 fol. 308v.]

Exempla de alleluys.

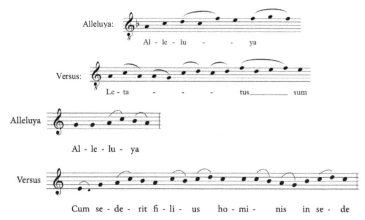

Alleluya: Al - le - lu -   ya

Versus: Le - ta -   tus_____ sum

Alleluya   Al - le - lu - ya

Versus   Cum se - de - rit fi - li - us   ho - mi -   nis   in se - de

Exempla[107] de sequentiis.

Sequentia   Iu - bi - le - mus om - nes u -   na

Exempla[108] de tractibus.

Tractus   Be - ne - di -   ctus   es   in fir - ma - men -   to

Exempla de offerendis.

Offerendum   Be - ne - di - xi -   sti do -   mi -   ne

aliud.

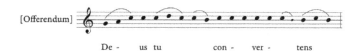

[Offerendum]   De -   us tu   con -   ver -   tens

[86v] Exempla de communionibus.

Communio   Qui   me - di - ta - bi - tur in le - [ge]

---

[107] Exemplum *Klundert*.   [108] Exemplum *Klundert*

Examples of Alleluias:

[Second Sunday in Advent: BnF lat. 1107 fol. 3v.][313]

[Several Martyrs: BnF lat. 1107 fols. 301r-v.]

Examples of the sequence:

[Fourth Sunday in Advent: BnF lat. 1107 fols. 341r-v.]

Examples of tracts:

[First week of Lent, Saturday: BnF lat. 1107 fol. 59v.]

Examples of offertories:

[Third Sunday in Advent: BnF lat. 1107 fol. 6r.]

Another:

[Second Sunday in Advent: BnF lat. 1107 fol. 4r.]

Examples of communions:

[Ash Wednesday: BnF lat. 1107 fol. 43v.]

Communio

Be - a - tus ser - vus quem cum

[2.4.0]

Capitulum .iiij. in quo ponuntur exempla de .iiij. tono. antiphona. huius toni cum neumate.

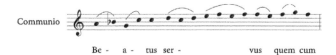

Quar - ta vi - gi - li - a ve - nit ad e - os

Modus intonandi super psalmos.

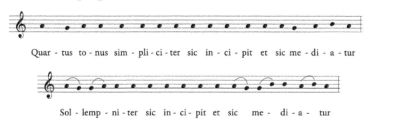

Quar - tus to - nus sim - pli - ci - ter sic in - ci - pit et sic me - di - a - tur

Sol - lemp - ni - ter sic in - ci - pit et sic me - di - a - tur

[2.4.1]

Prima differentia.

Et sic sem - per fi - ni - tur. E u o u a e

Et ista debetur. antiphonis. incipientibus in .cfaut. et ascendentibus isto modo.

Antiphona

Ne re - mi - ni - sca - ris

vel sic

Antiphona

Quid vo - bis

vel sic

Antiphona

E - rat vir do - mi - ni

[Confessor: BnF lat. 1107 fol. 310r.][314]

[2.4.0]
Chapter four, in which examples of the fourth tone are given. The antiphon of the fourth tone with its *neumata*:

[Matthew14:25 provides the text for the model antiphon for tone four.]

The way of intoning upon psalms:

[Simple psalm intonation for the third tone]

[Solemn psalm intonation for the third tone]

[2.4.1]
The first *differentia*:

[Termination formula with *seculorum amen*]

And this is assigned to antiphons beginning on C-faut and ascending in this way:

[From *Esther*: BnF lat. 17296 fol. 305v.]

Or thus:

[Eighteenth Sunday after Pentecost: BnF lat. 17296 fol. 326r.]

Or thus:

[St. Benedict: BnF lat. 17296 fol. 81v.]

Item incipientibus a. dsolre. ascendentibus isto modo.

Est se - cre - tum

vel sic

Am - bu - la - bunt

vel sic

Ni - si di - li - gen - ter

Item incipientibus ab elami descendendo sic.

Laus   de - o   pa - tri

vel ascendendo isto modo.

Te   de - um

vel sic

Iu - bi - la - te de - o

[87r] Item incipientibus ab. ffaut et descendentibus[109] isto modo.

Lau - da - bo

vel sic

Ma - ri - a

vel sic

Om - nis ter - ra

vel sic

Ha -   bi - ta - bit

---

[109] descentibus *corrected to* descendentibus **H2**.

Likewise to those beginning on D-solre, ascending in this way:

[St. Cecilia: BnF lat. 17296 fol. 255v.]

Or thus:

[Holy Innocents: BnF lat. 17296 fol. 38v.]

Or thus:

[St. Agatha: BnF lat. 17296 fol. 71r.]

Likewise to those beginning on E-lami descending thus:

[Holy Trinity: BnF lat. 17296 fol. 164v.]

or ascending in this way:

[Holy Trinity: BnF lat. 17296 fol. 168v.]

Or thus:

[Fridays throughout the year: BnF lat. 15181 fol. 69v.]

Likewise to those beginning on F-faut and descending in this way:

[Sunday in Septuagesima: BnF lat. 17296 fol. 85r.]

Or thus:

[Epiphany: BnF lat. 17296 fol. 48r.]

Or thus:

[Epiphany: BnF lat. 17296 fol. 44v.]

Or thus:

[Holy Saturday: BnF lat. 17296 fol. 133v.]

vel sic

Cre - do vi - de - re

vel sic

In fer - ven - tis

vel sic

Fa - ctum est

vel econtrario ascendentibus isto modo.

Di - co vo - bis

Be - ni - gne fac

Item illis que incipiunt a. gsolreut descendendo isto modo.

Ex - e - qui - e mar - ti - ni

vel sic

Ec - ce mer - ces san - cto - rum

[2.4.2]
Secunda differentia.

Et sic fi - ni - tur.   E u o u a e

Et hec proprie debetur illis que incipiunt a. gsolreut descendendo isto modo.

Cu - sto - dit do - mi - nus

Or thus:

[Holy Saturday: BnF lat. 17296 fol. 134r.]

Or thus:

[St. John the Evangelist: BnF lat. 17296 fol. 33r.]

Or thus:

[St. Peter: BnF lat. 17296 fol. 176r.]

or in reverse ascending in this way:

[Third Sunday after Pentecost: BnF lat. 17296 fol. 322v.]

[Saturdays throughout the year: BnF lat. 15181 fol. 76v.]

Likewise to those that begin from G-solreut descending in this way:

[St. Martin: BnF lat. 17296 fol. 247v.]

Or thus:

[Common of Several Martyrs: BnF lat. 1090 fol. 262v.]

[2.4.2]
The second *differentia*:

[Termination formula with *seculorum amen*]

And this is properly assigned to those that begin from G-solreut, descending in this way:

[Sunday in Septuagesima: BnF lat. 17296 fol. 85r.]

vel ascendendo isto modo.

[2.4.3]
Tertia differentia.

Et ista proprie debetur .antiphonis. illis que ab alamire incipientes ascendunt isto modo.

vel que incipientes ab elami sic ascendunt.

Nec mireris si ista differentia videatur similis quinte differentie primi toni. quia. antiphone. que habent istam differentiam huius toni vel in elami finiuntur sicut patet in duabus ultimis. vel si finiantur [87v] in alamire sicut accidit in duabus primis. tunc debent in fine cum .b. molli notari et sic ad .e. grave<m>[110] reduci idest ad primum elami. que ut dictum est supra in prima parte huius tractatus est finalis littera huius toni. antiphone. vero ille que habent quintam differentiam primi toni. vel in dsolre finiuntur vel si alibi terminentur sine .b. molli notantur in fine. et ita per consequens non ad .e. reducentur sed potius ad .d. idest ad dsolre que est finalis littera primi toni.

---

[110] gravem *Klundert*

or ascending in this way:

[Sundays throughout the year: BnF lat. 15181 fol. 184v,
though beginning on E and not G.]

[Assumption: BnF lat. 17296 fol. 208r.]

[2.4.3]
The third *differentia*:

[Termination formula with *seculorum amen*]

And this is properly assigned to those antiphons that, beginning on a-lamire, ascend in this way:

[Fourth week in Advent, Friday: BnF lat. 17296 fol. 17v.]

[First week in Advent, Friday: BnF lat. 17296 fol. 4v.]

Or that, beginning from E-lami, ascend thus:

[Holy Cross: BnF lat. 17296 fol. 213v.]

[Holy Cross: BnF lat. 17296 fol. 213v.]

Do not be surprised if this *differentia* seems similar to the fifth *differentia* of the first tone, because antiphons that have this *differentia* of this tone or finish on E-lami (as is evident in the last two), or if they finish on a-lamire (as happens in the first two), then they ought to be notated (at the end) with soft b. Thus they are understood to end on E grave, that is to the first E-lami which, as has been said above in the first part of this treatise, is the final letter of this tone. But indeed those antiphons that have the fifth *differentia* of the first tone either end on D-solre or, if terminated otherwise, are notated (at their end) without soft b. Consequently they are not understood to end on E but rather on D, that is, on D-solre, which is the final letter of the first tone.

[2.4.4]
Quarta differentia.

Et sic fi - ni - tur E u o u a___ e

Et ista debetur proprie illis antiphonis que incipientes a. csolfaut sic ascendunt ut supra primam sillabam. antiphone. sit unica notula et supra secundam due isto modo.

Antiphona: Val - de___ iam

Antiphona: Fac- tus___ sum,

Cuius contrarium est in differentia sequenti.

[2.4.5]
Quinta differentia.

Et sic fi - ni - tur   E   u   o   u a   e

Et ista econtrario ad precedentem debetur .antiphonis. illis que similiter incipientes a. csolfaut sic ascendunt ut supra primam. antiphone. sillabam sint due notule. supra. vero secundam unica tamen. ut sic.

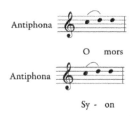

Antiphona   O   mors

Antiphona   Sy - on

[2.4.6]
Sexta differentia.

Et sic fi - ni - tur.   E u o u a e

Et ista proprie debetur .antiphonis. illis que incipientes a. gsolreut sic ascendunt.

[2.4.4]
The fourth *differentia*:

[Termination formula with *seculorum amen*]

And this is properly assigned to those antiphons that, beginning from c-solfaut, ascend thus, so that, beyond the first syllable of the antiphon, they should have a single little note and two above the second in this way:

[Thursday in the first week of Lent: BnF 17296 fol. 101v.][315]

[Holy Saturday: BnF lat. 17296 fol. 135r.][316]

The reverse of this is in the following *differentia*.

[2.4.5]
The fifth *differentia*:

[Termination formula with *seculorum amen*]

And in reverse this is assigned to the preceding one, likewise to those antiphons that, similarly beginning on c-solfaut, thus ascend so that there are two little notes above the first syllable of the antiphon, but above the second there is one, however, as thus:
[Holy Saturday: BnF lat. 17296 fol. 135v.]

[Second week in Advent, Wednesday: BnF lat. 17296 fol. 8v.]

[2.4.6]
The sixth *differentia*:

[Termination formula with *seculorum amen*]

And this is properly assigned to those antiphons that, beginning from G-solreut, ascend thus:

Be - ne - di - cta   tu

Antiphona

An - te tho - rum

Et consimilibus vel hoc modo.

Prop - ter   sy - on

Item illis que incipientes ab alamire primo per unam notulam descendunt. et statim ut precedentes postea reascendunt sic.

Post par - tum vir - go

Antiphona

Gau - de ma - ri - a

Et consimiles.

Notandum est autem quod secundum usum nostrum idem est modus intonandi tam simpliciter quam sollempniter quantum ad mediationem omnes huius toni differentias preter primam. credo tamen salvo meliori iudicio quod sequendo communiorem usum et consuetudinem in hac parte omnes iste intonari deberent quantum ad medium sollempniter sicut prima.

Exempla de responsoriis.

Di - ffu -   sa est gra - ti - a

Versus

Di - le - xi - sti

[88r]

Be - a - tis - si - mus

Versus

Et pa - ri - si - us

[First week in Advent, Thursday: BnF lat. 17296 fol. 4v.]

[Purification: BnF lat. 17296 fol. 66r.]

And to similar ones in this way:

[Fourth week in Advent, Wednesday: BnF lat. 17296 fol. 17r.]

Likewise to those that, beginning on a-lamire, descend at first through one little note, and immediately re-ascend afterwards as the preceding ones thus:

[Purification: BnF lat. 17296 fol. 66v.]

[Purification: BnF lat. 17296 fol. 66v.]

And similar ones.

It should be noted, however, that according to our use the way of intoning all the *differentiae* of this tone, both simply and solemnly, is the same in relation to the median note. Saving better judgment however, I believe, that, following the more common use and custom in this matter, all these ought to be intoned solemnly as regards the median note just like the first [*differentia*].

Examples of responsories:

[Feast of a Virgin: BnF lat. 17296 fol. 284v.]

[St. Denis: BnF lat. 17296 fol. 230r.]

Glo - ri - a   pa - tri et fi - li - o   et   spi - ri - tu - i san - cto

Exempla de invitatoriis. et venite.

[Invitatorium]

De - um ve - rum u - num

Psalmus

Ve - ni - te ex - ul - te - mus

Item aliud invitatorium.

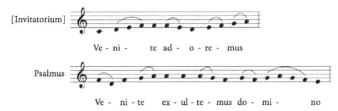

[Invitatorium]

Ve - ni - te ad - o - re - mus

Psalmus

Ve - ni - te ex - ul - te - mus do - mi - no

Aliud invitatorium.

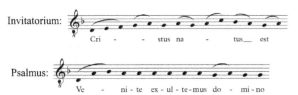

Invitatorium:

Cri - stus na - tus est

Psalmus:

Ve - ni - te ex - ul - te - mus do - mi - no

Aliud invitatorium.

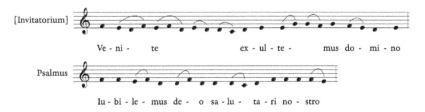

[Invitatorium]

Ve - ni - te   ex - ul - te - mus do - mi - no

Psalmus

Iu - bi - le - mus de - o sa - lu - ta - ri no - stro

Aliud invitatorium.

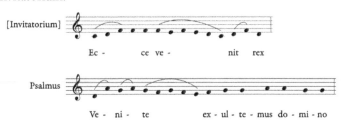

[Invitatorium]

Ec - ce ve - nit rex

Psalmus

Ve - ni - te   ex - ul - te - mus do - mi - no

Examples of invitatories and *Venite*:

[Saturday of Holy Trinity: BnF lat. 15182 fols. 90r-v.]

Likewise another invitatory:

[Assumption: BnF lat. 12044 fol. 175r.]

Another invitatory:

[Christmas Day: BnF lat. 17296 fol. 19v.]

Another invitatory:

[Mondays throughout the year: BnF lat. 15181 fol. 188v.]

Another invitatory:

[First Sunday in Advent: BnF lat. 15181 fols. 106r-v.]

Nec mireris si modo dictum sit istud ultimum venite esse quarti toni cum supra dictum sit istud idem esse primi toni. secundum enim magistrum iohannem de garlandia qui fuit magne reputationis musicus non est inconveniens idem venite esse diversorum tonorum diversis respectibus. scilicet. per respectum ad diversa invitatoria. sicut idem seculorum amen per respectum ad diversas antiphonas potest esse diversorum tonorum. prout notavi supra in tertia differentia huius toni post illam. antiphonam [**88v**] Tuam crucem. Alterum enim istorum[111] duorum necesse est dicere, videlicet. vel quod de quolibet venite secundum suum invitatorium seu invitatoria ad que applicatur debeat iudicari sicut dicit magister predictus. et sic quandoque idem venite sit diversorum tonorum vel quod non semper oportet invitatorio venite eiusdem toni applicari sed quandoque alterius toni. et hoc maxime et frequenter secundum usum presentis monasterii video evenire. non solum in predicto venite immo et etiam in primo venite huius toni quod .scilicet. aliquando invitatorio. Christum regem. et multis aliis sui toni .scilicet. quarti. aliquando vero invitatorio Regem regum dominum. et quibusdam aliis eiusdem toni cum ipso scilicet primi. necnon etiam interdum aliquibus secundi sicut invitatorio de angelis. scilicet. Regem celorum applicatur aliquando. et hoc sicut credo maxime fit propter festivitatem cantus ipsius et communitatem vel etiam venustatem. Et fortassis utrumque dictum potest esse verum satisque probabiliter sustineri.

---

[111] tonorum *struck through after* istorum.

You should not be surprised if it is said in this way that the last *Venite* should be of the fourth tone, when it was said above to be the same as the first tone. For according to Master John of Garland,[317] who was a musician of great reputation, it is not inappropriate for the same *Venite* of different tones to be different in certain respects, namely with respect to a different invitatory, just as the same *seculorum amen* can be of different tones with respect to different antiphons. This is just as I have noted above in the third *differentia* of this tone, after the antiphon *Tuam crucem*.[mmm 318] For it is necessary to speak of the other of those two, namely, that any *Venite* ought to be judged according to its invitatory or the invitatories to which it is applied (just as the aforementioned master says), and it is thus whenever the Venite is the same for different tones. For it is not always necessary to apply the *Venite* to the invitatory of that tone, but sometimes of another tone. And I see this occurring mostly and frequently according to the use of the present monastery, not only in the aforesaid *Venite*, indeed, but also in the beginning of the *Venite* of this tone, that, namely, sometimes in the invitatory *Christum regem*,[nnn] and in many others of its tone, namely the fourth. Indeed sometimes it happens in the invitatory *Regem regum dominum*,[ooo] and certain others of this tone with the same, namely the first, even sometimes in some others of the second, just as is applied sometimes in the invitatory of the angels, namely *Regem celorum*.[ppp] And this happens, as I believe, principally on account of the festivity and familiarity or even the charm of the chant itself. And perhaps each can be said to be true and be sustained credibly enough.

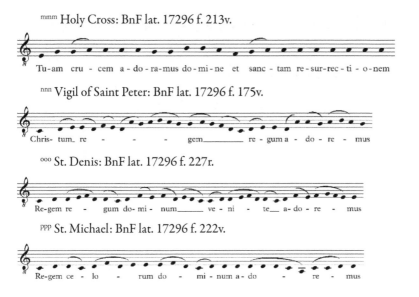

[mmm] Holy Cross: BnF lat. 17296 f. 213v.

Tu-am cru - cem a - do - ra-mus do - mi - ne et sanc - tam re - sur-rec - ti - o - nem

[nnn] Vigil of Saint Peter: BnF lat. 17296 f. 175v.

Chris- tum_ re - - - gem_____ re - gum a - do - re - mus

[ooo] St. Denis: BnF lat. 17296 f. 227r.

Re-gem re - gum do- mi - num_____ ve - ni - te_ a - do - re - mus

[ppp] St. Michael: BnF lat. 17296 f. 222v.

Re-gem ce - lo - rum do - mi - num a - do - re - mus

Exempla de hympnis.

Hympnus

An - nu - e cri - ste

Hympnus

I - ste con - fes - sor

Modus intonandi in officiis misse.

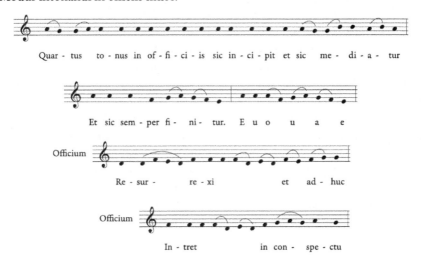

Quar - tus to - nus in of - fi - ci - is sic in - ci - pit et sic me - di - a - tur

Et sic sem - per fi - ni - tur. E u o u a e

Officium

Re - sur - re - xi et ad - huc

Officium

In - tret in con - spe - ctu

Exempla de responsoriis.

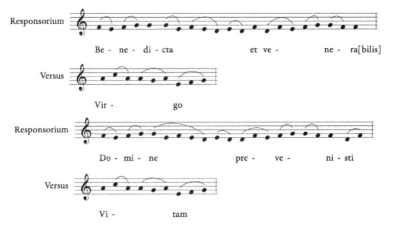

Responsorium

Be - ne - di - cta et ve - ne - ra[bilis]

Versus

Vir - go

Responsorium

Do - mi - ne pre - ve - ni - sti

Versus

Vi - tam

Examples of hymns:

[Common of Apostles: BnF lat. 15181 fol. 499v.]

[Concordant melody in tone 4 not found.]

The way of intoning in introits of the mass:

[Intonation formula for the fourth tone]

[Termination formula with *seculorum amen*]

[Easter Sunday: BnF lat. 1107 fol. 144r.]

[Several Martyrs: BnF lat. 1107 fol. 296v.]

Examples of responsories:

[Assumption: BnF lat. 1107 fol. 257v.]

[Common of one Confessor: BnF lat. 1107 fol. 309r.]

Exempla de alleluys.

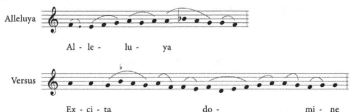

[89r]

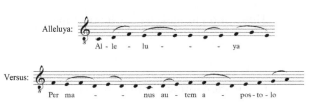

Exempla[112] de sequentiis.

Exempla[114] de tractibus.

Exempla de offerendis.

aliud.

Exempla de communionibus.

---

[112] Exemplum *Klundert*   *neumes erased.*
[113] alia Laude iocunda *struck through*;   [114] Exemplum *Klundert*

Examples of Alleluias:

[Third Sunday in Advent: BnF lat. 1107 fols. 5v-6r.]

[Common of Apostles: BnF lat. 1107 fol. 287r.]

Examples of sequences:

[Third Sunday in Advent: BnF lat. 1107 fol. 341r.]

Examples of Tracts:

[Saturday, 17th week after Pentecost: BnF lat. 1107 fol. 199r.]

Examples of offertories:

[St. John the Evangelist: BnF lat. 1107 fol. 20v.]

Another:

[Pentecost: BnF lat. 17307 fol. 138v.]

Examples of communions:

[Pentecost: BnF lat. 1107 fol. 178r.]

Mag - na est glo -   ri - a e - ius

[2.5.0]

Capitulum .v. in quo ponuntur exempla de .v. tono. antiphona huius toni cum suo neumate.[115]

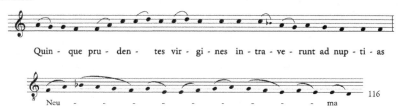

Quin - que pru - den -   tes vir - gi - nes in - tra - ve - runt ad nup - ti - as

Neu - - - - - - - - ma   116

[89v] Modus intonandi super psalmos.

Quin - tus to - nus sim - pli - ci - ter sic in - ci - pit et sic me - di - a - tur

Sol - lemp - ni - ter sic in - ci - pit et sic si - mi - li - ter me - di - a - tur

Et sic sem - per fi - ni - tur.   E u o u a e

Antiphona

Ec - ce ma - ri - a

Antiphona

Ex   quo om -   ni - a

---

[115] This heading, following the example "Magna est gloria eius" has been erased.

[116] Following the example, an extended passage has been struck through. See Appendix I.

[Common of a Martyr: BnF lat. 1107 fol. 294r.]

[2.5.0]
Chapter five, in which examples of the fifth tone are given. The antiphon of the
fifth tone with its *neumata*:

[Matthew 25:10 provides the text for the model antiphon for tone five.]

[Melisma associated with *Neuma*]qqq

The way of intoning upon psalms:

[Simple psalm intonation for the fifth tone]

[Solemn psalm intonation for the fifth tone]

[Termination formula with *seculorum amen*]

[Octave of Christmas: BnF lat. 17296 fol. 44r.]

[Holy Trinity: BnF lat. 17296 fol. 165r.]

---

qqq There appears to be some clef confusion; it should probably be:

Neu - - - - - - - ma

Exemplum[117] de responsoriis.

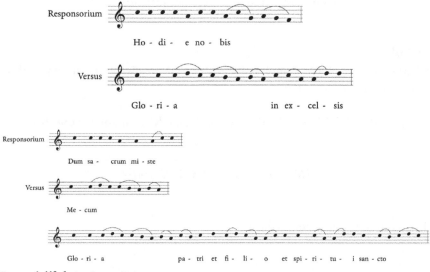

Exempla[118] de invitatoriis.

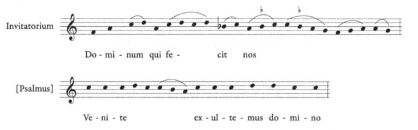

[90r] Exemplum de hympnis.

Iste hympnus cantatur de beato ludovico secundum usum pariensis ecclesie de quo licet non cantetur apud nos exemplum malui ponere quam in exemplo quoad hymnos quorum nullum huius toni habemus deficere.

Modus intonandi in officiis misse.

---

[117] Exempla *Klundert*   [118] "Exemplum" **K**

Examples of responsories:

[Christmas Day: BnF lat. 17296 fol. 20v.]

[St. Denis: BnF lat. 17296 fols. 230r-v.]

Example of invitatories:

[Third Sunday of Lent: BnF lat. 15181 fol. 240v.]

Example of hymns:

[St. Louis: BnF lat.1028 fol. 332v.]ᵀᵀ

This hymn is sung for Blessed Louis according to the use of the Church of Paris, for which, although it is not sung among us, I prefer to give an example rather than do without an example for hymns, of which we have none in this tone.

The way of intoning in introits of the mass:

[Intonation formula for the fifth tone]

ᵀᵀ The hymn Gaude mater ecclesia features at First Vespers in the Offices for St. Louis called Nunc Laudare and Lauda Celestis 1. See M. Cecilia Gaposchkin *The Making of Saint Louis: Kingship, Sanctity, and Crusade in the Later Middle Ages* (Cornell University Press, 2008) Appendix 2.1 pp. 253–83.

[2.5.1]
Prima differentia.

Et sic fi - ni - tur.   E u o u a e

Et hec differentia apud nos habetur in omnibus introitibus huius toni ubicumque incipiant verbi gratia.

Officium

Lo - que -   bar

aliud.

[Officium]

Ex - au - di de - us

aliud.

[Officium]

De -   us in lo -   co

aliud.

[Officium]

Cir-cum-de-de- runt_____

aliud.

[Officium]

Le - ta -   re   ie - ru - sa - lem

Exempla de responsoriis.

Responsorium

Be - ne - di -   ctus qui ve -   nit

Versus

A   do - mi - no

---

[119] *Corrected from* Circundederunt

[2.5.1]
The first *differentia*:

[Termination formula with *seculorum amen*]

We use this *differentia* in all introits of this tone wherever they begin, for example:

[Common of several confessor bishops: BnF lat. 1107 fol. 315v.]

Another:

[Fourth week of Lent: BnF lat. 1107 fol. 87v.]

Another:

[Eleventh Sunday after Pentecost: BnF lat. 1107 fol. 188v.]

Another:

[Septuagesima Sunday: BnF lat. 1107 fol. 35r.]

Another:

[Fourth Sunday of Lent: BnF lat. 1107 fol. 84v.]

Examples of responsories:

[Christmas Day: BnF lat. 1107 fol. 18v.]

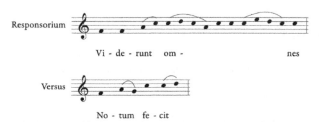

Responsorium

Vi - de - runt om - nes

Versus

No - tum fe - cit

Exempla de alleluys.

Alleluya:

Al - le - lu - ya

Versus:

An - te_____ thro - num

[90v]

Alleluya:

Al - le - lu - ya

Versus:

Dy - o - ni - si__ pa - ter____ al - me

Exempla[120] de sequentiis.

Sequentia:

Le - ta - bun - dus__ ex - ul - tet fi - de - lis

Hec tamen sequentia videtur esse mixta de .v°. tono et .vj°.[121]

Exempla de offerendis.

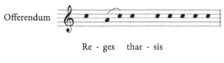

Offerendum

Re - ges thar - sis

aliud.

[Offerendum]

Be - ne - dic a - ni - ma

---

[120] Exemplum *Klundert*

[121] Hec tamen sequentia videtur esse mixta de .v°. tono et .vj°· **H2**

[Christmas Day: BnF lat. 1107 fol. 20r.]

Examples of Alleluias:

[Votive Office for Mary: BnF lat. 1028 fol. 342v.]

[St. Denis: unable to find source for this Alleluia and verse.]

Example of sequences

[Christmas Day: BnF lat. 830 fol. 302r]

This sequence, however, seems to be a mixture of the fifth and sixth tones.

Examples of offertories:

[Epiphany: BnF lat. 1107 fol. 28r.]

Another:

[First week of Lent, Friday: BnF lat. 1107 fol. 57v.]

Exempla de communionibus.

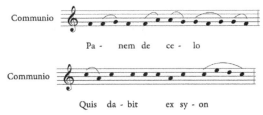

[2.6.0]

Capitulum .vi. in quo ponuntur exempla de tono .vi. antiphona huius toni cum suo neumate.[122]

Modus intonandi super. psalmos.

[91r] Exempla de responsoriis.

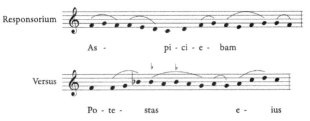

[122] "Capitulum .vi. in quo ponuntur exempla de tono .vi. antiphona huius toni cum suo neumate" H2 partially erased.

Examples of communions:

[Thirteenth Sunday after Pentecost: BnF lat. 1107 fol. 191v.]

[Third week of Lent, Monday: BnF lat. 1107 fol. 75v.]

[2.6.0]
Chapter six, in which examples of the sixth tone are given. The antiphon of the sixth tone with its *neumata*:

[John 4:6 provides the text for the model antiphon for tone 6.]

The way of intoning upon psalms:

[Simple psalm intonation for the sixth tone]

[Solemn psalm intonation for the sixth tone]

[Termination formula with *seculorum amen*]

[Dedication of a Virgin: BnF lat. 17296 fol. 287r.]

[Processional: BnF lat. 12044 fol. 177v.]

Examples of responsories:

[First Sunday in Advent: BnF lat. 17296 fol. 2r.]

Responsorium — Gra - ti - as ti - bi do - mi - ne

Versus — Quin - im - mo

Glo - ri - a pa - tri et fi - li - o et spi - ri - tu - i san - cto

Exempla de invitatoriis.

Invitatorium — Sur - rex - it do - mi - nus ve - re

Psalmus — Ve - ni - te ex - ul - te - mus do - mi - no iu - bi - le - mus de - o

aliud invitatorium.

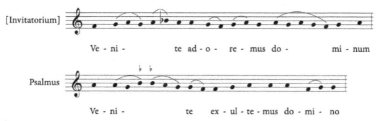

[Invitatorium] — Ve - ni - te ad - o - re - mus do - mi - num

Psalmus — Ve - ni - te ex - ul - te - mus do - mi - no

aliud invitatorium.

Invitatorium: — Re - gem cu - i om - ni - a_____ vi - vunt

Psalmus: — Ve - ni - te ex - ul - te - mus do - mi - no

Nota tamen quod si istud venite dicatur esse octavi toni non notaretur ut hic notatum est sed sicut infra in octavo tono videbitur.

Exemplum[123] de hympnis.

Hympnus: — Au-ro-ra lu-cis ru - ti-lat

---

[123] Exempla *Klundert*.

[St. Denis: BnF lat. 17296 fol. 229v.]

Examples of invitatories:

[Easter Monday: BnF lat. 15181 fol. 299v.]

Another invitatory:

[Holy Innocents: BnF lat. 17296 fol. 38v.]

Another invitatory:

[Office of the Dead: BnF n.a. lat. 1535 fol. 129r.]

Note, however, that if this *Venite* is said to be of the eighth tone, it is not notated as it is here but as will be seen below in the eighth tone.

Examples of hymns:

[Second Sunday after Easter: BnF lat. 15181 fol. 321v]

alius.

Hympnus:

Ser - mo - ne blan - do an - ge -lus

[91v] Modus intonandi in officiis misse.

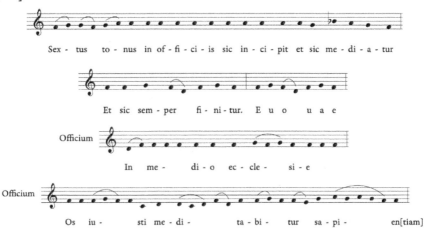

Sex - tus   to - nus in of - fi - ci - is sic in - ci - pit et sic me - di - a - tur

Et sic sem - per   fi - ni - tur. E u o   u a e

Officium

In me -   di - o ec - cle -   si - e

Officium

Os   iu -   sti me - di -   ta - bi -   tur sa - pi -   en[tiam]

Nota quod nullum .Responsorium. huius toni recolo me vidisse in toto gradali quod non sit vel irregulare vel mixtum cum quinto nisi forte istud. quod sequitur.

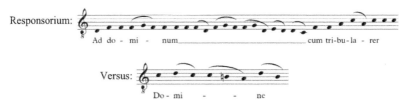

Responsorium:

Ad do - mi -   num_____   cum tri-bu-la - rer

Versus:

Do - mi -   - ne

Sciendum est tamen quod multa sunt Responsoria que ex isto tono et quinto mixta videntur et valde pulcram continent armoniam. quia tamen magis tendunt ad acuitatem et ad ascensum quam ad gravitatem vel descensum videntur potius esse quinti a dominio quam sexti. verbi gratia.

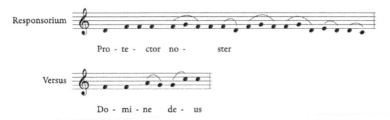

Responsorium

Pro - te - ctor no -   ster

Versus

Do - mi - ne   de - us

Another:

[Monday after the Easter Octave: BnF lat. 15181 fol. 311r.]

The way of intoning in introits of the mass:

[Intonation formula for the sixth tone]

[Termination formula with *seculorum amen*]

[St. John the Evangelist: BnF lat. 1107 fol. 22v.]

[Common of a Confessor: BnF lat. 1107 fol. 313v.]

Be aware that I recall having seen in the whole Gradual no responsory of this tone that is neither irregular nor mixed with the fifth [tone], except perhaps this one that follows:

[Second week of Lent, Friday: BnF lat. 1107 fol. 69r.][319]

It should be known, however, that there are many responsories that seem to be a mixture of this tone and the fifth and contain a very beautiful melody. Since, however, they tend more to height and ascent than to gravity and descent, they seem to be rather of the domain of the fifth than the sixth. For example:

[Second week of Lent, Friday: BnF lat. 1107 fol. 50v.]

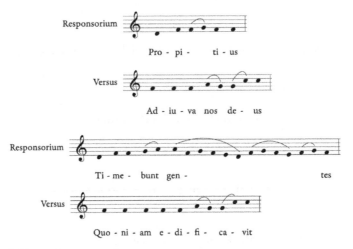

Et alia m[u]lta valde consimilia istis.

Exempla de alleluys.

[92r]

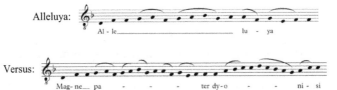

Exempla de sequentiis.

alia.

[First week of Lent, Saturday: BnF lat. 1107 fol. 58r.]

[Epiphany: BnF lat. 1107 fol. 33r.]

And many others very similar to these.

Examples of Alleluias:

[Seventeenth Sunday after Pentecost: BnF lat. 1107 fol. 194v.]

[St. Denis: not found in contemporary sources.]

Examples of sequences:

[Blessed Virgin Mary: BnF lat. 1107 fol. 375r.]

Another:

[St. Denis: London, Victoria and Albert Museum, MS 1346-1891][320]

Exempla de offerendis.

alia.

Exempla de communionibus.

alia.

[2.7.0]

Capitulum .vii. in quo ponuntur exempla de .vii. tono. antiphona. eiusdem toni cum suo neumate.

Modus intonandi super psalmos.

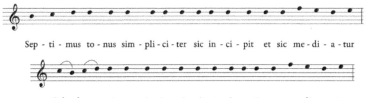

[2.7.1]

Prima differentia.

Et ista debetur illis .antiphonis. que incipientes a. gsolreut statim ascendunt in dlasolre isto modo.

[92v]

Examples of offertories:

> [Common of a Confessor: BnF lat. 1107 fol. 314r.]

Another:

> [Second week of Lent, Friday: BnF lat. 1107 fol. 69v.]

Examples of communions:

> [Common of a Martyr: BnF lat. 1107 fol. 293v.]

Another:

> [Second week of Lent, Thursday: BnF lat. 1107 fol. 68r.]

[2.7.0]
Chapter seven, in which examples of the seventh tone are given. The antiphon of the seventh tone with its *neumata*:

> [Revelations 4:5 provides the text for the model antiphon for tone 7.]

The way of intoning upon psalms:

> [Simple psalm intonation for the seventh tone]

> [Solemn psalm intonation for the seventh tone]

[2.7.1]
The first *differentia*:

> [Termination formula with *seculorum amen*]

And this is assigned to those antiphons that, beginning on G-solreut, immediately ascend to d-lasore in this way:

> [Octave of Epiphany: BnF lat. 17296 fol. 50r.]

vel sic magis gradatim.

De - scen -   di

vel sic

Re - dem - pti - o - nem

vel sic

Hic ac - ci - pi - et

vel sic

Do - mum tu - am do - mi - ne

vel sic

Vi - ri ga - li - le -   i

vel sic

Qui me dig - na - tus est

[2.7.2]
Secunda differentia.

Et sic fi - ni - tur.   E   u   o   u   a   e

Et ista debetur proprie illis .antiphonis. que incipiunt a. csolfaut. descendendo sic
et iterum ascendendo.

Cla - ma - ve -   runt

Do - mi - ne o - sten -   de

Or thus more step by step:

[Octave of the Assumption: BnF lat. 17329 fol. 226r]

Or thus:

[Christmas Day: BnF lat. 17296 fol. 25r.]

Or thus:

[Common of a Martyr: BnF lat. 17296 fol. 276v.]

Or thus:

[For dedications: BnF lat. 17296 fol. 289r.]

Or thus:

[Ascension: BnF lat. 17296 fol. 159r.]

Or thus:

[St. Agatha: BnF lat. 17296 fol. 73v.]

[2.7.2]
The second *differentia*:

[Termination formula with *seculorum amen*]

And this is properly assigned to those antiphons that begin on c-solfaut, descending thus and again ascending:

[Apostles: BnF lat. 17296 fol. 265r.]

[Saints Philip and James: BnF lat. 17296 fol. 153v.]

Et consimilibus. vel ascendendo sic quamvis raro hoc accidat.

Et in - gres - se

Item illis que a. bfabmi ita incipiunt.

Stel - la i - sta

Mi - sit do - mi - nus

[2.7.3]
Tertia differentia.

Et sic fi - ni - tur.   E u o u a e

Et ista proprie debetur .antiphonis. incipientibus a. dsolre isto modo.

Ad - iu - va - bit e - am

Spe - ci - e   tu - a

Et eis consimilibus vel sic.

A - ga - thes

Do - mi - ne la - bi - a

vel sic

Sit no - men do - mi - ni

Item incipientibus a csolfaut isto modo.

Lux   de   lu - ce

And similar ones. Or ascending thus, although this happens rarely:

[Easter antiphons: BnF lat. 17296 fol. 142v.]

Likewise, those that begin on b-fa-bi-mi thus:

[Epiphany: BnF lat. 17296 fol. 49v.]

[St. John the Baptist: BnF lat. 1107 fol. 169r.]

[2.7.3]
The third *differentia*:

[Termination formula with *seculorum amen*]

And this is properly assigned to those antiphons beginning on D-solre in this way:

[Purification: BnF lat. 17296 fol. 66r.]

[Purification: BnF lat. 17296 fol. 66r.]

And in similar ones or thus:

[St. Agatha: BnF lat. 15181 fol. 453v.]

[Second Sunday of Lent: BnF lat. 17296 fol. 104r.]

Or thus:

[Sundays throughout the year: BnF lat. 15181 fol. 80r.]

Likewise those beginning on c-solfaut in this way:

[Epiphany: BnF lat. 17296 fol. 49r.]

Item incipientibus ab alamire isto modo.

He - le - na san - cta

vel sic

In ver - bum tu - um

[2.7.4]
Quarta differentia.

Et sic fi - ni - tur.   E u o u a e

[93r] Et ista debetur illis .antiphonis. que incipientes a. gsolreut ascendunt statim in csolfaut et postea modicum descendunt et reascendunt isto modo.

Ca -   ri - tas

Pon - ti -   fi - ces

Item illis que ab eodem loco magis gradatim ascendunt isto modo.

Be - a - tus il - le   ser - vus

Exempla de responsoriis.

Mis - sus est

A -   ve   ma - ri - a

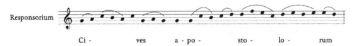

Ci -   ves   a - po -   sto -   lo -   rum

Au - di -   te

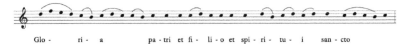

Glo -   ri - a   pa - tri et fi - li - o et spi - ri - tu - i   san - cto

Likewise those beginning on a-lamire in this way:

[Holy Cross: BnF lat. 17296 fol. 154v][321]

Or thus:

[Sunday in Septuagesima: BnF lat. 17296 fol. 88r.]

[2.7.4]
The fourth *differentia*:

[Termination formula with *seculorum amen*]

And this ought to be assigned to those antiphons that, beginning on G-solreut, ascend immediately to c-solfaut and afterwards descend a little and reascend in this way:

[Holy Trinity: BnF lat. 17296 fol. 166r.]

[St. Nicholas: BnF lat.17296 fol. 262r.]

Likewise for those that ascend from the same place more gradually in this way:

[Common of a Confessor: BnF lat.17296 fol. 282v.]

Examples of responsories:

[First week of Advent: BnF lat. 17296 fol. 2v.]

[Apostles: BnF lat. 15181 fols. 503r-v.]

Exempla[124] de invitatoriis.

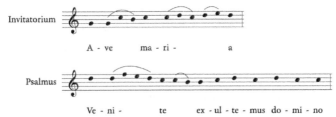

Invitatorium — A - ve ma - ri - a

Psalmus — Ve - ni - te ex - ul - te - mus do - mi - no

Exempla de hympnis.

Hympnus — For - tem fi - de - lem mi - li - tem

Hympnus — Re - rum de - us te - nax vi[gor]

Modus intonandi in officiis misse.

Sep - ti - mus to - nus in of - fi - ci - is sic in - ci - pit et sic me - di - a - tur

Et sic sem - per fi - ni - tur. E u o u a e

Officium — Pu - er na - tus est

Officium — Vi - ri ga - li - le - i

Exempla de responsoriis.
[93v]

Responsorium: — Ia - cta_____ co - gi - ta-tum

Versus: — Dum cla - ma - rem

[124] Exemplum *Klundert*

Examples of invitatories:

[Annunciation: BnF lat. 15181 fol. 467v.]³²²

Examples of hymns:

[St. Denis: Hymn possibly by Fortunatus not found with a melody in contemporary sources.]

[Hymn at Nones (St. Louis?): Attributed to St. Ambrose not found with a melody in contemporary sources.]

The way of intoning in introits of the mass:

[Intonation formula for the seventh tone]

[Termination formula with *seculorum amen*]

[Christmas Day: BnF lat. 1107 fol. 19v.]

[Ascension: BnF lat. 1107 fol. 162r.]

Examples of responsories:

[Thursday after Quinquagesima Sunday: BnF lat. 1107 fol. 44v.]

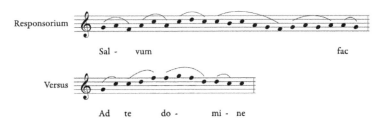

Responsorium

Sal - vum   fac

Versus

Ad   te   do -   mi - ne

Exempla de alleluys.

Alleluya

Al - le - lu -   ya

Versus

Pa - scha no -   strum

Alleluya

Al - le -   lu -   ya

Versus

Na - ti -   vi - tas

Exempla de sequentiis.

Sequentia

Zi - ma   ve - tus ex - pur - ge - tur

alia.

[Sequentia]

Cri - sto in - cli - ta can - di - da

Exemplum de tractibus.

Tractus

Be -   ne - di - ctus es do - mi - ne   de - us pa -   trum

Exempla de offerendis.

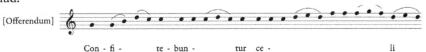

Offerendum

Pre - ca -   tus   est   mo - y - ses

aliud.

[Offerendum]

Con - fi -   te - bun -   tur ce -   li

[First week of Lent, Saturday: BnF lat. 1107 fol. 59r.]

Examples of Alleluias:

[Easter Sunday: BnF lat. 1107 fol. 144v.]

[Blessed Virgin Mary: BnF lat. 1107 fol. 263r.]

Examples of sequences:

[Tuesday of Holy Week: BnF lat. 1107 fol. 351r.]

Another:

[All Saints: BnF lat. 1107 fol. 385v.]

Example of tracts:

[First week in Advent, Saturday: BnF lat. 1107 fol. 11v.]

Examples of offertories:

[Second week of Lent, Thursday: BnF lat. 1107 fol. 67v.]

Another:

[Ascension: BnF lat. 1107 fol. 163av.]

Exempla de communionibus.

[2.8.0]

.viij^um. capitulum. in quo ponuntur exempla de .viij°. tono. antiphona. huius toni
cum suo neumate.

Modus intonandi super psalmos.

[94r]

[2.8.1]

Prima differentia.

Et ista debetur .antiphonis. incipientibus a. cfaut. ascendentibus sic

vel sic

vel sic

Examples of communions:

[Pentecost: BnF lat. 1107 fol. 169v.

[Third Sunday in Advent: BnF lat. 1107 fol. 6r.]

[2.8.0]
Chapter eight, in which examples of the eighth tone are given. The antiphon of the eighth tone with its *neumata*:

[Matthew 5:3-11 provides the text for the model antiphon for tone eight.]

The way of intoning upon psalms:

[Simple psalm intonation for the seventh tone]

[Solemn psalm intonation for the seventh tone]

[2.8.1]
The first *differentia*:

[Termination formula with *seculorum amen*]

And this ought to be assigned to antiphons beginning on C-faut ascending thus:

[Holy Innocents: BnF lat. 17296 fol. 39r.]

Or thus:

[From the Book of Wisdom: BnF lat. 17296 fol. 293r.]

Or thus:

[First Sunday after Ascension: BnF lat. 17296 fol. 160r.]

Item incipientibus a dsolre sic.

In - sig - nes pre - co - ni - is

Quamvis raro hoc accidat. Item incipientibus ab. ffaut. ascendendo sic.

Ho - di - e ma - ri - a vir - go

vel sic

Ma - gi

vel sic[125]

Io - cun - da - re

vel sic

Ma - ri - a no - li

vel sic

A - ni - me im - pi - o - rum

vel sic

A - ga - thes in - gres - sa

vel sic

E - gre - gi - o

Item incipientibus a. gsolreut isto modo descendentibus.

Dum me - di - um

vel sic

Pre - ce - dam vos

cccxlviii

---

[125] Iucundare **Klundert**.

Likewise for those beginning on D-solre thus:

[St. Denis: BnF lat. 17296 fol. 227r.]

although this happens rarely. Likewise those beginning on F-faut ascending thus:

[Assumption: BnF lat. 17296 fol. 207v.]

Or thus:

[Epiphany: BnF lat. 17296 fol. 44v.]

Or thus:

[First Sunday in Advent: BnF lat. 17296 fol. 4r.]

Or thus:

[Resurrection: BnF lat. 17296 fol. 144v.]

Or thus:

[Fifth Sunday of Lent: BnF lat. 17296 fol. 119v.]

Or thus:

[St. Agatha: BnF lat. 17296 fol. 70v.]

Or thus:

[St. Gregory: BnF lat. 17296 fol. 74r.]

Likewise for those beginning on G-solreut descending in this way:

[First Sunday after Christmas Day: BnF lat. 17296 fol. 25v.]

Or thus:

[Resurrection: BnF lat. 17296 fol. 143v.]

vel sic

Ec - ce   a - scen -   di - mus

vel sic

In   il -   la   di -   e

vel sic

Ad   om - ni -   a

Item ab eodem loco ascendentibus isto modo.

Tam - quam spon - sus

vel sic

Ne - mo   te con - demp - na -   vit

vel sic

Si   di - li -   gi - tis   me

vel sic[126]

Pe - trus a -   po - sto - lus

Item incipientibus ab alamire descendentibus isto modo.
[94v]

Sur - re -   xit do - mi - nus

vel sic

Com - ple -   ti   sunt

Et etiam ab eodem loco ascendentibus isto modo.

De fru - ctu

[126] apostolus **H2**

Or thus:

[Quinquagesima: BnF lat. 17296 fol. 96r.]

Or thus:

[First Sunday in Advent: BnF lat. 17296 fol. 3v.]

Or thus:

[St. John the Baptist: BnF lat. 17296 fol. 169r.]

Likewise for those ascending from the same place in this way:

[Christmas Day: BnF lat. 17296 fol. 19v.]

Or thus:

[Third Sunday of Lent: BnF lat. 17296 fol. 111r.]

Or thus:

[Pentecost: BnF lat. 17296 fol. 160v.]

Or thus:

[Apostles: BnF lat. 17296 fol. 181r.]

Likewise for those beginning on a-lamire descending in this way:

[Easter Sunday: BnF lat. 17296 fol. 143v.]

Or thus:

[Christmas Eve: BnF lat. 17296 fol. 19v.]

And also for those ascending from the same place in this way:

[Christmas Day: BnF lat. 17296 fol. 25v.]

Vi - den - ti - bus

vel sic

Tunc   va -   le - ri -   a -   nus

vel sic

Ce - ci - li -   a   me mi - sit

vel sic

Ad - iu - va me

[2.8.2]
Secunda differentia.

Et sic fi - ni - tur.   E u o u a e

Et ista debetur illis .antiphonis. que incipiunt a. csolfaut isto modo.

Do -   mi - nus

vel sic

Da - ta   sunt e -   i

vel sic

Antiphona:

Cir- cu[m] dan - tes

vel sic

Ve - ri - tas de ter - ra

vel sic

Ho - di - e sci - e -   tis

[Ascension Eve: BnF lat. 17296 fol. 159r.]

Or thus:

[St. Cecilia: BnF lat. 17296 fol. 253v.]

Or thus:

[St. Cecilia: BnF lat. 17296 fol. 253v.]

Or thus:

[Mondays throughout the year: BnF lat. 12044 fol. 32v.]

[2.8.2]
The second *differentia*:

[Termination formula with *seculorum amen*]

And this is assigned to those antiphons that begin on c-solfaut in this way:

[Ascension Eve: BnF lat. 17296 fol. 19v.]

Or thus:

[St. Michael: BnF lat. 17296 fol. 223r.]

Or thus:

[Palm Sunday: BnF lat. 17296 fol. 124v.]

Or thus:

[Christmas Day: BnF lat. 17296 fol. 20r.]

Or thus:

[Christmas Eve: BnF lat. 17296 fol. 18v.]

[2.8.3]
Tertia differentia.

Et sic fi - ni - tur.   E u o u a e

Et ista debetur antiphonis incipientibus ab alamire et ascendentibus statim in csolfaut sic.

Antiphona

Do - mi - ne in vir - tu - te

Antiphona

De   pro - fun - dis

Item incipientibus ab ipso. csolfaut ascendentibus isto modo.

Antiphona

Con - fir - ma hoc de -   us

vel sic

Antiphona

Tol -   le

vel ab eodem loco descendentibus sic.

Antiphona

Mag - nus san - ctus pau - lus

Antiphona

In do - mo   da - vid

Nota tamen quod sicut supra dixi de omnibus differentiis quarti toni licet apud
nos idem sit modus intonandi simpliciter et sollempniter omnes illas prima dumtaxat excepta, sequendo tamen communiorem usum et consuetudinem ceterorum
omnes potius intonari deberent sollempniter sicut prima. ita etiam et hic dico
salvo meliori atque saniori iudicio. quod licet apud nos non consuetum sit hactenus aliter intonare sollempniter quam simpliciter secundum istam differentiam
ultimam huius toni secundum tamen dicta musicorum. qui de tonis tractaverunt
nec istius [**95r**] differentie ad ceteras precedentes aliquam distinctionem quoad
modum intonandi fecerunt. videtur quod ista sollempniter potius sicut ille debeat
intonari. Istud tamen et omnia alia que hactenus dixi nostrorum potius arbitrio
seniorum iudicioque maiorum volo relinquere quam super hoc presumptuose
aliquid innovare vel temere diffinire.

[2.8.3]
The third *differentia*:

[Termination formula with *seculorum amen*]

And this is assigned to antiphons beginning on a-lamire and with immediate ascents on c-solfaut thus:

[St. Louis: Melbourne, State Library of Victoria, MS 096.1
[Poissy Antiphonal] fol. 313v.][323]

[Wednesdays throughout the year: BnF lat. 15181 fol. 193r.][324]

Likewise to those beginning on the same c-solfaut, with ascents in this way:

[Pentecost: BnF lat. 17296 fol. 160v.]

Or thus:

[Sunday in Septuagesima: BnF lat. 17296 fol. 89r.]

Or to those descending from the same point thus:

[St. Paul: BnF lat. 17296 fol. 182r.]

[Responsories from the Psalms: BnF lat. 17296 fol. 318r.]

Note, however, that just as I said above in relation to all the *differentiae* of the fourth tone, although amongst us the way of intoning all of these simply or solemnly is the same, except for the first yet, following more common use and custom, all of the rest ought rather to be intoned solemnly, just like the first. Also, therefore, I say this, saving better and wiser judgment, up to now amongst us it has not been the practice to intone this solemnly rather than simply according to this last *differentia* of this tone. Yet according to the sayings of the musicians who have dealt with the tones, and did not make any distinction in the way of intoning this differentia from the others preceding, it seems that this ought rather to be intoned solemnly like that one. This matter and all the others of ours that I have mentioned up to now, however, I leave to the decision of the elders and the judgment of betters rather than to introduce something presumptuously or define anything rashly.

[2.8.4]

Quarta differentia.

I- tem__ a - li-quan-do to-nus is - te sic in - ci-pit et sic me-di - a - tur

Et sic fi - ni- tur__   E u o u a e

Et ista differentia apud nos attribuitur solum isti .antiphone.

Antiphona

Nos qui vi - vi - mus be - ne - di - ci - mus do - mi - no

Istum autem cantum sicut dicunt communiter tractantes de tonis non tam ratio
quam voluntas et usus obtinuit. habet enim irregulare medium intonandi idest
non secundum formam et regulam octavi toni sed accommodatum potius a sexto
tono. unde et aliqui huiusmodi cantum appellant obliquum alii peregrinum. alii
abortivum.

Exempla de responsoriis.

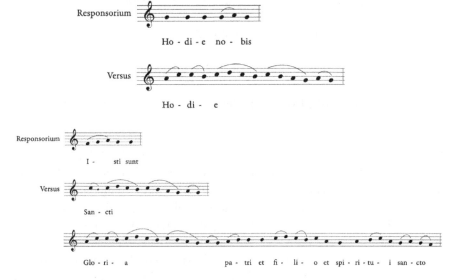

Responsorium

Ho - di - e no - bis

Versus

Ho - di - e

Responsorium

I -   sti sunt

Versus

San - cti

Glo - ri - a   pa - tri et fi - li - o et spi - ri - tu - i san - cto

[2.8.4]
The fourth *differentia*:

[Similarly, this tone sometimes begins and is mediated thus.]

[Termination formula with *seculorum amen*]

And this *differentia* is attributed amongst us only to this antiphon:

[Sundays throughout the year: BnF lat. 15181 fol. 80v.]

It is not so much reason, however, but will and custom that has maintained this chant, as those dealing with tones commonly say, for it has an irregular mediant in intoning that does not accord with the form and rule of the eighth tone but rather is adapted from the sixth tone. Hence some people call chant of this kind lopsided, others meandering, others addled.

Examples of responsories:

[Christmas Day: BnF lat. 17296 fol. 20v.]

[Apostles: BnF lat. 17296 fol. 274r.]

Notandum est quod sicut aliqui dicunt nullum est venite octavi toni. dicunt enim quod sicut sunt .vij. solum dies in ebdomada. et septem dona spiritus sancti. ita etiam spirituales ecclesie doctores. qui nos invitando ad postulandam septiformem spiritus sancti gratiam invitatoria statuerunt cantari. antiquitus incipiebant prima die ab invitatorio primi toni et sic deinceps. ita videlicet quod septimo die in invitatorio septimi toni finiebant et sic numerum invitatoriorum iuxta numerum .vij. dierum qui sunt in ebdomada statuerunt. Quicquid tamen sit de [**95v**] hoc, potest dici secundum magistrum iohannem predictum qui allegat usum parisiensis. ecclesie et magistrum petrum de cruce qui fuit optimus cantor et ambianensis ecclesie consuetudinem specialiter observavit, aliqua invitatoria sunt istius toni saltem duo. unum videlicet de quo ponit exemplum ille magister petrus quod[127] apud nos non est in usu nec eius venite. sed videntur esse de usu ambianensis ecclesie sumpta. scilicet preoccupemus. Aliud vero de quo ponit exemplum prefatus magister iohannes de garlandia. videlicet istud quod sequitur.

Exempla[128] de invitatoriis.

Invitatorium   Re - gem cu - i om - ni - a   vi - vunt

Psalmus   Ve - ni - te ex - ul - te - mus do - mi - no

Nec istud est contrarium illi quod supra dixi tractando et exempla ponendo de invitatoriis et venite sexti toni ubi istud invitatorium cum suo venite[129] positum fuit tamquam sexti toni. sicut enim ibi potest videri ambo notantur cum .b. rotundo vel molli et sic in .f. gravi idest in primo .ffaut. terminantur que ut dictum est in prima parte operis huius est finalis littera sexti toni. hic vero sine .b. molli vel rotundo notantur. et sic in .g. gravi. secundo idest in primo gsolreut. que est octavi toni finalis littera terminantur. et sic diversis respectibus possunt esse diversorum tonorum. sicut etiam supra dictum est de eodem seculorum amen respectu diversarum antiphonarum. et de eodem venite respectu diversorum invitatoriorum. Immo etiam si quis diligenter velit inspicere quandoque eadem antiphona secundum diversum modum notandi eam posset esse et est quandoque diversorum tonorum ita quod a quibusdam dicitur esse unius toni et ab aliis alterius sicut est de antiphona. me suscepit. mecum enim et aliis multis quare vero hoc accidat non est speculationis presentis.

---

[127] qui **H1**; quod *Klundert.*
[128] Exemplum *Klundert*

[129] neumate *struck through and corrected with* venite *inserted from left margin.*

It should be noted that just as some say there is no *Venite* of the eighth tone, for they say there are only seven days in the week and seven gifts of the Holy Spirit, thus also the spiritual doctors of the church decree that invitatories be sung inviting us to ask for the seven-fold grace of the Holy Spirit. In antiquity they began on the first day with the invitatory of the first tone, and so on. So clearly they concluded on the seventh day with the invitatory of the seventh tone and thus they decree the number of invitatories to be the same number, seven, as the days of the week. Yet whatever is the case about this it can be said according to the said Master John, who invokes the use of the Church of Paris, and Master Petrus de Cruce, who was the finest cantor and particularly observed the practice of the church of Amiens, that some invitatories are of this tone, at least two: namely one, for which Master Petrus gives an example, which is not in use among us nor its *Venite*, but they seem to be taken from the use of the church of Amiens, namely *Preoccupemus*.[325] The other is that for which the said Master John of Garland gives an example, namely that which follows.

Examples of invitatories:

[Office for the Dead: not found in chant sources][326]

This is not contrary to what I said above in treating and giving examples of invitatories and *Venites* of the sixth tone, where that invitatory with its *Venite* was placed as if of the sixth tone; for just as, in that place, it seems to be that they are notated with round or soft b, and thus they are terminated on F-grave, that is, on the first F-faut, which, as was said in the first part of this work, is the final letter of the sixth tone. But here they are notated without soft or round b, and similarly they are terminated on the second G-grave, that is, the first G-solreut, which is the final letter of the eighth tone. And thus they can be of different tones in different respects, just as was also said above about the same *seculorum amen* with respect to different antiphons, and about the same *Venite*, with respect to different invitatories. Rather, even if anyone wishes to carefully consider that sometimes the same antiphon can sometimes be of different tones, according to a different way of notating it, so that it is said to be of one tone by some people and by others to be of another, just as is the antiphon *Me suscepit*,[sss] *Mecum enim*[ttt] and many others—but why this happens is not at present under consideration.

Exempla de hympnis.

Hympnus

Ver - bum su - per - num pro - di - ens

Hympnus

I -   ste con - fes - sor

Modus intonandi in officiis misse.

O - cta - vus   to - nus in of - fi - ci - is sic in - ci - pit et sic   me - di - a - tur

[96r]

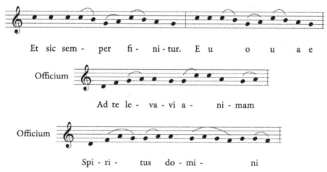

Et sic sem - per fi - ni - tur. E u   o   u   a e

Officium

Ad te le - va - vi a - ni - mam

Officium

Spi - ri - tus do - mi - ni

Exempla de responsoriis.

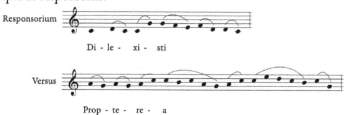

Responsorium

Di - le - xi - sti

Versus

Prop - te - re - a

Examples of hymns:

[Advent: BnF lat. 8882 fol. 151v but transposed up a tone.]

[Vespers Hymn: BnF lat. 1028 fol. 277v.]

The way of intoning in introits of the mass:

[Intonation formula for the eighth tone]

[Termination formula with *seculorum amen*]

[Advent: BnF lat. 1107 fol. 1r.]

[Pentecost: BnF lat. 1107 fol. 168r.]

Examples of responsories:

[Common of several Confessors: BnF lat. 1107 fols. 316r-v.]

ˢˢˢ Fourth week in Advent: BnF lat. 17296 f. 345v (see example below) which is in mixed tone 5/6. But see also BnF lat. 15182 f. 427v, in mixed tone 7/8 which illustrates Guy's point.

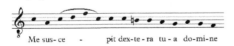

Me sus-ce -   pit dex-te - ra tu - a do-mi-ne

ᵗᵗᵗ St. Agnes: BnF lat. 17296 f. 59r which is in tone 5, but see also BnF lat. 15181 f. 425v (example below) which is in tone 8

Me-cum e -   nim__ ha - be - o cus - to - dem cor - por - is me - i

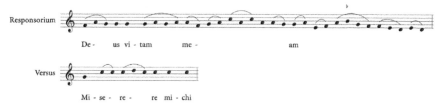

Responsorium

De - us vi - tam   me -   am

Versus

Mi - se - re -   re mi - chi

Exempla de alleluys.

Alleluya

A -   lle -   lu -   ya

Versus

O - sten -   de no - bis

Alleluya

A -   lle -   lu - ya

Versus

An - ge -   lus do - mi -   ni

Exempla de sequentiis.

Sequentia

E - pi - pha - ni - am do - mi - no

alia.

[Sequentia]

Ver - bum   bo - num et su - a - ve

Exempla de tractibus.

Tractus

De pro - fun -   dis

alius.

[Tractus]

Si - cut cer -   vus

alius.

[Tractus]

Qui re -   gis

[Third week of Lent, Monday: BnF lat. 1107 fol. 75r.]

Examples of Alleluias:

[First Sunday in Advent: BnF lat. 1107 fol. 1v.]

[Tuesday after Easter Sunday: BnF lat. 1107 fol. 148r.]

Examples of sequences:

[Epiphany: BnF lat. 1107 fol. 346v.]

Another:

[Assumption: BnF lat. 1107 fol. 367r.]

Examples of tracts:

[Septuagesima Sunday: BnF lat. 1107 fol. 36r.]

Another:

[Vigil of St. Felix: BnF lat. 1107 fol. 138v.]

Another:

[Saturday of the third week of Advent: BnF lat. 1107 fol. 12v.]

alius.

[Tractus]

Qui con - fi -   dunt

alius.

[96v]
Tractus:

Se- pe_____   ex - pu- gna - ve- runt___ me

Exempla de offerendis.

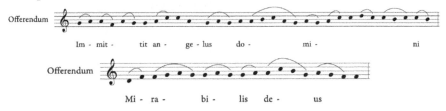

Offerendum

Im - mit -   tit an -   ge - lus   do -   mi -   ni

Offerendum

Mi - ra -   bi -   lis   de -   us

Exempla de communionibus.

Communio

Di -   co au - tem   vo -   bis

Communio

Lux e -   ter - na

Communio

O - por - tet te fi - li

Et hec de tonis. quantum precipue ad usum et consuetudinem nostri monasterii pertinet cui quantum commode potui me ipsum conformare studui de dictis
boecii. Guidonis monachi et aliorum quorundam ut a principio dixi ad presens
sufficiat collegisse illo mediante cui est honor et gloria in secula seculorum. amen.
Explicit tractatus de tonis a fratre guidone monacho monasterii sancti dyonisii in
francia compilatus.[130]

---

[130] hoc est Explicit tractus de tonis a
fratre guidone monacho monasterii sancti
dyonisii in francia compilatus *added* Gosselin (**H3**).

Another:

[Fourth week of Lent: BnF lat. 1107 fol. 85r.]

Another:

[Passion Sunday: BnF lat. 1107 fol. 97r.]

Examples of offertories:

[First week of Lent, Thursday: BnF lat. 1107 fol. 56r.]

[Common of several Martyrs: BnF lat. 1107 fol. 301v.]

Examples of communions:

[Common of several Martyrs: BnF lat. 1107 fol. 303r]

[Requiem Mass: BnF lat. 1107 fol. 330v.]

[Second week of Lent, Saturday: BnF lat. 1107 fol. 72r.]

And let it suffice that these things about the tones have been collected from the sayings of Boethius, Guido the monk, and certain others, as far as pertains particularly to the use and custom of our monastery, to which I have endeavored to conform myself as fittingly as I could; as I have said from the beginning to the present, this is through the mediation of Him to Whom is honor and glory forever and ever. Amen.

Here ends the treatise on the tones compiled by brother Guy, monk of the monastery of Saint-Denis in France.

NOTES

[1] "pre nimia brevitate...obscurior." See Horace, *Ars poetica* 25: "Denique sit quod uis, simplex dumtaxat et unum. Maxima pars uatum, pater et iuuenes patre digni, decipimur specie recti. Breuis esse laboro, obscurus fio; sectantem leuia nerui deficiunt animique; professus grandia turget; serpit humi tutus nimium timidusque procellae; qui uariare cupit rem prodigialiter unam, delphinum siluis adpingit, fluctibus aprum."

[2] "sic que scillam...in caribdim." Cf. Walter of Châtillon, *Alexandreis* 5:301, p. 133: "Incidis in Scillam cupiens uitare Charibdim." As with the name "Guido" in the *Tractatus*, the name Guillermus is spelt out in the *Alexandreis* in the initial letters of its chapters. This is a reference to Archbishop William of Rheims, to whom Walter dedicated the *Alexandreis*.

[3] "ex musica boecii," i.e. Boethius, *De institutione musica*.

[4] "omnis ars...difficili." Cf. Jacobus, *Speculum musicae* 7.45, vol. 3/7, p. 88. Ars enim, etsi dicatur esse de difficili, est tamen de bono et utili, cum sit virtus animam intellectu mediante perficiens." See also Aristotle, *Ethics* 1.1:1094a1–2: "Omnis ars et omnis doctrina similiter atuem et operatio et proheresis boni alicuius operatrix esse videtur;" *Ethics* 2.3:1105a9–10: "Circa difficiliosa vero semper ars virtusque consistit."

[5] "quod tonus in musica duobus modis accipitur." Grocheio, *Ars musice* 4.12, "Tonus autem multipliciter dicitur...uno enim modo dicitur de elevatione, depressione, et fine cantus...Alio modo dicitur de concordantia que consistit in aliqua proportione."

[6] "nam tropus...secundum guidonem." Cf. John Cotton, *De musica cum tonario* 10, p. 77: "Tropi a convenienti conversione dicti; quomodocumque enim cantus in medio varietur, ad finalem semper per tropos id est tonos convenienter convertitur. Quos autem nos modos vel tropos nominamus, Graeci phtongos vocant. Et sciendum, quod eos tonos appellari Guidoni incongruem videtur et abusivum." See Guido of Arezzo, *Micrologus* 10, p. 133: "Hi sunt quattuor modi vel tropi, quos abusive tonos nominant, qui sic sunt ab invicem naturali diversitate disiuncti, ut alter alteri in sua sede locum non tribuat, alterque alterius neumam aut transformet aut numquam recipiat." See also Jacobus, *Speculum musicae* 6.35, vol. 3/6, p. 86: "Nam dicuntur tropi, modi et toni. Graece dicuntur tropi. Est autem tropus conversio, a trophos vel strophos, quod est conversio."

[7] Grocheio, *Ars musice* 4.12: "uno enim modo dicitur de elevatione, depressione, et fine cantus, ut ecclesiastici accipiunt."

[8] "Tonus secundum aliquos...diiudicat." Cf. Pseudo-Odo, *Dialogus de musica* 8, p. 257: "Tonus vel modus est regula, quae de omni cantu in fine diiudicat." See also Grocheio, *Ars musice* 25.1: "Describunt autem tonum quidam, dicentes eum esse regulam que de omni cantu in fine iudicat."

[9] "qui cantus publicos...regulari." See Grocheio, *Ars musice* 25.1: "Sed isti videntur multipliciter peccare. Cum enim dicunt dicitur omni cantu: videntur cantum civilem et mensuratum includere. Cantus autem iste per toni regulas forte non vadit, nec per eas mensuratur;" Grocheio, *Ars musice* 26.1 Dico etiam cantum ecclesiasticum. ut excludantur cantus publicus et precise mensuratus, qui tonis non subiciuntur."

[10] "Tonus est regula...ad finem." See Grocheio, *Ars musice* 26.1: "Temptemus igitur aliter describere et dicamus quod tonus est regula per quam quis potest omnem cantum ecclesiasticum cognoscere et de eo iudicare. Inspiciendo ad initium. medium. vel ad finem."

¹¹ "Dicitur autem…tonando." Cf. John Cotton, *De musica cum tonario* 8, p. 68: "Tonus a tonando vocatur."

¹² "vel ab intonando…intonantur." See Guido of Arezzo, *Micrologus* 6, p. 116: "Tonus autem ab intonando, id est sonando, nomen accepit qui maiori voci novem, minori vero octo passus constituit." See also Jacobus, *Speculum musicae* 2.39, vol. 3/2, p. 97: "Tonus, secundum Guidonem, ab intonando dicitur, quia perfecte intonat, vel a 'tono, tonas', quia perfecte duarum vocum immediate sibi succedentium distantiam manifestat."

¹³ "Alio modo…concordantia appellatur." See Grocheio, *Ars musice* 2.2: "Principia autem musice solent consonantie et concordantie appellari."

¹⁴ I.e. the proportion of 9:8 (one and one extra part, an eighth, to one). See [1.1.6].

¹⁵ "que videlicet concordantia…consistens." Cf. Grocheio, *Ars musice* 4.12: "Alio modo dicitur de concordantia que consistit in aliqua proportione. et isto modo tonus est cum unus sonus alii continuatus eum in acuitate vel gravitate excedit vel exceditur ab eo in sexquioctava proportione sicut .9. se habet ad .8. vel econtrario."

¹⁶ "quia tamen … principia." See Grocheio, *Ars musice* 2.2: "Principia autem musice solent consonantie et concordantie appellari."

¹⁷ "ignoratis autem…ignorari." Cf. Jacobus, *Speculum musicae* 1.1, vol. 3/1, p. 12: "Sed iam ad narrationem descendamus, ubi praemittemus quaedam communia, quae scire convenit, cum, ignoratis communibus, ars ignoretur, licet, illis scitis, ars non sciatur, quae ex propriis procedit principiis." See also Aristotle, *Physics* 1.1 184a12: "Scire et intelligere contingit circa omnes scientias quarum principia sunt causa et elementa ex eorum cognitione."

¹⁸ "a boecio…pertractata." See Boethius, *De institutione musica* 1.10, pp. 197–198 ("Quemadmodum Pythagoras proportiones consonantiarum investigaverit"). Cf. Guido of Arezzo, *Micrologus* 20, pp. 228–233: ("Quomodo musica ex malleorum sonitu sit inventa").

¹⁹ "consonantia que omnem…usque ad auditum." See Boethius, *De institutione musica* 1.3, p. 189: "Consonantia, quae omnem musicae modulationem regit, praeter sonum fieri non potest, sonus vero praeter quendam pulsum percussionemque non redditur, pulsus vero atque percussio nullo modo esse potest, nisi praecesserit motus. Si enim cuncta sint inmobilia, non poterit alterum alteri concurrere, ut alterum inpellatur ab altero, sed cunctis stantibus motuque carentibus nullum fieri necesse est sonum. Idcirco definitur sonus percussio aeris indissoluta usque ad auditum." Cf. Peter of Auvergne, *Quodlibet* 6.16.413: "De primo dicendum est, quod harmonia seu consonantia musica non est sine sono. Musica enim per se considerat numerum in sonis. Sonus autem sine percussione et pulsu esse non potest. Hic autem motus quidam sunt locales. Unde, si omnia quiescerent, sonus omnino non esset, propter quod sonus materialiter definitur, quod est percussio continua usque ad auditam."

²⁰ "Motuum vero localium…non diutius tremit." See Boethius, *De institutione musica* 1.3, pp. 189–190: "Motuum vero alii sunt velociores, alii tardiores, eorundemque motuum alii rariores sunt alii spissiores…Et si tardus quidem fuerit ac rarior motus, graves necesse est sonos effici ipsa tarditate et raritate pellendi. Sin vero sint motus celeres ac spissi, acutos necesse est reddi sonos. Idcirco enim idem nervus, si intendatur amplius, acutum sonat, si remittatur, grave. Quando enim tensior est, velociorem pulsum reddit celeriusque revertitur et frequentius ac spissius aerem ferit. Qui vero laxior est, solutos ac tardos pulsus effert rarosque ipsa inbecillitate feriendi, nec diutius tremit." Cf. Peter of Auvergne, *Quodlibet* 6.16.413: "Motuum autem alii sunt tardiores, alii vero velociores, eorundem etiam quidam

sunt rariores, quidam spissiores. Rarior vero aut tardior si fuerit motus, sonum efficit gravere, si autem celer fuerit aut spissus, acutum. Propter quod, si eadem corda intendatur amplius, acutiorem sonum reddit, si vero remittatur, graviorem. Quanto enim tensior fuerit, velociorem pulsum reddit celeriusque revertitur et frequentius aerem percutit, quanto vero laxior, tardiores reddit pulsus, et propter inbecillitatem percussionis non diutius tremit."

[21] "Neque enim quando...celeribus atque spissis." Boethius, *De institutione musica* 1.3, p. 190: "Neque enim quotiens chorda pellitur, unus edi tantum putandus est sonus aut unam in his esse percussionem, sed totiens aer feritur, quotiens eum chorda tremebunda percusserit. Sed quoniam iunctae sunt velocitates sonorum, nulla intercapedo sentitur auribus et unus sonus sensum pellit vel gravis vel acutus, quamvis uterque ex pluribus constet gravis quidem ex tardioribus et rarioribus acutus vero ex celeribus ac spissis."

[22] Quoniam ergo acute...et inequalitate distantes." See Boethius, *De institutione musica* 1.3, pp. 190–191: "Igitur quoniam acutae voces spissioribus et velocioribus motibus incitantur, graves vero tardioribus ac raris, liquet additione quadam motuum ex gravitate acumen intendi, detractione vero motuum laxari ex acumine gravitatem. Ex pluribus enim motibus acumen quam gravitas constat. In quibus autem pluralitas differentiam facit, ea necesse est in quadam numerositate consistere. Omnis vero paucitas ad pluralitatem ita sese habet, ut numerus ad numerum comparatus. Eorum vero, quae secundum numerum conferuntur, partim sibi sunt aequalia partim inaequalia. Quocirca soni quoque partim sunt aequales, partim vero sunt inaequalitate distantes." Cf. Peter of Auvergne, *Quodlibet* 6.16.413: "Quoniam igitur voces acutae a spissioribus et velocioribus causantur motibus, graves vero a tardioribus et raris, manifestum est, quadam additione motuum ex gravitate in acumen intendi, subtractione vero eorundem laxari ex acumine in gravitatem. In quibus autem pluralitas differentiam facit, necesse est in quadam numerositate consistere. Omnis vero paucitas ad pluralitatem sic se habet ut numerus ad numerum comparatus. Eorum vero, quae secundum numerum conferuntur, quaedam sunt aequalia, quaedam autem inaequalia, et ideo sonorum quidam aequales, quidam autem inaequales."

[23] "In hijs autem ...proprie loquendo consonantia." Cf. Boethius, *De institutione musica* 1.3, p. 191: "Sed in his vocibus, quae nulla inaequalitate discordant, nulla omnino consonantia est."

[24] "sed magis aliquid...musicalium est mensura" Cf. Peter of Auvergne, *Quodlibet* 6.16.413: "Et in his, qui simpliciter sunt aequales, non est proprie consonantia vel harmonia musica proprie, sed aliquid perfectius et sicut mensura omnium consonantiarum vel harmoniarum musicalium."

[25] "quod consonantia est...in unum concordia." See Boethius, *De institutione musica* 1.3, p. 191: "Est enim consonantia dissimilium inter se vocum in unum redacta concordia."

[26] "Licet autem...videantur differentiam" E.g. John of Garland, *De mensurabili musica* 9, p. 67: "Sequitur de consonantiis in eodem tempore. Consonantiarum quaedam dicuntur concordantiae, quaedam discordantiae."

[27] "Consonantia namque est...perfectam efficiunt melodiam." Cf. Grocheio, *Ars musice* 2.2: "Consonantiam autem dico quando duo soni vel plures simul uniti et in uno tempore unam perfectam armoniam reddunt."

[28] "ille voces sunt...nec suavem sonum." See Boethius, *De institutione musica* 4.1, p. 302: "Consonae quidem sunt, quae simul pulsae suavem permixtumque inter se coniungunt sonum. Dissonae vero, quae simul pulsae non reddunt suavem neque permixtum sonum."

[29] "Concordantia vero ut...per ascensum et descensum." Cf. Jacobus, *Speculum musicae* 2.10, vol. 3/2, p. 31: "ratione accentus est quidam cantus, et tamen, in moderato accentu, locum habet solus unisonus, non sic in gravi et acuto, in quibus proceditur secundum arsim vel thesim, id est secundum elevationem vel depositionem. Item aves cantare dicuntur et tamen in ipsarum cantibus male potest discerni qua utantur consonantia, nisi unisono."

[30] *Armonice*, derived from *armonia*, often loosely translated as "harmony," is a term with a range of meanings in medieval music theory and is most often understood as a well-ordered arrangement of pitches in a system. In general terms it refers to a joining together or adjustment of parts. See Thomas J. Mathiesen. "Harmonia (i)." *Grove Music Online. Oxford Music Online.* Oxford University Press. [Subscriber access required].

[31] "Vel ut aliqui...temporis continuatur alteri." Cf. Grocheio, *Ars musice* 2.2: "Dico autem concordantiam quando unus sonus cum alio armonice continuatur. Sicut una pars temporis vel motus cum alia continua est."

[32] "ita scilicet armonice...excedatur ab eo." Cf. Grocheio, *Ars musice* 4.12: "Alio modo dicitur de concordantia que consistit in aliqua proportione. et isto modo tonus est cum unus sonus alii continuatus eum in acuitate vel gravitate excedit vel exceditur ab eo."

[33] "de numero relato ad sonum." Cf. Boethius, *De institutione musica* 1.7, p. 194: "Illud tamen esse cognitum debet, quod omnis musicae consonantiae aut in duplici aut in triplici aut in quadrupla aut in sesqualtera aut in sesquitertia proportione consistant; et vocabitur quidem, quae in numeris sesquitertia, diatessaron in sonis..." See also Grocheio, *Ars musice* 5.1: "Dicentes eam esse de numero relato ad sonos;" John of Garland, *Musica plana, reportatio* 1.8, p. 3: "Alia est relata de qua est musica in qua determinatur de numeris relatis ad sonos."

[34] "vel de sono armonice numerato." Cf. Grocheio, *Ars musice* 5.3: "musica est ars vel scientia de sono numerato armonice;" Cf. Robert Kilwardby, *De ortu scientiarum* pp. 51-2: paragraph 128: "et ideo posuerunt recte musicam audibilem esse de sono harmonice numerato vel de numero sonorum harmonico."

[35] "sicut arismetica...absolute considerato" Cf. John of Garland, *Musica plana, reportatio* 1.8, p. 3: "...quia alia est absoluta de qua est Arismetica, in qua determinatur de numeris absolute."

[36] "Unde secundum...corruptio melodie." Cf. Grocheio, *Ars musice* 2.7: "Si enim proportio consonantie causa esset ubi esset talis proportio ibi esset talis consonantia. Quod non videtur intuenti sonum tonicus cum alio ei habenti proportionem. Non enim armoniam faciunt. sed potius organum auditus corrumpunt."

[37] "concordantes sonos...melodie appellat." See Boethius, *De institutione musica* 1.8, p. 195: "Sonus igitur est vocis casus emmeles, id est aptus melo, in unam intensionem."

[38] "discordantes autem...melodie ineptos." See Boethius, *De institutione musica* 5.6, p. 357: "Potest enim distantium sibique dissimilium vocum differentia deprehendi, in quibus, qui iuncti efficere melos possunt, emmeles dicuntur, ekmeles autem, quibus iunctis melos effici non potest."

[39] "Quamvis autem...dixerunt infinitas." Grocheio, *Ars musice* 2.4: "Quidam autem vulgaliter loquentes dixerunt esse consonantias infinitas. Sed sue positionis nullam assignaverunt rationem;" Grocheio, *Ars musice* 4.5: Quibusdam vero videtur concordantias infinitas esse. Sed ad hoc nullam probabilitatem adducunt."

[40] "Alii vero .xiii....et dyapason." John of Garland, *Musica plana, reportatio* 1.60, p. 7: "Sciendum quod diatonici generis sunt XIII species, uidelicet unisonus, diapason,

diapente, diatessaron, tonus, semitonium maius, ditonus, semiditonus, tonus cum diapente, semitonium cum diapente, <semiditonus cum diapente>, ditonus cum diapente,
tritonus." Cf. Grocheio, *Ars musice* 4.7: "Alii finitas esse dicunt et sub numero determinato.
plures tamen quam .7. puta .13. qui volunt dictum suum per experientiam declarare. sicut
magister .Iohannes. de garlandia."

⁴¹ "Quidam vero...et dyapason." Grocheio, *Ars musice* 2.5: "Alii autem rationabiliter
loquentes tres consonantias esse asserunt. volentes per numeros sui dicti rationem osten-
dere;" Grocheio, *Ars musice* 3.3: Est enim una prima armonia quasi mater, que dyapason
ab antiquis dicta est: Et alia quasi filia in ista contenta dyapente dicta. Et tertia ab eis procedens que dyatessaron appellatur."

⁴² "consonantias secundarias...cum dyapente." Cf. Grocheio, *Ars musice* 4.10: "Antequam autem aliorum experientia dissolvatur, oportet videre quid unaqueque istarum sit. et
qualiter sic dicatur. Dicimus autem eas. Unisonum. Tonum. Semitonum. Dytonum. Semiditonum vel dyatessaron. Dyapente, et dyapason." See also John of Garland, *De mensurabili musica* 9, p. 69: "Sic apparet, quod sex sunt species concordantiae, scilicet unisonus,
diapason, diapente, diatessaron, ditonus, semiditonus"

⁴³ "Secundum tamen...ad .vii." Grocheio, *Ars musice* 4.8: "Alii autem omnes ad .7.
reducunt. Qui modo subtiliori investigant."

⁴⁴ "tonus. semitonus...et dyapason." Cf. Grocheio, *Ars musice* 1.4: "Et sic invenit pytagoras quid esset. Dyesis. Tonus. Ditonus. Semiditonus. Dyatessaron. Dyapente. Dyapason.
Et ex hiis composita. Ista autem principia sunt et materia qua utitur omnis musicus."

⁴⁵ "melius est...principiis contradicat." Grocheio, *Ars musice* 4.8: "Melius enim est
pauca principia supponere, cum pluralitas principiis contradicat."

⁴⁶ "Cum enim...penitus imitari." Grocheio, *Ars musice* 4.9: "...homo ut ait plato et
aristoteles. est quasi mundus. unde et microcosmus .idest. minor mundus ab eis dicitur.
unde et leges et operationes humane debent legem divinam ut possibile est penitus imitari."

⁴⁷ "Ad diversitatem...virtutibus suffecerant." Grocheio, *Ars musice* 4.9: "Ad diversitatem autem generationum et corruptionum totius universi .vii. stelle cum earum virtutibus
suffecerunt."

⁴⁸ "sicut ergo .vii....annus mensuratur." Grocheio, *Ars musice* 4.8: "...et in septimana .7.
dies. quibus multotiens resumptis totus annus mensuratur."

⁴⁹ "vii. que sunt dona spiritus sancti." Grocheio, *Ars musice* 4.8: "dicentes esse .7. dona
spiritus."

⁵⁰ "Ita rationabile...sufficere videantur." Grocheio, *Ars musice* 4.9 "Et ideo rationabile
fuit ponere in arte humana .vii. principia que omnium diversitatum sonorum cum armonia
cause essent, que quidem cause concordantie appellantur."

⁵¹ "Etsi que...principia aliarum." Cf. Grocheio, *Ars musice* 4.18: "que concordantie
composite et non simplices debent dici. Nos autem solum hic intendimus de hiis ut sunt
simplices et principia aliarum."

⁵² The intervals constructed here are the tritone or augmented fourth (*diabolus in
musica*) and the major 6th. "qui enim...potest efficere." Grocheio, *Ars musice* 4.18: "Qui
enim scit quid tonus. quid dytonus. potest de levi per additionem toni tritonum efficere.
Et qui cognoscit quid dyapente potest ex additione toni tonum cum dyapente efficere."

⁵³ "Restat igitur...ac dyapason." Cf. Grocheio, *Ars musice* 4.10: "...oportet videre quid

unaqueque istarum sit. et qualiter sic dicatur. Dicimus autem eas. Unisonum. Tonum. Semitonum. Dytonum. Semiditonum vel dyatessaron. Dyapente, et dyapason."

[54] "Tonus igitur est...exceditur ab eodem." Cf. Grocheio, *Ars musice* 4.12: "Alio modo dicitur de concordantia que consistit in aliqua proportione. et isto modo tonus est cum unus sonus alii continuatus eum in acuitate vel gravitate excedit vel exceditur ab eo in sexquioctava proportione sicut .9. se habet ad .8. vel econtrario."

[55] "unde quod est proportio sexquioctava in numeris. hoc est tonus...in sonis musicis." Boethius uses a similar phrasology to describe the *diatessaron.* Boethius, *De institutione musica* 1.7, p. 194: "quae in numeris sesquitertia, diatessaron in sonis."

[56] "Est autem sexquioctava...pars octava." Cf. Lambert, *Tractatus de musica*, p. 257: "Sicut enim in numeris videmus quod aliquis numerus continet alium numerum et octavam partem ejus, sicut novem continet octo et ejus octavam partem que est unitas; sic quando vox una super aliam in octava parte elevatur, hic proprie tonus appellatur."

[57] "Dicitur autem tonus...sonus latine." Cf. Boethius, *De institutione musica* 1.8, p. 195: "Sonum vero non generalem nunc volumus definire, sed eum, qui graece dicitur phthongos, dictus a similitudine loquendi, id est phthengesthai." See also John Cotton, *De musica cum tonario* 4, p. 58: "Solus dumtaxat discretus, qui etiam proprie phthongus vocatur, ad musicam pertinet."

[58] "si enim non sonaret. non audiretur tonus." Cf. Peter of Auvergne, *Quodlibet* 6.16.413: "De primo dicendum est, quod harmonia seu consonantia musica non est sine sono."

[59] Cf. John Cotton, *De musica cum tonario* 8, p. 68: "Tonus a tonando vocatur. Est autem tonare potenter sonare, et tonus fortem habet sonum respectu semitonii."

[60] "et per consequens...remissus sonus." Grocheio, *Ars musice* 4.13: "Semitonus autem vel dyesis dicitur non quia medietatem toni contineat. Sed quia ab eius perfectione deficit. Est enim quasi tonus remissus vel imperfectus."

[61] "Dicitur autem semitonus...toni contineat." Cf. Boethius, *De institutione musica* 2.28, p. 260: "Videntur enim semitonia nuncupata, non quod vere tonorum sint medietates, sed quod sint non integri toni."

[62] "sed quia tamquam...toni deficiat." Grocheio, *Ars musice* 4.13: "Semitonus autem vel dyesis dicitur non quia medietatem toni contineat. Sed quia ab eius perfectione deficit."

[63] "sicut et semivir...imperfectus vir." Cf. John Cotton, *De musica cum tonario* 8, pp. 68–69: "Semitonium, a Platone limma vocatum, dictum est, quod sit non plenus tonus sed imperfectus, non ut quidam imperiti resolvunt dimidius tonus. Virgilius semiviri Phryges, id est non pleni viri, quia more feminarum se vestiunt."

[64] "Sciendum est...maius et minus." Boethius, *De institutione musica* 1.16, p. 203: "Sed utraque semitonia nuncupantur, non quod omnino semitonia ex aequo sint media, sed quod semum dici solet, quod ad integritatem usque non pervenit. Sed inter haec unum maius semitonium nuncupatur, aliud minus."

[65] "tonus enim...non potest." Boethius, *De institutione musica* 1.16, p. 202: "Rursus tonus in aequa dividi non potest, cur autem, posterius liquebit; nunc hoc tantum nosse sufficiat, quod nunquam tonus in gemina aequa dividitur."

[66] "Maius ergo semitonium...non pervenit." Boethius, *De institutione musica* 2.30, p. 263: "Reliqua igitur pars, quae maior est, apotome nuncupatur a Graecis, a nobis vero potest vocari decisio...Quantum igitur semitonium minus integro dimidio toni minus est, tantum apotome toni integrum superat dimidium."

[67] "Minus vero semitonium...non attingit." Boethius, *De institutione musica* 2.27, p. 260: "huiusque spatii, quod nunc quidem semitonium nuncupamus, apud antiquiores autem limma vel diesis vocabatur, hic modus est. Cum enim ex sesquitertia proportione, quae diatessaron est, duae sesquioctavae habitudines, quae toni sunt, auferuntur, relinquitur spatium, quod semitonium nuncupatur."

[68] i.e. 1 + 13/243. "Et secundum doctrinam...quadragesimas tertias." Cf. Boethius, *De institutione musica* 1.17, p. 204: Restat comparatio ducentorum .LVI. ad .CCXLIII. quorum differentia est .XIII. qui octies facti medietatem ducentorum .XL. trium non videntur inplere. Non est igitur semitonium, sed minus a semitonio. Tunc enim integrum esse semitonium iure putaretur, si eorum differentia, quae est .XIII. facta octies medietatem ducentorum .XL. trium numerorum potuisset aequare; estque verum semitonium minus ducentorum quadraginta trium ad .CCLVI. comparatio."

[69] "Notandum est...melodiam facere." Grocheio, *Ars musice* 4.13: "Semitonus autem vel dyesis...Eius autem proprietas est cum tono omnem cantum et omnem concordantiam aliam mensurare et melodiam in cantu facere."

[70] "in aliis tamen...vocum mutatio." Cf. Grocheio, *Ars musice* 7.7: "Et in una dictione oportuit plures voces esse, ut in eodem tono fieret vocum mutatio propter earum continuationem."

[71] "excepto .bfabmi....semitonio distant." Cf. Grocheio, *Ars musice* 7.7: "Septem autem voces tono sunt ad se invicem differentes: mifa exceptis, que semitonio differunt."

[72] "eo scilicet...non possunt." Cf. Grocheio, *Ars musice* 7.7: "Sed in bfabmi nullam dixerunt esse mutationem. eo quod mi. et fa. in eodem tono concordare non possint."

[73] "Antiqui tamen musici...etiam .♮. quadratum." Guido of Arezzo, *Micrologus* 8 ("De aliis affinitatibus et .b. et .♮."), p. 124: ."b. vero rotundum, quod minus est regulare, quod adiunctum vel molle dicunt, cum .F. habet concordiam; et ideo additum est, quia .F. cum quarta a se .♮. tritono differente nequibat habere concordiam; utramque autem .b.♮. in eadem neuma non iungas."

[74] "per primum b...integrum designantes." Cf. Grocheio, *Ars musice* 7.7: "Sibi tamen duo signa sive .2. litteras attribuerunt. per unam autem tonum completum per aliam semitonum signaverunt."

[75] "Moderni vero musici...locum habet." Cf. Grocheio, *Ars musice* 7.8: "Moderni vero propter descriptionem consonantiarum et stantipedum et ductiarum aliud addiderunt quod falsam musicam vocaverunt. quia illa duo signa .scilicet. b. et .♮. que in bfabmi tonum et semitonum designabant: In omnibus aliis faciunt hoc designare. Ita quod ubi erat semitonus per .♮. illud ad tonum ampliant ut bona concordantia vel consonantia fiat. Et similiter ubi tonus inveniebatur illud per .b. ad semitonum restringunt."

[76] "sicque ipsum...notatum inveni." Cf. John of Garland, *Introductio musice* 224–225, pp. 89–90. "Quando ergo incipit in .f. coniuncta uel diuisa de propinquo uel remoto unius ibi est b mol sine signo. Similiter a superiori. Cuius causa exempla ponantur ne valeas aberrare et non solum unius toni, sed per ordinem singulorum...Exempla quinti toni."

[77] "ut ad musicam boecii" Boethius, *De institutione musica* 2.30, pp. 263–264 ("De maiore parte toni, in quibus minimis numeris constet"); 2.28, pp. 260–261 ("De semitonio, in quibus minimis numeris constet"); 2.29, pp. 262–263 ("Demonstrationes non esse .CCXLIII. ad .CCLVI. toni medietatem").

[78] "Ditonus vero...in numeris." Grocheio, *Ars musice* 4.14: "Dytonus autem est

concordantia continens .2. tonos que sono precedenti comparata sic proportionari videtur sicut .81. ad .64." Cf. John of Garland, *Musica plana, reportatio* 3.102, p. 47: "Ditonus dicitur superpartiens decimas septimas ut 81 ad 64."

[79] "inter istas...proportio repperitur." Cf. Boethius, *De institutione musica* 1.7, p. 194: "Illud tamen esse cognitum debet, quod omnis musicae consonantiae aut in duplici aut in triplici aut in quadrupla aut in sesqualtera aut in sesquitertia proportione consistant."

[80] "Semiditonus autem...in numeris." Cf. John of Garland, *Musica plana, reportatio* 3.109, p. 48: "Semiditonus dicitur super quinque partiens septimas ut 32 ad 27."

[81] "et inter eas...proportio repperitur." Cf. Boethius, *De institutione musica* 1.7, p. 194: "Illud tamen esse cognitum debet, quod omnis musicae consonantiae aut in duplici aut in triplici aut in quadrupla aut in sesqualtera aut in sesquitertia proportione consistant."

[82] "Dyatessaron vero...et excedit." Cf. Grocheio, *Ars musice* 4.15: "Semidytonus autem vel dyatessaron est concordantia .2. tonos cum uno semitonio continens que precedenti sono comparata eum in sexquitertia proportione excellit."

[83] "quod est enim...in sonis musicis." Boethius, *De institutione musica* 1.7, p. 194. "et vocabitur quidem, quae in numeris sesquitertia, diatessaron in sonis."

[84] "Est autem...eius partem." Boethius, *De institutione musica* 1.4, p. 191: "...id est cum maior numerus minorem numerum habet in se totum et unam eius aliquam partem eamque vel dimidiam...ut quattuor ad tres, et vocatur sesquitertia."

[85] "sicut se...ad .ix." Cf. Grocheio, *Ars musice* 4.15: "In qua proportione se habent .4. ad .3. vel .12. ad .9."

[86] "et talis...boecio dicitur" Cf. Boethius, *De institutione musica* 1.10, p. 197: "Cum igitur ante Pythagoram consonantiae musicae partim diapason partim diapente partim diatessaron, quae est consonantia minima, vocarentur..."

[87] "Dicitur autem...ex .iiij^{or}. vocibus." Cf. John of Garland, *Musica plana, reportatio* 3.100, p. 47: "Diatesseron dicitur sesquitercium ut 4 ad 3 et dicitur a *dia* quod est de et *tessar* quod est quatuor quasi de 4 vocibus."

[88] "Dyapente autem...et excedit." Cf. Grocheio, *Ars musice* 4.16: "Dyapente autem est concordantia .3. tonos cum uno semitonio continens, que precedenti sono comparata eum superat in sexquialtera proportione."

[89] "eum in sexquialtera...in sonis musicis." Boethius, *De institutione musica* 1.7, p. 194: "quae in numeris sesqualtera, diapente appellatur in vocibus."

[90] "Est autem sexquialtera...eius partem." Boethius, *De institutione musica* 1.4, p. 191: "id est cum maior numerus minorem numerum habet in se totum et unam eius aliquam partem eamque vel dimidiam, ut tres duorum, et vocatur sesqualtera proportio."

[91] "Et talis concordantia...consonantiarum dicitur." Cf. John of Garland, *De mensurabili musica* 9.10, vol. 1, p. 69: "Media dicitur esse illa, quando duae voces iunguntur in eodem tempore, quod nec dicitur perfecta vel imperfecta, sed partim convenit cum perfecta et partim cum imperfecta, et duae sunt species, scilicet diapente et diatesseron."

[92] "Dicitur autem dyapente...constet vocibus." Cf. John of Garland, *Musica plana, reportatio* 3.99, p. 47: "Diapente...dicitur a *dia* quod est de et *penta* quod est qunque quasi continens quinque uoces."

[93] "Dyapason vero...et excedit." Cf. Grocheio, *Ars musice* 4.17: "Dyapason autem est concordantia continens .5. tonos et duo semitonia...Que sono immediate precedenti comparata eum in dupla proportione excellit."

[94] "quod enim est...in sonis musicis." Boethius, *De institutione musica* 1.7, p. 194: "quae vero in proportionibus dupla est, diapason in consonantiis."

[95] "Est autem proportio...alium continet." Cf. Boethius, *De institutione musica* 1.4, p. 191: "Est vero multiplex, ubi maior numerus minorem numerum habet in se totum vel bis vel ter vel quater ac deinceps, nihilque deest, nihil exuberat. Appellaturque vel duplum vel triplum vel quadruplum atque ad hunc ordinem in infinita progreditur."

[96] "et ista concordantia que mater consonantiarum dicitur" Cf. Grocheio, *Ars musice* 3.3: "Est enim una prima armonia quasi mater, que dyapason ab antiquis dicta est..."

[97] "nulla enim...suam octavam." Guido of Arezzo, *Micrologus* 5, p. 113: "Nulla enim vox cum altera praeter octavam perfecte concordat."

[98] "Dicitur autem dypason...de omnibus." Cf. John of Garland, *Musica plana, reportatio* 3.99, p. 47: "Diapason...dicitur a *dia* quod est de et *pan* quod est totum quasi continens omnes species alias in se."

[99] "omnes enim concordantias...coniunctione resultat." Cf. Grocheio, *Ars musice* 4.17: "que ex coniunctione dyatessaron cum dyapente resultat."

[100] "ex ipsa etiam...cum dyapason." Cf. Grocheio, *Ars musice* 4.18: "Et qui cognoscit quid dyapente potest ex additione toni tonum cum dyapente efficere. que concordantie composite et non simplices debent dici."

[101] "Sicut ergo manifeste...consonantie appellantur." Grocheio, *Ars musice* 2.5: "Alii autem rationabiliter loquentes tres consonantias esse asserunt." Grocheio, *Ars musice* 4.8: "Alii autem omnes ad .7. reducunt. Qui modo subtiliori investigant."

[102] Superior in the sense of greater in that there are more concords than consonances.

[103] "Trinam itaque armoniam...in trinitate perfecta" Cf. Grocheio, *Ars musice* 3.2: "Dicamus igitur quod omnium sublimis creator, a principio in sonis trinam armoniam inseruit perfectam, ut in eis suam bonitatem ostenderet, et per illos nomen suum laudaretur."

[104] "ut in istis tribus...est creatus" Cf. Grocheio, *Ars musice* 3.4: "Dicamus ergo quod anima humana immediate a primo creata speciem vel ymaginem retinet creatoris. Que ymago a Iohanne damasceno. ymago trinitatis dicitur: mediante qua naturalis cognitio est ei innata. Et forte ista naturali cognitione in sonis trinam perfectionem apprehendit."

[105] "a sui...non posset." Cf. Grocheio, *Ars musice* 3.2: "Et etiam ut nullus possit se excusare a laude divina. Sed omnis lingua in sonis nomen glorie fateatur."

[106] "Tres siquidem...efficiunt melodiam" Cf. Grocheio, *Ars musice* 3.3: "Et iste tres [*dyapason, dyapente* and *dyatessaron*] simul ordinate consonantiam perfectissimam reddunt."

[107] "prima armonia...eis procedens." Cf. Grocheio, *Ars musice* 3.3: "Est enim una prima armonia quasi mater, que dyapason ab antiquis dicta est: Et alia quasi filia in ista contenta dyapente dicta. Et tertia ab eis procedens que dyatessaron appellatur."

[108] "Et hoc...inclinatione ducti." Cf. Grocheio, *Ars musice* 3.3: "Et forte hoc senserunt quidam pytagorici naturali inclinatione ducti."

[109] "in creaturis...alibi declarari." Cf. Grocheio, *Ars musice* 3.2 and 3.4, *op. cit.*

[110] "hoc tamen...methafora loquebantur." Cf. Grocheio, *Ars musice* 3.3: "non ausi tamen sub talibus verbis exprimere sed in numeris sub methaphora loquebantur."

[111] "de hoc...reperta fuisse." Cf. Boethius, *De institutione musica* 1.10, p. 197: "Cum igitur ante Pythagoram consonantiae musicae partim diapason partim diapente partim diatessaron, quae est consonantia minima, vocarentur, primus Pythagoras hoc modo repperit, qua proportione sibimet haec sonorum concordia iungeretur."

[112] "Ad cuius evidentiam...si velimus. " Boethius, *De institutione musica* 1.1, p. 187: "ut ex his omnibus perspicue nec dubitanter appareat, ita nobis musicam naturaliter esse coniunctam, ut ea ne si velimus quidem carere possimus."

[113] "enim infantes...musicis adiunguntur." Boethius, *De institutione musica* 1.1, pp. 179–80: "...verum per cuncta diffunditur studia et infantes ac iuvenes nec non etiam senes ita naturaliter affectu quodam spontaneo modis musicis adiunguntur, ut nulla omnino sit aetas, quae a cantilenae dulcis delectatione seiuncta sit."

[114] "ut nulla omnino...proferant delectantur. " Boethius, *De institutione musica* 1.1, p. 186: "Et qui suaviter canere non potest, sibi tamen aliquid canit, non quod eum aliqua voluptate id quod canit afficiat, sed quod quandam insitam dulcedinem ex animo proferentes, quoquo modo proferant, delectantur."

[115] "quod cum...ipse decerpat." Boethius, *De institutione musica* 1.1, p. 187: "Quid? quod, cum aliquis cantilenam libentius auribus atque animo capit, ad illud etiam non sponte convertitur, ut motum quoque aliquem similem auditae cantilenae corpus effingat; et quod omnino aliquod melos auditum sibi memor animus ipse decerpat?"

[116] "Cum igitur musica ...ignorasse videntur." Cf. Grocheio, *Ars musice* 1.2: "Licet enim homines semper quasi a principio cantaverint: eo quod musica sit eis naturaliter innata...Principia tamen cantus et musice ignorabant usque ad tempus pytagore."

[117] "Licet enim...nomen traxisse." Cf. Grocheio, *Ars musice* 1.1: "Fabulose loquentes dixerunt musicam inveniri a musis iuxta aquas habitantibus. Et inde nomen accipere."

[118] "Quidam vero ab iubal...musicam adinvenit." Cf. Petrus Comestor, *Historia scholastica* 29, CCCM 119, p.54: "*Nomen fratris eius Iubal, pater canentium in cithara, et organo* [Genesis 4.21]. Non instrumentorum quidem que longe post inventa fuerunt, sed inventor fuit musice, id est consonantiarum, ut labor pastoralis quasi in deliciis verteretur. ... Sella genuit Tubalcaim, qui ferrariam artem primus invenit, res bellicas decenter exercuit, sculpturas operum in metallis in libidinem oculorum fabricavit. Quo fabricante Iubal, de quo dictum est, sono malleorum delectatus, ex ponderibus eorum proportiones et consonantias eorum que ex eis nascuntur excogitavit."

[119] "secundum tamen boecium...pitagora philosopho " Boethius, *De institutione musica* 1.10, pp. 196–98: "Quemadmodum Pythagoras proportiones consonantiarum investigaverit.;" Guido of Arezzo, *Micrologus* 20, p. 229: "Cum Pythagoras quidam magnus philosophus forte iter ageret, ventum est ad fabricam in qua super unam incudem quinque mallei feriebant...;" Grocheio, *Ars musice* 1.2: "Sed boetius...Ait enim in libro suo de armonia musicali. quod pictagoras principia musice adinvenit."

[120] "qui tempore cambisys...legitur floruisse" Cf. Vincent of Beauvais, *Speculum historiale* 3.19, p. 93: "*Ex chronicis.* Cyro successit filius eius Cambyses anno quintae aetatis 61. mundi vero terio millesimo 424. et regnavit annis 8." See also Vincent of Beauvais, *Speculum historiale* 3.23, p. 94: "*Eusebius in chroni.* Anno Cambysis 7. Pythagoras Physicus Philosophus habetur clarus."

[121] "qui que primus...antea dicebantur" Cf. Vincent of Beauvais, *Speculum historiale* 3.23, p. 94: "*Aug. de civit. Dei lib. 8 cap. 2....* Authorem habuit Pythagoram Samium: a quo etiam ferunt ipsum Philosophiae nomen exortum, nam cum antea sapientes appellarentur...quid profiteretur? Philosophum se esse respondit id est studiosum vel amatorem Sapientiae...;" Vincent of Beauvais, *Speculum historiale* 3.24, p. 95: "*Valerius lib. 9....*Interrogatus quo cognomine censeretur, ne sapientem se diceret: iam enim illud

nomen 7. viri sapientes occupaverant, se amatorem sapientiae, hoc est philosophum dixit."

[122] "sed certa...fuerunt inventa." Cf. Boethius, *De institutione musica* 1.10, pp. 197–98: "Cum interea divino quodam nutu praeteriens fabrorum officinas pulsos malleos exaudit ex diversis sonis unam quodam modo concinentiam personare...;" Grocheio, *Ars musice* 1.3: "Ductus enim fuit ut narrat boetius quasi divino spiritu ad fabrorum officia." Guido of Arezzo, *Micrologus* 20, pp. 228-9

[123] "Erant antiquitus...sed ceca." Guido of Arezzo, *Micrologus* 20, p. 228: "Erant antiquitus instrumenta incerta et canentium multitudo, sed caeca."

[124] "nullus enim...nutu disponeret. " Guido of Arezzo, *Micrologus* 20, pp. 228–229: "nullus enim hominum vocum differentias et symphoniae descriptionem poterat aliqua argumentatione colligere. neque posset unquam certum aliquid de hac arte cognoscere, nisi divina tandem bonitas, quod sequitur suo nutu disponeret."

[125] "cum pitagoras...versari cognovit." Guido of Arezzo, *Micrologus* 20, pp. 229–230: "Cum Pythagoras quidam magnus philosophus forte iter ageret, ventum est ad fabricam in qua super unam incudem quinque mallei feriebant, quorum suavem concordiam miratus philosophus accessit primumque in manuum varietate sperans vim soni ac modulationis existere, mutavit malleos. Quo facto sua vis quemque secuta est. Subtracto itaque uno qui dissonus erat a caeteris alios ponderavit, mirumque in modum divino nutu primus XII, secundus IX, tertius VIII, quartus VI, nescio quibus ponderibus appendebant. Cognovit itaque in numerorum proportione et collatione musicae versari scientiam."

[126] Boethius, *De institutione musica* 1.10, p. 197; Guido of Arezzo, *Micrologus* 20, p. 229.

[127] "pitagoras .iiij[or]. ...dyapason dicitur." Cf. Grocheio, *Ars musice* 1.3: "et ponderans eos. Invenit unum in dupla proportione ad alterum sicut sunt .12. ad .vi. Et isti adinvicem reddebant consonantiam que dyapason appellatur."

[128] "Ille vero...consistit, resonabat." Cf. Grocheio, *Ars musice* 1.3: "Et ad alium se habebat in sexquitertia proportione sicut .12. ad .9. qui dyatessaron resonabant."

[129] "Ad tertium...proportione reddebat." Cf. Grocheio, *Ars musice* 1.3: "Ille idem malleus ad duos alios medios in sexquialtera proportione et sexquitertia se habebat pondere— Ita quod ad unum in sexquialtera sicut 12 ad [8] qui dyapente reddebant."

[130] "Isti etiam duo...se habebant." Cf. Grocheio, *Ars musice* 1.3: "Similiter etiam isti duo cum subduplo in proportione sexquialtera et sexquitertia se habebant et consonantiam dyatessaron et dyapente resonabant."

[131] "sicut sunt .ix....sexquioctava, reddebat." Cf. Grocheio, *Ars musice* 1.3: "Sed isti duo in proportione sexquioctava se habebant sicut .9. ad .8. et tonum adinvicem resonabant."

[132] "Quintus vero...potius corrumpebat." Cf. Grocheio, *Ars musice* 1.3: "Quintus autem malleus omnibus improportionalis erat. Et ob hoc nullam reddebat armoniam. sed potius corrumpebat."

[133] "Ex istis...istis composita." Cf. Grocheio, *Ars musice* 1.4: "Et sic invenit pytagoras quid esset. Dyesis. Tonus. Ditonus. Semiditonus. Dyatessaron. Dyapente. Dyapason. Et ex hiis composita."

[134] "immo etiam...monocordium composuit." Guido of Arezzo, *Micrologus* 20, p. 233: "Per supradictas species voces ordinans monochordum primus ille Pythagoras composuit."

[135] "Est autem monocordium...circa in spissitudine" John of Garland, *Musica plana*,

reportatio 1.16, p. 4: "Unde monochordum est quoddam instrumentum trium palmorum in longitudine in latitudine uero unius palmi uel circa, habens unicam cordam sub qua proportionantur omnes <proportiones> armoni<c>e sumpte."

[136] "sapientibus in...diligenti notitia" Guido of Arezzo, *Micrologus* 20, p. 233: "in quo quia non est lascivia sed diligenter aperta artis notitia, sapientibus in commune placuit..."

[137] "quod priores...potius posuerunt." Cf. John Cotton, *De musica cum tonario* 10. p. 76: "Sed cum nunc octo sint, quondam dumtaxat quattuor erant, ad similitudinem fortasse quattuor temporum."

[138] "in cronicis," i.e. Sigebert of Gembloux, *Chronica* [anno 1028].

[139] "guidonis aretini...omnis cantus." Sigebert of Gembloux, *Chronica* [anno 1028] MGH SS, 6, p. 356: "Claruit hoc tempore in italia guido aretinus, multi inter musicos nominis in hoc etiam philosophis preferendus quod ignotos cantus etiam pueri facilius discunt per eius regulam quam per vocem magistri aut per usum alicuius instrumenti. Dum sex litteris vel sillabis modulatim appositis ad sex voces quas solas regulariter musica recipit his que vocibus per flexuras digitorum levae manus distinctis per integrum diapason se oculis et auribus ingerunt intentae et remissae elevationes vel depositiones earundem vi vocum." Cf. Guido of Arezzo, *Micrologus*, p. 85: "Cum me et naturalis conditio et bonorum imitatio communis utilitatis diligentem faceret, cepi inter alia musicam pueris tradere. Tandem affuit divina gratia, et quidam eorum imitatione chordae ex nostrarum notarum usu exercitati ante unius mensis spatium invisos et inauditos cantus ita primo intuitu indubitanter cantabant, ut maximum plurimis spectaculum praeberetur dum sex litteris vel sillabis modulatim appositis ad sex voces. quas solas regulariter musica recipit."

[140] "Harum ergo vocum...sonum efficiant" Cf. Guido of Arezzo, *Micrologus* 2, pp. 93–95: "Notae autem in monochordo hae sunt: In primis ponitur G graecum a modernis adiunctum. Sequuntur septem alphabeti litterae graves ideoque maioribus litteris insignitae hoc modo: .A.B.C.D.E.F.G. Post has eaedem septem litterae acutae repetuntur, sed minoribus litteris describuntur, in quibus tamen inter .a. et .♮. aliam .b. ponimus quam rotundam facimus, alteram vero quadravimus, ita: .a.b. ♮ .c.d.e.f.g. Addimus his eisdem litteris, sed variis figuris tetrachordum superacutarum, in quo .b.. ♮. similiter duplicamus, ita: aa. bb.. ♮ ♮. cc. dd."

[141] "Et secundum guidonem...gamatis que sunt. " Cf. Guido of Arezzo, *Micrologus* 7, pp. 117–118: "Cum autem septem sint voces, quia aliae ut diximus, sunt eaedem, septenas sufficit explicare, quae diversorum modorum et diversarum sunt qualitatum. Primus modus vocum est, cum vox tono deponitur et tono et semitonio duobusque tonis intenditur, ut .A. et .D. Secundus modus est, cum vox duobus tonis remissa semitonio et duobus tonis intenditur, ut .B. et .E. Tertius est qui semitonio et duobus tonis descendit, duobus vero tonis ascendit, ut .C. et .F. Quartus vero deponitur tono, surgit autem per duos tonos et semitonium, ut .G." There should probably only be three affinals, namely a, b ♮ and c, as b♭ has no affinity with the E below.

[142] "Sed beatus gregorius...potius distinxerunt." Cf. e.g. Aribo, *De musica*, p. 31: "Patet admodum, beatum Gregorium totius pene ecclesiastici cantus auctorem duplicem eius cognovisse operationem, qui in tetrardo non potius autenticas, quam plagales diligit odas."

[143] "sicut guido...predicti commemorat." Guido of Arezzo, *Micrologus* 12, pp. 147–149: "De divisione quattuor modorum in octo"

[144] "dicit enim...essent octo." Guido of Arezzo, *Micrologus* 12, pp. 148–149: "Interea

cum cantus unius modi, utpote proti, ad comparationem finis tum sint graves et plani, tum acuti et alti, versus et psalmi et siquid ut diximus, fini aptandum erat uno eodemque modo prolatum, diversis aptari non poterat. Quod enim subiungebatur si erat grave, cum acutis non conveniebat; si erat acutum a gravibus discordabat. Consilium itaque fuit ut quisque modus partiretur in duos, id est acutum et gravem, distributisque regulis acuta acutis et gravia convenirent gravibus; et acutus quisque modus diceretur autentus, id est auctoralis et princeps, gravis autem plaga vocaretur, id est lateralis et minor. Qui enim dicitur stare ad latus meum minor me est, caeterum si esset maior ego aptius dicerer stare ad latus eius. Cum ergo dicatur autentus protus et plagis proti et similiter de reliquis, qui naturaliter in vocibus erant quattuor in cantibus facti sunt octo."

[145] "Fuit olim...que orci. " Cf. Servius, *In Vergilii Aeneidos librum tertium commentarius* 3.420: "Scylla autem ipsa Phorci et Creteidos nymphae filia fuit."

[146] "Alii vero...glauci uxorem." Cf. Servius, *In Vergilii Aeneidos librum tertium commentarius* 3.420: "hanc amabat Glaucus, quem Circe diligebat."

[147] "Alii autem...ad genua." Cf. Servius, *In Vergilii Aeneidos librum tertium commentarius* 6.286: "Scyllaeque biformes bene plurali usus est numero: nam et illa Nisi secundum alios in avem conversa est, secundum alios in piscem. ergo etiam ipsa biformis fuit, sicut haec in Siciliae freto. dictum autem est per poetae scientiam vel licentiam."

[148] "quam etiam dicit...mare mergebant." Vergil, *Aeneid* 3.420–432: "dextrum Scylla latus, laeuum implacata Charybdis obsidet, atque imo barathri ter gurgite uastos sorbet in abruptum fluctus rursusque sub auras erigit alternos, et sidera uerberat unda. at Scyllam caecis cohibet spelunca latebris ora exsertantem et nauis in saxa trahentem. prima hominis facies et pulchro pectore uirgo pube tenus, postrema immani corpore pistrix delphinum caudas utero commissa luporum. praestat Trinacrii metas lustrare Pachyni cessantem, longos et circumflectere cursus, quam semel informem uasto uidisse sub antro Scyllam et caeruleis canibus resonantia saxa."

[149] "Habuisse quoque...illa pertimebat." Cf. Maurus Servius Honoratus, *In Vergilii Aeneidos librum tertium commentarius* 3.420: "dextrum scylla latus laevum inplacata charybdis de Ionio venientibus. Scylla enim in Italia est, Charybdis in Sicilia."

[150] Vergil, *Aeneid* 3.420–432.

[151] "dicit enim eneam...patiebantur ignari." Vergil, *Aeneid* 3.684–686: "contra iussa monent Heleni, Scyllamque Charybdinque inter, utrimque uiam leti discrimine paruo, ni teneam cursus: certum est dare lintea retro."

[152] Cf. Ovid, *Metamorphoses* 5.

[153] "Sed istud dictum...sonum efficiunt." Cf. Grocheio, *Ars musice* 5.6: "Qui vero sic dividunt, aut dictum suum fingunt: aut volunt pytagoricis vel aliis magis quam veritati obedire. aut sunt naturam et logicam ignorantes. Prius enim dicunt universaliter musicam esse de sono numerato. Corpora vero celestia in movendo sonum non faciunt, quamvis antiqui hoc crediderunt. nec findunt orbes secundum aristotelem."

[154] Anon., *Libellus de tonis ac eorum origine antiquo*. Not found.

[155] "sic enim audiebatur...navis vociferans" Cf. Vergil, *Aeneid* 8.115–116: "Tum pater Aeneas puppi sic fatur ab alta paciferaeque manu ramum praetendit olivae."

[156] "et alter minor...urbique propinquant." Cf. Virgil, *Aeneid* 8.100–104: "ocius advertunt proras urbique propinquant. Forte die sollemnem illo rex Arcas honorem Amphitryoniadae magno divisque ferebat ante urbem in luco. Pallas huic filius una,

una omnes iuvenum primi pauperque senatus tura dabant, tepidusque cruor fumabat ad aras."

[157] Anon., *Libellus de tonis ac eorum origine antiquo.* Not found.

[158] "Greci tamen...exultationem designans." Cf. e.g., Priscian, *Institutiones grammaticae* 90:12–15, ed. by Heinrich Keil (1859): "...interiectio tamen non solum quem dicunt Graeci sceliasmon significat sed etiam voces, quae cuiuscumque passionis animi pulsu per exclamationem intericiunter. habent igitur diversas significationes: gaudii, ut 'euax'; doloris, ut 'ei'."

[159] The source for this quote has not been found.

[160] "dans plurima officiorum. responsoriorum vel antiphonarum exempla." Another possible translation of this passage is "examples of introits, responsories or antiphons."

[161] "ita quisque...et minor." Guido of Arezzo, *Micrologus* 12, p. 148: "ut quisque modus partiretur in duos, id est acutum et gravem, distributisque regulis acuta acutis et gravia convenirent gravibus; et acutus quisque modus diceretur autentus, id est auctoralis et princeps, gravis autem plaga vocaretur, id est lateralis et minor."

[162] "qui enim ut...stare dicerer." Guido of Arezzo, *Micrologus* 12, p. 148: "Qui enim dicitur stare ad latus meum minor me est, caeterum si esset maior ego aptius dicerer stare ad latus eius."

[163] "ita etiam...qualitatibus variatur." Guido of Arezzo, *Micrologus* 13, p. 150: "Igitur octo sunt modi, ut octo partes orationis et octo formae beatitudinis, per quos omnis cantilena discurrens octo dissimilibus qualitatibus variatur."

[164] "quod sicut octo...qualitatibus variatur." Guido of Arezzo, *Micrologus* 10, p. 149: "...pro autento proto et plagis proti primus et secundus, pro autento deutero et plagis deuteri tertius et quartus, pro autento trito et plagis triti quintus et sextus, pro autento tetrardo et plagis tetrardi septimus et octavus."

[165] "Solent etiam...femininos appellant." Cf. Grocheio, *Ars musice* 26.3: "eos communi nomine et numerali appellaverunt. puta primus. secundus. tertius. et cetera. Dicentes impares, principales. Autenticos masculinos. pares vero, differentiis contrariis nuncupando."

[166] "sicut ab aristotele .viij°. politice." Aristotle, *Politics* 8.5.1340a18–1340b9 and 8.7.1342a28–1342b434; Cf. Peter of Auvergne, *In libros politicorum* 8.2.24 (1312) and 8.3.12 (1339), p.429 and p. 437. The *hypo-* and *hyper-* modes are not mentioned in Aristotle's *Politics* and the Hypermixolydian mode is not mentioned in Peter of Auvergne's commentary.

[167] The more usual name for the eighth tone, hypomixolydian, is not used by Guy. Hypermixolydian is the term used by Boethius to explain the discrepancy between the seven octave species and the eight tones. "Septem quidem esse praediximus modos, sed nihil videatur incongruum, quod octavus super adnexus est. Huius enim adiectionis rationem paulo posterius eloquemur. ... in eo modo qui inscribitur hypermixolydius." Boethius *De institutione musicae* 4.17 pp. 343-4. Hypermixolodian became hypomixlydian to establish consistency with the other three plagal modes.

[168] "abusio quedam...et octavum." Guido of Arezzo, *Micrologus* 12, p. 149: "Abusio autem tradidit latinis dicere pro autento proto et plagis proti primus et secundus, pro autento deutero et plagis deuteri tertius et quartus, pro autento trito et plagis triti quintus et sextus, pro autento tetrardo et plagis tetrardi septimus et octavus."

[169] See the struck through chapter 1.3.4a [Appendix I] for an explanation of

"transposition" and the use of B flat beside the clef as a sign of this. Guy's use of "in fine" in this passage is translated here as "at the start," meaning at the left-hand end.

[170] See chapter 1.3.4a. [Appendix I]

[171] Guy is discussing octave transposition here, as is made clear in the citation from John of Garland below. It is nonetheless interesting to compare examples of the same chant from BnF lat. 17296 fol. 58v and BnF lat. 15181 fol. 425r.

[172] "secundum magistrum Iohannem de garlandia...reducuntur." Cf. John of Garland, *Introductio musice* 202–205, p. 87. "Quatuor littere finales sunt hec: .D. .E. .F. .G. graues in grauibus constitute. Et ratio quare in grauibus pocius ordinantur quam in acutis est quia si fuissent in acutis non habuissent tantum plenum assensum supra finales nec humiliassent per naturalem depositionem; quia omne simile requirit suum simile, id est originale fundamentum vult habere suum fundamentum naturale, Et propter hoc moderni et correctores musice rationabilius quatuor finales litteras in grauibus ordinauerunt." This reference has been taken as an allusion to a now-missing tonary by John of Garland; see *De mensurabili musica,* vol. 1, pp. 9–10.

[173] Theodore Karp notes that although this chant has been designated *protus* (mode 1) in modern editions, it includes a *deuterus* (third-mode) cadence. *Alleluia Laetatus* is found on a-acute in French sources, an apparent solution to the mixed-mode character of this chant; see Karp, "The Analysis of the *Alleluia Laetatus sum,*" *Studia Musicologica Academiae Scientiarum Hungaricae* 39 (1998), pp. 215–222.

[174] *Paratum panem* occurs in the Octave of Corpus Christi as an antiphon in MS Arras, Bibliothèque municipale, 893 fol. 257r without music, but is not found as a responsory verse in any contemporary source nor in any of the known versions of the Office of Corpus Christi, edited and studied by Barbara R. Walters, Vincent Corrigan and Peter T. Ricketts (University Park, PA: Pennsylvania State University Press, 2006). The phrase *paratum panem* does occur within the antiphon *Angelorum esca*, found in a little diffused early version of the Office, attributed to Thomas Aquinas (ed. by Walters et al., p. 1888, for Vespers), but this does not seem to be what Guy is referring to here, implying that he is drawing on an otherwise unknown early version of the Office.

[175] Cf. Psalm 33.9: "gustate et videte quoniam suavis est Dominus beatus vir qui sperat in eo."

[176] "audientium mentes...interdum conferre." Cf. Peter of Auvergne, *Quodlibet* 6.16.412: "Consequenter ponuntur quaestiones pertinentes ad accidentia in particulari; et fuerunt duae circa idem: prima fuit, utrum harmoniae musicales sint excitativae passionum, puta raptus vel aliarum huiusmodi; secunda fuit, utrum faciant ad mores."

[177] "Ad quorum evidentiam...ut dicit damascenus" Cf. Peter of Auvergne, *Quodlibet* 6.16.413: "De secundo vero dicendum est, quod secundum Johannem Damascenum secundo libro vicesimo secundo capitulo passio, quamvis dicatur multipliciter, prout tamen hic sumitur, est motus partis animae sensibilis in imaginatione boni vel mali. Et secundum Eustratium super secundum Ethicae passio animae est motus partis appetitivae sub phantasia boni vel mali." Guy was reliant on Peter of Auvergne for this rationale concerning the use of music in arousing the passions and connecting the thinking of John the Damascene in *De fide orthodoxa* to that of Eustratius in his commentary on the *Nichomachean Ethics* of Aristotle.

[178] Cf. Augustine, *De Trinitiate* 10.1: "Ac primum quia rem prorsus ignotam amare

omnino nullus potest, diligenter intuendum est cuiusmodi sit amor studentium, id est non iam scientium sed adhuc scire cupientium quamque doctrinam.;" Peter of Auvergne, *Quodlibet* 6.16.414: "Passiones etiam huiusmodi actus, qui sunt partis animae appetitivae, quae in actu suo sequitur ordine naturae apprehensionem boni sub ratione convenientis vel disconvenientis."

[179] Cf. Peter of Auvergne, *Quodlibet* 6.16.414: "Et ideo ponitur in definitione praedicta 'sub phantasia boni vel mali'. Ex his apparet, secundum quid scilicet est passio animae et circa quid."

[180] "Dicuntur autem...philosopho .vij. phisicorum" Cf. Peter of Auvergne, *Quodlibet* 6.16.414: "Dicitur autem esse motus non, qui est actus imperfecti, ut in potentia ad ulteriorem perfectionem, quia huiusmodi motus non est in parte animae appetitiva vel sensitiva, sicut probatum est septimo Physicae, sed secundum quod est actus perfecti vel perfectio de potentia ad actum, quae est mutatio indivisibilis." See also Aristotle, *Physics* 7.2, 245a21: "Si quidem igitur sensibiles quidem sunt passiones, per hec autem alteratio fit, hoc igitur manifestum est quod patiens et passio simul, et horum nullum est medium."

[181] "mutatio autem ...ubi supra." Cf. Peter of Auvergne, *Quodlibet* 6.16.414: "Mutationes autem indivisibiles sunt fines motuum. Et ideo passio animae ordine naturae sequitur alterationem in qualitatibus primis activis et passivis, secundum quas primo alterantur, quaecumque alterantur secundum Philosophum, ubi prius."

[182] "Cum enim appetitiva...qualitatum sequuntur." Cf. Peter of Auvergne, *In libros politicorum* 8.3.6 (1333): "Et quia pars animae appetitiva est virtus quaedam in corpore et organo; ideo sequitur in esse et operatione sua dispositionem materiae et corporis; et ideo huiusmodi passiones ipsius aliquam dispositionem qualitatum primarum sequuntur."

[183] "unde et anime...contractionem eorum." Cf. Peter of Auvergne, *Quodlibet* 6.16.414: "Similiter se habet et in aliis, propter quod definiuntur huiusmodi passiones materialiter per huiusmodi qualitates. Unde dicimus, quod ira est accensus sanguinis vel spiritus circa cor, timor autem remissio eorundem, delectatio vero diffusio spirituum et caloris, tristitia vero contractio eorundem."

[184] "Qualitates autem...proportionem permixtum" Cf. Peter of Auvergne, *Quodlibet* 6.16.414: "Istae autem qualitates non sunt simplices in animali, sed permixtae ex extremis secundum aliquam proportionem numerabilem, puta calidum animalis non est simpliciter calidum sed remissum per frigidum, sic nec humidum eius est humidum purum, sed permixtum cum sicco secundum aliquam proportionem."

[185] "et ideo...vero minus." Cf. Peter of Auvergne, *In libros politicorum* 8.3.6 (1333): "Et quia huiusmodi dispositio qualitatum in omnibus hominibus est, inquantum omnes compositi sunt ex ipsis sicuti ex materia, sed tamen magis et minus secundum quod quidam magis calidi, quidam minus, et secundum quod quidam magis frigidi, quidam autem minus sunt."

[186] "Ex quo contingit...in ipsis." Cf. Peter of Auvergne, *In libros politicorum* 8.3.6 (1333): "propter hoc omnes huiusmodi passiones quadam aptitudine et virtute sunt in omnibus. Sed in quibusdam magis secundum actum et intense; in quibusdam autem magis secundum potentiam et remisse. ...quoniam passiones quae fiunt in animalibus quorumdam secundum excellentiam quamdam, secundum quod quidam sunt excellenter audaces, quidam excellenter timidi, et sic de aliis...secundum magis et minus, secundum quod magis vel minus dominantur qualitates, quae disponunt ad eas."

[187] Cf. Peter of Auvergne, *In libros politicorum* 8.3.6 (1334): "Harmoniae autem musicae similiter in quadam media ratione sonorum existunt, quae similes sunt aliquando proportioni in qua consistit passio aliqua, aliquando autem dissimiles."

[188] Cf. Peter of Auvergne, *Quodlibet* 6.16.414: "Harmoniae autem seu consonantiae musicae ratione soni harmonici agunt et per motum localem, ut dictum est prius, et per alterationem secundum primas qualitates spirituum, qui sunt organum primum auditus et universaliter omnium virtutum sensitivarum et motivarum."

[189] Cf. Peter of Auvergne, *In libros politicorum* 8.3.6 (1334): "Visibilia enim movent visum sola quadam alteratione tenui, et quasi insensibili. Audibilia autem movent secundum alterationem quamdam, et secundum motum quemdam localem medii et organi."

[190] Cf. Peter of Auvergne, *Quodlibet* 6.16.414: "Prima vero est quia: omne, quod agit, per aliquam formam primo in agendo assimilat sibi passum."

[191] Cf. Peter of Auvergne, *Quodlibet* 6.16.414: "Passum enim in principio contrarium est, in fine simile; in medio autem compositum est ex simili et contrario secundum Commentatorem super secundum De anima." See also" "...passivum enim, antequam patiatur, est contrarium agenti, et cum passio completur, est simile, et dum patitur, est admixtum ex simili et contrario." Averroes, *Commentarium Magnum In Aristotelis De anima* 2.54, p. 213.

[192] Cf. Peter of Auvergne, *Quodlibet* 6.16.414: "Igitur assimilant eos sibi alteratos ipsos secundum qualitates primas harmonicas harmonia sibi simili."

[193] Cf. Peter of Auvergne, *Quodlibet* 6.16.415: "Cum igitur passiones sequantur per se dispositiones aliquas primarum qualitatum commixtas secundum aliquam proportionem numeralem, ut probatum est prius, si aliqua harmonia musica sit in eadem proportione vel propinqua et agat in spiritus secundum quod huiusmodi, eos assimilabit sibi, et per consequens causabit vel excitabit passionem existentem in simili proportione..."

[194] Cf. Peter of Auvergne, *Quodlibet* 6.16.415: "Secunda, quae sumitur ex parte operationis appetitivae per se, est: quoniam omnis operatio partis animae appetitivae, quae fit secundum inclinationem naturalem, delectabilis est secundum intentionem Philosophi secundo Rhetoricae. Septimo etiam Ethicae dicit, quod delectatio est operatio connaturalis habitus non impedita."

[195] Cf. Peter of Auvergne, *Quodlibet* 6.16.416: "Sed operatio ipsius, quae fit ab harmonia simili ei, in qua consistit passio aliqua eius, puta ira vel timor, fit secundum inclinationem eius naturalem, ut in tali passione consistit vel bene dispositus est ad eam, igitur sibi est delectabilis, sed delectatio secundum aliquam operationem adauget operationem illam et corrumpit contrariam, sicut dicit Philosophus decimo Ethicae, igitur harmonia musica factiva huiusmodi delectationis inducit et auget passionem, quae in simili proportione consistit, et corrumpit contrariam ab ipsa purgando, propter quod dicit Philosophus octavo Politicae quasdam esse purgativas. Quae enim generativa est unius, corruptiva est contrariae."

[196] Cf. Peter of Auvergne, *Quodlibet* 6.17.419: "Simile enim agendo disponit ad sibi simile."

[197] Cf. Peter of Auvergne, *Quodlibet* 6.16.414: "Ex dictis potest apparere duplex ratio, propter quam consonantiae vel musicae harmoniae causant vel excitant passiones..."

[198] Cf. Peter of Auvergne, *Quodlibet* 6.17.419: "Sed passiones ad medium reductae disponunt ad virtutes, quoniam sunt materia earum. Virtutes enim per se sunt moderativae earum. Igitur consonantiae quaedam musicae, quae scilicet magis ad medium reductae sunt, valent et disponunt ad virtutes."

¹⁹⁹ Cf. Peter of Auvergne, *Quodlibet* 6.17.412: "Ad istam quaestionem dicendum est consequenter primo, quod quaedam consonantiae musicae valent et disponunt ad mores seu virtutes."

²⁰⁰ Cf. Peter of Auvergne, *Quodlibet* 6.17.418: "Cuius ratio primo apparet ex dictis, quoniam si aliquis agit vel disponit ad aliquid, ipsum magis factum agit et disponit ad magis tale..."

²⁰¹ Cf. Peter of Auvergne, *Quodlibet* 6.17.418: "...quoniam si simpliciter ad simpliciter et magis ad magis et maxime ad maxime. Sed soni consonantes secundum aliquas harmonias agunt ad passiones et excitant eas, sicut apparet ex praecedenti quaestione..."

²⁰² Cf. Peter of Auvergne, *Quodlibet* 6.17.418: "...ergo magis consonantes et ad medium reducti agunt et disponunt ad passiones moderatas et ad medium reductas magis."

²⁰³ Cf. Peter of Auvergne, *Quodlibet* 6.17.419: "Igitur harmoniae musicae quaedam valent et disponunt ad virtutes."

²⁰⁴ Cf. Peter of Auvergne, *In libros politicorum* 8.2.24 (1312): "Deinde cum dicit in melodiis declarat, quod in audibilibus manifeste inveniuntur similitudines morum.... In prima parte dicit, quod in ipsis melodiis musicalibus manifeste inveniuntur imitationes morum..." See also Aristotle, *Politics* 8.5.1340a37: "In melodiis autem ipsis sunt imitationes morum."

²⁰⁵ Cf. Peter of Auvergne, *Quodlibet* 6.17.419: "Igitur harmoniae vel consonantiae musicae bene proportionatae valent et disponunt ad virtutes, improportionatae autem ad contraria."

²⁰⁶ Cf. Vincent of Beauvais, *Speculum historiale* 21.14, p. 93: "*Sigebertus in chronicis.* Eodem tempore Symmachus Patricius Rempublicam Romanam illustravit, et cum eo gener eius Boethius vir consularis...;" Cf. Sigebert of Gembloux, *Chronica* [anno 517], col. 97: "(Beda) Anastasius imperator fulmine a Deo percussus periit, post quem Justinus senior annis 11 regnavit. Boetius annitente sibi Simmacho, cum auctoritatem Romani senatus contra Theodericum regem."

²⁰⁷ Cf. Boethius, *De institutione musica* 1.1, pp. 179–180: "Unde fit ut, cum sint quattuor matheseos disciplinae, ceterae quidem in investigatione veritatis laborent, musica vero non modo speculationi verum etiam moralitati coniuncta sit. Nihil est enim tam proprium humanitatis, quam remitti dulcibus modis, adstringi contrariis..."

²⁰⁸ Cf. Boethius, *De institutione musica* 1.1, p. 180: "Unde Plato etiam maxime cavendum existimat, ne de bene morata musica aliquid permutetur."

²⁰⁹ Cf. Boethius, *De institutione musica* 1.1, pp. 180–181: "Negat enim esse ullam tantam morum in re publica labem quam paulatim de pudenti ac modesta musica invertere. Statim enim idem quoque audientium animos pati paulatimque discedere nullumque honesti ac recti retinere vestigium, si vel per lasciviores modos inverecundum aliquid, vel per asperiores ferox atque immane mentibus illabatur."

²¹⁰ Cf. Boethius, *De institutione musica* 1.1, p. 181: "Nulla enim magis ad animum disciplinis via quam auribus patet. Cum ergo per eas rythmi modique ad animum usque descenderint, dubitari non potest, quin aequo modo mentem atque ipsa sunt afficiant atque conforment."

²¹¹ Cf. Boethius, *De institutione musica* 1.1, p. 181: "Fuit vero pudens ac modesta musica, dum simplicioribus organis ageretur. Ubi vero varie permixteque tractata est, amisit gravitatis atque virtutis modum et paene in turpitudinem prolapsa minimum antiquam speciem servat."

²¹² Cf. Boethius, *De institutione musica* 1.1, p. 181: "Unde Plato praecipit minime oportere pueros ad omnes modos erudiri sed potius ad valentes ac simplices."

²¹³ Cf. Boethius, *De institutione musica* 1.1, p. 181: "Idcirco magnam esse custodiam rei publicae Plato arbitratur musicam optime moratam pudenterque coniunctam, ita ut sit modesta ac simplex et mascula nec effeminata nec fera nec varia. Quod Lacedaemonii maxima ope servavere..."

²¹⁴ Cf. Boethius, *De institutione musica* 1.1, p. 184: "Tanta igitur apud eos fuit musicae diligentia, ut eam animos quoque obtinere arbitrarentur."

²¹⁵ Cf. Boethius, *De institutione musica* 1.1, pp. 185–186: "In tantum vero priscae philosophiae studiis vis musicae artis innotuit, ut Pythagorici, cum diurnas in somno resolverent curas, quibusdam cantilenis uterentur, ut eis lenis et quietus sopor inreperet. Itaque experrecti aliis quibusdam modis stuporem somni confusionemque purgabant, id nimirum scientes quod tota nostrae animae corporisque compago musica coaptatione coniuncta sit."

²¹⁶ Cf. Boethius, *De institutione musica* 1.1, p. 184: "Vulgatum quippe est, quam saepe iracundias cantilena represserit, quam multa vel in corporum vel in animorum affectionibus miranda perfecerit."

²¹⁷ Cf. Boethius, *De institutione musica* 1.1, pp. 184–185: "Cui enim est illud ignotum, quod Pythagoras ebrium adulescentem Tauromenitanum subphrygii modi sono incitatum spondeo succinente reddiderit mitiorem et sui compotem? Nam cum scortum in rivalis domo esset clausum atque ille furens domum vellet amburere, cumque Pythagoras stellarum cursus, ut ei mos, nocturnus inspiceret, ubi intellexit, sono phrygii modi incitatum multis amicorum monitionibus a facinore noluisse desistere, mutari modum praecepit atque ita furentis animum adulescentis ad statum mentis pacatissimae temperavit."

²¹⁸ Cf. Boethius, *De institutione musica* 1.1, p. 185: "Quod scilicet Marcus Tullius commemorat in eo libro, quem de consiliis suis composuit, aliter quidem..."

²¹⁹ Cf. Boethius, *De institutione musica* 1.1, p. 185: "...cum vinolenti adulescentes tibiarum etiam cantu, ut fit, instincti mulieris pudicae fores frangerent, admonuisse tibicinam ut spondeum caneret Pythagoras dicitur. Quod cum illa fecisset, tarditate modorum et gravitate canentis illorum furentem petulantiam consedisse." Note that the spelling *petulentiam* is used in Jerome of Moravia's citation of this passage; see *Tractatus de musica* 8, p. 38.

²²⁰ Cf. Boethius, *De institutione musica* 1.1, pp. 186–187: "Nonne illud etiam manifestum est, in bellum pugnantium animos tubarum carmine accendi? Quod si verisimile est, ab animi pacato statu quemquam ad furorem atque iracundiam posse proferri, non est dubium quod conturbatae mentis iracundiam vel nimiam cupiditatem modestior modus possit adstringere."

²²¹ Cf. Guido of Arezzo, *Micrologus* 14, p. 160: "Ita quondam legitur quidam phreneticus canente Asclepiade medico ab insania revocatus."

²²² Cf. Guido of Arezzo, *Micrologus* 14, p. 161: "Item et David Saul daemonium cithara mitigabat et daemoniacam feritatem huius artis potenti vi ac suavitate frangebat."

²²³ Cf. Boethius, *De institutione musica* 1.1, p. 185: "Ismenias vero Thebanus Boeotiorum pluribus, quos ischiadici doloris tormenta vexabant, modis fertur cunctas abstersisse molestias."

²²⁴ Cf. Boethius, *De institutione musica* 1.1, p. 185: "Sed ut similia breviter exempla

conquiram, Terpander atque Arion Methymneus Lesbios atque Iones gravissimis morbis cantus eripuere praesidio."

[225] Batholomew of England, *De proprietatibus rerum* 19.1393, p. 511: "...ars musica sive armonia contraria et disparata conciliat gravia acutis et acuta gravibus modificat et adaptat. affectiones contrarias et adversas reconciliat. malitiosos animorum motus reprimit et refrenat. sensus debilitatos reparat et confortat. unitatem exemplaris divini in operibus contrariis et diversis manifestissime preconizat. terrenis celestia celestibusque terrena posse uniri in concordia manifestat. letos animos magis letificat et tristes magis tristificat quia ut dicit beatus augustinus. ex quadam occulta anime et armonie consimili proprietate melodia anime affectionibus se conformat. et inde est quod dicunt auctores quod instrumenta musicalia letum reddunt letiorem et tristem tristiorem efficiunt."

[226] Cf. Peter of Auvergne, *Quodlibet* 6.16.414: "Et ideo passio animae ordine naturae sequitur alterationem in qualitatibus primis activis et passivis, secundum quas primo alterantur, quaecumque alterantur secundum Philosophum, ubi prius. Istae autem qualitates non sunt simplices in animali, sed permixtae ex extremis secundum aliquam proportionem numerabilem, puta calidum animalis non est simpliciter calidum sed remissum per frigidum, sic nec humidum eius est humidum purum, sed permixtum cum sicco secundum aliquam proportionem. Similiter se habet et in aliis, propter quod definiuntur huiusmodi passiones materialiter per huiusmodi qualitates."

[227] The same as *"O iuda"* above.

[228] Aristotle, *De anima* 2.2 (141a11–12): "Actus activorum sunt in patiente predisposito." Cf. Peter of Auvergne, *In libros politicorum* 8.1.2 (1260): "actus activorum fiunt in patiente bene disposito."

[229] Cf. Boethius, *De institutione musica* 1.1, p. 180: "Lascivus quippe animus vel ipse lascivioribus delectatur modis vel saepe eosdem audiens emollitur ac frangitur. Rursus asperior mens vel incitatioribus gaudet vel incitatioribus asperatur."

[230] Jerome, *Commentariorum In Epistolam Beati Pauli Ad Galatas* 1 (3:1) PL 26, col. 347AB: "...quod unaquaeque provincia suas habeat proprietates. Cretenses semper mendaces, malas bestias, ventres pigros, vere ab Epimenide poeta dictos, Apostolus comprobat. Vanos Mauros, et feroces Dalmatas, Latinus pulsat historicus. Timidos Phrygas, omnes poetae lacerant. Athenis expeditiora nasci ingenia, philosophi gloriantur. Graecos leves, apud C. Caesarem suggillat Tullius...Ipsum Israel, gravi corde, et dura cervice, omnes Scripturae arguunt. In hunc ergo modum arbitror et Apostolum Galatas regionis suae proprietate pulsasse."

[231] Jerome, *Commentariorum In Esaiam Prophetam* 1(2:8), CCSL 73, p.32: "Quod historiae quoque tam Graecae narrant quam Latinae, nihil Iudaeorum et Romanorum gente esse avarius."

[232] Cf. Isidore, *Etymologiae* 9.2.105: "Inde Romanos graves, Graecos leves, Afros versipelles, Gallos natura feroces atque acriores ingenio pervidemus, quod natura climatum facit."

[233] Cf. Isidore, *Etymologiae* 9.2.97: "Germanicae gentes dictae, quod sint inmania corpora inmanesque nationes saevissimis duratae frigoribus; qui mores ex ipso caeli rigore traxerunt, ferocis animi et semper indomiti, raptu venatuque viventes."

[234] John the Damascene, *De fide orthodoxa* 21.10.

[235] Cf. Boethius, *De institutione musica* 1.1, p. 180: "Amica est enim similitudo, dissimilitudo odiosa atque contraria."

[236] Cf. Boethius, *De institutione musica* 1.1, p. 180: "...neque enim fieri potest, ut mollia duris, dura mollioribus adnectantur aut gaudeant, sed amorem delectationemque, ut dictum est, similitudo conciliat."

[237] Cf. Boethius, *De institutione musica* 1.1, p. 181: "Nam quae asperiores sunt, Getarum durioribus delectantur modis, quae vero mansuetae, mediocribus..."

[238] Cf. Boethius, *De institutione musica* 1.1, p. 180: "Hinc est quod modi etiam musici gentium vocabulo designati sunt, ut lydius modus et phrygius. Quo enim quasi una quaeque gens gaudet, eodem modus ipse vocabulo nuncupatur."

[239] Cf. Guido of Arezzo, *Micrologus* 17, pp. 194–195: "...quod huic displicet ab illo amplectitur, et hunc oblectant nunc consona ille magis probat diversa; iste continuationem et mollitiem secundum suae mentis lasciviam quaerit, ille utpote gravis, sobriis cantibus demulcetur; alius vero ut amens in compositis et anfractis vexationibus pascitur."

[240] Cf. Grocheio, *Ars musice* 6.1–2 and 26.1: "Partes autem musice plures sunt et diverse secundum diversos usus: diversa ydiomata, vel diversas linguas in civitatibus vel regionibus diversis....Unum autem membrum dicimus de simplici musica vel civili, quam vulgalem musicam appellamus...Dico etiam cantum ecclesiasticum. ut excludantur cantus publicus et precise mensuratus..."

[241] Dionysius, *Epistula ad Polycarpum*, PG 3, col. 1078: "...quilibet enim affirmat se habere regium numisma, et fortassis habet particulae cujusdam verae fallacem aliquam imaginem..."

[242] Cf. Guido of Arezzo, *Micrologus* 17, p. 195: "...et unusquisque eum cantum sonorius multo pronuntiat, quem secundum suae mentis insitam qualitatem probat."

[243] John the Deacon, *Vita S. Gregorii Papae*, PL 75 cols 90D–91A: "Hujus modulationis dulcedinem inter alias Europae gentes Germani seu Galli discere crebroque rediscere insigniter potuerunt, incorruptam vero tam levitate animi, quia nonnulla de proprio Gregorianis cantibus miscuerunt, quam feritate quoque naturali, servare minime potuerunt. Alpina siquidem corpora, vocum suarum tonitruis altisone perstrepentia, susceptae modulationis dulcedinem proprie non resultant, quia bibuli gutturis barbara feritas, dum inflexionibus et repercussionibus mitem nititur edere cantilenam, natarali quodam fragore, quasi plaustra per gradus confuse sonantia rigidas voces jactat, sicque audientium animos, quos mulcere debuerat, exasperando magis ac obstrependo conturbat..."

[244] Aristotle, *Politics* 8.1–8.7; Peter of Auvergne, *In libros politicorum* 8.1.1 (1100)–8.3.15 (1342).

[245] Cf. Peter of Auvergne, *In libros politicorum* 8.2.24 (1312): "Aliae autem sunt quae raptos faciunt, sicut ea quae dicitur Phrygia, quae est melodia tertii toni...;" Cf. Aristotle, *Politics* 8.5.1340b: "raptos autem quae Phrygiste..."

[246] Cf. Peter of Auvergne, *In libros politicorum* 8.2.17 (1305): "Causa autem ipsius per se et naturalis videtur esse intensio vehemens animae circa aliquid, quae est vel ex vehementi desiderio attingendi ad aliquid vel fugiendi ab aliquo..."

[247] Cf. Peter of Auvergne, *In libros politicorum* 8.2.17 (1305): "Ex hoc enim quod aliquis vehementer intendit circa aliquid intrinsecum, contingit quod anima revocet spiritum qui est primum instrumentum sensus et motus ab exterioribus ad sensitivum et cogitativum primum, circa quae magis tunc laborat."

[248] Cf. Peter of Auvergne, *In libros politicorum* 8.2.17 (1305): "Hoc enim est de

proprietatibus naturae mittere spiritum ad locum ubi magis indiget: et per consequens sensus exteriores et membra immobilitantur, et efficitur homo quasi immobilis..."

²⁴⁹ Cf. Peter of Auvergne, *In libros politicorum* 8.2.17 (1305): "...quae propter fortem percussionem in vocibus fortissime revocat spiritus ab exterioribus ad interiora, quod disponit ad raptum."

²⁵⁰ Cf. Peter of Auvergne, *In libros politicorum* 8.3.10 (1337): "...illam enim eamdem naturam et virtutem quam habet fistula inter organa, habet melodia Phrygia inter harmonias, ambo enim provocant iram, et sunt illativa passionis ad quam disponit calidum propter fortitudinem motus et percussionis, ratione quorum habent excitare caliditatem in spiritibus." See also Aristotle, *Politics* 8.7.1342b: "Habet enim eamdem potentiam Phrygista harmoniam, quam quidem fistula inter organa: ambo enim iram provocantia, et passionis illativa."

²⁵¹ Cf. Peter of Auvergne, *In libros politicorum* 8.2.24 (1312): "Est autem Lydia mixta *melodia* vel *cantilena* septimi toni, quae propter acumen magnarum vocum, fortiter percutit spiritus et retrahit ad interiora, propter quod ad compassionem disponit."

²⁵² Cf. Peter of Auvergne, *In libros politicorum* 8.2.24 (1312): "sed in audiendo quasdam efficiuntur planctivi, et quasi contracti per retractionem spirituum ad interiora." See also Aristotle, *Politics* 8.5.1340b: "...sed non eodem modo se habeant ad utramque ipsarum, sed ad quasdam quidem planctive, et contrarie magis, velut ad eam quae vocatur Mixolydiste..."

²⁵³ Cf. Peter of Auvergne, *In libros politicorum* 8.2.24 (1312): "Alias autem audientes, puta remissas, magis disponuntur ad mollitiem, cuiusmodi sunt forte ea quae dicitur Lydia, quae est *melodia* quinti toni, et ea quae dicitur hypolydia, quae est sexti toni, quae propter remissionem vocum et motuum maxime per semitonia, quae frequenter accipiunt, manifeste videmus movere ad mollitiem."

²⁵⁴ Song of Songs 4:9: "Vulnerasti cor meum, soror mea, sponsa, vulnerasti cor meum in uno oculorum tuorum et in uno monili torquis tui."

²⁵⁵ Cf. Peter of Auvergne, *Quodlibet* 6.16.415: "quod harmoniae secundi et octavi toni excitant ad compassionem vel misericordiam."

²⁵⁶ Cf. Peter of Auvergne, *Quodlibet* 6.16.415: "unde tractus et cantus mortuorum in ecclesia ut in pluribus sunt illorum tonorum ad excitandum fideles ad compassionem."

²⁵⁷ Cf. Peter of Auvergne, *In libros politicorum* 8.2.24 (1312): "Talis autem est illa quae dicitur Dorica sola, quae est cantilena primi toni, quae maxime moralis est."

²⁵⁸ Cf. Peter of Auvergne, *In libros politicorum* 8.3.12 (1339): "...Dorica maxime sit moralis; dicens, quod Dorica melodia loquentes omnes universaliter confitentur, quod inter omnes melodias stabilissima existit; propter quod convenit cum virtute ad quam requiritur constantia mentis in his quae sunt secundum rationem, et maxime habet morem virilem idest virtuosum." See also Aristotle, *Politics* 8.7.1342b10: "de Dorista autem omnes confitentur tamquam stabilissima existente et maxime habente morem virilem."

²⁵⁹ Cf. Peter of Auvergne, *In libros politicorum* 8.3.12 (1339): "Melodia autem Dorica rationem medii habet respectu aliarum; non enim ita excellenter acuta est sicut illa, quae dicitur Lydia mixta, quae est septimi toni."

²⁶⁰ Cf. Peter of Auvergne, *In libros politicorum* 8.2.24 (1312): "Est autem Lydia mixta melodia vel cantilena septimi toni, quae propter acumen magnarum vocum, fortiter percutit spiritus et retrahit ad interiora, propter quod ad compassionem disponit."

[261] Cf. Peter of Auvergne, *In libros politicorum* 8.2.24 (1312): "Aliae autem sunt quae raptos faciunt, sicut ea quae dicitur Phrygia, quae est melodia tertii toni, quae propter fortem percussionem in vocibus fortissime revocat spiritus ab exterioribus ad interiora."

[262] Cf. Peter of Auvergne, *In libros politicorum* 8.3.12 (1339): "nec etiam ita depressa in gravitate, sicut hypodorica, vel hypophrygia, quae est secundi, vel quarti toni."

[263] Cf. Galatians 4:26: "illa autem quae sursum est Hierusalem libera est quae est mater nostra."

[264] Guy makes reference to a tradition that the *Te Deum laudamus* was spontaneously composed alternately by Saints Ambrose and Augustine on the night of Augustine's baptism (387). This tradition is referred to in the middle of the ninth century by Hincmar of Reims in *De praedestinatione*, PL 125, col. 290BC: "Et quomodo intelligi debeat quod sanctus dixit Ambrosius: Tu ad liberandum suscepturus hominem: quia ut a majoribus nostris audivimus, tempore baptismatis sancti Augustini hunc hymnum beatus Ambrosius fecit, et idem Augustinus cum eo confecit, in capite libri de Bono conjugii exponit dicens: 'Quoniam, inquit, unusquisque homo humani generis pars est, et sociale quoddam est humana natura, magnumque habet et naturale bonum, vim quoque amicitiae, ob hoc ex uno Deus voluit omnes homines condere, ut sua societate, non sola similitudine generis, sed etiam cognationis vinculo tenerentur.' Exponitur etiam in hoc hymno quia omnium naturam pro omnibus liberandis Christus assumpsit, sed credentibus regna coelorum aperuit." The chant is now credited to Hilary, Bishop of Poitiers, in the 4th century, Hilary of Arles or Nicetas of Remesiana, in the 5th, amongst others.

[265] Honorius of Autun, *Speculum Ecclesiae* PL 172, col. 995: "Romani vero destinaverunt eis Augustinum, scientes eum rhetorica arte egregie peritum. Qui cum saepius audisset Ambrosium de Deo et aeterna vita sermocinantem, credidit et uterque Spiritu sancto plenus ymnum Te Deum laudamus tunc in primis cecinit. Ab Ambrosio itaque habunde in divinis instructus, patriam revertitur, ibique populo Dei episcopus praeficitur."

[266] Aristotle, *Ethics* 1.3.1094b27: "Sermones inquirendi sunt secundum materiam de qua sunt."

[267] Cf. Guido of Arezzo, *Micrologus* 15, p. 174: "Item ut rerum eventus sic cantionis imitetur effectus, ut in tristibus rebus graves sint neumae, in tranquillis iocundae, in prosperis exultantes et reliqua."

[268] Cf. Guido of Arezzo, *Micrologus* 14, p. 161: "Quae tamen vis solum divinae sapientiae ad plenum patet, nos vero quae in aenigmate ab inde percepimus."

[269] See for example, John Beleth, *Summa de ecclesiasticis officiis* 38, ed. by Douteil, CCCM 44:69: "Est autem differentia inter neuma, neume et pneuma, pneumatis. Neuma in feminino genere est iubilus sicut in fine antiphonarum, pneuma etiam in neutro genere Spiritus sanctus."

[270] Grocheio, *Ars musice* 29.6: "Est autem neupma quasi cauda vel exitus sequens ad antiphonam. quemadmodum in viella post cantum coronatum vel stantipedem exitus quem modum viellatores appellant."

[271] See for example, Guido of Arezzo, *Micrologus* 9, ed. by Smits van Waesberghe, pp. 130–32: "...ita similes faciunt neumas adeo ut unius tibi cognitio alteram pandat. In quibus vero nulla similitudo monstrata est vel quae diversorum modorum sunt, altera alterius neumam cantumque non recipit... Ubi enim diversa est tonorum semitoniorumque positio, fiat necesse est et neumarum."

[272] See for example, Grocheio, *Ars musice* 29.7: "Et sunt primi toni ut. Primum querite regnum dei. cum suo neupmate...Secundi vero. ut. O sapientia. et eius neupma;" William of Auxerre, *Summa de officiis ecclesiasticis* 1.1 and 2.5, ed. by Franz Fischer, 2007 http://www.thomasinst.uni-koeln.de/sdoe/tca/tca_full.html: "Additur in fine antiphone neuma siue iubilus ad designandum ineffabilem iocunditatem mentis... Cantatur autem sine neumate, quia sufficit habere simplicem caritatem."

[273] See for example, John Beleth, *Summa de ecclesiasticis officiis* (*Rationale divinorum officiorum*) 59, ed. by Douteil, CCM 44, p. 108: "pro Spiritu autem sancto dicitur Graece hoc pneuma, pneumatis."

[274] Luke 24:39: "videte manus meas et pedes quia ipse ego sum palpate et videte quia spiritus carnem et ossa non habet sicut me videtis habere."

[275] The eight Latin intonation formulas: mode 1: *Primum querite regnum dei*; mode 2: *Secundum autem simile est huic*; mode 3: *Tertia dies est quod hec facta sunt*; mode 4: *Quarta vigilia venit ad eos*; mode 5: *Quinque prudentes virgines*; mode 6: *Sexta hora sedit super puteum*; mode 7: *Septem spiritus sunt ante tronum dei*; mode 8: *Octo sunt beatitudines*.

[276] Guido of Arezzo, *Micrologus* 13, ed. by Smits van Waesberghe, pp. 150–51: "Ad quos in cantibus discernendis etiam quaedam neumae inventae sunt..."

[277] Guido of Arezzo, *Micrologus* 13, ed. by Smits van Waesberghe, p. 151: "...ex quarum aptitudine ita modum cantionis agnoscimus sicut saepe ex aptitudine corporis quae cuius sit tunica, reperimus, ut Primum quaerite regnum Dei."

[278] Guido of Arezzo, *Micrologus* 13, ed. by Smits van Waesberghe, p. 154: "Mox enim ut cum fine alicuius antiphonae hanc neumam bene viderimus convenire, quod autenti proti sit non opus est dubitare; sic et de reliquis."

[279] Cf. William of Auxerre, *Summa de officiis ecclesiasticis* 5.1, ed. by Franz Fischer, 2007: "Sed in maioribus sollempnitatibus consuetudo est in quibusdam ecclesiis, quod, antequam legat euangelium, incipit antiphonam, que perficitur a choro. Et per hoc significatur, quod ille, qui lecturus est euangelium, debet habere caritatem; unde petro dictum est, iohannis xxi post medium: Petre, amas me pasce oues meas. Cantatur autem sine neumate, quia sufficit habere simplicem caritatem."

[280] William of Auxerre, *Summa de officiis ecclesiasticis* 1.1, ed. by Franz Fischer, 2007: "Additur in fine antiphone neuma siue iubilus ad designandum ineffabilem iocunditatem mentis, que est de re ineffabili. Iubilus enim est, ut ait gregorius in moralibus, exultatio mentis habita de eternis, que nec penitus exprimi potest nec uoce taceri."

[281] Sigebert of Gembloux, *Chronica* [anno 387], MGH SS 6, p. 303: "Ambrosius episcopus ritum antiphonas in aecclesia canendi primus ad latinos transtulit a grecis apud quos hic ritus iamdudum inoleverat ex instituto ignatii antioceni episcopi et apostolorum discipuli qui per visionem in caelum raptus vidit et audivit quomodo angeli per antiphonarum reciprocationem ymnos sanctae trinitati canebant."

[282] Cf. Dionysius, *De divinis nominibus* 4.12, PG 3, col. 710: "Scribit enim divinus Ignatius: 'Meus amor crucifixus est.'" See also Ignatius, *Epistola ad Romanos* 7, PG 5, col. 693–694: "Meum desiderium crucifixum est."

[283] Sigebert of Gembloux, *Chronica* [anno 387], MGH SS 6, p. 303: "...qui per visionem in caelum raptus, vidit et audivit, quomodo angeli per antiphonarum reciprocationem ymnos sanctae Trinitati canebant."

[284] Sigebert of Gembloux, *Chronica* [anno 391], MGH SS 6, p. 303: "Ambrosius post Hilarium Pictavensem ymnos in aecclesia canendos primus composuit."

[285] E.g. Sigebert of Gembloux, *Chronica* [anno 597], MGH SS 6, p. 320: "Gregorius papa, quod ipse olim facere intenderat, Augustinum cum aliis ad predicandum destinat in Anglia."

[286] John the Deacon, *Vita S. Gregorii papae,* 2.6, PL 75, col. 90C: "Deinde in domo Domini, more sapientissimi Salomonis, propter musicae compunctionem dulcedinis, Antiphonarium centonem cantorum studiosissimus nimis utiliter compilavit; scholam quoque cantorum...constituit; eique cum nonnullis praediis duo habitacula, scilicet alterum sub gradibus basilicae beati Petri apostoli, alterum vero sub Lateranensis patriarchii domibus fabricavit, ubi usque hodie lectus ejus, in quo recubans modulabatur, et flagellum ipsius, quo pueris minabatur, veneratione congrua cum authentico Antiphonario reservatur..."

[287] John the Deacon, *Vita S. Gregorii papae,* 2.9, PL 75, col. 91B: "Sed et Carolus noster patricius, rex autem Francorum, dissonantia Romani et Gallicani cantus Romae offensus, cum Gallorum procacitas cantum a nostratibus quibusdam naeniis argumentaretur esse corruptum, nostrique e diverso authenticum Antiphonarium probabiliter ostentarent..."

[288] John the Deacon, *Vita S. Gregorii papae,* 2.9, PL 75, col. 91C: "Respondentibus fontem prudenter adjecit: Ergo et nos qui de rivo corruptam lympham usque hactenus bibimus, ad perennis fontis necesse est fluenta principalia recurramus."

[289] Cf. Sigebert of Gembloux, *Chronica* [anno 592], MGH SS 6, p. 320: "Gregorius Romanae aecclesiae 60us presidet. Hic inter cetera pietatis opera animam Trajani Romanorum quondam imperatoris, quamvis pagani, a poenis inferni liberari, miserando et plorando a Deo optinuit. Hic inter multa, quae utilia aecclesiae fecit et instituit, antiphonarium regulariter centonizavit et utiliter compilavit. Kyrrieleyson a clero ad missas cantari precepit; Alleluia ad missas extra quinquagesimam dici fecit. In canone hostiae tria verba superaddidit: *Diesque nostros in tua pace disponas, atque ab aeterna damnatione nos eripi et in electorum tuorum jubeas grege numerari.* Orationem quoque dominicam post canonem super hostiam censuit recitari."

[290] John the Deacon, *Vita S. Gregorii papae* 2.9, PL 75, 91C–92A: "Sed cum multa post tempora, defunctis his qui Romae fuerant educati, cantum Gallicanarum Ecclesiarum a Metensi discrepare prudentissimus regum vidisset, ac unumquemque ab alterutro vitiatum cantum jactantem adverteret: Iterum, inquit, redeamus ad fontem. Tunc regis precibus, sicut hodie quidam veridice astipulantur, Adrianus papa permotus, duos in Galliam cantores misit, quorum judicio rex omnes quidem corrupisse dulcedinem Romani cantus levitate quadam cognovit, Metenses vero sola naturali feritate paululum quid dissonare praevidit. Denique usque hodie quantum Romano cantui Metensis cedit, tantum Metensi Ecclesiae cedere gallicanarum Ecclesiarum Germaniarumque cantus, ab his qui meram veritatem diligunt comprobatur."

[291] Guido of Arezzo, *Regule rithmice*, ed. by Pesce, p. 382: "Ita sane procuratum sit antiphonarium per Apulienses cunctos et vicinos Calabros, quibus tales misit neumas per Paulum Gregorius."

[292] See for example, *Guido of Arezzo, Regule rithmice*, ed. by Pesce, p. 372 and p. 374: "Incipit de notis....Causa vero breviandi neume solent fieri, qui si curiose fiant, habentur pro litteris..."

[293] Cf. Guido of Arezzo, *Regule rithmice*, ed. by Pesce, p. 361 and p. 378: "Relique iam vero voces valde sibi dissident: suam queque facit neumam alteri dissimilem, neque sue sedis locum neume dat extranee." "Illud quoque quod predixi valde erit utile: similis figure neumas si cures inspicere..."

[294] Guido of Arezzo, *Regule rithmice*, ed. by Pesce, p. 382. This is probably Paul the Deacon who had an important role to play in the liturgical concerns of the eighth century. See Thomas Forrest Kelly, *The Beneventan Chant*, (Cambridge: Cambridge University Press, 1989), p. 22, where he says "We cannot be certain that Paul himself was the intermediary of the Roman rite in the south, but his career exemplifies the cultural currents which brought the Gregorian liturgy from the Carolingian north to the Lombard south."

[295] Cf. Jacobus, *Speculum musicae* 6.113, ed. by Bragard, vol. 7, p. 310: "Nec est increpandus Boethius si pauciora de tonis tetigit et secundum alium modum quam ceteri ipsum sequentes musici. Non sit etiam ambiguum quin, pro tempore suo, Romani, de quorum natione Boethius erat, tonis aliter et cantibus ac musicis notis uterentur quam secundum modum quem recitat Boethius, etiam in ecclesia Dei sancta, cum Boethium praecessissent beati Ambrosius et Gregorius qui cantus aliquos condiderunt et illos ad Dei laudem et sanctorum in officio ecclesiae cantandos instituerunt, et alii etiam ante ipsos, ut beatus Ignatius. Et cantus illi minime Boethio latuerunt qui fuit vir vere catholicus."

[296] Cf. Guido of Arezzo, *Micrologus* 13, ed. by Smits van Waesberghe, pp. 150–151: "Ad quos in cantibus discernendos etiam quaedam neumae inventae sunt, ex quarum aptitudine ita modum cantionis agnoscimus..."

[297] Cf. Grocheio, *Ars musice* 29.2: "Differunt enim intonationes in diversis modis a parte principii. medii. et finis." A complete psalmodic formula consists of the opening intonation or *initium*; the tenor or reciting tone and various cadences, namely the flexa (only used for moderately long intonations), the median (*mediatio*) at the middle of the verse, and termination at the end of the verse, (*terminatio*). The example provided in Appendix II may be useful.

[298] Cf. Grocheio, *Ars musice* 29.2: "Nam primus cum sexto fa. sol. la. semper habeto. tertius octavus ut re. fa. sicque secundus. La. sol. la. quartus ut. mi. sol. sit tibi quintus. Septimus est mi. fa. sol. sic omnes esse recordor." On the early sources of *Primum cum sexto*, see Lebedev, "Zu einigen *loci obscuri* bei Johannes de Grocheio," in *Quellen und Studien zur Musiktheorie des Mittelalters* 2, ed. by M. Bernhard (Munich: Bayerische Akademie der Wissenschaften, 1997), p. 100.

[299] Cf. Petrus de Cruce, *Tractatus de tonis*, ed. by Harbinson, p. VII: "Primum cum sexto cantu. fa. sol. la. teneto. Tertius octavus. ut. re. fa. Sicque secundus. Septimus incipiet .mi.fa.sol. Quartusque la. sol.la Nunc quintum dicas/ quem. fa. lare. fa. bene cantas." See also Lebedev, "Zu einigen *loci obscuri*," p. 100.

[300] Cf. Grocheio, *Ars musice* 29.3: "A parte vero medii sic differunt et conveniunt. quoniam primus et sextus et septimus fa. mi. re. mi. dant. Secundus quintus. octavus. quisque .fa. sol. fa. Tertius sol. fa. mi. fa. Sed quartus dat ut. re. mi. re."

[301] Cf. Petrus de Cruce, *Tractatus de tonis*, ed. by Harbinson, p. VII: "Septimus et sextus dant. fa. mi. re. mi. quoque primus. Quintus et octavus. fa. fa. sol. fa. sic que secundus. Sol. fa. mi. fa. tertius. re. ut. re. mi. re. quarterus."

[302] Cf. Grocheio, *Ars musice* 29.2: "Et ista supra .8. dictiones figurant. puta pater. In filio. filius In patre. Spiritus sanctus ab utroque procedens."

[303] Cf. Grocheio, *Ars musice* 29.4: "Sed a parte finis multipliciter differunt. et istas differentias appellant seculorum Amen. Differunt enim secundum diversos modos. et adhuc in eodem tono differunt secundum diversos usus ecclesiarum et etiam secundum diversarum antiphonarum inceptiones."

[304] Cf. Guido of Arezzo, *Micrologus* 17, ed. by Smits van Waesberghe, p. 194: "Illud praeterea scire te volo quod in morem puri argenti cunctus cantus quo magis utitur, coloratur, et quod modo displicet, per usum quasi lima politum postea collaudatur... ."

[305] In the authentic modes, the rule of thumb is that the mediant is the scale step that lies a third below the reciting tone (or tenor), namely "f" in mode 1 (Dorian); "a" in modes 3 and 5 (Phrygian and Lydian) and "b" in mode 7 (Mixolydian).

[306] See Appendix II for an explanation of these intonation formulae.

[307] See M. Cecilia Gaposchkin, "Philip the Fair, the Dominicans and the liturgical Office for Louis IX: new perspectives on *Ludovicus Decus Regnantium*," *Plainsong and Medieval Music*, (2004) vol. 13 #1, pp. 33–61.

[308] This source does not have the flat signature for this example.

[309] For further on Guy of St. Denis and his treatment of the Invitatory see Anne Walters Robertson, *The Service-Books of the Royal Abbey of Saint-Denis: Images of Ritual and Music in the Middle Ages* (Oxford, 1991), pp.113–128.

[310] For further on this see Charles M. Atkinson, *The Critical Nexus: Tone-System, Mode, and Notation in Early Medieval Music* (Oxford, 2009), p.87.

[311] The Psalm *Venite exultemus* is omitted from BnF lat. 17296. But see BnF lat. 15181 fol. 546v and 15182 fols. 285v-286r for related versions of this. See Anne Walters Robertson, *The Service-Books of the Royal Abbey of Saint-Denis: Images of Ritual and Music in the Middle Ages* (Oxford, 1991) p.120.

[312] This mode 3 antiphon is included in the office that was celebrated at St. Denis and the complete texts for the office are provided as *Lauda Celestis 3* in Appendix 2.1 (pp. 253-83) of M. Cecilia Gaposchkin, *The Making of Saint Louis: Kingship, Sanctity, and Crusade in the Later Middle Ages* (Cornell University Press, 2008). Gaposchkin makes no reference to the chants in use for this office and the melody for *Hostem pestis* is not found. See also Anne Walters Robertson, *The Service-Books of the Royal Abbey of Saint-Denis: Images of Ritual and Music in the Middle Ages* (Oxford, 1991), pp. 77–8.

[313] Note that the B flat at the beginning of the example indicates that this Alleluia is transposed; *Alleluia laetatus sum* is found in other sources in Mode 1 starting on the final D.

[314] Like *Alleluya Laetatus sum, Beatus servus quem cum* is transposed to begin on A rather than on the usual tone 3 final, E. See Guy's explanation for the necessity of this in Book 1 at 1.3.10. Further explanation is provided in Charles M. Atkinson, *The Critical Nexus: Tone-System, Mode, and Notation in Early Medieval Music* (Oxford, 2009) pp. 235–7.

[315] Manuscript sources present this as *Vade iam.*

[316] This source does not use the B flat signature.

[317] This appears to be a reference to a now-missing tonary attributed to Johannes de Garlandia; see Reimer, ed., *Johannes de Garlandia*, vol. 1, pp. 9–10.

[318] See above at [2.4.3] for the explanation about the nature of this antiphon.

[319] In this source the responsory appears as *Ad dominum dum tribularer* with a B flat key signature, starting on G (though ending on F). The *Versus* follows Guy's example exactly.

[320] London, Victoria and Albert Museum, MS 1346–1891contains six sequences one of which is *Ave pater gallie*. See Matthew Martin Franke, 'Singing for a Patron Saint: Musical Strategies and Political Subtexts in Sequences from the Abbey of Saint-Denis' Masters Thesis (The University of North Carolina at Chapel Hill, 2009), p.10.

[321] This source is not a perfect match since it starts on g rather than a.

[322] For further on this see Anne Walters Robertson, *The Service-Books of the Royal Abbey of Saint-Denis: Images of Ritual and Music in the Middle Ages* (Oxford, 1991), pp. 113-128 and specifically pp. 125-6.

[323] The antiphon in this source begins on G rather than A and is a psalm verse rather than an antiphon.

[324] This source provides a remarkably similar melodic outline for this antiphon, though it commences on C rather than A.

[325] St. Sebastian: BnF lat. 17296 fol. 52r. "De octavo tono exemplum...invitatorium. Preoccupemus. Psalmus. Venite exsultemus domino." Petrus de Cruce Ambianensis, *Tractatus de tonis*, ed. by Denis Harbison, Corpus scriptorum de musica 29 (Rome: American Institute of Musicology, 1976), pp. xxiii–xxiv.

[326] This Invitatory is found in chant sources clearly in mode 6 and starting on C. The example given here seems to be only found in theoretical sources. See Anne Walters Robertson *The Service Books of the Royal Abbey of Saint-Denis: Images of Ritual and Music in the Middle Ages* (Oxford, 1991), pp. 126–7.

Appendices

Appendix I: Deleted Materials

1.3.4a: deleted passage (f. 67r)

Sciendum est autem quod si contingat cantus aliquos huius toni finiri in .g. grave, idest in primo .gsolreut. causa videlicet necessitatis alicuius vel quia aliter notari non possunt prout consueverunt cantari. tunc in fine cum .b. rotundo vel molli notari debent, ut sic videlicet non in .ut. vel .sol. sed in .re. finiantur; et ita .g. gravis ad .d. gravem idest ad dsolre. reducetur. et talis reductio locum habere videtur in Responsorio *Germanus plenus spiritu sancto* et in antiphona illa *Oramus te.* et in Responsorio. *Pater insignis. Deus omnipotens.* et quibusdam aliis cantibus[1] quorum nonnullos si vera sunt. immo quia vera sunt que de tonis senserunt musici salva nostrorum pace non solum irregulares esse constat immo nec umquam ab expertis in musica prout apud nos cantantur ad presens fuisse compositos. Sed magis scriptorum vicio vel correctionis negligentia depravatos. de quorum sibi quia similium correctione alias forsitan erit locus.

2.5.0: deleted passage (f. 89r-v)

Non potest notari aliter quam per falsam musicam de qua dictum est supra prima parte huius operis primo capitulo ubi videlicet de semitonio agebatur notando scilicet ipsum prout apud nos consuevit cantari et communiter apud alios multos. Aliqui tamen sine falsa musica ipsum notant et bene si ita consuetum est apud eos cantari videlicet isto modo:

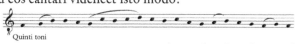

Quinti toni

A quodam etiam satis experto cantare quandoque [89v] audivi predictum neuma aliter posse cantari et notari sine falsa musica videlicet isto modo:

Iterum quinti toni

Sed si quis diligenter inspiciat primum neuma respectu aliorum duorum que sine falsa musica sunt notata quasi in medio se tenet. minus enim ascendit quam tertium. plus vero quam secundum. unde quamvis ut falsa musica sit notatum. communius tamen et potius quam alia duo apud nos et alios multos habetur in usu.

[1] *Germanus ... aliis cantibus* **H2** over erasure.

Appendix I: Deleted Materials

1.3.4a: translation of deleted passage (fol. 67r)

However, it should be known that if certain chants of this tone happen to end on G grave, that is to say on the first g solreut because of a certain necessity or because they cannot be notated other than as they have habitually been sung, then they ought to be notated with a round or soft b at the end [i.e. at the clef]; so that clearly they finish not on ut, or sol, but on re, and thus G grave is transposed to D grave, that is to d-solre. Just such a transposition seems to occur in the responsory *Germanus plenus spiritu sancto*[1] and in that antiphon *Oramus te*[2] and in the responsory *Pater insignis*,[3] *Deus omnipotens*[4] and in certain other chants; of these, it is clear that several (if the things music theorists sensed about the tones are true, or rather because they are true, keeping peace with our own) are not only irregular but rather it is the case that they were never composed by those experienced in music in the way that they are sung among us at present. But they have been corrupted more by the fault of scribes or carelessness in correction. Concerning the correction of similar things there will perhaps be place elsewhere.

2.5.0: deleted passage (fols. 89r–v)

It cannot be notated otherwise than through musica falsa, spoken about in the first part of this work in chapter one, where there was discussion of notating the semitone namely how it has been customarily sung among us and commonly among many others. Some however notate it without musica falsa and do so well if it is customary to be sung in this way amongst them.

[Fifth tone notated without musica falsa]

I have sometimes heard from someone sufficiently expert in singing that the said Neuma can be sung otherwise and notated without musica falsa, namely in this way.

[Fifth tone neuma notated without musica falsa]

But if anyone looks carefully at the first Neuma with respect to the two others that are notated without musica falsa it is as if in between. For it ascends less than a third but more than a second, so although it is notated with musica falsa it is yet held more often in use than the two others among us and many others.

[1] St Germanus: BnF lat.17296 fol. 199v:

Ger_ ma - nus___ ple - nus // pu - er de_____ mor - te.

[2] St Benedict: BnF lat.17296 fol. 82r:

O - ra - mus. te // dig - ne - ris_ ex - is - te - re.

[3] St Benedict: BnF lat. 17296 fol. 77r: (this chant opens in untransposed tone 2 and ends in transposed form on G.)

Pa - ter in - sig - nis // doc- tor_____ in_ or - be.

[4] St Cucuphas: BnF lat. 17296 fol. 197v:

De-us om - ni-po- tens_____ do-mi-ne_ // in-tro-i - re_ me - re - ar.

Appendix II Explanatory Material

(1) Hexachords, registers and pitch

The hexachords interlock with the pitch letter names within the three registers and provide the individual names for each pitch. The three hexachords are the Natural starting on C, the Hard starting on G, and the Soft, starting on F.

Note: there is no B♭ available in the Grave register; e'-la lies beyond the super-acute register and is considered to be *extra manum*; B natural is only found in the hard hexachord and B flat is only found in the soft hexachord.

Register	GRAVE								ACUTE								SUPERACUTE					
Pitch letter names	Γ	A	B	C	D	E	F	G	a	b♭	b♮	c	d	e	f	g	a'	b'♭	b'♮	c'	d'	e'
Natural hexachord				Ut	re	mi	fa	sol	la			Ut	re	mi	fa	sol	la					
Hard hexachord	Ut	re	mi	fa	sol	la		Ut	re		mi	fa	sol	la		Ut	re		mi	fa	sol	la
Soft hexachord							Ut	re	mi	fa		sol	la		Ut	re	mi	fa		sol	la	

(2) Mnemonic for the beginnings of the intonations for each tone in order. See 2.0.15

1.Pa - ter   2.In fi - li - o.   3.Fi - li - us.   4.In__ pa - tre.   5.Spi - ri - tus.

6.Sanc- tus.__   7.Ab__ u - tro- que.   8.Pro - ce- dens.

This is a melodic mnemonic in which each numbered phrase reminds the singer of how to get from the starting note of the chant to the reciting pitch for each tone. Thus for tone 1 the starting note is F and the tenor is A; for tone 2 the starting note is C and the tenor is F, and so on. Given that chant could begin on any of several pitches other than the final of the tone, but that the reciting pitch was fixed, this mnemonic must have been very useful. The rule of thumb is that the reciting pitch or tenor is a fifth above the final in authentic tones and a third below the reciting pitch or tenor in the respective plagal. In tones three and eight however, where the tenor falls on B it is moved to C.

(3) Intonation formulae

A complete psalmodic formula consists of the opening intonation or *initium*; the tenor or reciting tone and various cadences, namely the flexa (only used for moderately long intonations), the median at the middle of the verse, (*mediatio*) and termination at the end of the verse, (*terminatio*). Guy's explanation of the system is both clear and reliable.

Intonation   tenor   flexa   tenor   median   tenor   termination

Pri- mus_mo-dus sic in-ci-pi-tur sic flec-ti-tur et sic me-di-a-tur at-que sic fin-i - tur.

Chant Sources and Concordances Table:
Explanatory Notes

THE CHANT SOURCES table provides a convenient cross reference tool that compiles all chant citations and examples given in Books 1 and 2 of the *Tractatus de tonis* of Guy de Saint-Denis. The chants referred to in Book 1 have no notated musical examples, while those in Book 2 are generally illustrated with an accompanying music incipit. Where there is an occasional lack of music examples in Book 2, this is distinguished by an asterisk in the "Paragraphs" column.

The table aims to validate the mode of each chant melody from a concordant manuscript example exemplifying locality and liturgical practice where possible. The important notated manuscripts from Saint-Denis, the Antiphonal BnF lat. 17296 and the Missal BnF lat. 1107 have been used in the main, supplemented by Parisian manuscripts and those further afield where necessary. Some chants not able to be located in accessible digitised formats have been noted as 'not found' for the present. The folios given represent the beginning of the chant, and verses and psalms are also cited separately. Bracketed text is given at times to amplify short incipits presented in the *Tractatus*, to avoid ambiguity and clarify spelling variants where needed. Medieval orthography is adhered to generally, although proper names are distinguished by respectful capitals.

In the "Tone" column, additional mode alternatives given for a single chant may suggest both modal combinations being represented within the chant, or at other times alternative interpretations of mode. Alternatives given in the manuscript example columns are various instances of the same melody, the first generally being the melody in full followed by shorter incipits. The CAO numbers are given when they concur with both melody and text as represented by the Cantus ID in the Cantus database, hosted by the University of Waterloo and maintained by Jan Koláček and Debra Lacoste. (http://cantusdatabase.org, accessed 20 June, 2015)

Legend for Chant Sources and Concordances Table
An = Antiphon; Al = Alleliua; Av = Alleliua verse; C = Communion; G = Gloria Patri; Gl = Gloria in excelsis; H = Hymn; In = Introit/Officium; Inv = Invitatory; O = Offertory; Ps = Psalm; R = Responsory; Rv = Responsory verse; S = Sequence; T = Tract; tr = transposition; * indicates that no music example is given in *Tractatus de tonis* Book 2.

Incipit	Harley 281	Paragraphs	Type	Tone	BnF lat. 17296	BnF lat. 1107	Other MSS	CAO/ Cantus
Ad celebres	76v	2.0.2*	S	7/2		380r		
Ad dominum cum tribularer-Rv. Domine	91v	2.6.0	R	6		69r		
Adiutor [in opportunitatibus]-Rv. Quoniam non	86r	2.3.2	R	3		35v		850361
Adiutorium nostrum	81r	2.1.4	An	1			lat. 15181-191v	1279
Adiuva me	94v	2.8.1	An	8			lat. 12044 - 32v	1281
Adiuva nos deus [Resp. Propitius esto]	69v/91v	1.3.22/2.6.0	Rv	5/6		58r		
Adiuvabit eam	92v	2.7.3	An	7	66r/210v/284r			1282
A domino [Resp. Benedictus qui venit]	90r	2.5.1	Rv	5		18v		6251
Ad omnia [que]	94r	2.8.1	An	8	169r			1249
Ad quantam vero	85v	2.3.2	An	3	261v			1251
Ad te domine [Resp. Salvum fac populum]	93v	2.7.4	Rv	7		59v		
Ad te domine levavi	87r	2.4.3	An	4 tr	17v			1255
Ad te levavi animam	96r	2.8.4	In	8		1r		
Eterna Christi munera	85v	2.3.2	H	3			lat. 15181-518v	8252
Agathes ingressa	94r	2.8.1	An	8	70v			1305bis
Agathes [letrissime]	92v	2.7.3	An	8	70v - start error?		lat. 15181-453v	1306
Alleluia, Angelus domini	96r	2.8.4	Al	8		148r		
Alleluia, Ante thronum	90r	2.5.1	Al	5			lat. 1028 - 342v-Av	
Alleluia, Cum sederit filius hominis	86r	2.3.2	Al	3		301r		
Alleluia, Deus iudex	91v	2.6.0	Al	5/6/7/8		194v		
Alleluia, Dies sanctificatus	84v	2.2.1	Al	2		20r		
Alleluia, Dionysi pater alme	90v	2.5.1	Al	5			Not found	
Alleluia, Excita domine	88v	2.4.6	Al	4		5v		
Alleluia, Iusti epulen[tur]	83r	2.1.12	Al	1		163ar		
Alleluia, Letatus sum	68r/86r	1.3.10/2.3.2	Al	3 tr		3v		
Alleluia, Magne pater Dionysi	92r	2.6.0	Al	5/6			Not found	

Alleluia, Nativitas [gloriose virginis]	93v	2.7.4	Al	7		263r		
Alleluia, Ostende nobis [domine misericordiam]	96r	2.8.4	Al	8		1v/327v		
Alleluia, Pascha nostrum	93v	2.7.4	Al	7		144v		
Alleluia, Per manus autem apostolo[rum]	89r	2.4.6	Al	4		287r		
Alleluia, Sancte Nichole [qui in celis]	83r	2.1.12	Al	1		282r		
Alleluia, Surrexit Christus [qui]	84v	2.2.1	Al	2		157r		
Alma redemptoris	69r	1.3.20	An	5	341r		1356	
Ambulabunt [mecum in albis]	86v	2.4.1	An	4	38v		1364	
Angelus domini [Alleluia]	96r	2.8.4	Av	8		148r		
Angelus domini descendit	69v	1.3.20	R	3	136v–137r		6093	
Angelus domini vocavit Abraham	67v	1.3.8	R	2 tr	94v/93r		6098	
Anime impiorum	94r	2.8.1	An	8	119v		1419	
Annue Christe	88v	2.4.6	H	4			8264	lat. 15181-499v
Ante thorum [torum huius virginis]	68r/87v	1.3.12/2.4.6	An	4 tr	66r/206v/210v		1438	lat. 1028 - 342v
Ante thronum [Alleluia]	90r	2.5.1	Av	5				
Apertis [thesauris suis]	81r	2.1.3	An	1	48r/48v		1447	
Aspiciebam-Rv. Potestas eius	91r	2.6.0	R	6	2r		6128	
Assumpsit Iesus discipulos	67v	1.3.8	An	2 tr	101v		1501	
Audite-Gloria patri [Resp. Cives apostolorum]	93r	2.7.4	Rv	7	267v		6289	lat. 15181-503v
Auge in nobis	85v	2.3.2	An	3	164r		1531	
Aurea virga	76v	2.0.2*	S	7/8		364v		
Aurora lucis rutilat	91r	2.6.0	H	6			8271	lat. 15181-321v
Ave Maria	70r/80v	1.3.23/2.1.1	An	1	13v/84r/239r			
Ave Maria	75v/84v	1.4.19/2.2.1	T	2		232r	1539	
Ave Maria-Ps. Venite exultemus domino	93r	2.7.4	Inv	7	84r/206v - no ps		1041	lat. 15181-467v
Ave Maria [Resp. Missus est]	93r	2.7.4	Rv	7	2v/84v		7170	
Ave Maris stella	82v	2.1.11	H	1	84r - blank		8272	lat. 15181-467r
Ave pater Gallie	92r	2.6.0	S	?				GB: Lva 1346-1891 -419r

Incipit	Harley 281	Paragraphs	Type	Tone	BnF lat. 17296	BnF lat. 1107	Other MSS	CAO/ Cantus
Ave regina celorum	68v/90v	1.3.15/2.6.0	An	6 tr	340v - tr		lat. 12044 - 177v	1542
Ave virgo virginum	92r	2.6.0	S	5/6 tr		375r		1570
Beata mater	83v	2.2.0	An	2	206r/210v			6190
Beatissimus [Dionysius]-Rv. Et Parisius-Gloria patri	88r	2.4.6	R	4	230r		lat. 17329-245v - Gloria	
Beatus ille servus	93r	2.7.4	An	7	282v/283r			1634
Beatus servus quem cum	68r/86v	1.3.10/2.3.2	C	3 tr	27r	310r		1665
Beatus Stephanus	81v	2.1.7	An	1				
Benedic anima	90v	2.5.1	O	5		57v		
Benedicimus deum celi	89r	2.4.6	C	4		178r		
Benedicta tu	87v	2.4.6	An	4 tr	4v/65v			1709
Benedictus es domine deus patrum	93v	2.7.4	T	7		11v		
Benedictus es in firmamento	86r	2.3.2	T	3		59v		
Benedictus qui venit-Rv. A domino	90r	2.5.1	R	5		18v		6251
Benedixisti domine	86r	2.3.2	O	3		6r		
Benigne fac	87r	2.4.1	An	4			lat. 15181 - 76v	1736
Candida virginitas	67r	1.3.4	R	1	1r			6262
Caritas [Karitas pater est]	93r	2.7.4	An	7	166r			1773
Cecilia me misit	94v	2.8.1	An	8	253v			1748
Christi virgo	82r	2.1.9	An	1	56r/57r			1787
Christo inclita candida	93v	2.7.4	S	8/2		385v		
Christum regem	88v	2.4.6*	Inv	4	175v			1051
Christus natus est-Ps. Venite exultemus domino	88r	2.4.6	Inv	4	19v/43r			1055
Circumdantes [circumdederunt]	94v	2.8.2	An	8	124v			1809
Circumdederunt	90r	2.5.1	In	5		35r		
Cives apostolorum-Rv. Audite-Gloria patri	93r	2.7.4	R	7	267v		lat. 15181-503r-v	6289

Clamaverunt	92v	2.7.2	An	7	265r/273r			1823
Clamavi	81r	2.1.3	An	1			lat. 12044 - 33v	1824
Completi sunt	94v	2.8.1	An	8	19v/343r			1862
Conclusit vias	69r	1.3.20	R	8	121v			6306
Confessio et pulchritudo	86r	2.3.2	In	3		55r/255r		
Confirma hoc	89r	2.4.6	O	3/4		169v - tr	lat. 17307 - 138v	
Confirma hoc deus	94v	2.8.3	An	8	160v			1873
Confitebuntur celi	93v	2.7.4	O	7		163av		
Congaudentes exultemus	83r	2.1.12	S	1		389v		
Cornelius centurio	67r	1.3.4	R	1	175r			6340
Credo videre	87r	2.4.1	An	4	134r			1948
Crucem tuam	87r	2.4.3	An	4	213v			1953
Cum appropinquaret [dominus Ierusalem]	80v	2.1.1	An	1	324r			1975
Cum esset in accubitu	68v	1.3.15	R	6 tr			Poissy - 313r	
Cum sederit filius hominis [Alleluia]	86r	2.3.2	Av	3		301r		
Cum venerit [Convenerit] paraclitus	94r	2.8.1	An	8	160r			2043
Custodit dominus [alleluia alleluia alleluia]	87r	2.4.2	An	4	85r			2085
Data sunt ei	94v	2.8.2	An	8	223r			2102
De fructu	94v	2.8.1	An	8	25v			2106
De ore leonis-Gloria patri [Resp. Erue a framea]	83v	2.2.0	Rv	2	119v			6671
Deponet omnes iniquitates nostras [Resp. Qui venturus est]	75v	1.4.18	Rv	6	9v			7485
De profundis	75v/96r	1.4.19/2.8.4	T	8		36r	lat. 15181 - 193r	
De profundis	94v	2.8.3	An	8			lat. 17329 - 226r	2116
Descendi [in hortum/ortum]	92v	2.7.1	An	7				2155
Desiderium anime	92r	2.6.0	O	6		314r		
De Syon veniet [dominus/qui regnaturus]	70r/80v	1.3.23/2.1.1	An	1	17r		lat. 15182 - 90r-v	2120/2121
Deum verum unum-Ps. Venite exultemus	88r	2.4.6	Inv	4	165r - no ps			1061

Incipit	Harley 281	Paragraphs	Type	Tone	BnF lat. 17296	BnF lat. 1107	Other MSS	CAO/Cantus
Deus deus meus respice	75v	1.4.19	T	2		107v		
Deus in loco	90r	2.5.1	In	5		188v		
Deus iudex [Alleluia]	91v	2.6.0	Av	5/6/7/8		194v		6429
Deus omnipotens [domine Iesu]/erased	67r	1.3.4	R	2 tr	197v	4r		
Deus tu convertens	86r	2.3.2	O	3		75r		
Deus vitam meam-Rv. Miserere michi	96r	2.8.4	R	8		243r		
De ventre matris	82v	2.1.12	In	1		6r		
Dicite pusillanimes	93v	2.7.4	C	7		303r		
Dico autem vobis [amicis meis]	96v	2.8.4	C	8				
Dico vobis [gaudium]	87r	2.4.1	An	4	322v			2208
Dies sanctificatus [Alleluia]	84v	2.2.1	Av	2		20r		
Diffusa est gratia-Rv. Dilexisti	87v	2.4.6	R	4	284v/255v			6446
Dilexisti [Resp. Diffusa est gratia]	88r	2.4.6	Rv	4	284v/255v			6446
Dilexisti-Rv. Propterea	96r	2.8.4	R	8		316r		
Dinumerabo eos [Resp. Nimis honorati sunt]	84v	2.2.1	Rv	2		286r		7216
Dionysi pater alme [Alleluia]	90v	2.5.1	Av	5			Not found	
Dixit dominus [Resp. Iuravit dominus]	86r	2.3.2	Rv	3		308v		
Dixit Iesus ad legis	81v	2.1.7	An	1	325v			2293
Docebit nos-Rv. Venite ascendamus	83v	2.2.0	R	2	6r			6481
Domine [Resp. Ad dominum cum tribularer]	91v	2.6.0	Rv	6		69r		
Domine deus [Resp. Protector noster]	69v/91v	1.3.22/2.6.0	Rv	5/6		50v		
Domine Iesu Christe [magister]	70r	1.3.23	An	2	261r			2352
Domine in auxilium	92r	2.6.0	O	6		69v		
Domine in virtute	94v	2.8.3	An	8			Not found/Poissy - 313v - Ps	
Domine labia	92v	2.7.3	An	7	104r			2355
Domine mi rex	85r	2.3.1	An	3	209v			2358

Incipit								
Domine non sum dignus	81r	2.1.5	An	1	96v			2363
Domine ostende	92v	2.7.2	An	7	153v			2366
Domine prevenisti-Rv. Vitam	88v	2.4.6	R	4		309r		6505
Domine puer meus	81r	2.1.5	An	1	96v			2368
Dominum qui fecit nos-Ps. Venite exultemus domino	89v	2.5.0	Inv	5	106r/313r - no ps		lat. 15181 - 240v	1066
Dominus [iudicabit/defensor]	81r	2.1.5	An	1	19v/43r		lat. 15181 - 193r	2414/2404
Dominus [dixit ad]	94v	2.8.2	An	8	17v			2406
Dominus legifer noster	85r	2.3.1	An	3				2415
Domum tuam domine	92v	2.7.1	An	7	289r			2425
Domus mea	80v	2.1.1	An	1	100v/289v			2428
Dum clamarem [Resp. Iacta cogitatum]	93v	2.7.4	Rv	7		44v		
Dum medium	94r	2.8.1	An	8	25v			2461
Dum sacrum myste[rium]-Rv. Mecum-Goria patri	89v	2.5.0	R	5	230r/288r			6559
Ecce apparebit dominus	67r	1.3.4	R	1	9r			6578
Ecce ascendimus [Ierusolimam]	94r	2.8.1	An	8	96r			2495
Ecce Maria	89v	2.5.0	An	5	44r			2523
Ecce merces sanctorum	87r	2.4.1	An	4	39r - tr		lat. 1090 - 262v	2524
Ecce nomen domini	80v	2.1.1	An	1	1r - missing		lat. 15181 - 106r	2527
Ecce venit rex-Ps. Venite exultemus domino	88r	2.4.6	Inv	4	1v/6r - no ps		lat. 15181-106r-v	1074
Ecce vir prudens	75v	1.4.19	T	2	237r - R		lat. 17329 - 86r - R	
Ego autem in iustitia	83r	2.1.12	In	1		68r		
Egregio	94r	2.8.1	An	8	74r			2615
Epiphaniam domino	77r/96r	2.0.3*/2.8.4	S	8		346v		
Erat vir domini	86r	2.4.1	An	4	81v			2662
Erue a framea-Rv. De ore leonis-Gloria patri	83v	2.2.0	R	2	119r			6671
Est secretum	86v	2.4.1	An	4	255v			2680
Etenim sederunt	83r	2.1.12	In	1	21r			

Incipit	Harley 281	Paragraphs	Type	Tone	BnF lat. 17296	BnF lat. 1107	Other MSS	CAO/Cantus
Et ingresse	92v	2.7.2	An	7	142v			2707
Et Parisius-Gloria patri [Resp. Beatissimus Dionysius]	88r	2.4.6	Rv	4	230r			6190
Etsi [Et si] coram hominibus	83v	2.1.12	C	1		303r		
Exaudi deus	90r	2.5.1	In	5		87v		
Excita domine [Alleluia]	88v	2.4.6	Av	4		5v		
Exclamaverunt [ad te domine]	82v	2.1.12	In	1		235r		
Ex Egypto vocavi	68r/87r	1.3.12/2.4.3	An	4 tr	4v			2743
Ex quo facta	81r	2.1.5	An	1	17v - tr		lat. 12044 - 3v	2750
Ex quo omnia	89v	2.5.0	An	5	165r			2751
Exsequie Martini	87r	2.4.1	An	4	247v			2802
Exsistens maculis	85v	2.3.2	An	3	350v			2804
Exurge [quare obdormis]	82v	2.1.12	In	1		37r		
Facti sumus	81r	2.1.3	An	1			lat. 12044 - 34r	2839
Factum est [ut quedam]	87r	2.4.1	An	4	176r			2844
Factus est repente	93v	2.7.4	C	7		169v		6717
Factus sum	87v	2.4.4	An	4 tr	135r			2849
Felix namque es-Rv. Ora pro populo-Gloria patri	82r	2.1.11	R	1			lat. 15182 - 310v–311r	6725
Fidelia	87r	2.4.2	An	4			lat. 15181 - 79v/184v	2865
Fortem fidelem militem	93r	2.7.4	H	7			Not found	
Fulgebunt iusti [sicut sol]	82r	2.1.10	An	1	38v/39r			2908
Fundamenta eius	81r	2.1.4	An	1			lat. 15181 - 195r	2911
Gaudeamus [omnes in domino]	82v	2.1.12	In	1		225r/257r		
Gaude Maria	68r/87v	1.3.12/2.4.6	An	4 tr	66v			2924
Gaude mater ecclesia nove laudis preconio	90r	2.5.0	H	5			lat. 1028 - 332v	
Gaude prole Grecia	83r	2.1.12	S	1		381r		

			R	1/2 tr			
Germanus plenus spiritu sancto/erased	67r	1.3.4	R		199v		6771
Germinavit radix	80v	2.1.1	An	1	44r/48v		2941
Gloria in excelsis	76r	1.4.21	Gl	4		lat. 1112 - 259r/lat. 14819-36v	
Gloria in excelsis [Resp. Hodie nobis.... gaudet exercitus]	69v/89v	1.3.20/2.5.0	Rv	5	20v		6858
Gloria patri [Resp. Beatissimus Dionysius-Rv. Et Parisius]	88r	2.4.6	G	4		lat. 17329 - 245v	6190
Gloria patri [Resp. Cives apostolorum-Rv. Audite]	93r	2.7.4	G	7		lat. 15181 - 503v	6289
Gloria patri [Resp. Dum sacrum myste[rium]-Rv. Mecum]	89v	2.5.0	G	5		Not found	6559
Gloria patri [Resp. Erue a framea-Rv. De ore leonis]	83v	2.2.0	G	2		Not found	6671
Gloria patri [Resp. Felix namque es-Rv. Ora pro populo]	82v	2.1.11	G	1		lat. 15182 - 311r	6725
Gloria patri [Resp. Gratias tibi domine-Rv. Quin immo]	91r	2.6.0	G	6		Poissy - 3r	6791
Gloria patri [Resp. Salvatorem exspectamus-Rv. Sobrie]	85v	2.3.2	G	3		Not found	7562
Gratias tibi domine-Rv. Quin immo-Gloria patri	91r	2.6.0	R	6	229v	Poissy - 3r - Gloria	6791
Habitabit	87r	2.4.1	An	4	133v/276v		2987
Hec est que nescivit	85r	2.3.2	An	3	66r		3001
Helena sancta	92v	2.7.3	An	7	154v		3024
Hic accipiet	92v	2.7.1	An	7	276v/280r		3047
Hodie [Resp. Hodie nobis [de celo]]	95r	2.8.4	Rv	8	20v		6859
Hodie Maria virgo	94r	2.8.1	An	8	207v		3105

Incipit	Harley 281	Paragraphs	Type	Tone	BnF lat. 17296	BnF lat. 1107	Other MSS	CAO/Cantus
Hodie nobis [celorum...gaudet exercitus]- Rv. Gloria in excelsis	69v/89v	1.3.20/2.5.0	R	5	20v			6858
Hodie nobis [de celo]-Rv. Hodie	95r	2.8.4	R	8	20v			6859
Hodie scietis	94v	2.8.2	An	8	18v		Not found	3119
Hostem pestis	85r	2.3.2	An	3				
Iacta cogitatum-Rv. Dum clamarem	93r	2.7.4	R	7		44v		7031
Ierusalem cito veniet	73r	1.4.9	R	4	6r			7034
Ierusalem surge	84v	2.2.1	C	2		4r		
Iesu salvator seculi [redemptis]	82v	2.1.11	H	1			Poissy - 416v	8333
Immittit angelus domini	96v	2.8.4	O	8		56r		3228
Inclina domine	67r	1.3.4	In	1		192v		
In domo David	94v	2.8.3	An	8	318r			3234
In ferventis	87r	2.4.1	An	4	33r			3244
In illa die	94r	2.8.1	An	8	3v			
In medio ecclesie	91v	2.6.0	In	6		22v		3262
In omnem terram	70r	1.3.23	An	2	239r/265r			3272
In prole mater	87r	2.4.2	An	4	208r			
Inquirentes [Resp. Timete dominum]	83r	2.1.12	Rv	1		299r		
Insignes preconiis	94v	2.8.1	An	8	227r			3355
Insurrexerunt in me	69v	1.3.20	R	3	123r			6973
Intret in conspectu	88v	2.4.6	In	4		296v		
Inveni David	84v	2.2.1	O	8/2 tr		310r - tr		6986
Inveni David-Rv. Nichil proficiet	83r	2.1.12	R	1		308v		
In verbum tuum	92v	2.7.3	An	7	88r			3308
Invocantem	80v	2.1.1	An	1	280r			3399
Iocundare [filia Syon]	94r	2.8.1	An	8	4r			3509

Ipsi soli	82r	2.1.9	An	1	57r			3406
Iste confessor [domini sacratus]	88v	2.4.6	H	4			Not found	8323
Iste confessor [domini sacratus]	95v	2.8.4	H	8			lat. 1028 - 277v	8323
Isti sunt [viri]-Rv. Sancti-Gloria patri	95r	2.8.4	R	8	274r			7026
Iubilate deo	86v	2.4.1	An	4			lat. 15181 - 69v	3508
Iubilate deo [universa]	83r	2.1.12	O	1		32r		
Iubilemus deo salutari nostro [Inv. Venite exultemus domino]	88r	2.4.6	Ps	4			lat. 15181 - 188v	1179
Iubilemus omnes una	86r	2.3.2	S	3		341r		
Iudea et Ierusalem/O Iuda	73r	1.4.9	R	4	19v			7040/7271bis
Iuravit dominus-Rv. Dixit dominus	86r	2.3.2	R	3		308v		
Iusti epulen[tur] [Alleluia]	83r	2.1.12	Av	1		163ar		
Iustorum anime	94r	2.8.1	An	8	39r/201r/216v			3538
Laudabo [alleluia alleluia alleluia]	87r	2.4.1	An	4	85r			3583
Lauda celestis	80v	2.1.1	An	1			Not found	
Laudate dominum de celis	81v	2.1.6	An	1	92r			3585
Laudes crucis	69v	1.3.22	S	8/7		377v		
Laudum carmina	84v	2.2.1	S	2		362r		
Laus deo patri	86v	2.4.1	An	4	164v			3600
Lazarus	81r	2.1.5	An	1	115v			3603
Letabundus exsultet fidelis	69v/90v	1.3.22/2.5.1	S	5/8 tr		342r - not tr	lat. 830 - 302r	508017
Letare Ierusalem	90r	2.5.1	In	5		84v		
Letatus sum [Alleluia]	68r/86r	1.3.10/2.3.2	Av	3 tr		3v		
Levate capita	70r	1.3.23	An	1	19r			3608
Loquebar	90r	2.5.1	In	5		315v		
Loquere domine	80v	2.1.1	An	1	289v			
Lux eterna	96v	2.8.4	C	8		330v		3636

Incipit	Harley 281	Paragraphs	Type	Tone	BnF lat. 17296	BnF lat. 1107	Other MSS	CAO/ Cantus
Lux de luce	92v	2.7.3	An	7	49r			3649
Lux orta est super nos	82r	2.1.9	An	1	25r			3652
Magi [viderunt stellam]	94r	2.8.1	An	8	44v			3655
Magna est gloria eius	89r	2.4.6	C	4		294r		8130
Magne pater Dionysi [Alleluia]	92r	2.6.0	Av	5/6			Not found	
Magnus sanctus Paulus	94v	2.8.3	An	8	182r			3683
Maria [et flumina]	87r	2.4.1	An	4	48r			3700
Maria noli	94r	2.8.1	An	8	144v			3703
Mecum enim [habeo]/[est]	95v	2.8.4*	An	5/7	59r/228v		lat. 15181 - 425v	3729/3728
Mecum-Goria patri [Resp. Dum sacrum myste[rium]]	89v	2.5.0	Rv	5	230v/288r			6559
Me suscepit	95v	2.8.4*	An	5/7	345v		lat. 15182 - 427v	3725
Mirabilis deus	96v	2.8.4	O	8		301v		
Miserere michi [Resp. Deus vitam meam]	96r	2.8.4	Rv	8		75r		
Misereris omnium	83r	2.1.12	In	1		42r		
Misit dominus [manum/angelum]	92v	2.7.2	An	7	169r/180r/192v			3785/3783/ 3784
Missus est-Rv. Ave Maria	93r	2.7.4	R	7	2v/84v			7170
Nativitas [Alleluia]	93v	2.7.4	Av	7		263r		
Nativitas gloriose	84v	2.2.1	C	2	212r - R	264r		
Nato canunt omnia	76v	2.0.3*	S	8/7		341v		
Nemo te condemnavit	94r	2.8.1	An	8	111r			3873
Ne reminiscaris	86v	2.4.1	An	4	305v			3861
Nichil proficiet [Resp. Inveni David]	83r	2.1.12	Rv	1		309r		6986
Nimis honorati sunt-Rv. Dinumerabo eos	84v	2.2.1	R	2 tr		286r		7216
Nisi diligenter	86v	2.4.1	An	4	71r			3881

Non auferetur [sceptrum]	81v	2.1.7	An	1	9r/84r			3902
Nos qui vivimus benedicimus domino	95r	2.8.4	An	8			lat. 1535 - 36v	3960
Notum fecit [Resp. Viderunt omnes]	90r	2.5.1	Rv	5		20r		
Nunc scio vere	86r	2.3.2	In	3		245v		
O beata [et benedicta]	81v	2.1.7	An	1	168r/242v			3992
O beate Dionysi	81v	2.1.7	An	1	152r/232v/240r			3999
Octo sunt beatitudines	93v	2.8.0	An	8	Model Antiphon			
O Iuda [et Ierusalem]/Iudea et Ierusalem	73r	1.4.9	R	4	19v			7271bis/7040
Omnia [quecumque voluit]	85v	2.3.2	An	3			lat. 15181 - 90v/194v	4139
Omnipotens adorande	67v	1.3.8	R	2 tr	58v - tr/a		lat. 15181 - 425v - tr/d'	7318
Omnipotentem semper adorant	89v	2.4.6	T	4		199r		
Omnis terra [adoret]	87r	2.4.1	An	4	44v			4155
O mors	87v	2.4.5	An	4 tr	135v			4045
O pastor eterne	81v	2.1.7	An	1	261r			4051
Oportet te fili	96v	2.8.4	C	8		72r		
O quam metuendus est	90v	2.6.0	An	6	287r			4065
O quantus luctus	82r	2.1.8	An	1	251r			4074
Oramus te [beatissime confessor dei]/erased	67r	1.3.4	An	2 tr	82r			4175
Ora pro populo-Gloria patri [Resp. Felix namque es]	82v	2.1.11	Rv	1			lat. 15182 - 311r	6725
Oravit Iacob	69r	1.3.19	R	8 tr	103v			7334
Orietur [diebus]	85v	2.3.1	An	3	20r/43r			4194
O sapientia	70r/83v	1.3.23/2.2.0	An	2	13v			4081
Os iusti meditabitur sapien[tiam]	91v	2.6.0	In	6		313v		
Ostende nobis [Alleluia]	96r	2.8.4	Av	8		1v/327v		
Panem de celo	90v	2.5.1	C	5		191v		
Pange lingua gloriosi	85v	2.3.2	H	3 tr			lat. 15181 - 261v	8367
Paratum panem	68v	1.3.15	R/Rv	6			Not found	

Incipit	Harley 281	Paragraphs	Type	Tone	BnF lat. 17296	BnF lat. 1107	Other MSS	CAO/ Cantus
Pascha nostrum [Alleluia]	93v	2.7.4	Av	7		144v		8435
Pater insignis [confessor Benedicte]/erased	67r	1.3.4	R	2 tr	77r - unclear		lat. 17329 - 240r - tr	7361
Pater manifestavi	81v	2.1.7	An	1	156r			4237
Peccata mea	81v	2.1.7	An	1	312v			4255
Per manus autem apostolo[rum] [Alleluia]	89r	2.4.6	Av	4		287r		
Petrus apostolus [et Paulus]	94r	2.8.1	An	8	181r/182v			4284
Pontifices	93r	2.7.4	An	7	262r			4309
Post partum virgo	87v	2.4.6	An	4 tr	66v/210v/242v			4332
Postulavi	80v	2.1.1	An	1	136r			4342
Posuerunt	80v	2.1.1	An	1	133v			4343
Posuerunt mortalia	83v	2.1.12	C	1		302v		
Posuisti domine	92r	2.6.0	C	6		293v		
Potestas eius potestas eterna [Resp. Aspiciebam]	75v/91r	1.4.18/2.6.0	Rv.b	6	2r			6128
Precatus est moyses	93v	2.7.4	O	7		67v		
Precedam vos	94r	2.8.1	An	8	143v/138r			4352
Predicans [preceptum domini]	80v	2.1.1	An	1	276r			4359
Preoccupemus	95v	2.8.4*	Inv	7	52r		Mode 8 not found	1115/1117
Preter rerum seriem [rerum ordinem]	84v	2.2.1	O	2	Model Antiphon	398v		
Primum querite regnum dei	77r/80r	2.0.5*/2.1.0	An	1				4377
Prophete predicaverunt	80v	2.1.1	An	1	17r			4392
Propitius esto [domine peccatis-Rv. Adiuva nos deus]	69v/91v	1.3.22/2.6.0	R	5/6		58r		
Propterea [Resp. Dilexisti]	96r	2.8.4	Rv	8	17r	316v		
Propter Syon	87v	2.4.6	An	4 tr				4400
Protector noster-Rv. Domine deus [virtutum]	69v/91v	1.3.22/2.6.0	R	5/6		50v		
Pueri Hebreorum [tollentes/vestimenta]	80v	2.1.1	An	1	125v			4415/4416

Puer natus est	93r	2.7.4	In	7	43v	19v	4441	
Quando natus est	85r	2.3.2	An	3				
Quarta vigilia venit ad eos	86v	2.4.0	An	4	Model Antiphon		7465	
Quatuor animalia	68v	1.3.15	R	6 tr	270v		4425	
Que est ista	80v	2.1.1	An	1	207v			
Querentes eum	85r	2.3.2	An	3	105v			
Qui celorum [contines thronos]	81v	2.1.7	An	1	309r		4460	
Qui confidunt	96r	2.8.4	T	8		85r		
Qui custodiebant	67r/69r	1.3.4/1.3.20	R	1	118r		7475	
Qui de terra est	85r	2.3.2	An	3	43r		4464	
Quid vobis	86v	2.4.1	An	4	326r		4533	
Qui habitat	75v/84v	1.4.19/2.2.1	T	2		48r		
Qui Lazarum [Resp. Requiem]	84r	2.2.1	Rv	2		329v	7533	
Qui manducat carnem meam	92r	2.6.0	C	6		68r		
Qui me dignatus est	92v	2.7.1	An	7	73v		4480	
Qui meditabitur in le[ge]	86v	2.3.2	C	3		43v		
Quin immo-Gloria patri [Resp. Gratias tibi domine]	91r	2.6.0	Rv	6	230r		6791	
Quinque prudentes virgines-Neuma	89r	2.5.0	An	5		Model Antiphon	4543	
Qui regis	96v	2.8.4	T	8		12v		
Qui regis sceptra	89r	2.4.6	S	4		341r		
Quis dabit ex Syon	90v	2.5.1	C	5		75v		
Qui seminant	75v	1.4.19	T	8		225v		
Quod autem [cecidit]	81v/82r	2.1.7/2.1.10	An	1	92v/93r		4557	
Quoniam [in seculum/eternum]	85v	2.3.2	An	3			4567	lat. 15181 - 91r
Quoniam edificavit [Resp. Timebunt gentes]	91v	2.6.0	Rv	5/6		33r		
Quoniam non [Resp. Adiutor] [in opportunitatibus]	86r	2.3.2	Rv	3		36r	850361	

Incipit	Harley 281	Paragraphs	Type	Tone	BnF lat. 17296	BnF lat. 1107	Other MSS	CAO/ Cantus
Redemptionem	92v	2.7.1	An	7	25r			4587
Regem celorum dominum adoremus	84r/88v	2.2.0/2.4.6*	Inv	2	222v			1128
Regem cui omnia vivunt-Ps. Venite exultemus domino	91r	2.6.0	Inv	6			nal.1535 - 129r	1131
Regem cui omnia vivunt-Ps. Venite exultemus domino	95v	2.8.4	Inv	8			Not found	1131
Regem precursoris dominum-Ps. Venite exultemus domino	85v	2.3.2	Inv	3			lat. 15182 - 207r/ 15181 - 547r	1140
Regem regum dominum	88v	2.4.6*	Inv	1	152r/227r/239r			1146
Regem sempiternum pronis mentibus- Ps. Venite exultemus	84r	2.2.0	Inv	2	188v		lat. 15181 - 546v/ 15182 - 285v	1148
Reges Tharsis	81r	2.1.2	An	1	44v			4594
Reges Tharsis	90v	2.5.1	O	5		28r		
Requiem-Rv. Qui Lazarum	84r	2.2.1	R	2 tr		329r		7533
Rerum deus tenax vi[gor]	93r	2.7.4	H	7			Not found	
Resurrexi et adhuc	88v	2.4.6	In	4		144r		
Rorate [celi de super]	82v	2.1.12	In	1	1r - missing folio? 6v			
Salus autem	83v	2.1.12	In	1		297r		
Salvator [mundi]	81v	2.1.7	An	1	243v			4689
Salvatorem exspectamus-Rv. Sobrie-Gloria patri	85v	2.3.2	R	3	3r			7562
Salve regina	69v	1.3.20	An	1			lat. 15182 - 313r	204367
Salve sancta parens	84r	2.2.1	In	2		322v		
Salvum fac [populum]-Rv. Ad te domine	93v	2.7.4	R	7		59r		
Sancte Nichole [Alleluia]	83r	2.1.12	Av	1		282r		
Sanctificavit	80v	2.1.1	An	1	287v			4748
Sancti-Gloria patri [Resp. Isti sunt]	95r	2.8.4	Rv	8	274r			7026

						lat. source	
Sapientia clamitat	94r	2.8.1	An	8	293r/296v		4811
Sapientiam sanctorum	83r	2.1.12	In	1	297r		
Scio cui	83r	2.1.12	In	1	220r		
Secundum autem simile est huic	83v	2.2.0	An	2	Model Antiphon		
Senex puerum portabat	70r	1.3.23	An	2	69r		4864
Sepe expugnaverunt me	75v/96v	1.4.19/2.8.4	T	8	97r		
Septem sunt spiritus ante thronum dei	92r	2.7.0	An	7	Model Antiphon		
Sermone blando angelus	91r	2.6.0	H	6		lat. 15181 - 311r	8271e
Serve nequam	85r	2.3.2	An	3	327r		4873
Servite domino	85r	2.3.1	An	3		lat. 12044 - 32v	4875
Sexta hora sedit super puteum	90v	2.6.0	An	6	Model Antiphon		7657
Sicut cedrus	69r	1.3.20	R	4	206/7 - missing f?	lat. 15182 - 306v	7657
Sicut cervus	75v/96r	1.4.19/2.8.4	T	8	138v		
Sint lumbi vestri	82r	2.1.8	An	1	240v/283v		4968
Syon renovaberis/Syon noli	68r/87v	1.3.12/2.4.5	An	4 tr	8v/4v		4970/4969
Sit nomen domini	92v	2.7.3	An	7		lat. 15181 - 80r	4971
Sobrie-Gloria patri [Resp. Salvatorem exspectamus]	85v	2.3.2	Rv	3	3r		7562
Specie tua	92v	2.7.3	An	7	66r/206v/210v/284r	4987	
Speciosus forma	82r	2.1.9	An	1	43r		4989
Spiritus domini	96r	2.8.4	In	8	168r		
Spiritus sanctus [patri]	67r	1.3.4	R	1	162v		7692
Stella ista	92v	2.7.2	An	7	49v		5022
Stetit angelus	83r	2.1.12	O	1	269r		
Super salutem et omnem-Rv. Valde eam	85v	2.3.2	R	3	294r/211r	lat. 15182 - 309v	7727/7726
Surrexit Christus [qui] [Alleluia]	84v	2.2.1	Av	2	157r		
Surrexit dominus [de sepulcro]	94v	2.8.1	An	8	143v/140v/154r		5079

Incipit	Harley 281	Paragraphs	Type	Tone	BnF lat. 17296	BnF lat. 1107	Other MSS	CAO/Cantus
Surrexit dominus vere-Ps. Venite exultemus domino iubilem	91r	2.6.0	Inv	6	138r		lat. 15181 - 299v	1166
Tanquam sponsus	94r	2.8.1	An	8	19v			5101
Tantam gratiam	80v	2.1.1	An	1	79v			5105
Te deum laudamus	76r	1.4.21	H	4	168v		Poissy - 396r	909010
Te deum [patrem]	86v	2.4.1	An	4	168v			5117
Tenebre facte sunt	69r	1.3.20	R	8	132v			7760
Tertia dies est que [quod] hec facta sunt	84v	2.3.0	An	3	Model Antiphon			
Te unum	83v	2.2.0	An	2 tr	165r - tr		lat. 15182 - 90v	5126
Tibi Christe splendor patris	84r	2.2.1	H	2			lat. 15182 - 375r	8403
Timebunt gentes-Rv. Quoniam edificavit	91v	2.6.0	R	5/6		33r		
Timete dominum-Rv. Inquirentes	83r	2.1.12	R	1		299r		
Tolle [quod]	94v	2.8.3	An	8	89r			5157
Tuam crucem [adoremus domine et sanctam]	87r/88v	2.4.3/2.4.6*	An	4	213v			5226
Tu Bethleem	85r	2.3.1	An	3	16v			5195
Tu es pastor ovium-Ps. Venite exultemus domino	82v	2.1.11	Inv	1	180v			5207
Tui sunt celi	89r	2.4.6	O	4		20v		
Tunc Valerianus [perrexit]	94v	2.8.1	An	8	253v			5253
Una hora	68v	1.3.17	R	7 tr	128v - no tr		lat. 15181 - 282v	7807
Universi qui te exspectant	67r	1.3.4	R	1		1r		
Unum opus feci	85r	2.3.1	An	3	115r			5275
Unus est enim	81v	2.1.7	An	1	105r			5278
Ut queant laxis resonare fibris	84r	2.2.1	H	2	101v		lat. 15182 - 206v	8406
Vade [Valde] iam	87v	2.4.4	An	4 tr				5301
Valde eam [Resp. Super salutem et omnem]	85v	2.3.2	Rv	3			lat. 15182 - 309v	7726
Valde honorandus est	80v	2.1.1	An	1	32r			5310

Chant							
Veniet dominus	81r	2.1.3	An	1	10v/84r		5337
Venite adoremus dominum-Ps. Venite exultemus domino	91r	2.6.0	Inv	6	38v/201v		1173
Venite adoremus [regem regum]-Ps. Venite exultemus	88r	2.4.6	Inv	4	206v	lat. 12044 - 175r	1177
Venite ascendamus [Resp. Docebit nos]	83v	2.2.0	Rv	2	6r		6481
Venite exultemus domino [Inv. Ave Maria]	93r	2.7.4	Ps	7		lat. 15181 - 467v	1041
Venite exultemus domino [Inv. Christus natus est]	88r	2.4.6	Ps	4	19v		1055
Venite exultemus [domino] [Inv. Deum verum unum]	88r	2.4.6	Ps	4		lat. 15182 - 90v	1061
Venite exultemus domino [Inv. Dominum qui fecit nos]	90r	2.5.0	Ps	5	106r/93r	lat. 15181 - 240v	1066
Venite exultemus domino [Inv. Ecce venit rex]	88r	2.4.6	Ps	4		lat. 15181 - 106v	1074
Venite exultemus domino [Inv. Regem cui omnia vivunt]	91r	2.6.0	Ps	6	65v	nal. 1535 - 129r	1131
Venite exultemus domino [Inv. Regem cui omnia vivunt]	95v	2.8.4	Ps	8		Not found	1131?
Venite exultemus domino [Inv. Regem precursoris dominum]	85v	2.3.2	Ps	3		lat. 15181 - 547r	1140
Venite exultemus domino [Inv. Regem sempiternum]	84r	2.2.0	Ps	2		lat. 15181 - 546v/15182 - 286r	1148
Venite exultemus domino iubilemus deo [Inv. Surrexit dominu]	91r	2.6.0	Ps	6		lat. 15181 - 299v	1166
Venite exultemus domino [Inv. Tu es pastor ovium]	82v	2.1.11	Ps	1	65v/116r/142r		1167
Venite exultemus domino [Inv. Venite adoremus dominum]	91r	2.6.0	Ps	6	38v/201v		1173

Incipit	Harley 281	Paragraphs	Type	Tone	BnF lat. 17296	BnF lat. 1107	Other MSS	CAO/Cantus
Venite exultemus [domino] [Inv. Venite adoremus [regem re	88r	2.4.6	Ps	4			lat. 12044 - 175r	1177
Venite exultemus domino - Ps. Iubilemus deo salutari nostro	88r	2.4.6	Inv	4			lat. 15181 - 188v	1179
Verbum bonum et suave	96r	2.8.4	S	8		367r		
Verbum supernum prodiens	95v	2.8.4	H	1/2/8 tr			lat. 771 - 241r/lat. 8882 - 151v	
Veritas de terra	94v	2.8.2	An	8	20r/43v/45r			5368
Veritas mea	84v	2.2.1	O	2		309v		
Veterem [hominem]	75r/92v	1.4.17/2.7.1	An	7	50r			5373
Videntibus [illis]	94v	2.8.1	An	8	159r			5392
Viri Galilei	92v	2.7.1	An	7	159r			5458
Viri Galilei	93r	2.7.4	In	7		162r		
Vitam [Resp. Domine prevenisti]	88v	2.4.6	Rv	4		309r		6505
Volo pater	81r	2.1.2	An	1	279r			5491
Vos qui reliquistis	81v	2.1.7	An	1	193v			5501
Vultum tuum	84r	2.2.1	In	2		316r		
Zima vetus expurgetur	93v	2.7.4	S	7		351r		

Works Cited

Chant Manuscript Sources

Arras, Bibliothèque mununicipale MS 893 [Saint-Vaast Breviary]
London, Victoria and Albert Museum, MS 1346–1891
London, British Library, Harley 281 [Saint-Denis]
Melbourne, State Library of Victoria, MS 096.1 [Poissy Antiphonal]
Paris, BnF lat. 830 [Paris Missal]
Paris, BnF lat. 1028 [Sens Breviary]
Paris, BnF lat. 1090 [Marseille Antiphonal]
Paris, BnF lat. 1107 [Saint-Denis Missal]
Paris, BnF lat. 8882 [Auxerre Antiphonal]
Paris, BnF lat. 12044 [Saint-Maur de Fosse Antiphonal]
Paris, BnF lat. 15181 [Paris, Notre Dame winter Breviary]
Paris, BnF lat. 15182 [Paris, Notre Dame summer Breviary]
Paris, BnF lat. 17307 [Compiègne Sacramentary]
Paris, BnF lat. 17329 [Compiègne Gradual]
Paris, BnF lat. 17296 [Saint-Denis Antiphonal]
Paris, BnF n. a. lat. 1235 [Nevers Gradual]
Paris, BnF n. a. lat. 1535 [Sens Antiphonal]

Primary Sources

Albertus Magnus [Albert the Great]. *Commentarius in Aristotelis libros I-VIII Politicorum.* In *Opera Omnia.* Edited by E. Borgnet. vol. 8. Paris: Vives, 1891.

Anonymous. *Compendium musicae mensurabilis artis antiquae (MS Faenza, Biblioteca Communale 117).* Edited by F. Alberto Gallo. CSM 15. Rome: American Institute of Musicology, 1971. pp. 66–72. [Cited throughout as Anonymous.]

Anonymous. *Tonale sancti Bernardi.* In Christian Meyer, "Le tonaire cistercien et sa tradition," *Revue de Musicologie,* 89 (2003), 57–92. (The tonary runs between pp. 77 and 92).

Anonymous 3. *De cantu mensurabili.* In *Scriptorum de musica medii aevi nova series a Gerbertina altera.* Edited by Edmond de Coussemaker. Paris: Durand, 1864–76; Hildesheim: Olms, 1963. 1:319–27.

Anonymous of St. Emmeram. *De musica mensurata: The Anonymous of St. Emmeram.* Edited by Jeremy Yudkin. Bloomington: Indiana University Press, 1990.

Aribo Scholasticus. *De musica*. Edited by Joseph Smits van Waesberghe. CSM 2. Rome: American Institute of Musicology, 1951.

Aristotelis [Aristotle]. *De anima*. Translated by James of Venice. Edited by Jos Decorte and Jozef Brams. AL 12.1. Turnhout: Brepols, 2003.

———. *Aristotelis Ethica Nicomachea*. Translated by Robert Grosseteste. AL 26.1–3. Edited by R. A. Gauthier. Turnhout: Brepols, 1973. [Cited throughout as Aristotle, *Ethics*.]

———. *Politica*. Translated by William of Moerbeke. Edited by Franz Susemihl. 3rd edn. AL 29.2. Leipzig: Teubner, 1872. [Cited throughout as Aristotle, Politics.]

———. *Physica*. Translated by James of Venice. Edited by Fernand Bossier and Jozef Brams. AL 7.1. Leiden: Brill, 1990. [Cited throughout as Aristotle, *Physics*.]

Augustinus [Augustine]. *De Trinitate libri XV*. Edited by W. J. Mountain and F. Glorie. CCSL 50–50A. Turnhout: Brepols, 1968.

———. *Confessionum libri XIII*. Edited by L. Verheijen. CCSL 27. Turnhout: Brepols, 1981. [Cited throughout as Augustine, *Confessions*.]

Averroës. *Commentarium magnum in Aristotelis De anima libros*. Edited by F. Stuart Crawford. Cambridge, MA: Mediaeval Academy of America, 1953.

Bartholomaeus Anglicanus [Bartholomew of England]. *De proprietatibus rerum*. Edited by Baudouin van den Abeele. Turnhout: Brepols, 2007.

Boethius. *De institutione musica*. In *Anicii Manlii Torquati Severini Boetii De institutione arithmetica libri duo. De institutione musica libri quinque. Accedit geometria quae fertur Boetii*. Edited by Gottfried Friedlein. Leipzig: Teubner, 1867.

Dionysius (Areopagita). *Epistula ad Polycarpum*. Edited by Jacques-Paul Migne. In *Patrologia Graeca* 5, cols. 1078–1084. Paris: Garnier, 1894.

———. *De divinis nominibus*. Edited by Jacques-Paul Migne. In *Patrologia Graeca* 3, cols. 585–996. Paris: Garnier, 1894.

Elias Salomo. *Scientia artis musicae*. In *Scriptores ecclesiastici de musica sacra potissimum*. Edited by Martin Gerbert, 3:16–64. St. Blaise: Typis San-Blasianis, 1784; reprint Hildesheim: Olms, 1963.

Eustratius. *Commentary on the Nichomachean Ethics*. In *The Greek Commentaries on the Nicomachean Ethics in the Latin Translation of Robert Grosseteste, Bishop of Lincoln (1253)*. Corpus Latinum commentariorum. In Aristotelem Graecorum. pp. 1–193. Leiden: Brill, 1973.

Franco of Cologne. *Ars cantus mensurabilis*. Edited by Gilbert Reaney and André Gilles. CSM 14. Dallas: American Institute of Musicology, 1974.

Johannes de Grocheio. *Ars musice*. Edited by Constant J. Mews, John N. Crossley, Catherine Jeffreys, Leigh McKinnon and Carol J. Williams. Kalamazoo: Medieval Institute Publications, Western Michigan University, 2011.

Guido Augensis. *Regulae*. In *La réforme cistercienne du plain-chant: étude d'un traité théorique*. Edited by Claire Maître. pp. 108–233. Brecht: Cîteaux, Commentarii Cisterienses, 1995.

Guido of Arezzo. *Micrologus*. Edited by Joseph Smits van Waesberghe. CSM 4. Rome: American Institute of Musicology, 1955.

———. *Regulae Rhythmicae*. In *Guido d'Arezzo's Regule rithmice, Prologus in antiphonarium, and Epistola ad michahelem: a critical text and translation with an introduction, annotations, indices, and new manuscript inventories.* Edited by Dolores Pesce. Ottawa: Institute of Mediaeval Music, 1999.

Guido of Saint-Denis. *Tractatus de tonis.* Edited by Sieglinde van der Klundert. Bubenreuth: Hurricane Publishers, 1998.

Hincmar of Reims. *De praedestinatione.* Edited by Jacques-Paul Migne. In *Patrologia Latina* 125, cols. 65–474. Paris: apud Editorem, 1852.

Honorius of Autun. *Speculum ecclesiae.* Edited by Jacques-Paul Migne. In *Patrologia Latina* 172, cols. 813–1108. Paris: apud Editorem, 1854.

Horace. *Ars poetica.* Edited by D. R. Shackleton Bailey. 3rd ed. pp. 310–332. Leipzig: Teubner, 1995.

Ignatius. *Epistola ad Romanos.* Edited by Jacques-Paul Migne. In *Patrologia Graeca* 5, cols. 686–696. Paris: Garnier, 1894.

Isidore [of Seville]. *Etymologiae.* Edited by W. M. Lindsay. Oxford: Oxford University Press, 1911.

Jacobus Leodiensis (Jacques de Liège, Jacobus de Ispania). *Speculum musicae.* Edited by Roger Bragard. CSM 3 [Rome:] American Institute of Musicology, 1973.

Jerome [Hieronimus]. *Commentariorum in Epistolam Beati Pauli ad Galatas.* Edited by Jacques-Paul Migne. In *Patrologia Latina* 26, cols. 307–438D. Paris: apud Editorem, 1855–66.

———. *Commentariorum in Esaiam [Isaiam] prophetam.* Edited by M. Adriaen. CCSL 73–73A Turnhout: Brepols, 1963.

Jerome of Moravia. *Tractatus de musica.* Edited by Christian Meyer and Guy Lobrichon. CCCM 250. Turnhout: Brepols, 2012.

Johannes de Muris. *Notitia artis musicae.* Edited by Ulrich Michels. CSM 17 [Rome]: American Institute of Musicology, 1972.

John [Johannes] Beleth. *Summa de ecclesiasticis officiis.* Edited by H. Douteil. CCCM 44–44. Turnhout: Brepols, 1976.

John Cotton. *De musica cum tonario.* Edited by Joseph Smits van Waesberghe. CSM 1 [Rome:] American Institute of Musicology, 1950.

John of Garland. *De mensurabili musica.* Edited by Erich Reimer. Wiesbaden: Franz Steiner, 1972.

———. *Introductio musice.* In *Scriptorum de musica medii aevi nova series a Gerbertina altera.* Edited by Edmond de Coussemaker, Paris: Durand, 1864–76, 1:157–75.

———. *Musica plana.* Edited by Christian Meyer. Baden-Baden: V. Koerner, 1998.

Saint John Damascene. *De fide orthodoxa.* Edited by Eligius M. Buytaert. St. Bonaventure, NY: Franciscan Institute, 1955.

John the Deacon. *Vita S. Gregorii papae.* Edited by Jacques-Paul Migne. In *Patrologia Latina* 75, cols. 61–242. Paris: apud Editorem, 1849.

John Wylde. *Musica manualis cum tonale.* Edited by Cecily Sweeney. CSM 28 [Rome]: American Institute of Musicology, 1982.

Lambert [Pseudo Aristotle]. *Tractatus de musica.* Edited by Christian Meyer and translated by Karen Desmond. In *The Ars Musica Attributed to Master Lambert/Aristoteles.* Farnham: Ashgate, 2015.

Ovid. *Metamorphoses.* Edited by W. S. Anderson. Leipzig: Teubner, 1981.

Peter Comestor. *Historia scholastica.* Edited by A. Sylwan. CCCM 119. Turnhout: Brepols, 2005.

Petrus de Cruce. *Tractatus de tonis*. Edited by Denis Harbinson. CSM 29. [Rome]: American Institute of Musicology, 1976.

Petrus de Sancto Dionysio. *Tractatus de musica*. Edited by Ulrich Michels, CSM 17 [Rome]: American Institute of Musicology, 1972.

Petrus Picardus. *Ars motettorum compilata breviter*. Edited by F. Alberto Gallo, CSM 17. [Rome]: American Institute of Musicology, 1971.

Peter of Auvergne. *Quodlibet VI*. In *Quaestiones*. Edited by Frank Hentschel, "Der verjagte Dämon: Mittelalterliche Gedanken zur Wirkung der Musik aus dem Zeit um 1300, mit einer Edition der Quaestiones 16 und 17 aus Quodlibet VI des Petrus d'Auvergne." In *Miscellanea Mediaevalia: Veröffentlichungen des Thomas-Instituts der Universitäts zu Köln*. Edited by Jan A. Aersten and Andreas Speer. pp. 412–21. Berlin: Walter de Gruyter, 2000.

———. *In libros politicorum*. In Petri de Alvernia Continuatio S. Thomae in Politicam. Edited by Raimondo M. Spiazzi. Turin: Marietti, 1951.

———. *Quaestiones supra librum De caelo et mundo*. Edited by Griet Galle. Leuven (Belgium): Leuven University Press, 2003.

Priscian. *Institutiones grammaticae*. Edited by Cirilo Garcia Roman and Marco A. Gutierrez Galindo. Hildesheim: Olms, 2001.

Pseudo Odo. *Dialogus de musica*. Edited by Martin Gerbert. In *Scriptores ecclesiastici de musica sacra potissimum*, pp. 251–64. St. Blaise: Typis San-Blasianis, 1784; reprinted. Hildesheim: Olms, 1963.

Robert Kilwardby. *De ortu scientiarum*. Edited by Albert G. Judy. Auctores Britannici Medii Aevi. London: British Academy, 1976.

Servius in Vergilii Aeneidos librum tertium commentarius. Edited by Hermann Hagen and Georg Thilo. In *Servii Grammatici qui feruntur in Vergilii carmina commentarii*. Leipzig: Teubner, 1878.

Sigebert of Gembloux. *Chronica*. Edited by Ludwig Conrad Bethmann. Monumenta Germaniae Historica. Scriptores 6. pp. 300–84. Hanover: Hahn, 1844.

Stephen of Liège. *Officium sanctae Trinitatis*. Edited by Ritva Jonsson. In *Historia. Études sur la genèse des offices versifiés*. pp. 221–24 Stockholm: Almquist & Wiksell, 1968.

Thomas Aquinas. *Summa theologiae*. Edited by Leonina. In *Sancti Thomae Aquinatis Opera Omnia*, vols. 4–12. Rome: various imprints, 1888–1905.

———. *In libros politicorum Aristotelis expositio*. Edited by Raimondo M. Spiazzi. Turin-Rome: Marietti, 1951.

———. *In Aristotelis libros Metaphysicorum*. Edited by M. R. Cathala and Raimondo M. Spiazzi. Turin-Rome: Marietti, 1950.

———. *De caelo et mundo expositio*. Edited by Leonina. In *Sancti Thomae Aquinatis, Opera omnia*, vol. 3. Rome, 1886.

Vincent of Beauvais. *Speculum historiale*. In *Speculum Maius*, vol. 4. Douai, 1624; repr. Graz: Akademische Druck, 1964.

Virgil. *Aeneid*. Edited by O. Ribbeck. Leipzig: Teubner, 1895.

Walter of Châtillon. *Alexandreis*. Edited by Marvin L. Colker. In *Galteri de Castellione Alexandreis*. Padua: Antenor, 1978.

———. *Alexandreis*. Edited by David Townsend. In *The Alexandreis: a twelfth-century epic*. Peterborough, Ont.: Broadview Press, 2007.

William of Auxerre. *Summa de officiis ecclesiasticis*. Edited by Franz Fischer. In *Magistri Guillelmi Autissiodorensis Summa de officiis ecclesiasticis: Kritisch-digitale Erstausgabe*. PhD thesis. Cologne: University of Cologne, 2007.

Secondary Sources

Anzulewicz, Henryk. "Peter of Auvergne and Albert the Great as Interpreters of the *De caelo*." In *Peter of Auvergne: University Master of the 13th century*. Edited by Flueler et al. Scrinium Friburgense 26. Fribourg: De Gruyter, 2015. pp. 107–34.

Atkinson, Charles M. *The Critical Nexus: Tone-System, Mode and Notation in Early Medieval Music*. Oxford: Oxford University Press, 2009.

Baltzer Rebecca A. "Johannes de Garlandia." In *Grove Music Online* (Oxford University Press) [subscriber access required].

Bent, Margaret. "Jacobus de Ispania? – Ein Zwischenbericht." In *Nationes, Gentes und die Musik im Mittelalter*. Edited by Frank Hentschel and Maria Winkelmuller. Berlin: De Gruyter, 2014. pp. 407–22.

Bent, Margaret. *Magister Jacobus de Ispania, Author of the Speculum musicae*. Farnham: Ashgate, 2015.

Bianchi, Luca. "Peter of Auvergne and the Condemnation of 1277." In *Peter of Auvergne: University Master of the 13th Century*. Edited by Flueler et al. Scrinium Friburgense 26. Fribourg: De Gruyter, 2015. pp. 29–50.

Bianchi, Luca. *Il vescovo e i filosofi: La condanna parigina del 1277 e l'evoluzione dell'aristotelismo scolastico*. Bergamo: Lubrina, 1990.

Bruzelius, Caroline Astrid. *The 13th-Century Church at St-Denis*. New Haven: Yale University Press, 1985.

Close, Florence. "L'Office de la Trinité d'Étienne de Liège (901–920). Un témoin de l'héritage liturgique et théologique de la première réforme carolingienne à l'aube du Xe siècle." *Revue belge de philologie et d'histoire* 86 (2008): 29–51.

Crocker, Richard L. "Matins Antiphons at St. Denis." *Journal of the American Musicological Society* 39 (1986): 441–90.

Crocker, Richard L. "*Les Tonaires: Inventaire, Analyse, Comparaison* by Michel Huglo." *Journal of the American Musicological Society* 26 (1973): 490–95.

Crocker, Richard L. *Studies in Medieval Music Theory and the Early Sequence*. Variorum collected studies series. Brookfield, VT: Variorum, 1997.

Courtenay, William J. "Peter of Auvergne, Master in Arts and Theology in Paris." In *Peter of Auvergne: University Master of the 13th century*. Edited by Flueler et al. Scrinium Friburgense 26. Fribourg: De Gruyter, 2015. pp. 11–28.

Delaborde, H.–François. "Notes sur Guillaume de Nangis." *Bibliothèque de l'école des chartes* 44 (1883): 192–201.

Delisle, Léopold. *Le Cabinet des manuscrits de la Bibliothèque impériale*. 4 vols. Paris: Imprimerie impériale, 1868–1881.

Denifle, Heinrich Suso, ed. *Chartularium Universitatis Parisiensis*. 4 vols. Paris: Delalain, 1889–97 reprinted Brussels: Culture et civilisation, 1964.

Desmond, Karen. "Sicut in grammatica: Analogical Discourse in Chapter 15 of Guido's Micrologus." *The Journal of Musicology* 16 (1998): 467–93.

Félibien, Michel. *Histoire de l'abbaye royale de Saint-Denys en France.* Paris: Frédéric Lonard, 1706.

Flueler, Christoph, Lidia Lanza, and Marco Toste, eds. *Peter of Auvergne. University Master of the 13th Century.* Scrinium Friburgense 26. Fribourg: de Gruyter, 2015.

Flueler, Christoph. *Rezeption und Interpretation der Aristotelischen Politica im späten Mittelalter.* 2 vols. Amsterdam: B. R. Grüner, 1990.

Fourquin, Guy. "Les débuts du fermage. L'exemple de Saint-Denis." *Études rurales* 22–24 (1966): 7–81.

Franke, Matthew Martin. "Singing for a Patron Saint: Musical Strategies and Political Subtexts in Sequences from the Abbey of Saint-Denis." Master's Thesis (University of North Carolina at Chapel Hill, 2009).

Galle, Griet. "A Comprehensive Bibliography of Peter of Auvergne." *Bulletin de philosophie médiévale* 42 (2000): 53–79.

Gaposchkin, M. Cecilia. "Philip the Fair, the Dominicans, and the Liturgical Office for Louis IX: New Perspectives on Ludovicus Decus." *Plainsong and Medieval Music* 13 (2004): 33–61.

Gaposchkin, M. Cecilia. "The Monastic Office for Louis IX of France." *Revue Mabillon* 20 (2009): 55–86.

Gaposchkin, M. Cecilia. *The Making of Saint Louis. Kingship, Sanctity, and Crusade in the Later Middle Ages.* Ithaca: Cornell University Press, 2008.

Gauthier, R. A. "Notes sur Siger de Brabant. II. Siger en 1272–1275. Aubry de Reims et la scission des Normands." *Revue des sciences philosophiques et théologiques* 68 (1984): 3–49.

Geraud, Hércule, ed. *Chronique latine de Guillaume de Nangis de 1113 à 1300 avec les continuations de cette chronique de 1300 à 1368.* 2 vols. Paris: Renouard, 1844.

Glorieux, Palémon. *La faculté des arts et ses maîtres au XIIIe siecle.* Paris: Librairie Philosophique J. Vrin, 1971.

Glorieux, Palémon. *Répertoire des maîtres en théologie de Paris au XIIIe siècle.* 2 vols. Paris: Librairie Philosophique J. Vrin, 1933.

Hentschel, Frank. "Der verjagte Dämon. Mittelalterliche Gedanken zur Wirkung der Music aus der Zeit um 1300. Mit einer Edition der Questiones 16 und 17 aus Quodlibet VI des Petrus d'Auvergne." In *Geistesleben im 13. Jahrhundert.* Edited by Andreas Speer Jan A. Aertsen. Berlin, New York: 2000. pp. 395–421.

Hentschel, Frank. *Sinnlichkeit und Vernunft in der mittelalterlichen Musiktheorie: Strategien der Konsonanzwertung und der Gegenstand der musica sonora um 1300,* vol. 47, *Beihefte zum Archiv für Musikwissenschaft.* Stuttgart: F. Steiner, 2000.

Hesbert, Dom René-Jean. *Corpus Antiphonalium Officii.* 6 vols. Rome: Herder, 1963–79.

Hiley, David. *Western Plainchant: A Handbook.* Oxford: Clarendon Press, 1993.

Hissette, Roland. *Enquête sur les 219 articles condamnés à Paris le 7 mars 1277.* Louvain: Publications Universitaires, 1977.

Hughes, Andrew. "Modal Order and Disorder in the Rhymed Office." *Musica Disciplina* 37 (1983): 29–51.

Huglo, Michel. *Les tonaires: inventaire, analyse, comparaison.* Paris: Société française de musicologie, 1971.

Huglo, Michel. "Les chants de la Missa greca de Saint-Denis." In *Essays presented to E. Wellesz.* Edited by J. Westrup. Oxford: Oxford University Press, 1966. pp. 74–83.

Huglo, Michel. "Guy de Saint-Denis." In *Grove Music Online* (Oxford University Press) [subscriber access required].

Huglo, Michel. "Der Prolog des Odo zugeschriebenen *Dialogus de Musica*." *Archiv für Musikwissenschaft* 28 (1971): 134–46.

Huglo, Michel. "La Musica du Fr. Prêcheur Jérome de Moray." In *Max Lütolf zum 60 Geburtstag: Festschrift*. Edited by Bernhard Hangartner and Ursula Fischer. Basel: Wiese Verlag, 1994. pp. 113–6.

Jeffreys, Catherine. "The Exchange of Ideas About Music in Paris c. 1270–1304: Guy of Saint-Denis, Johannes de Grocheio, and Peter of Auvergne." In *Communities of Learning: Networks and the Shaping of Intellectual Identity in Europe, 1100–1500*. Edited by Constant J. Mews and John N. Crossley. Turnhout: Brepols, 2011. pp. 151–75.

Jeffreys, Catherine. "Some Early References to Aristotle's *Politics* in Parisian Writings about Music." In *Identity and Locality in Early European Music*. Edited by Jason Stoessel. Aldershot: Ashgate, 2009. pp. 83–106.

Karp, Theodore. "The Analysis of the *Alleluia Laetatus sum*." *Studia Musicologica Academiae Scientiarum Hungaricae* 39 (1998): 215–22.

Kelly, Thomas Forrest. *The Beneventan Chant,* Cambridge Studies in music. Cambridge: Cambridge University Press, 1989.

Lambertini, Roberto. "Peter of Auvergne, Giles of Rome and Aristotle's 'Politica.'" In *Peter of Auvergne: University Master of the 13th Century*. Edited by Fleuler et al. Scrinium Friburgense 26. Fribourg: De Gruyter, 2015. pp. 51–69.

Lanza, Lidia. "Aspetti della ricezione della 'Politica' aristotelica nel XIII secolo: Pietro d'Alvernia." *Studi Medievali* 35 (1994): 643–94.

Lebedev, Sergey N. "Zu einigen loci obscuri bei Johannes de Grocheio." In *Quellen und Studien zur Musiktheorie des Mittelalters*. Edited by Michael Bernhard. Munich: Bayerische Akademie der Wissenschaften, 1997. pp. 92–108.

Lemoine, Jean, ed. *Chronique de Richard Lescot, religieux de Saint-Denis (1328–1344) suivie de la continuation de cette chronique (1344–1364)*. Paris: Renouard, 1896).

Maître, Claire. *La réforme cistercienne du plain-chant: Etude d'un traite théorique*. Brecht, Belgium: Citeaux, Commentarii Cistercienses, 1995.

Mathiesen, Thomas J. "The Office of the New Feast of Corpus Christi in the Regimen Animarum." *The Journal of Musicology* 2 (1983): 13–44.

Mathiesen, Thomas J. "Harmonia (i)." In *Grove Music Online* (Oxford University Press) [subscriber access required].

Mews, Constant J., John N. Crossley, Catherine Jeffreys, Leigh McKinnon, and Carol Williams. "Guy of Saint-Denis and the Compilation of Texts about Music in London, British Library, Harl. MS. 281." In *Electronic British Library Journal* (2008): Article 6, pp. 1–34.

Mews, Constant J., John N. Crossley, and Carol J. Williams. "Guy of St Denis on the Tones: Thinking about Chant for Saint-Denis c. 1300." *Journal of Plainsong and Medieval Music*, 23 (2014): 151–76.

Mews, Constant J. "Gregory the Great, the Rule of Benedict and Roman liturgy: The Evolution of a Legend." *Journal of Medieval History* 37 (2011): 125–44.

Mews, Constant J. "Questioning the Music of the Spheres: Aristotle, Johannes de Grocheio, and the University of Paris 1250–1300." In *Knowledge, Discipline and Power in the Middle Ages, Essays in Honour of David Luscombe.* Edited by Joseph Canning, Edmund King and Martial Staub. Leiden: Brill, 2011. pp. 95–117.

Meyer, Christian. "Le tonaire cistercien et sa tradition." *Revue de Musicologie* 89 (2003): 57–92.

Morin, Gervais. "L'office Cistercien pour la Fête-Dieu comparé avec celui de saint Thomas d'Aquin." *Revue Bénédictine,* 27 (1910): 236–46.

Nebbiai-Dalla Guarda, Donatella. "Le collège de Paris de l'abbaye de Saint-Denis-en-France (XIIIe–XVIIIe siècle)." In *Sous la règle de Saint Benoît: Structures monastiques et sociétés en France du Moyen Age à l'époque moderne, Abbaye bénédictine Sainte Marie de Paris, 23–25 octobre 1980.* Geneva: Droz, 1982. pp. 461–88.

Nebbiai-Dalla Guarda, Donatella. *La Bibliothèque de l'abbaye de Saint-Denis en France du IXe au XVIIIe siècle.* Paris: CNRS, 1985.

Nebbiai-Dalla Guarda, Donatella. "Des rois et des moines: Livres et lecteurs à l'abbaye de Saint-Denis (XIIIe–XVe siècles)." In *Saint-Denis et la royauté. Etudes offerts à B. Guenée.* Edited by Françoise Autrand, Claude Gauvard and Jean-Marie Moeglin. Paris: Publications de la Sorbonne, 1999. pp. 355–74.

Page, Christopher. "Johannes de Grocheio on Secular Music: a Corrected Text and a New Translation." *Plainsong and Medieval Music,* 2 (1993): 17–41 (reprinted in Christopher Page, ed. *Music and Instruments of the Middle Ages: Studies on Texts and Performance.* [Aldershot: Ashgate, 1997]).

Riethmuller, Albrecht. "Probleme der spekulativen Musiktheorie in Mittelalter." In *Rezeption des antiken Fachs im Mittelalter.* Edited by Michael Bernhard. Darmstadt: Wissenschaftliche Buchgesellschaft, 1990. pp. 197–201.

Robertson, Anne Walters. *The Service-Books of the Royal Abbey of Saint-Denis: Images of Ritual and Music in the Middle Ages.* Oxford: Clarendon Press 1991.

Robertson, Anne. "The Reconstruction of the Abbey Church at Saint-Denis (1231–81): The Interplay of Music and Ceremony with Architecture and Politics." *Early Music History,* 5 (1985): 187–238.

Rouse, Richard H. "Manuscripts Belonging to Richard de Fournival." *Revue d'histoire des textes* 3 (1973): 253–69.

Smits van Waesberghe, Joseph, Pieter Fischer, Michel Huglo, and Christian Meyer. *The Theory of Music from the Carolingian era up to 1400: Descriptive Catalogue of Manuscripts,* 6 vols. *Répertoire international des sources musicales.* B. Munich-Duisberg: G. Henle, 1961.

Spiegel, Gabrielle M. *The Chronicle Tradition of Saint-Denis: A Survey.* Brooklyn: Classical Folia Editions, 1978.

Stinson, John. "The Poissy Antiphonal: A Major Source of Late Medieval Chant." *La Trobe Library Journal,* 51–52 (1993): 50–59.

Sweeney, C. "The Regulae organi Guidonis abbatis and the 12th Century Organum/Discantus treatises." *Musica Disciplina,* 43 (1989): 7–31.

Tempier, Étienne and Kurt Flasch. *Aufklärung im Mittelalter? Die Verurteilung von 1277 das Dokument des Bischofs von Paris, Excerpta classica.* Mainz: Dieterich Verlagsbuchhandlung, 1989.

Théry, P. G. "Documents concernant Jean Sarrasin." *Archives d'histoire doctrinale et littéraire du moyen âge,* 18 (1950): 45–87.

Thijssen, J. M. M. H. *Censure and Heresy at the University of Paris, 1200–1400.* Philadelphia: University of Pennsylvania Press, 1998.

Udovich, JoAnn. "Modality, Office Antiphons, and Psalmody: The Musical Authority of the Twelfth-Century Antiphonal from St.-Denis." (PhD thesis, University of North Carolina at Chapel Hill, 1985).

Waite, William G. "Johannes de Garlandia, Poet and Musician." *Speculum,* 35 (1960): 179–95.

Walters, Barbara R., Vincent Corrigan, and Peter T. Ricketts. *The Feast of Corpus Christi.* University Park, PA: Pennsylvania State University Press, 2006.

Weiss, Roberto. "Lo studio del greco all'abbazia di San Dionigi durante el medio evo." *Rivista di storia della chiesa in Italia* 6 (1952): 426–38.

Whitcomb, Pamela. "Teachers, Booksellers and Taxes: Reinvestigating the Life and Activities of Johannes de Garlandia." *Plainsong and Medieval Music,* 8 (1999): 1–13.

Wippel, John F. "The Condemnations of 1270 and 1277 at Paris." *Journal of Medieval and Renaissance Studies* 7 (1977): 169–201.

Lexicon

Entries are under the nominative or infinitive. Variations, e.g. derived adjectives or adverbs, are included under the noun or verb. Entries under a given item, e.g. *cantus,* are listed in English alphabetical order.

Specific antiphons may be found in the Chant Sources and Concordances Table.

accensio: inflaming [of the blood] [1.4.2]; incited [by the sound of flutes] [1.4.7]; aroused [by the call of trumpets] [1.4.7]

actio: action [1.4.12]

acutus: high [of sound, musical note] [1.1.2, 1.1.3, 1.1.6, 1.2.2, 1.2.3, 1.2.4, 1.2.9, 1.3.3, 1.3.5, 1.3.7, 1.3.8, 1.3.9, 1.3.10, 1.3.11, 1.3.12, 1.3.13, 1.3.14, 1.3.15, 1.3.16, 1.3.17, 1.3.18, 1.3.19, 1.3..22, 1.4.20]; higher [1.2.8];

affectio: disposition [of the spirits] [1.4.7, 1.4.8]

affinal: affinals [ending notes] [1.2.3, 1.3.5, 1.3.6, 1.3.8, 1.3.10, 1.3.12, 1.3.15, 1.3.17, 1.3.19]

alatus: winged [1.4.17]

amor: love [1.4.13, 1.4.14, 1.4.18, 2.0.7]

anima: soul [1.1.5, 1.4.4, 1.4.6, 1.4.12, 1.4.15, 1.4.6, 1.4.8, 1.4.15]; see also *passio*

animal: animal [1.4.2]

animus: spirit [1.1.16, 1.4.1, 1.4.6, 1.4.7, 1.4.8, 1.4.14]; [lascivious] disposition [1.4.10]; [laxity of] spirit [1.4.14]

antiphona: antiphon [1.1.1, 1.2.8, 1.4.22.

2.0.1–2.0.9, 2.0.19–2.1.11, 2.2.0, 2.3.0–2.4.1, 2.4.3–2.5.0, 2.6.0, 2.7.0–2.8.4]

apothome: apothome or remnant [1.1.8]

aptitudo: aptitude [1.4.2, 2.0.5]

arismetica: arithmetic [1.1.4, 1.4.6]

armatus: armed [1.4.17]

armonia: harmony, melodic quality [1.1.3, 1.1.15, 1.1.18, 1.1.20, 1.3.20, 1.4.1, 1.4.3, 1.4.4, 1.4.5, 1.4.20, 1.4.22, 2.6.0]; [first] harmony [= diapason] [1.1.15]; [triple] harmony [1.1.15]; see also *sonus, proportio*

ars: art [of iron- and metal-work] [1.1.17]; art [of the tones and music] [1.1.17, 1.1.19, 1.2.1, 1.2.4, 1.2.8, 1.3.4, 1.4.6, 1.4.7, 2.0.17, 2.1.11]; [human] art [1.1.5]; [other] arts [1.2.6]

arsis: arsis [as opposed to thesis] [1.1.4]

asperitas: hardness [in second and eighth tones] [1.4.19]

astronomia: astronomy [1.4.6]

audacia: boldness [1.4.2, 1.4.16, 1.4.17]

autenticus: authentic [tone] [1.2.10, 1.3.1, 1.3.2, 1.3.4, 1.3.22, 1.3.23, 2.0.5]; authentic [chant] [2.0.8] *autentus*: authentic [protus, deuterus, tritus, tetradus] [1.2.9, 1.4.10]

avarius: avaricious [1.4.11]

b molle: soft b [1.1.9, 1.3.8, 1.3.10, 1.3.12, 1.4.18, 2.0.18, 2.4.3, 2.8.4]

b rotundum: round b [1.1.9, 1.3.4a, 1.3.5, 1.3.8, 1.3.10, 1.3.12, 1.4.18, 2.0.18, 2.8.4]

bestia: beast [1.2.5, 1.4.11]

calidas: warmth [1.4.16]; see also animal

cantandum: singing [1.1.1, 1.1.17, 1.2.6, 1.2.9, 1.4.6, 1.4.7, 1.4.0, 1.4.13, 1.4.14, 1.4.22, 1.3.4]

cantare: sing [1.1.9, 1.1.17, 1.2.3, 1.3.4a, 2.0.18]; see also decantare

cantilena: lyric song [1.1.1, 1.1.16, 1.2.5, 1.2.6, 1.2.9, 1.4.6, 1.4.7, 1.4.14]

cantio: singing [1.4.22, 2.0.5]

cantor: cantor [1.3.4, 1.4.22]

cantus: chant, song [1.1.1, 1.1.9, 1.2.1, 1.2.3, 1.2.4, 1.3.3, 1.3.4, 1.3.15, 1.3.21, 1.3.22, 1.3.23, 1.4.9, 1.4.10, 1.4.13, 1.4.14, 1.4.19, 1.4.21, 1.4.22, 2.0.3, 2.0.5]; sound [of flutes] [1.4.7]; [irregular] chant [1.3.3, 1.3.7, 1.3.9, 1.3.151.3.18, 1.3.19, 1.3.20, 1.3.21]; *cantus coronatus* [2.0.4]; *cantus ecclesiatici*: ecclesiatical chants [1.1.1, 1.2.4, 1.3.21, 1.4.9, 1.4.19, 1.4.22]; *cantus gregoriani*: Gregorian chant [1.3.4, 1.3.20, 1.4.14]; *cantus mensuratus*: measured song [1.1.1, 1.1.9]; *cantus publici et civiles*: public and civic chants [1.1.1, 1.4.14]; see also *irregulariter, licencialiter*

causa: cause [1.4.12]; cause [of rapture] [1.4.15]; [particular and related] cause [1.4.12]; [universal] cause [1.4.12]

celestia: celestial [poles] [1.2.6]; heavenly bodies [1.4.12]; heavenly things [1.4.8]

cervix: [stiff] neck [1.4.11]

cignus: swan [1.4.18]

cithara: cithara [1.1.17, 1.4.7]

complexio: [diverse] complexions [1.4.12]; [natural] constitution [1.4.12]

concordantia: concord [1.1.1, 1.1.5, 1.1.6, 1.1.7, 1.1.9, 1.1.10, 1.1.11, 1.1.12, 1.1.3, 1.1.14, 1.1.15, 1.1.17, 1.1.18]; [difference between consonance and] concord [1.1.4] [1.1.14]; [seven] concords [1.1.5]; see also *sonos*

consona: consonance [1.4.13]

consonantia: consonance [1.1.1, 1.1.2, 1.1.3, 1.1.4, 1.1.5, 1.1.15]; [difference between] consonance [and concord] [1.1.4]; [hammers rendered the] consonance [1.1.18]; [mother of] consonances [1.1.14]; [musical] consonances [1.1.1, 1.4.1, 1.4.3, 1.4.15]; [perfect] consonances [1.1.14]; [seven] consonances [1.1.5]; [three aforesaid] consonances [1.1.15]

conversio: [Latin for trope] [1.1.1]

cor: [hard] heart [1.4.11]

corda: [vibrating] string [1.1.2]; string [on monochord] [1.1.19]

corona: crown [1.4.20]

corruptio: corruption [by custom] [1.1.5, 2.0.19]; corruption [of the melody] [1.1.4]; corrupts [its opposite passion] [1.4.4]

Cretenses: [lying] Cretans [1.4.11]

crines: hair [streaming in the wind] [1.4.16, 1.4.22]

cupiditas: desire, lust [1.4.7]

Dalmata: [fierce] Dalmatian [1.4.11]

deuterus: see *tonus, plaga*

dies: days [in a week] [1.1.5, 2.8.4]

differentia: difference [between audible and visible things] [1.4.3]; difference [between authentic and plagals] [1.3.2]; difference [between consonance and concord] [1.1.4]; *differentia* [end of intonations] [2.0.17, 2.0.18]; examples of *differentiae* [2.1.1–2.8.4]; [plurality makes the] difference [1.1.3]; [variety of] pitches [1.1.17]

dilectio: delight [1.4.13]

disciplina: discipline [of music] [1.2.6]; [mathematical] disciplines [1.4.6]

discipulus: disciple [1.2.10, 2.0.7]

dispositio: disposition [of men] [1.4.10]; disposition [of qualities] [1.4.9]; disposition [of the hearers] [1.4.9]; [bodily] dispositions [1.4.12]; [varieties of] disposition [1.4.10]

ditonus cum dyapente: see *tonus*

ditonus: see *tonus*

diversitas: diversity [of appearances of the heavens] [1.4.12, 1.4.13], diversity [of men] [1.4.13]; diversity [of generations] [1.1.5]; diversity [of tropes] [1.4.10]; diversity [of minds] [1.4.10]; diversity [of musical sounds] [1.1.5]; diversity [of regions and customs of men] [1.4.14, 2.0.17]

dona: gifts [of the Spirit] [1.1.5, 2.8.4]

dorius: see *modus*

dulcedo: sweetness [from the spirit] [1.1.16]; sweetness [of song] [1.1.16, 2.0.8]

dupla proportio (4:2, 12:6, 2:1): see *proportio*

dyapason: see *tonus*

dyapente: see *tonus*

dyatessaron: see *tonus*

dyesis: semitone [1.1.9]; see also *tonus*

ekmeles: discordant sound [1.1.4]

emmeles: "suited to a tune or melody" [1.1.4]

equus: horse [1.4.16]

excitare: excite [passions] [1.4.1, 1.4.5, 1.4.6, 1.4.9, 1.4.15]; excite [spirits] [1.4.16]

exempla: examples, see the appropriate item: *sequentia, etc.*

feritas: wildness [of the Teutons] [1.4.14]; ferocity [of Saul] [1.4.7]

feste: [special] feasts [1.4.21, 2.0.6]

fistula: pipe [1.2.7, 1.4.16]

fragilitas: [human] frailty [1.1.15]

Frigas: Phrygian [mode] [1.4.7, 1.4.15, 1.4.17]; [name of] Phrygians [1.4.13]; [timid] Phrygians [1.4.11]; see also *modus*

frigus: cold [prime quality] [1.4.1, 1.4.2]; frigid [bodies] [1.4.12]

gama: gamut [1.1.9, 1.2.1, 1.2.2, 1.2.3]

gamaut: Gamma-ut [1.3.7];

garrulitas: babbling [of the seventh tone] [1.4.10]

geometria: geometry [1.4.6]

gramatica: grammar [1.1.7, 1.3.20]

Greci: Greeks [1.2.6, 1.2.7]

habitus: disposition [1.4.4, 1.4.12]

hoqueti: hockets [1.1.1]

humidum: cold [prime quality] [1.4.1, 1.4.2]

inflexio: inflexions [in lyric songs] [1.4.14]

insania: madness [1.4.7]

intonandum: intoning [1.1.1, 2.0.1, 2.0.2, 2.0.9, 2.0.10, 2.0.13, 2.0.14, 2.0.16–2.0.21, 2.1.11, 2.2.0, 2.2.1, 2.3.0, 2.3.2, 2.4.0, 2.4.6, 2.5.0, 2.6.0, 2.7.0, 2.7.4, 2.8.0, 2.8.3, 2.8.4]

invidius: jealous [people] [1.4.2]

iocunde: happy [1.4.22]

ira: anger [1.4.2, 1.4.4, 1.4.7, 1.4.16, 1.4.17]

irregularis: irregular [1.3.15, 1.3.20, 2.6.0, 2.8.4]; see also *cantus*

iuvenes: children [1.1.16]; [drunken] youth [1.4.7]

lancea: lance [1.4.18]

lascivia: lascivious [modes of singing [1.4.6, 1.4.10]; playfulness [1.1.19], sensuousness [1.4.18]

letitias: happiness [1.4.8]; joy [1.2.7]; joyful [spirits] [1.4.8]; [chants of] happiness [1.4.19]

licencialiter: by license [1.3.3, 1.3.4, 1.3.7, 1.3.9, 1.3.11, 1.3.13, 1.3.14, 1.3.15, 1.3.16, 1.3.18]

Lidius: Lydian [mode] [1.2.11, 1.4.13]

lima: lima [Greek word] [1.1.8]

limites: limits [1.3.3, 1.3.20]

luctus: grief [1.4.19]

malleus: hammer [1.1.17, 1.1.18]

mathematica: mathematical disciplines [1.4.5]

medium: half [1.1.7, 1.1.8, 1.1.13]; intermediate [1.1.15, 1.1.18, 1.4.3, 1.4.5, 1.4.20, 1.4.21]; middle [of chant] [1.1.1, 2.0.10, 2.0.13, 2.0.14, 2.0.16, 2.0.18, 2.4.6, 2.8.4]

melodia: melody [1.1.4, 1.1.9, 1.1.15, 1.2.5, 1.2.6, 1.3.4, 1.3.20, 1.4.1, 1.4.3, 1.4.8, 1.4.9, 1.4.15, 1.4.16, 1.4.17, 1.4.18, 1.4.20, 1.4.21]

mens: mind [1.2.8, 1.3.20, 1.4.1, 1.4.6, 1.4.7, 1.4.10, 1.4.13, 1.4.14, 1.4.15, 1.4.18, 1.4.20, 2.0.6]; spirit [1.4.10]

mensura: measure [1.1.3, 1.1.5, 1.1.9]

missa: mass [1.4.21, 2.0.20, 2.1.11, 2.3.2, 2.4.6, 2.5.0, 2.6.0, 2.7.3, 2.8.4]; [for the dead] [1.4.19]

modulatio: modulation [1.4.14, 2.0.3–2.0.5]

modus cantandi: see *cantare* and *intonandum*

modus: mode [types of mode]: Dorian (see also [1.4.20]), Hypodorian, Frigian [Phrygian], Hypofrigian [Hypophrygian], Lydian, Hypolidian, Mixolidian, Hypermixolydian [1.2.11]; see also *tonus*

mollitio: softness [1.4.13, 1.4.18, 2.0.19]

monocordium: monochord [1.1.19]

moralitas: morality [1.4.6]

mores: behavior [1.4.1, 1.4.5, 1.4.6, 1.4.11, 1.4.12, 1.4.14, 1.4.20]

mortalitas: [human] mortality [1.4.21]

motetus: motet [1.1.1, 1.1.9]

motus: motion [1.1.2, 1.1.4, 1.2.6, 1.4.1, 1.4.8, 1.4.10, 1.4.12, 1.4.15, 1.4.16]

mulier: woman [1.4.7]

mulus: mule [1.4.21]

musae: Muses [1.1.17]

musica falsa: [1.1.9]

musica recta: [1.1.9]

musicus: music theorist, musician [1.1.9, 1.2.0, 1.2.1, 1.2.4, 1.2.8, 1.2.9, 1.2.10, 1.3.3, 1.3.4, 1.3.4a, 1.3.7, 1.3.9, 1.3.14, 1.3.20, 1.4.7, 1.4.22, 2.0.9]

neuma: [1.1.9, 1.4.22, 2.0.2–2.0.9, 2.1.0, 2.2.0, 2.3.0, 2.4.0, 2.5.0, 2.6.0, 2.7.0, 2.8.0]

noannoeane: [1.2.5]

noeagis: [1.2.5]

noioeane: [1.2.5]

notare, nota, notula: notate, note, little note [1.1.9, 1.2.3, 1.3.4a, 1.3.5, 1.3.8, 1.3.10, 1.3.12, 2.0.8, 2.0.9, 2.0.10, 2.1.8, 2.1.11, 2.3.1, 2.3.2, 2.4.3–2.4.6, 2.8.4]

nudus: naked [1.4.18]; drawn [sword] [1.4.19]

numerus: number [1.1.4, 1.1.6, 1.1.8, 1.1.10, 1.1.11, 1.1.12, 1.1.13, 1.1.14, 1.1.15, 1.2.1, 1.2.4, 1.2.9, 1.2.12, 2.0.17, 2.8.4]

olor: swan [1.4.18]

operatio: operation [1.0.2, 1.1.5, 1.4.2, 1.4.4, 2.0.1, 2.0.9]

organum: organ [bodily, of hearing] [1.4.2, 1.4.3, 1.4.6, 2.0.8]

passio: passions [of the soul] [1.4.1, 1.4.2, 1.4.3, 1.4.4, 1.4.5, 1.4.6, 1.4.7, 1.4.9, 1.4.10, 1.4.15, 1.4.16]

pavo: peacock [1.4.19]

percussio: beating [of air, string] [1.1.2, 1.4.16]; reverberation, beating [in voices] [1.4.15, 1.4.16]

plaga: plagal [1.2.7, 1.2.9, 1.2.10, 1.3.1, 1.3.2, 1.3.22, 1.3.23, 1.4.10]

planetum: planet [1.1.5, 1.2.6, 1.4.12]

plaustrum: wagon [1.4.14]

pluralitas: plurality [1.1.3, 1.1.5]

Postcommunion: postcommunion [2.0.20]; for specific postcommunions see Chant Sources and Concordances Table

potentia: potential [1.4.2]

proportio: proportion [between pitches] [1.1.7]; proportion [in science of

music] [1.1.17]; proportions [of
hammers] [1.1.17]; proportion
[of *diapason*] [1.1.14]; proportion
[of *diatessaron*] [1.1.13, 1.1.14];
proportion [of ditone] [1.1.10];
proportion [of semiditone, 32:27
ratio] 1.1.11]; proportion [of
semitone] [1.1.9]; double proportion
[1.1.14, 1.1.18]; numerical proportion
[1.1.4]; sesquialter proportion [3:2
ratio] [1.1.13, 1.1.18]; sesquioctave
proportion [9:8 ratio] [1.1.1, 1.1.18];
sesquitertian proportion [4:3 ratio]
[1.1.12, 1.1.18]; superpartiens
proportion [e.g., 256:243] [1.4.8];
[harmonic] proportions [1.1.19]
prothus: first tone [1.2.4, 2.0.5]
psalmus: [1.1.1, 1.2.4, 2.0.6, 2.0.9, 2.0.10,
2.0.14, 2.0.16, 2.0.18–2.0.21, 2.1.0,
2.2.0, 2.3.0, 2.4.0, 2.5.0, 2.6.0, 2.7.0,
2.8.0]
ptongos: see *tonus* [1.1.6]
pulsus: beat [1.1.4]; pulse [1.1.2]
qualitates primas: first qualities [1.4.1,
1.4.2, 1.4.3, 1.4.9]
raptus: rapture [1.3.20, 1.4.15, 1.4.16, 2.0.7]
regio: region [1.4.10, 1.4.11, 1.4.12,
1.4.13, 1.4.14]
regula: rules [of the art of singing] [1.2.1,
1.2.8, 2.0.9, 2.0.10, 2.0.13, 2.0.14,
2.0.17. 2.0.18, 2.8.4]; rule [for plagal]
[1.3.23]; [tone is a] rule [1.1.1]
regulares termini: regular terminations [of
chants] [1.3.3, 1.3.20, 1.3.21]
regulariter: regularly [1.3.2, 1.3.3, 1.3.7,
1.3.9, 1.3.11, 1.3.13, 1.3.14, 1.3.16,
1.3.18, 1.3.22]; (cf. *licencialiter*)
remissio: shrinking [of blood around the
heart] [1.4.2]
repercussio: repercussion [1.4.14, 2.3.1]
repetitio: repetition [1.1.5, 2.3.1]
responsorium: responsory [1.2.8, 2.0.3,
2.0.20]; for specific responsories see
Chant Sources and Concordances
Table.

rotundellus: rondeau [1.1.1]
sagitta: arrow [1.4.19]
saltus: leap [of the deuterus] [1.4.10]
sanguis: blood [1.4.2]
semiditonus cum dyapente: see *tonus*
semiditonus: see *tonus*
semiton[i]us: [1.1.7, 1.1.8, 1.1.9,
1.1.11–1.1.14, 1.1.19, 1.3.13, 1.4.18,
2.0.18]; see also *tonus*
semitonius cum dyapente: see *tonus*
sequentia: sequence [1.1.1, 1.1.9, 1.3.22,
2.0.3, 2.0.9, 2.0.20, 2.5.1]
sexquitertia (sesquitertia): see *proportio*
siccus: dryness [1.4.1, 1.4.2]
simphonia: symphony [1.1.17]
sompnus: sleep [1.4.6]
sonus: sound [1.1.4, 1.2.6, 2.0.18];
[consonant] sounds [1.4.5]
sopor: sleep [1.4.6]
speculatio: speculation, theory [1.0.2,
1.1.9, 1.4.6, 2.0.1]
spiritus: spirit [1.1.16, 1.4.1, 1.4.2, 1.4.3,
1.4.9, 1.4.15, 1.4.16, 1.4.17, 1.4.20,
2.0.2, 2.0.4]; [Holy] Spirit 1.1.5, 2.0.2,
2.0.15, 2.8.4]; breath [of wind] [1.2.7]
spondeus: spondee [1.4.7]
stantipedes: stantipede [1.1.9, 2.0.4]
suavitas: sweetness [1.3.20]; smoothness
[1.4.10]
superacutus: superacute [1.2.2, 1.4.17]
superpartiens: see *proportio*
terminus: [regular] limit [1.3.20, 1.3.21,
2.4.3, 2.8.4]
terrena: earthly things [1.4.8]
tetrardus: see *tonus*
thesis: thesis [1.1.4]
tibia: flutes [1.4.7]
tibicina: flute player [1.4.7]
tonando: tonando [1.1.6]
tonus: eight tones [1.2.12]; [ancient
four] tones [1.2.4, 1.2.7, 1.2.9];
[etymology of] tone [1.1.6]; [kinds
of] tone [*dyesis vel semitonus, ditonus,
semiditonus, dyatessaron. dyapente,
semitonium cum dyapente, tonum cum*

dyapente, semiditonum cum dyapente, ditonum cum dyapente, dyapason] [1.1.5, 1.1.19]; see also *modus*

tristitia: sadness [1.1.4, 1.4.2, 1.4.19]

tritus see *tonus*

tropus: trope [1.1.1, 1.4.10]; see also *modus*

tuba: trumpet [1.1.17]

unisonus: unison [1.1.3, 1.1.5, 2.0.18]

usus: practice [1 .1.1]; use [in a church] [1.2.8, 2.0.7, 2.0.16, 2.0.17, 2.0.20, 2.1.1, 2.1.11, 2.2.1, 2.4.6, 2.5.0, 2.8.3, 2.8.4]; usage [of authors in grammar] [1.3.20]

venter: glutton [1.4.11]

ventus: wind [1.2.7, 1.4.16]

versiculus: versicles [1.4.10, 1.4.18, 1.4.21]

vexillum: banner [1.4.20]

virtus: power [1.0.3, 1.4.0, 1.4.1, 1.4.3]; force [1.1.5, 1.1.17]

virtutis: virtue [1.4.5, 1.4.6, 1.4.7, 1.4.10, 1.4.12, 1.4.16, 1.4.20, 1.4.21, 1.4.22]

vitium: vice [1.4.12]

voluptas: indulgence [1.4.10]

voluptuosus: voluptuous [1.4.18]

vox: pitch [1.1.3, 1.1.4, 1.1.6, 1.1.7, 1.1.9, 1.1.11, 1.1.12, 1.1.13, 1.1.14, 1.1.17, 1.1.19, 1.2.4, 1.3.2, 1.3.3, 1.3.4, 1.3.7, 1.3.9, 1.3.11, 1.3.13, 1.3.14, 1.3.16, 1.3.18, 1.3.19, 1.3.23, 1.4.17, 1.4.22, 2.0.3, 2.0.4, 2.0.8]; [solmization] syllable [1.1.9, 1.2.1, 1.2.2]; voice [1.2.1, 1.2.5, 1.2.7, 1.4.14, 1.4.15, 1.4.16, 1.4.19]; voicing [1.2.5]

vulnus: wound [1.4.18]

ypermixolodius: see *modus*

ypodorius: see *modus*

ypofrigius: see *modus*

ypolidius: see *modus*

Glossary

Acutus [1.2.2]: Acute, the middle of the three registers of pitch from a-lamire to g-solreut [7 pitches]:

a/lamire b/fa b/mi c/solfaut d/lasolre e/lami f/faut g/solreut

Affinales [1.2.3]: Affinals, three pitches, namely a-lamire, b-mi, and c-solfaut that have "affinity" with the first 3 finals, D-solre, E-lami and F-faut and operate as finals themselves when the tones have been transposed.

a/lamire b/mi c/solfaut

Alleluys [2.8.4]: Alleluia, a Proper chant of the Mass sung in a responsorial manner after the gradual except on liturgical occasions associated with penitence, fasting or sorrow, when it may be replaced by the Tract. First the word 'alleluia' is sung concluding with an extended melismatic phrase, the *jubilus*; then a verse (sometimes 2 or 3 verses) is sung and finally the alleluia is repeated.

Antiphona [1.1.1]: Antiphon, a chant with a prose text sung before and after a psalm to reinforce or interpret its meaning.

Antiphonarius [2.0.1]: Antiphoner, Antiphonary, liturgical book containing the antiphons and other choir chants sung at the service of the Divine Office.

Armonia [1.1.3]: Harmony, the pleasing combination or juxtaposition of different elements of the same class, for example, a higher and a lower pitch.

Autentus [1.2.7]: Authentic tones are the odd numbered ones; they have the final as the lowest note of the range. As an example, tone 1, with final D, is authentic protus:

Cantus coronatus [2.0.4]: *Chanson couronnée*, "crowned song," a term used by Johannes de Grocheio in reference to specific *trouvère* songs which had been awarded a prize or crown of esteem. These songs belong to the generic *grand chans*.

Communio [1.3.10]: Communion, originally a chant with an antiphon and psalm to be sung during the distribution of Communion. By the 12th century only the antiphon is provided in the sources.

Deuterus [1.2.4]: The second of the four mode pairs, or tones 3 and 4, the Phrygian and Hypophrygian. The final is E:

Final

Dies Profestus [2.0.6]: Ordinary days, days with no particular feast assigned to them which generally occur within two periods of ordinary time between Epiphany, or the Baptism of Christ up to Ash Wednesday, and from Pentecost Monday to the first Sunday of Advent.

Diapason [1.1.5]: The proportion 2:1 known as the octave or perfect 8th.

Diapente [1.1.5]: The proportion 3:2; the interval expressed by ut – sol and re – la; known now as the perfect 5th.

Diatessaron [1.1.5]: The proportion 4:3; the interval expressed by ut – fa, re – sol and mi – la; known now as the perfect 4th.

Differentia [2.0.16]: Difference, or termination, the formula with which a psalm tone may end, and lead back to the beginning of the antiphon. Since antiphons could start on one of several pitches other than their final, there needed to be a choice of *differentia* for the singer to select from.

Ditonus [1.1.5]: Ditone, the proportion 81:64; the interval expressed by ut – mi and fa – la; known now as the major 3rd.

Doxology: See *Gloria Patri*.

Festum Sollemne [2.0.6]: Solemn feasts, feast days of the highest rank in the liturgical calendar celebrating a mystery of faith such as the Trinity, an event in the life of Christ, the Virgin Mary or other important saint.

Finales [1.2.3]: Finals, the pitches D, E, F and G of the Grave register. A final is the regular concluding pitch of any chant in any of the eight modes or tones.

Gammaut-gamatis [1.1.9]: Gamut, the whole pitch range from Γ ut to e' la:

Gloria Patri [2.0.15, 2.1.11]: Doxology, an expression of praise sung to the Holy Trinity of the Father, the Son and the Holy Spirit and often used as a final statement in worship. The full text of this doxology is "Gloria Patri, et Filio, et Spiritui Sancto. Sicut erat in principio, et nunc, et semper, et in secula seculorum. Amen." It is called the lesser doxology or minor doxology to distinguish it from the great doxology "Gloria in Excelsis Deo."

Gradale [1.3.10]: Gradual, a response sung between the Epistle and Gospel in the Mass; or a liturgical book containing the chants for the Proper of the Mass.

Gravis [1.2.2]: Grave, the lowest of the three registers of pitch, from Γ ut – G solreut [8 pitches]:

G/ut A/re B/mi C/faut D/solre E/lami F/faut G/solreut

Iuncturae manus levae [1.2.1]: Guidonian hand, a mnemonic device in which the hexachord syllables, assigned to pitch letter names throughout the gamut are affixed to the 19 locations on the left hand. Though Guido of Arezzo did not write about this, it is likely that he developed it for its pedagogic use.

Hymnus [1.4.21]: Hymn, a strophic composition sung in the Divine Office with a metrical poetic text and a mainly syllabic melody.

Intono [1.1.1]: Intoning (of the Psalms) Psalms are chanted to melodic formulas known as psalm tones; each of the 8 psalm tones has its own intonation, reciting pitch, median and final cadences. These formulas are usually sung to a monotone but with the beginning, middle, and end of each verse punctuated by brief intonation, flex, median and cadential formulas. Each psalm concludes with a doxology (*Gloria Patri*) and is preceded and followed by an antiphon. The intonation could be either simple or solemn according to the nature of the feast in which it was performed.

Invitatorium [2.8.4]: Invitatory, a fixed psalm (Vulgate psalm xciv "Venite exultemus Domino") opening a service of the Divine Office sung in alternation with an antiphon and concluded with the minor doxology. The antiphon is sung in full before the psalm and after each of the odd-numbered sections. After the even-numbered sections and the doxology, only the final section of the antiphon was sung.

Iubilus [2.0.7]: Jubilus, derived from the notion of expressing a joy beyond speech and is usually associated with the melismatic vocalization on the penultimate syllable of the alleluia. In the Middle Ages it is associated with melismatic chant more broadly and included under the term *Neuma* q.v.

Maneriae: The modes without distinguishing between authentic and plagal forms. This term is not used by Guy of St Denis.

Medium [2.8.4]: Mediant, in any of the tones, the scale step that lies a 3rd below the tenor or reciting tone. See above *Intono*.

Missa pro mortuis [1.4.19]: Mass for the Dead, Requiem Mass, a votive mass on behalf of the dead, sung on the day of burial and on succeeding anniversaries. It is also celebrated on All Souls' Day, 2 November.

Monocordium [1.1.19]: Monochord, said to have been invented by Pythagoras, is a single string, teaching instrument which was used to demonstrate intervals throughout the medieval era. The string is stretched across two fixed bridges and a third, movable, bridge divides the string into two sections which when sounded demonstrates the connection between the proportion of the string sections and the interval sounded.

Motetus [1.1.1]: Motet, a polyphonic composition in which the slow moving tenor line is usually a segment of chant while the faster moving one, two or three upper lines have different melodies with either Latin and/or French lyrics. It could serve a liturgical purpose but was most commonly performed for ceremonial or other secular purposes. *Motetus* can also refer to the first texted line above the tenor.

Musica falsa [1.1.9]: Used in opposition to *musica vera,* or *musica recta* to refer to "false" locations of hexachords on pitches other than C, F or G.

Musica recta [1.1.9]: The product of the hexachords built on G, C and F comprising the "white" notes of the diatonic scale with the addition of B flat throughout the gamut.

Mutatio [1.1.9]: Mutation, the process of switching from one hexachord to another. A complex set of rules governed when and where mutation could occur.

Neuma [1.1.9]: (1) Broadly refers to a musical phrase but in tonaries, refers to the special melismas or textless melodies added to the model antiphons for each tone.

Neuma [2.0.8]: (2) Note, the notational sign element used to locate pitch by its positioning within the staff.

Neumata [2.0.8]: Melismatic phrase, another term for the special melismas or textless melodies added to the model antiphons for each tone.

Noannoeane (*noioeane, noieane*), *noeagis,* (*noieagis*) [1.2.7]: Known collectively as *Echema* they are melodic intonation formulae sung to nonsense words. The terms *noannoeane* and *noioeane* were used for the authentic tones and *noeagis* (or *noeane*) for the plagal.

Notae [2.0.8]: Notes, often called neumes, are the notational symbols used to depict pitch on the staff.

Notulae [2.0.8]; Little notes, notational symbols used to depict pitch on the staff. It is unclear what the distinction between *notae* and *notulae* is.

Offerendum [2.8.4]: Offertory, a responsorial chant of the mass sung while the bread and wine are prepared for the Eucharist. The offertory chant consisted of a choral refrain with 2 or 3 verses sung by a soloist. The *repetendum* or final phrase of the refrain was repeated after each verse.

Officium [1.2.8]: (1) Office, a series of services performed in the course of the day and night. There are eight services, each associated with a particular time of day: Matins, after midnight and often around 3 a.m.; Lauds, at sunrise; Prime, at 6 a.m.; Terce, at 9 a.m.; Sext, at noon; Nones, at 3 p.m.; Vespers, at sunset; and Compline, before bedtime. See also *Divinum Officium* [2.0.8].

Officium [1.3.4]: (2) Introit, the first of the Proper chants of the Mass. An entrance chant, it is sung during the entrance of the priest at the beginning of the Mass.

Ordinarium: Ordinary chants (see *Proprium*).

Plagalis [1.2.7]: Plagal, the even-numbered tones with an *ambitus* or range which includes the octave lying between the fourth below and the fifth above its final. The plagal tones adopt the prefix 'hypo' with the exception of tone 8, the Hypermixolydian. As an example, tone 2 with final D is the plagal protus or Hypodorian:

Final

Proprium: Proper chants, those chants from both Mass and Office on special occasions, whose texts vary from day to day as distinct from the Ordinary chants whose texts remain constant. The annual cycle of liturgical observances in honor of the saints is called the Proper of the Saints and the Proper of the Time covers the annual cycle of celebrations determined by the date of Easter.

Protus [1.2.4]: The first of the four mode pairs, or tones 1 and 2, the Dorian and Hypodorian with a final D:

Final

Responsorium [1.2.8]: Responsory, responsorial chant in which the choir responds with a refrain to verses sung by the cantor. The Responsory usually consisted of a choral respond, a single solo psalm verse and the *repetendum* (the last part of the responsory repeated).

Seculorum amen or *EVOVAE* [2.0.17]: Of the ages amen. *Evovae* is a pseudo word formed from the vowels of the last 6 syllables of the doxology '*seculorum amen*' used as an abbreviation at the end of an antiphon to indicate the psalm tone with its appropriate ending (*differentia*) to be used for the following psalm.

Semiditonus [1.1.5]: Semiditone, the proportion 32:27; the interval expressed by re – fa and mi – sol; known now as the minor 3rd.

Semitonium minus [1.1.8]: Minor semitone, the proportion 256:243 and the interval expressed by mi – fa.

Sequentia [1.3.22]: Sequence, an extended composition with its Latin text set syllabically. The text usually comprises a series of couplets, each having lines of the same length sung to the same melody though each couplet is different from the preceding one in both melody and length.

Sex voces [1.2.1]: Hexachord syllables, elements of the system of aural recognition which uses interlocking hexachords of syllables, ut, re, mi, fa, sol, la, on the fixed pitches C, F and G, as a mnemonic device for indicating melodic intervals.

Stantipes [1.1.9]: Stantipedes (Fr. *Estampies*), instrumental and vocal dance form described by Grocheio.

Superacutus [1.2.2]: Superacute, the highest of the three registers from a' lamire to d' lasol [4 pitches]:

a'/lamire b'/fa b'/mi c'/solfa d'/lasol

Tenor [2.0.4]: Tenor, reciting note, the note on which most of a psalm verse or other chant sung to a recitation formula, is sung.

Tetrardus [1.2.4]: the fourth of the four mode pairs, or tones 7 and 8, the Mixolydian and Hypermixolydian with a final G.

Final

Tonarius: Tonary, liturgical book containing chant incipits organized according to the eight tones. Its main repertory covers antiphons and responsories from the Office, and sometimes from the Mass, though it may also include other forms, for example hymns and sequences.

Tonus [1.0.0]: (1): Tone Tones may refer to the complex of meanings now associated with modes, or, more specifically to the formulas for singing psalm verses or responsory verses.

Tonus [1.1.1]: (2): Tone is the proportion 9:8 and the interval expressed by ut – re, re – mi, fa – sol and sol – la.

Tractus [1.4.19]: Tract, an elaborate solo chant replacing the alleluia of the Mass on selected penitential occasions. It is sung by a soloist with the verses following one after the other without the intervention of choral responses. The repertory of Tracts is small and most of them are of either the second or eighth tone.

Tritus [1.2.4]: The third of the four mode pairs, or tones 5 and 6, the Lydian and Hypolydian with a final F:

Final

Tropus [1.1.1]: Trope, a term for octave species used interchangeably as a term for tone or mode.

Venite [2.8.4]: Venite (Come!), the opening chant of Matins, properly "Venite exultemus Domino" (Psalm xciv) sung in alternation with an antiphon. (See *Invitatorium*.)

Versus [1.2.4]: Verse, a line of a psalm, or a sentence from a biblical text, such as those used in graduals, alleluias and introits, usually sung by a soloist.

Versiculus[1.4.9]: Versicle, any short text followed by an answer or response from the congregation or choir. The combination of versicle and response is often called *versus* in liturgical sources.

Viella [2.0.4]: Vielle, Fiddle, a bowed string instrument most commonly played at the shoulder, with a waisted shape to allow greater facility with the bow, and strung with gut.

Vox [1.1.9]: Syllable, namely the specific syllables ut, re, mi, fa, sol and la.

Onomastic Index

Adrian, Pope [2.0.8]

Aeneas [1.2.6]

Africans [1.4.11]

Agnes, Saint [1.3.8]

Alberic xv, xlv (n.)

Albert the Great xvi, xlvi (nn.)

Alfonso the Wise xxxiii

Ambrose, Saint [1.4.21, 2.0.7] xxxii, xl

Amiens [2.1.11, 2.8.4]

Apostle, The, (Paul) [1.4.11, 1.4.21]

Apulians [2.0.8, 2.0.9]

Aristotle (aka The Philosopher) [1.1.5, 1.2.6, 1.2.11, 1.4.4, 1.4.5, 1.4.8, 1.4.10, 1.4.15–1.4.17, 1.4.20] xi, ii, xvi, xviii, xxi–xxiv, xxx, xxxi, xxxiii, xlv–xlviii (nn.), l (nn.), li (n.)

———, De Anima [1.4.3] xxiv

Aristotle, De Caelo xv, xvi, xxi,, xii, xlv (n.), xlvi (n.), l (nn.)

———, Ethics [1.4.1] xviii, xlviv (n.)xlviii (nn.)

———, Metaphysica xv, xxxiii, li (n.)

———, Politics [1.2.11, 1.4.5, 1.4.15] xv, xvi, xxiii, xxiv, xxx, xlv (n.), xlvi (nn.)

———, De Proprietatibus Rerum [1.4.8] liii (n.)

Asclepiades [1.4.7]

Athens [1.4.11]

Augustine, Saint [1.4.1, 1.4.8, 1.4.21, 1.4.22]

———, Confessions xxxi, liii (n.)

Avicenna xiv

Bartolomeus Anglicus, De proprietarum rerum [1.4.8] xxxi, liii (n.)

Benedict XII, Pope xxxv, xliii (n.)

Bernard of Clairvaux, Tonale (mis-attributed) xix, xxv, xlviii (nn.)

Boethius [1.0.1, 1.1.1–1.1.4, 1.1.8–1.1.12, 1.1.15–1.1.18, 1.2.8, 1.4.6, 1.4.7, 1.4.10, 1.4.13, 2.8.4] xxi–xxiv, xxvi, xxvii, xxix–xxxi, xxxiii, xxxvii–xxxix, xlvi (n.), l (n.), li (n.), liv (n.)

———, De institutione musice xxi, xxii, xxiv, xxvi, xlvi (n.), l (n.)

———, De Consiliis [1.4.7]

Boniface VIII, Pope xiii

Caesar [1.4.11]

Calabrians [2.0.8, 2.0.9]

Cambyses, King of the Persians [1.1.17]

Carthaginians [1.4.11]

Charlemagne [2.0.8] xviii, xl

Charybdis [1.0.1, 1.2.5, 1.2.6]

Chronicles (Peter Comestor) [1.1.17] 219 (n.); (Sigebert of Gembloux) [1.2.1, 2.0.7, 2.0.8] xiii, xiv, 221 (n.)

Cicero, Marcus Tullius [1.4.7, 1.4.11] 228 (n.), 229 (n.)

Circe [1.2.5]

Clement V, Pope xx, xlvi (n.)

Compiègne xxxii

Coutances, Normandy i

Cretans [1.4.11]

Cucuphas, Saint xii, xxxii

Cyrus, King [1.1.17]

Dagobert, King xii

Dalmatians [1.4.11]

Damascene, The, see John of Damascus

David (Davidic harp) [1.4.7]

Dionysius, see Pseudo-Denis

Dionysius the Areopagite xiv, xliv (n.), liv (n.), 230 (n.), 233 (n.)

Eleanor of Castile xxxiii, liii (n.)

Epimenides [1.4.11]

Europe [1.4.14]

Eustratios of Nicaea xxiv

Eustrat[i]us, *Commentary on Aristotle's Ethics* [1.4.1]

Feasts: Augustine [1.4.22]; Catherine [1.4.22]; Corpus Christi (Eucharist) [1.3.15] xvii, xxxiv, xlvi (n.), xlvii (n.); Easter [1.3.20, 1.4.19, 2.0.18]; Holy Trinity [1.4.22, 2.02, 2.07] xviii, xxxviii; Louis [1.4.22]; Mary Magdalene [1.4.22]; Nicholas [1.4.22]; Purification [1.3.23, [1.3.14] (n.)] see also [1.3.11], [1.4.21], [2.0.6], [2.4.6], xii, xiv, xviii–xx, xxxii, xxxiv, xxxv

Jacques Fournier (Pope Benedict XII) xxxv

Franco of Cologne xii,xxxiii, xlix (n.)

———, *Ars cantus mensurabilis* xxi

French [1.4.14]

Fulrad, Abbot of Saint-Denis xviii

Galatians (Epistle to the) [1.4.11]

Gauls [1.4.11, 1.4.14, 2.0.8]

Gerard of Abbeville xxx

Germany [1.4.12]

Giffard, Renaud xiii

Gilles of Pontoise xiii, xvii, xxxiv, liv (n.)

Glaucus [1.2.5] 222 (n.)

Gosselin de Vire, Jean [2.8.4] (n.), xxv, xxxvi, liv (n.)

Greek (language) [1.1.1, 1.1.6, 1.1.8, 1.2.7, 1.2.12]

Greeks [1.2.6, 1.2.7, 1.4.11, 2.0.7]

Gregory, Pope and Saint [1.2.4, 1.4.14, 2.0.8, 2.0.9] xii, xvii, xxxii, xl, xliii (n.); see also Paul the Deacon

Grocheio, Johannes de xxvi, xxxiii, xxxiv, xxxvi, xxxvii, xliv (n.)

———, *Ars musice* i, xiv–xvi, xxii–xxv, xxvii, xxx, xlii (n.), xlvi (n.), l (nn.), li (n.)

Guido of Arezzo [1.0.1, 2.0.4, 2.0.5, 2.0.8, 2.0.17, 2.8.4] i, xii, xvii-xix, xxi, xxiii, xxv-xxx, xxx, xxxiii, xxxv, xxxix, xlii (n.), xlvii (n.), li (nn.), lii (nn.), liv (n.)

———, *Dialogus* xix, xx, li (nn.)

———, *Epistola ad Martinum [pro Michaelem]* xxv, li (n.)

———, *Micrologus* [1.1.17, 1.2.4, 1.2.5, 1.2.9] xxv–xxviii, xxx, xlviii (n.), li (nn.), lii (nn.

———, *Regule rhythmice* xxix, xxx, xlviii (nn.), liii (n.)

Guy of Châtres xiii, xiv, xxxiv, xxxv, xliii (n.), xliv (n.)

———, *Sanctilogium* xiii, xxxiv-xxxvi, liv (nn.)

Guido Augensis, Abbot (Guy of Eu) [1.2.8], xix, xxix, xxx, xlviii (nn.), lii (n.)

Guy of Saint-Denis [2.8.4]

Harley, Robert xxxvi

Hilduin, Abbot of Saint-Denis xviiii

Honorius, *Speculum Ecclesie* [1.4.21]

Horace [1.0.1]

Ignatius, Bishop of Antioch [2.0.7]

Isaiah [1.4.11]

Isidore of Seville [1.4.12] xxi, xxx

Ismenias the Theban [1.4.7]

Israel [1.4.11]

Italians [1.4.14]

Jacobus de Voragine, *Golden Legend* xxxiv

Jacobus Leodiensis, Jacobus de Ispania xxxiii, liii (nn.), liv (n.), 210 (nn.), 211 (n.), 213 (n.), 235 (n.)

Jean de Venette xliii (n.)

Sarrazin, Jean xiv

Jerome, St, *Commentary on Isaiah* [1.4.11]; *Commentary on the Epistle to the Galatians* [1.4.11]

Jerome of Moray (Hieronymus de Moravia) xxi, xxii, xlix (nn.), l (n.)

———, (Hieronymus de Moravia), *Tractatus de Musica*

Jerusalem [1.4.21]

Jews [1.4.11]

Johannes de Muris (Jehan des Murs) xxxiii, liii (n.)

John of Damascus [1.4.1, 1.4.12] xxiv

John of Garland, *De Musica* [1.1.19, 2.4.6, 2.8.4] xvi, xxi–xxiii, xlix (nn.), l (nn.)

———, *De mensurabili musica*

Jubal [1.1.17]

Juliana of Cornillon xvii

Kalkar, Heinrich Eger von l (n.)

Lacedemonians [1.4.6]

Lescot, Richard xiv, xliii (n.)

Louis IX, Saint and King [1.3.17 n., 1.4.22, 2.1.1], xiii, xviii, xx, xxxiv, xlix (nn.)

Marcus Tullius, see Cicero

Martin IV, Pope xv

Matthew of Vendôme xiii, xiv

Metz [2.0.8]

Odo of Cluny, *Dialogus* (attributed by Guy to Guido of Arezzo) xix

Paris [2.2.1, 2.5.0] xii–xvi, xxi–xxiv, xxx, xxxii, xxxiv–xxxvi, xli, xlii (n.), xliii (nn.), xliv–l (nn.), lii (n.), liii (nn.)

Parisians [1.4.14]

Paul the Deacon, *Life of the Blessed Pope Gregory* [1.4.14, 2.0.8, 2.0.9]

Pepin xviii

Peter of Auvergne xv, xvi, xxi, xxiii–xxv, xxvii, xxxiii, xxxiv, xliv–xlvi (nn.)

———, *Quaestiones*

Petrus de Cruce [2.1.11, 2.4.6, 2.8.4] xv, xx–xxii, xxxiii, xliv (n.), xlix (n.), li (n.)

Peter of Limoges xxi

Petrus de Cruce, *Tractatus de tonis* xi, xv, xxii, xxv, xxvii

Petrus de Sancto Dionysio xxxiii, xliii (n.), xliv (n.)

Petrus Picardus xlix (n.)

Petrus Picardus, *Ars motettorum compilata breviter* xxi

Philip IV, King xx, xlviii (n.)

Philosopher, The, see Aristotle

Phorcus [1.2.5]

Phrygians [1.4.11] see also *Frigas* in the Lexicon

Plato [1.1.5, 1.2.6, 1.4.6] xxxix

Pseudo-Denis, (Blessed), *Epistula ad Polycarpum* [1.4.14, 2.0.7]

Pseudo-Odo xxiii, xxvi, xxx, li (n.)

———, *Dialogus de musica* xxv, l (n.), liii (n.), 210

Pythagoras [1.1.15, 1.1.17–1.1.19, 1.4.7] also the Introduction xxiii, xxxviii, xxxix

Pythagoreans [1.1.15, 1.2.6, 1.4.6] xxi, xxii, xxxviii

Richard of St. Victor xxi

Romans [2.0.8]

Rome [2.0.8]

Saint-Denis (abbey) [2.8.4] also introduction xi–xiv, xvii, xviii, xx, xxvii, xxxii–xxxvii, xl, xli, xlii–xliv (nn.), xlvi (n.), xlix (n.), liii (n.), liv (nn.)

Sainte-Chapelle xx

Scylla [1.0.1, 1.2.5, 1.2.6]

Septuagesima [1.4.19]

Sigebert of Gembloux see *Chronicles*

Siger of Brabant xv, xvi, xlv (n.)

Simon de Brion xv

St. Barbara Abbey, Cologne xxii

Solomon [2.0.8]

Spaniards [1.4.14]

Stephen of Liège xviii, xlvii (n.)

Stephen II, Pope xviii

Stephen Tempier xvi

Thomas Aquinas, Saint xv–xvii, xxi, xxiii, xxiv, xxviii, xlvi (nn.), xlvii (n.), xlix (n.), li (n.)

———, Saint, *Summa Theologia* xvi, xxiv, xlvi (n.)

Teutons [1.4.14]

Tubalchaim [1.1.17]

Urban IV, Pope xvii

Usuard, *Martyrologium* xxxiv

Vincent of Beauvais, *Speculum historiale* xxxiv

Vergil [1.2.5, 1.2.6] 222 (nn.)

Walter of Châtillon, *Alexandreis* xxviii, lii (n.)

William Gap xiv

William of Auxerre, *Summa de officio* [2.0.6] 233 (n.)

William of Moerbeke xvi

William of Nangis, *Chronicle* xiii, xliii (nn.)

William, first abbot of Rievaulx xix, xx

Christopher Wren the Younger xxxvi

Typeset in 11/13 Garamond Premier Pro
Composed by Tom Krol

Printed and bound by CPI Group (UK) Ltd, Croydon, CR0 4YY

Medieval Institute Publications
College of Arts and Sciences
Western Michigan University
1903 W. Michigan Avenue
Kalamazoo, MI 49008-5432
http://www.wmich.edu/medievalpublications

 WESTERN MICHIGAN UNIVERSITY